Logic: Modern and Traditional

Henry J. Ehlers

University of Minnesota
Duluth

Charles E. Merrill Publishing Company
A Bell & Howell Company
Columbus, Ohio

Published by
Charles E. Merrill Publishing Company
A Bell & Howell Company
Columbus, Ohio 43216

This book was set in Century Schoolbook.
The Production Editor was Linda Lowell.
The cover was designed by Will Chenoweth.

PROPERTY OF JOHN FAUVER TECHNICAL LIBRARY
2121 G. WHEELER ROAD MIDLAND MICHIGAN 48640
U.S.A.

ISBN:0-675-08676-0

Library of Congress Catalog Card Number: 75-16936

1 2 3 4 5 6 7 8—83 82 81 80 79 78 77 76

Printed in the United States of America

As the total amount of human knowledge increases and the journey from ignorance to the frontier of discovery lengthens, it becomes more and more important to hasten the process and to make the journey as easy as possible.

—Bertrand Russell

Preface

It is impossible to explain the contents of a logic book without using words which the book itself studies in considerable detail—words such as *is, and, or, not, if, then, only, some, all, tautological, self-contradictory, contingent, relevant, true, false, doubtful, valid, invalid, vague, ambiguous, discursive, reasoning,* and *probable.* What ordinary language expresses somewhat vaguely and ambiguously, logical symbolism expresses quite clearly and precisely. This symbolism helps students not only to see the *structure* of statements and arguments, but also to attain levels of reasoning far beyond the reach of unaided language.

Although the main emphasis of the book is on formal deductive logic, chapter 3, "Informal Logic," relates logic to ordinary language, and chapter 5, "Inductive Logic and Science," emphasizes the interdependence of the inductive and deductive aspects of reasoning. These two chapters also provide contrast and diversion from the hard-core logic found in the other chapters.

This book contains more than one hundred exercises and over 1500 problems. This number would be excessive were it not for the fact that answers are given for nearly all odd-numbered problems. This usage enables students, while studying, to immediately reinforce what they have learned. It also frees instructors from some of the mechanics of logic, so that more class time may be given to the discussion of related topics—historical, epistemological, or philosophical. Most important, students completing this text will not only understand *that* logicians can solve problems in a variety of ways, but they will also acquire *know-how* because they have solved many specific problems themselves.

Very early in the book the similarities among three of logic's most basic operations (conjunction, disjunction, and negation) and the three basic operations of modern mathematics (intersection, union, and complementation) are discussed. These concepts are understood by the majority of current high school graduates. Other similar concepts are the laws of commutation, association, distribution, and double negation. By emphasizing what logic and mathematics have in common, this text not only builds on what students already know, it also illustrates how formal logic, like mathematics, employs precisely defined symbols and operators as aids to thinking.

Although strictly modern, perhaps the most unique feature of the book is the manner in which it incorporates most features of traditional Aristotelian-scholastic logic, while discarding other features. The procedures and symbolisms which make this possible are explained in chapter 6.

The materials in this book have been tested and retested with a variety of classes, most of them consisting of college freshmen and sophomores. In a one-quarter five-credit course, a course having fifty fifty-minute class meetings, nearly all classes cover the entire book. However since different students manifest different interests, and since almost every chapter lends itself to more extended treatment, some classes have omitted as much as 10 to 15 percent of the total.

Now a few brief words of thanks. For their constant help I am indebted to my wife and to two secretaries, Mrs. Jo Ann Larson and Mrs. Mary Bowman. For the privilege of several single-quarter leaves and a sabbatical, I am grateful to the University of Minnesota. Several Minnesota colleagues or former colleagues have been of great assistance with various sections of this text. They include Robert Evans, David Mayo, Robert Sessions, Herbert Feigl, and Wilfred Sellars concerning "Inductive Logic and Science" (chapter 5); also, Ervin Dorff and Peter Longley concerning laws common to logic and mathematics (chapters 1 and 7). I am especially obligated to some 3000 students who, over the years, have served as guinea pigs for the several trial runs of this book.

Finally my appreciation to other logicians, ancient as well as modern, who, over the centuries, have given form and structure to an extremely diverse body of materials, or who have helped to make an ancient subject meaningful and modern. Although *Logic: Modern and Traditional* has several distinctive features, it is primarily a bouquet of other men's flowers.

Contents

chapter 1

PRELIMINARIES

1.1 The Domain of Logic

THOUGHT AND LANGUAGE.   Human beings are superior to other animals largely because of their ability to use language. Logic is the study of those aspects of language which enable humans to express ideas more clearly and to make inferences more validly. The thinking of animals is largely confined to that which is immediately present in time and space, as when a monkey joins two sticks to reach a banana, or a dog associates the stimulus "Lie down" with the act of lying down.

In contrast, human thinking is able to dissociate words and ideas from their natural settings and to recombine them with other words and ideas. For example, the two nouns "door" and "mouth," the two verbs "open" and "close," and the two conjunctions "and" and "or" may be combined in many different ways, as in "open door," "close mouth," "open mouth and door," "open or close mouth," and "open and close mouth or door." Again, if we have experienced the presence of green grass and white swans, the concepts "green," "white," "grass," and "swan" can be reshuffled, enabling us to think of each concept by itself, or to anticipate the possibility of a "green swan" or "white grass." Freed from confinement to the specific, the mind is able to form a multitude of new combinations of words and ideas, many of which have not been, and may never be, actually experienced. Because of this unique ability to recombine words and ideas into new and creative patterns, all humans are able to transcend their environment.

Mankind is distinguished from other animals by its use of language: civilized man by written language; modern man by printing; and twentieth-century man by the use of telegraphy, radio, TV and other forms of instant communication. Insofar as the study of logic adds to our understanding of language, it gives us a better understanding of what is most distinctive and important about human beings.

Exercise 1.1A.   Reason and Human Excellence

Directions: Defend or criticize any one of the following statements:

A.   While it is not the business of education to prove every statement made, any more than to teach every possible item of information, it is its business to cultivate deep-seated effective habits of discriminating tested beliefs from mere assertions, guesses and opinions, to develop a lively, sincere and open-minded preference for conclusions that are properly grounded and to ingrain into the individual's working habits methods of inquiry and reasoning appropriate to the various problems that present themselves. No matter how much an individual knows as a matter of hearsay and information, if he has not attitudes and habits of this sort he is not intellectually educated.—*John Dewey*[1]

B.   We may insist as often as we like that man's intellect is powerless in comparison with his instinctual life, and we may be right in this. Nevertheless, there is something peculiar about this weakness. The voice of the intellect is a soft one, but it does not rest till it has gained a hearing. Finally, after a countless succession of rebuffs, it succeeds. This is one of the few points on which one may be optimistic about the future of mankind, but it is in itself a point of no small importance. And from it one can derive yet other hopes . . . [such as hope in] the love of man and the decrease of suffering.—*Sigmund Freud*[2]

C.   The fact that we can liberate ourselves [however slightly] from purely causal determination—from circumstances, custom, fashion, habit, prejudice, superstition, merely associative thinking, instinct and appetite—is much too remarkable to be merely admitted and recorded. . . .

   We are out of space and time so far as we know them. We are exempt from causality every time we discover a causal law, since we can do this only when our thinking is not the mere resultant of mental and cerebral antecedents but is a free weighing of evidence. And not only when we seek truth are we loosed from the tyranny of space, time and causality, but also when we check an impulse in favour of a principle, when we do something because we are convinced that it is right, and when, instead of taking matter and sensations and ideas as we find them, or making them serve as merely utilitarian ends, we rehandle them radically to make them beautiful. Truth is excellence of thinking, goodness is excellence of disposition and conduct, and beauty is excellence of form. Excellence is the element common to and constitutive of ideals, and because man can conceive it, can analyze its requirements, can choose it and embody it in every department of his life, he is a unique kind of creature, not to be thought of in purely natural terms without doing appalling damage to the evidence. . . . Science itself, even the science that studies matter, is a world of propositions, and propositions are not in Nature; they are nowhere and nowhen, and they are not connected causally but logically or evidentially; and the world of logic and evidence is constituted by the ideals of truth, and therefore collapses if this be discredited.—*T. E. Jessup*[3]

THOUGHT AND LANGUAGE PATTERNS.   Our ways of thinking, no less than our manner of speaking, are acquired from the linguistic community in which we live and grow. Of the many possible combinations of sound, only a few are meaningful in a given speech community. In English the syllables *if*, *in*, and *it* make sense, but *ig* and *iw* do not; *bid*, *did*, *hid*, *kid*, *lid*, *rid*, and *Sid* are meaningful, whereas *jid*, *nid*, *pid*, and *zid* are not. Patterns apply to sentences as well as to words, so that "Man eats meat," and "The cat sat on the mat" are meaningful, whereas "Meat eats man," and "Mat the on sat cat the" are not. Logic will include a study of some of these meaningful sentence patterns, with emphasis on the ways in which words and ideas may be related to one another in a clear and consistent manner.

---

[1] John Dewey, *How We Think* (New York: Holt, Rinehart and Winston, 1911), p. 27. Dewey's view with respect to the scope of logic is discussed again near the end of sec. 5.2.

[2] Sigmund Freud, *The Future of an Illusion*, ed. and trans. James Strachey et al., in *The Complete Psychological Works of Sigmund Freud* (London: Hogarth Press, 1961), 21:53.
   See also W. T. Stace, *What Are Our Values?* (Lincoln: University of Nebraska Press, 1959), pp. 30–40.

[3] T. E. Jessup, *The Freedom of the Individual in Society* (Toronto: Ryerson Press, 1948), chap. 2. Read also Edna St. Vincent Millay's poem, "Euclid Alone Knew Beauty Bare."

REASON AND MEMORY.   Reasoning depends on memory, and complicated chains of logical reasoning cannot be performed unless our memories are aided by some system of concise symbolism. To appreciate the interdependence of reason and memory, try to memorize the following series of numerals. Then observe how easily the same numerals are recalled when arranged according to a pattern (as shown in the footnote).

1 4 9 1 6 2 5 3 6 4 9
1 2 3 1 4 9 2 3 4 4 9 16[4]

As another example, try to memorize one of the following series of words in its present form. Then unscramble the line of words to form a sentence, and see how easily the very same words may be remembered.

1. the no whole truth contains epigram
2. as as him a is that man big annoy things the
3. summarizes experience proverb a a short long
4. Lyman Beecher fire logic on eloquence as defined
5. cobwebs cables as as and habits begin end
6. Voltaire fools of defined reason prejudice the as

Since memory retains ideas that are structured into patterns, and since reason is very dependent on memory, *brevity* is often an aid to clarity and to logical thought. For example, it is much easier to remember, and to reason about, "1 + 2 = 3" than to remember and reason about "if any object is added to a pair of objects, one will invariably obtain a group of three objects." To appreciate how important symbols are to mathematical reasoning, try to translate into ordinary language the algebraic equation $x^2 - y^2 = (x + y)(x - y)$.

CONSISTENCY.   The ability of the human mind to recognize some concepts as compatible, others as contradictory, is the foundation of logic. Memory is necessary before we can react to words, but reason actively intervenes to interpret what we read or hear. Ordinary language often implies much more than is stated explicitly, and a brilliant literary style generally combines ideas which have many implications. To appreciate this point, study the two statements below; then list all the ideas that are *explicitly* stated, and all that are *implied* or suggested.

"If silicon had been a gas, I would have been a major-general," said the painter Whistler, recalling that his failure to pass an examination in chemistry had debarred him from West Point.

An accommodating Vicar, who was twice a Papist and twice a Protestant, denied the charge of being an opportunist, by declaring, "Not so. For if I changed my religions, I am sure I kept true to my principle, which is to live and die the Vicar of Bray."

Careful analysis of the many meanings contained in the above statements will reveal that we pursue hints and follow suggestions by making logical implications. In short, a good literary style assumes that the reader is able to perform logical inferences.

Thackeray begins one of his novels with this story: An old abbé declared to a party of ladies in his parish, "A priest has strange experiences; why, ladies, my first penitent was a murderer." A moment later, the mayor of the

---

[4] 1 4 9 16 25 36 49
1 2 3, 1^2 2^2 3^2, 2 3 4, 2^2 3^2 4^2

town entered the room and said, "Ah, Abbé, here you are. Do you know, ladies, that I was the Abbé's first penitent, and I promise you my confession astonished him!" Thackeray leaves it to the reader to derive the inference that these statements entail.

What is true of a good literary style is also true of ordinary speech. Given the proper context, a husband will find it easy to translate the statement of his nonmechanical wife, "I put those *do-dads* and *what-you-may-call-ems* right next to your *thing-a-ma-jig* on the work bench" to mean, "I put those *bolts* and *screws* right next to your *hammer* on the work bench."

Communication is a constant compromise between brevity and clarity. If we explain everything, our conversation becomes tedious and boring. If we leave too many things unexplained, we will be misunderstood. Here is a conversation that took place in a railway station:

> *Visitor:* Manx?
> *Station Agent:* No. 6:20 express.

To understand this conversation we must realize (1) that "Manx" is a species of cats that has no tail, and (2) that in the context of this conversation, there was a tail-less cat in the railway station. More fully expanded, this conversation would read something like this:

> *Visitor:* Is that tail-less cat a Manx cat?
> *Station Agent:* No. It is a tail-less cat because its tail was run over and cut off by the 6:20 express train.

Charleton Laird gives the following example of abbreviated conversation:

> "Home?"
> "Not yet. Appointment."
> "The boss?"
> "Nope. Boss's secretary."[5]

If you know that this conversation takes place between two stenographers at closing time, you can easily fill in the missing details.

It is because we enjoy making inferences that we prefer colorful analogies to plain statements of fact. Consider the following six proverbs, each of which speaks analogically or indirectly by way of metaphor:

1. "The early bird catches the worm."
2. "Haste makes waste."
3. "Nothing ventured, nothing gained."
4. "Look before you leap."
5. "He who hesitates is lost."
6. "An ounce of prevention is worth a pound of cure."

The tendency of the human mind to retain easily recalled patterns is so strong that most of us believe ("believe" in the sense that we have memorized) all of the above six proverbs. Yet there is a sense in which (1) is inconsistent with (2), (3) with (4), and (5) with (6). But reason is so dependent upon patterns (forms, structures) of thought that it must rely upon memory even in cases which provide logical difficulties.

What happens when the mind discovers that it is holding incompatible beliefs? The following analogy may provide an explanation. Many wartime stories tell of enemy troops who, during the dark of night, set up positions close to one another. Without mutual recognition, there is no contest. But at

---

[5] Charleton Laird, *The Miracle of Language* (New York: World, 1953), p. 205.

the break of day, the opposing troops recognize one another, and then either the weaker side is defeated by the stronger, or the enemy troops retreat to a safer, more distant position. In analogous manner, within the dark recesses of our minds, there are hidden many incompatible beliefs; and we may hold onto them for years without realizing that they are incompatible. But when the daylight of conscious exposure reveals their incompatibility, either the weaker opinion gives way to the stronger, or each opinion is thereafter confined to a more restricted area.

Logically, it is impossible that a thing should be round and also that it should be square; but psychologically there seems to be little difficulty in holding such incompatible beliefs. All that is needed is to keep these beliefs in separate compartments and to use them in turn as may be convenient. As an example, study the following ten pairs of proverbs (where we consider a proverb as a colorful memory-aid) and decide which of these pairs tend to reinforce one another, which ones tend to refute each other:

1A. A thing of beauty is a joy forever.

1B. Gather ye rosebuds while ye may.

2A. A stitch in time saves nine.

2B. Destroy the lion while it is young.

3A. Every man has his price.

3B. True gold fears no fire.

4A. Little strokes fell great oaks.

4B. Rome was not built in a day.

5A. Young saint, old devil.

5B. As the twig is bent, the tree is inclined.

6A. Barking dogs seldom bite.

6B. Empty vessels make the most noise.

7A. Absence makes the heart grow fonder.

7B. Absence makes the heart grow fonder—for someone else.

8A. Two can live as cheaply as one.

8B. Marriage doubles joys, halves sorrows, and quadruples expenses.

9A. A rolling stone gathers no moss.

9B. Plants oft removed never thrive.

10A. You will soon ruin the bow if you keep it stretched: All work and no play makes Jack a dull boy.

10B. Hold your nose to the grindstone: All work and no play makes—"jack."

WORDS ARE NOT PHYSICAL OBJECTS. Language sometimes leads us to confuse words with things. When we say "no square circles exist," the very act of denial seems to affirm a type of "existence" (or "subsistence") to a class of objects that has no members. Because we employ the same linguistic pattern to say "It (the road) goes to town" and "It (the line) goes to infinity," we tend to ascribe the same type of reality to "infinity" that we ascribe to "town." Because "Somebody came" and "Nobody came" have the same formal structure, we may be misled into believing that "Nobody" is some sort of person. Lewis Carroll lampooned this confusion in *Through the Looking Glass:*

"I see nobody on the road," said Alice.

"I only wish *I* had such eyes," the King remarked in a fretful tone. "To be able to see Nobody! And at this distance, too! Why, it's as much as *I* can do to see real people, by this light!"

Mark Twain had great sport with this tendency to identify language with reality. Returning from Europe, he complained that in Germany he had to eat *kraut,* in France *chou,* and was glad to get back to America where they called this food what it really is, *cabbage.* In *Huckleberry Finn* Jim could not understand why Frenchmen say "polly-voo-franzy?" when they mean "Do you speak French?" If a Frenchman is a man, argued Jim, then he ought to speak like a man; he ought to speak English.

The Book of Genesis (2:19–20) reads: "And out of the ground the Lord God formed every beast of the field, and every fowl of the air; and brought them unto Adam to see what he would call them: and whatsoever Adam called every living creature, that was the name thereof. And Adam gave names to all cattle, and to the fowl of the air, and to every beast of the field." Mark Twain wrote that one of these animals gave Adam great difficulty and he appealed to Eve for help: "What name shall I give to this animal?" he asked. "Call it a horse," answered Eve. "But why?" "Well," said Eve, "it looks like a horse, doesn't it?"

"Horse" is not the same as horse. "Horse" is an English word, even as "pferd" is a German word, and "cheval" a French word. Each of these words is conventional in the sense that the English, German, and French peoples accept these different words to signify real horses.

ABSTRACT TERMS.   Overanxious to avoid confusing words with things, or to use words that cannot be related to life, some writers have argued that the only meaningful words are those which refer, directly or indirectly, to physical objects or to concrete events. This line of thought makes it difficult to know what to do with words such as "meaningful," "meaningless," "non-physical," "abstract," and even with some of the basic terms employed in logic.

To further appreciate the distinction between concrete and abstract words, and between sense perception and rational conception, consider the following story about Johnnie and his schoolteacher.

> *Teacher:* Johnnie, stop making that noise.
> *Johnnie:* I'm not making *that* noise, teacher, I'm making another noise like it.

There is a sense in which Johnnie was correct. Considered as a sense perception, every noise is a unique event, an unrepeatable perception, like Johnnie's "*that* noise." However, the teacher was also right because unique events may be grouped with other events of a similar nature, like the teacher's "that *noise.*" A little reflection will show that, unless unique events are given common names, communication and rational discourse are impossible.

Abstract words make communication more brief and more precise. "Treason," for example, says in one word what would otherwise be weakly conveyed by "the violation of allegiance toward one's country, especially by waging war against it or purposely acting to aid its enemies." That is why every organized body of knowledge, from chemistry to logic, has its own lexicon— not to intimidate the layman but to communicate with brevity and clarity.

The more advanced a civilization (and the more developed its accompanying language) the more words there are to express abstract or general ideas. Even as a child learns the meaning of "dog" and "cat" before he learns about "mammal" or "vertebrate," so the language of primitive cultures reflects the tendency of the mind to begin with terms which refer to the concrete and the specific. On this point Otto Jesperson has written:

The aborigines of Tasmania had a name for each variety of gum-tree and wattle-tree, but they had no equivalent for the expression "a tree"; neither could they express abstract qualities such as hard, soft, warm, cold, long, short, round, etc. The Mohicans have words for cutting various objects, but none to convey *cutting* simply. The Zulus have no word for "cow," but words for "red cow," "white cow," etc. ... Many languages have no word for "brother," but have words for "elder brother," "younger brother." ... The nomenclature of a remote past was un-doubtedly constructed upon similar principles to those which are still preserved in a word-group like *mare, stallion, foal, colt,* instead of she-horse, he-horse, young horse, etc.[6]

Twentieth century English holds on to many of these ancient usages. In an age when every child learns that the number three designates *any* group of objects which come in threes, the child also learns that "trio" refers to music, "triple" denotes baseball, "triplet" suggests childbirth, and so on. It is obvious that the mathematician's number "3" can be abstracted from a musician's "trio," from a sportsman's "triple," from an obstetrician's "triplets," and from other specific contexts. But are we to conclude from this that the numbers of mathematics have *nothing whatsoever* to do with the world of concrete objects? By no means. We may validly conclude only this: the relationship between abstract numbers and specific events is *less immediate* and *less direct.* However we should also realize that it is *because* of this fact that mathematical computation is usable in many different fields. It is for precisely the same reason that logic may also be applied in many different fields.

OBJECT WORDS AND FUNCTIONAL WORDS. Some words—such as "is," "or," "and"—are used to *connect* other words, but do not refer to objects outside of language itself. W. H. Werkmeister calls such words "functional words" and distinguishes them from "object words":

"Object words ... refer to, designate, or mean some particular object, or group of objects, of experience; they are names for things, qualities, states, or events; they are signs that have a referent. Functional words, on the other hand, indicate something about the employment of language, something about the combination of object words and about the linguistic structure of statements. Object words pertain to the content or subject matter of thought, whereas functional words have syntactical or formal significance only. Object words designate the referent about which we say something, and signify what we say about it; functional words are but linguistic aids in the construction of our statements.[7]

This book will study in considerable detail some of these functional words and phrases—also called "connectives" or "operators"—such as "and," "or," "not," "is," "if ... then," "if and only if," "all," "some," and "only."

Since a large dictionary contains hundreds of thousands of words, the question may arise how the study of a few logical connectives can be very significant. The answer revolves around the fact that some words are used much more frequently than others. Numerous word-counts have been made, and these show that the 3,000 most frequently used words constitute more than 95 percent of all words used. Of these 3,000 the most frequently used 300 constitute about 75 percent, and the most frequently used 30 comprise almost 50 percent. These much-used words include "is," "and," "or," and

---

[6] Otto Jesperson, *Language: Its Nature, Development and Origin* (New York: Henry Holt, 1922), chap. 21, p. 429 f.

[7] W. H. Werkmeister, *An Introduction to Critical Thinking,* rev. ed. (Lincoln, Nebraska: Johnsen, 1957), p. 147.

others to be studied in this book. Because one or another of these logical connectives occur in almost every sentence we speak, a study of them helps us understand the basic patterns of language and of thought.

USE AND MENTION.   In most discourse we *use* a word to point to referents other than itself, as in "Paris is a city" and "A city is a place where there are many people." But if we turn our attention to the word itself, as in " 'Paris' is a five-lettered noun," " 'City' is a four-lettered noun," we are said to *mention* (to speak about) the words "Paris" and "City." In brief, *"mention"* connotes *names* and generally requires the use of quotation marks; *"use"* connotes *things* named by names, and seldom requires quotation marks.

Suppose someone asks us to give a logical explanation of the following absurdity: "Al is short, and Al is tall; hence, a short person may be a tall person." The ambiguity results from failure to distinguish *use* (the word "Al" as referring to a real man) and *mention* (the word "Al" considered merely as a two-lettered word). To clear up the ambiguity we would rewrite the so-called argument as follows: " 'Al' is a short name, but Al is a tall person." We now immediately see that there is no logical connection between "person" and "name." Here are some other illustrations of the distinction between *use* and *mention*—the first clause of each sentence illustrating *mention*, the second clause illustrating *use:*

> "Constantinople" is larger than "Tokyo," but Tokyo is larger than Constantinople.
> "One eighth," "$\frac{1}{8}$," "$12\frac{1}{2}\%$," "0.125," and "0.124999 . . . " are different symbols; but mathematicians would say that they all have the same numerical value.
>
> "The boiling point of water," "212°F" and "100°C" are *conventional symbols* by means of which English-speaking people communicate; whereas steam is a *natural sign* on the basis of which men infer the presence of boiling water.
>
> The statement "John is tall" is true, because John is tall.

Here we should observe that there is no universally accepted convention concerning the employment of single quotes (as in 'use' and 'mention'), double quotes (as in "use" and "mention"), or italics (as in *use* and *mention*). Also, in deference to the principle of least effort, common usage will generally omit quotation marks, and logicians may omit them too, except in contexts where misunderstanding is likely to occur.

Exercise 1.1B.   Use and Mention: Use of Quotation Marks

Directions: Assume that each sentence in this exercise is a true statement. Then, by the proper use of single and double quotation marks, indicate which words are being *used* and which words are being *mentioned*. Do the odd-numbered problems first, and check your answers against those at the end of the chapter. Then do the evens.

1. Tom is a cat is true if and only if Tom is a cat.
2. Lincoln was assassinated is false if and only if Lincoln was not really assassinated.
3. It is true that the sentence The word *logic* contains five letters contains exactly four words is false.
4. Students try to learn is true.
5. In John is a name the single quotes refer to a name and not to the bearer of that name.
6. It was and I said not or.
7. Smoke and the visible exhalation given off by a burning or smoldering substance, especially the gray, brown, or blackish mixture of gases and suspended carbon particles resulting from the combustion of wood, peat, coal, or other organic matter

are examples of *conventional symbols* used by English-speaking people; whereas real smoke is a *natural sign* on the basis of which men infer the existence of fire.

8. The symbol $\vee$ is a logical connective meaning or.
9. The algebraic identity $(x + y)(x - y) = x^2 - y^2$ is well known.
10. In The last letter of the alphabet is z the letter z may be written either with or without single quotes around it.
11. If is is not is and is not is not is not, is not is not is and is is not?
12. I said that that that that that that man used was used correctly.

We conclude with an exercise listing twenty-five of logic's most frequently used words. Students should already know these words well enough to match each word with its appropriate definition, and they should realize that a beginning course in logic aims at more precise definitions and deeper understandings of these words.

Exercise 1.1C.   Twenty-Five Terms Used in Logic

Directions: Below are fifteen nouns, each of which is widely used in logic. After each numbered definition, indicate by letter which of the 15 nouns is being defined. Most of these definitions are in Basic English, which has a vocabulary of only 850 words.

A. Argument	F. Experience	K. Premise
B. Conclusion	G. Fact	L. Proof
C. Consistency	H. Fallacy	M. Reason
D. Element	I. Implication	N. Relation
E. Essence	J. Logic	O. Set

1. (Knowledge got from) observation of facts or events.   1. _____
2. Thing which is certainly true or taken to be so; event.   2. _____
3. Class; collection of well-defined, clearly distinguishable objects— including objects of thought as well as objects of perception.   3. _____
4. A simple part of something complex.   4. _____
5. Most important, necessary quality of a thing; that which makes a thing what it is.   5. _____
6. Reason or reasoning for or against anything; having discussion with one taking a different view.   6. _____
7. (Facts put forward as) argument for, cause of, something; mind's power of judging, seeing connections.   7. _____
8. Fact(s) or reasoning making clear that something is true; test.   8. _____
9. Connection; any aspect or quality which makes two or more things alike.   9. _____
10. Statement(s) on which some other statement(s) or chain of reasoning is based.   10. _____
11. A statement or belief reached by reasoning.   11. _____
12. Relations between statements whereby the truth of some statement(s) make some other statement(s) true.   12. _____
13. Invalid argument; misleading connection of words.   13. _____
14. Quality of being all in harmony; agreement.   14. _____
15. The study of systematic rules for the justification and criticism of reasoning.   15. _____

Directions: Apply the same directions to the following ten verbs.

A. Analyze	F. Imply
B. Associate	G. Persuade
C. Believe	H. Postulate
D. Define	I. Preconceive
E. Illustrate	J. Think

16. (Of statements) make, if true, some other statements true.   16. _____
17. See or make a connection between; be much in the company (of).   17. _____

18. Make clear the sense of (words, writing, etc.); limit; mark out clearly. 18. _____
19. Make clear by examples, pictures, stories, comparisons. 19. _____
20. Make division of into its separate parts. 20. _____
21. Be using one's mind; have (thoughts) in one's mind; have opinion that; have idea how. 21. _____
22. Have no doubt that a statement is true, or that a person is saying what is true. 22. _____
23. Put forward, take, as fact to be reasoned from; assume. 23. _____
24. Get an idea about something before experiencing it. 24. _____
25. Get person to do by talk or argument; win over to do or believe. 25. _____

More will be said about logic and language in chapter 3 which deals with informal logic. As a further introduction to formal logic, sections 1.2 and 1.3 will review some concepts and laws that are basic to both mathematics and logic.

1.2   Modern Logic and Mathematics:
Three Common Operators

Like Darwin's theory of evolution, or Einstein's theory of relativity, Cantor's theory of sets is one of the great unifying theories of modern times. It provides the underlying concepts for many and varied branches of mathematics and logic, and it is the basis for the computer industry. Since nearly all students now entering college are familiar with "the new math," they should already have a speaking acquaintance with the elementary concepts of set theory that are used in this book. In should be noted, however, that set theory as taught in college mathematics courses, presupposes a knowledge of calculus, and deals with concepts far more difficult than those to be used in this introductory logic book.

SET OR CLASS.   This is logic's most basic undefined term. Synonyms are "aggregate," "collection," "group," or "assemblage." The objects that constitute a set are called its *elements* or *members*, and each set is uniquely determined by its members. Sets having the same members are identical.

SET THEORY SYMBOLISM.   Lower case letters are usually employed to signify *elements* (or *members*) of sets. Thus the five letters, a, e, i, o, and u are the members of the set "the five English vowels." Likewise, 1, 2, 3, 4, 5, 6, 7, 8, and 9 are the nine elements which comprise the set of single-digit natural numbers.

SETS.   Capital letters are generally employed to signify sets. Thus "A" might symbolize apples; "B," boys; "D," doughnuts; "G," green things; "N," nouns; "S," single-digit natural numbers; "V," vowels. Sets may also be symbolized by listing the elements of that set within braces. For example:

$$V = \{a, e, i, o, u\}$$
$$S = \{1, 2, 3, 4, 5, 6, 7, 8, 9\}$$

Note that the order or the repetition of elements does not change a set's meaning: $\{1, 2\} = \{2, 1\} = \{1, 2, 1, 2, 2\}$. Note also that, although members of a set usually have something in common, this need not be so. The three sets $\{1, 2, 3\}$, $\{a, b, c\}$ and $\{Kennedy, Nixon, Ford\}$ each have common properties. But the sets $\{a, 2, Taft, book, dream\}$ or $\{John, rock, angel, democracy, square\}$ do not.

ELEMENTS.   In most books on set theory, "is an element of" is symbolized by "ϵ," as in "$a \; \epsilon \; V$" for "a is a vowel." But to keep our discussion of set theory to a minimum, we shall not use the symbol "ϵ." When dealing with singular propositions (chapter 6), we shall symbolize "*a* is a vowel" by "*Va*," and symbolize "*b* is not a vowel" by " ~ *Vb*."

SUBSETS.   Sometimes two sets are related in such a manner that every element of one set is also a member of the second set. For example, each member of the set of vowels is also a member of the set of letters of the alphabet. If we let "*V*" signify the set of vowels, and let "*A*" signify the letters of the alphabet, then every element of *V* is also an element of *A*, and we say that the set *V* is a *subset* of the set *A*.

This relationship between sets is denoted by the symbol "⊂." We write $V \subset A$ for "Every member of the set of Vowels is also a member of the set of letters in the Alphabet." We write $A \subset F$ for "All Apples are Fruits." The following exercise should serve to review what we have been saying.

Exercise 1.2A.   Sets and Subsets

Part A. Directions: Let each of the following signify sets. For each one, give three examples of subsets.

1. Books	4. Mammals
2. Trees	5. Flowers
3. Students	6. Fine Arts

Part B. Directions: Name a set under which the following would all be subsets:

1. cats, lions, tigers, leopards, jaguars, lynxes
2. dogs, wolves, foxes, hyenas, jackals, coyotes
3. sharks, trout, bass, halibut, herring, pike, sardines
4. canines, felines, rodents, marsupials, ungulates
5. hawks, crows, robins, wrens, canaries, jays
6. fish, mammals, birds, reptiles, amphibians

IDENTITY OR EQUALITY OF SETS.   Two sets are *identical* or *equal* if and only if the two sets have exactly the same members. For example, if we let *A* = the set of equiangular triangles, and *L* = the set of equilateral triangles, then $A = L$. We may define " = " in terms of "⊂" thus: given two sets *A* and *B*, if and only if $A \subset B$ and $B \subset A$, then $A = B$. Proof of this is contained in the notion of "⊂": if $A \subset B$, then each element of *A* is also an element of *B* (by the definition of "⊂"). Similarly, every element of *B* is an element of *A*. Hence, every element of *A* is an element of *B*, and every element of *B* is an element of *A*. But this means that sets *A* and *B* have exactly the same members, or that $A = B$.

SUBSETS AND PROPER SUBSETS.   By definition, if every element of set *A* is also an element of set *B*, then $A \subset B$, even when $A = B$. By the same definition, $A \subset A$, that is, every set is a subset of itself. This calls for a distinction: if *A* and *B* are sets such that $A \subset B$ and $A \neq B$, then we speak of *A* as a proper subset of *B*. Thus $\{a, b\}$ is a subset, but not a proper subset of $\{a, b\}$; whereas $\{a, b\}$ is a proper subset of $\{a, b, c\}$.

In mathematics the symbol "<" means "is less than" and the symbol "≤" means "is equal to or less than." Many books on set theory employ an analogous usage, so that "$A \subset B$" means that *A* is a *proper* subset of *B*, whereas "$A \subseteq B$" means either that *A* is a proper subset of *B* or that *A* is equal to *B*. Some of these books also employ the symbols "⊃" and "⊇," on the analogy of ">" and " ≥." But we restrict ourselves to the symbol "⊂" as defined above.

INFINITE SETS.   Although infinite sets are not dealt with in this book, it is interesting to note how set theory gave some measure of precision to a subject previously viewed as obscure and enigmatic. In set theory, three dots are used to mean "etc." or "and so forth without end," as in $\{1, 2, 3, \ldots\}$. Any set S is defined as infinite if and only if there is a proper subset P of S such that each element of S may be paired off with, or matched against, a unique element in the proper subset P; for example, where $S = \{0, 1, 2, 3, 4, \ldots\}$ and $P = \{0, 2, 4, 6, 8, \ldots\}$. Because this logic book deals almost exclusively with finite sets, it has less need of the term "proper subset" than would be true of a mathematics book dealing with infinite sets.

DOMAINS OF DISCOURSE: UNIVERSAL SETS.   In most discussions, all sets are subsets of a larger set, called the *universe of discourse*, or the *universal set*, which we here symbolize by "U." Thus in zoology, Animals might be the universal set under whose domain would fall such subsets as Fish, Birds, and Horses. Again, Fish might be the universal set under whose domain would be such subsets as Pike, Trout, and Halibut. Still again, People might be considered the universal set within whose domain would fall subsets such as Americans, Baptists, and Carpenters. When a plumber, an organist, and a smoker employ the word "pipe" in their three different contexts, there is no ambiguity so long as it is clearly understood that the word "pipe" means different things when used in different domains of discourse. Some fifty years ago, logicians spoke of "the set of all sets"; but such a concept is not a specific domain of discourse, and it led to troublesome logical paradoxes. In this book, when we employ the symbol "U" to signify a universal set, we always restrict the meaning to a limited domain, to a universe of discourse more definite, and less general, than "the set of all sets."

The notion of "universal set" makes it possible for logic to do justice to the evolution of language and the changing meanings of terms. What is "essential" or "accidental" will depend upon the context in which that term is used. As an illustration of this point, consider the following definitions of baking soda (sodium bicarbonate):

From the viewpoint of chemistry, "sodium bicarbonate is a carbonate (*genus*) compounded with sodium (Na) and hydrogen (H) (*specific difference*) to form $NaHCO_3$ (definition)." Its general properties (*propria*) include: white, powdery solid, soluble in water, mildly basic or antacid, usually prepared by the formula: $Na_2CO_3 + H_2O + CO_2 \rightarrow 2NaHCO_3$. Its accidental properties are that it is used in medicine to counteract stomach acidity, that it is used in the soda-acid type of fire extinguisher, that it is sold by most grocers as baking soda, that the sample we have here was purchased from the XYZ chemical company, and so on.

Now suppose our general context (*genus*) is that of medicine. Our definition now becomes: "Sodium bicarbonate is a medicine (*genus*) widely used as a cure for stomach acidity (*specific difference*)." The *propria* would again include "white, powdery solid, soluble in water, etc." But in the context of medicine, the propria would also include "chemical formula is $NaHCO_3$"—which in the context of chemistry was part of the essential meaning (definition) of sodium-bicarbonate. In this new context, the fact that sodium bicarbonate is usually prepared by the formula $Na_2CO_3 + H_2O + CO_2 \rightarrow 2NaHCO_3$ now becomes quite as "accidental" as the fact that it is sold by the XYZ chemical company.

Now suppose our context (*genus*) is "fire extinguishers." In this context, the specific difference might be "using CO_2," and our formal definition now becomes "Sodium bicarbonate is a carbon dioxide type (*specific difference*) of fire extinguisher (*genus*)." In this context, properties which were essential (*genus-species*) properties in the context of chemistry or medicine, turn out to be mere *propria*, for example, that sodium bicarbonate has a chemical formula of $NaHCO_3$, that it is used in medicine to counteract stomach acidity. From the standpoint of "fire extinguishers" it is quite "accidental" that CO_2 which helps put out fires is the same CO_2 that is exhaled by animals and needed by plants—an "accidental" property which from the viewpoint of a biologist is most essential.

The point to be drawn from these examples is this: the basis of our classification—the context, the point of view—will determine which properties are essential and which ones are merely accidental. As a biologist, Aristotle very neatly classified man as *Homo sapiens*. But from the viewpoint of a shoe manufacturer, the most significant thing about man is not his rationality, but the size of shoes he wears, or the style of shoes he desires. A botanist can summarize basic information concerning thousands of different species of trees employing structural properties in a hierarchy of Phylum-Class-Order-Family-Genus-Species-Variety (or of Superset-Set-Subset, and so on). But a landscape architect may find it more meaningful to classify these same trees according to the soil in which they thrive; the color of their bark, leaves, and blossoms; or their normal height.

The notion of "context," or of "universal set," will explain why the "Morning Star" and "Evening Star" are both (1) the same, since they refer to the same planet Venus, and (2) different, since they are seen from different perspectives, or in different contexts.

In summary, the concept of "universal set" or "domain of discourse" means that we must first clarify our context, our general point of view. If this is carefully done, many ambiguities in logic automatically disappear.

We may conclude with a remark by G. K. Chesterton: "The most important part of any picture is its frame." In logic, this means: "The most important part of any thinking is its context," where "context" includes "basic assumptions." Only when thinking is based on clearly defined concepts, that is, when sets and subsets are placed within a universal set, do vagueness and ambiguity give way to clarity and precision.

OPERATORS, CONNECTIVES.   From elementary arithmetic, we are all familiar with the four operations by which numbers are changed to other numbers: addition, subtraction, multiplication, and division. Set theory and logic also have operators, or connectives, namely:

    (1) *Conjunction* or *Intersection* [Symbol: the dot $(\cdot)$]
    (2) *Disjunction* or *Alternation* or *Union* [Symbol: the wedge $(\vee)$]
    (3) *Negation* or *Complementation* [Symbol: the tilde $(\sim)$]

CONJUNCTION (INTERSECTION).   The conjunction (intersection) of two sets A and B is the set composed of those elements that are in A and also in B. The symbol for conjunction is the dot. "$A \cdot B$" reads "the conjunction (intersection) of the sets A and B." "$A \cdot B$" might also be expressed as "that which is *both* A and B," or "A which is also B," or "A dot B." For example, if "F" denotes the set of "flags," and if "G" denotes the set of "green objects," then "$F \cdot G$" would denote the set "green flags." Again, given that $A = \{1, 2, 3\}$ and $B = \{3, 4, 5\}$, the conjunction $A \cdot B = \{3\}$. $A \cdot B$ is the set of elements which belong to *both* A and B.

The greater the number of sets that are conjoined, the fewer elements the conjunction will have. Medieval logicians stated this idea thus: "The greater the comprehension of an idea, the smaller its extension; and the greater its extension, the smaller its comprehension." To illustrate this rule, suppose we examine equal-sized maps of (1) the Chicago Loop, (2) Chicago, (3) Illinois,

(4) the United States, (5) North America, and (6) the World. Obviously, the larger the territory, the less the detail; or, conversely, the greater the detail the smaller the territory. Thus there are fewer "large female Collie dogs" than "female Collie dogs" than "Collie dogs" than "dogs." The only exception to this rule is a class which has no extension: there are exactly as many "red square circles" as there are "square circles"—zero in each case. Here is a modern adaptation of the famous "Tree of Porphyry" (233–304 A.D.) illustrating this principle:

Comprehension (Intention)	Set Theory Symbolism	Extension (Referents)
Body	B	Minerals, Plants, Animals, Men
Body with Life	$B \cdot L$	Plants, Animals, Men
Body with Life and Sensation	$B \cdot L \cdot S$	Animals, Men
Body with Life, Sensation, and Reason	$B \cdot L \cdot S \cdot R$	Men

The following are examples from ordinary English of conjunctions of two sets:

"Dogs that are Mammals" $(D \cdot M)$. *Note:* Since $D \subset M$, $D \cdot M = D$.
"Horses that are Mammals" $(H \cdot M)$. Again, since $H \subset M$, $H \cdot M = H$.
"Dogs that are White" $(D \cdot W)$.
"White things that are Dogs" $(W \cdot D)$.

But now consider the following conjunction: "Dogs that are Horses" $(D \cdot H)$.

THE NULL SET.   What are we to say about such conjunctions? We have two alternatives: we can consider $D \cdot H$ as defined only when D and H have common members, and if D and H do not have members in common we can consider the phrase "dogs that are horses" as a meaningless combination of words, and the set $D \cdot H$ also as a meaningless symbol. Or, we can give a name to sets which have *no* members. Aristotle and medieval logicians took the first alternative, so for them the set "dogs that are horses" is meaningless. Modern logicians prefer the second alternative, for it produces a system that is more elegant and more comprehensive. On the second alternative, every conjunction of two sets is defined to produce a new set, even though this conjunction may result in a set that has no members. Sets which have no elements in common are called *disjoint* sets. Thus in modern logic, for any two sets A and B, the conjunction $A \cdot B$ is always defined, but it may be *empty*. An empty set is also called the *null* set, and is symbolized by "$\{\ \}$" or by "$\varnothing$". The use of the null set in modern logic is analogous to the use of zero in arithmetic.

Set theory should be viewed as a refinement of Aristotelian logic, not as a competing or opposing view. The null set gives a precise meaning and a neat symbolism to what Aristotle was saying in his Law of Self-Contradiction (section 1.3); and the universal set in modern logic is a precise, yet highly flexible, way of expressing what Aristotle was probably trying to express in his theory of the ten categories.[8]

Exercise 1.2B.   Conjoining Sets; The Null Set

Part A.   Directions: Let "V" signify the set of all Vertebrates; "M" the set of all Mammals; "D," Dogs; "F," Fish; "C," Collies; and let "L" signify the one-membered set (the unique dog) Lassie. Then find the following sets:

---

[8] Aristotle's categories were: Substance, Quality, Quantity, Relation, Action, Passion, Space, Time, Posture, Habit. For a list of twenty-five modern categories (universal sets) plus a twenty-sixth category allowing for flexibility, read Hugh Walpole, *Semantics: The Nature of Words and Their Meanings* (New York: Norton, 1941), esp. pp. 121–40, and 188.

1. $M \cdot D$ 6. $F \cdot (C \cdot D)$
2. $V \cdot F$ 7. $V \cdot M$
3. $M \cdot F$ 8. $V \cdot M \cdot D$
4. $D \cdot F$ 9. $V \cdot M \cdot D \cdot C$
5. $F \cdot (D \vee V)$ 10. $V \cdot M \cdot D \cdot C \cdot L$

Part B. Directions: Using words in their ordinary context, indicate which of the following twelve sets are null sets. Observe that null sets may have *meaning* even when they have *no referents.*

1. _____ square circles.
2. _____ mammals that are dogs.
3. _____ unicorns that are square circles.
4. _____ red tulips.

5. _____ large circles.

6. _____ unicorns.

7. _____ herbivorous lions.
8. _____ carnivorous cows.
9. _____ oak evergreens.
10. _____ carnivorous cows that are herbivorous lions.
11. _____ bachelors who are also students.
12. _____ Pegasus.

THE NUMBER OF SUBSETS IN A SET. Suppose we adopt the convention that the null set is a subset of every set. Let us now see why this convention is useful in determining the number of subsets in any set. We begin with a one-membered set, call it "$\{a\}$." This set will have exactly two ($= 2^1$) subsets: $\{a\}$ and $\emptyset$. A set consisting of exactly two elements, a and b, may be defined as the set $\{a, b\}$, and this set $\{a, b\}$ will contain exactly four ($= 2^2$) subsets: $\{a, b\}$; $\{a\}$; $\{b\}$; and $\emptyset$. A set $\{a, b, c\}$ consisting of three elements will contain exactly eight ($= 2^3$) subsets: $\{a, b, c\}$; $\{a, b\}$; $\{a, c\}$; $\{b, c\}$; $\{a\}$; $\{b\}$; $\{c\}$; and $\emptyset$. A set consisting of four elements will contain exactly 16 ($= 2^4$) subsets; a set consisting of five elements will contain exactly 32 ($= 2^5$) subsets; and, in brief, a set consisting of n elements will contain exactly 2^n subsets. This formula has numerous applications and adds greatly to the neatness of modern logic and mathematics.

DISJUNCTION (UNION, ALTERNATION). If A and B are sets, then the *union* (disjunction, alternation) of A with B includes every member of A, every member of B, and every member that is in both A and B. The union of the sets A and B is written "$A \vee B$." For example, $\{1, 2, 3\} \vee \{3, 4\} = \{1, 2, 3, 4\}$. Most mathematicians symbolize union by "$\cup$," and speak of $A \cup B$ as "A union B." Nearly all logic books employ the wedge ($\vee$) and speak of "A wedge B," or "the two disjuncts A and B," or "the two alternatives A and B," or "the disjunction, A wedge B," or "A cup B." Since the wedge looks like a cup, it may be a helpful memory device to note that "A cup B" ($A \vee B$) "holds more" than "A dot B" ($A \cdot B$).

For any three sets A, B, and C, the following relationships hold:

$A \subset A \vee B$	$A \cdot B \subset A$	$\emptyset \subset A$	$A \cdot \emptyset = \emptyset$
$B \subset A \vee B$	$A \cdot B \subset B$	$\emptyset \subset U$	$A \vee \emptyset = A$
$A \vee B \subset A \vee B \vee C$	$A \cdot B \cdot C \subset A$	$\emptyset \subset \emptyset$	$A \cdot U = A$
$A \vee C \subset A \vee B \vee C$	$A \cdot B \cdot C \subset A \cdot B$	$A \subset U$	$A \vee U = U$
$B \subset A \vee B \vee C$	$A \cdot B \cdot C \subset B \cdot C$	$A \vee B \subset U$	$U \cdot \emptyset \subset A$

NEGATION (COMPLEMENTATION). For every set A within a universal set U there is another set non-A, symbolized $\sim A$. $\sim A$ is called the *complement*, or the negation of set A. For example, if $U = \{a, b, c, d, e\}$, and if $A = \{b, c\}$, then $\sim A = \{a, d, e\}$. Again, if $U = \{1, 2, 3, 4\}$ and if $A = \{1, 2\}$, then $\sim A = \{3, 4\}$. Any subset and its negation (its "complement") should total the universal set. That all animals (universal set) are either dogs (set D) or nondogs (set

$\sim D$) means that "dogs" and "nondogs" are complementary sets. In symbols (where $D = \{$dogs$\}$ and $U = \{$animals$\}$), $D \vee \sim D = U$.

The principle just enunciated is known as the principle of *Excluded Middle*, that is, between D and $\sim D$ there is no middle ground. Every element x, within U, is contained either in D or in $\sim D$. More will be said about the principle of Exclusive Middle in section 1.3.

It should be clear to the student that if A is a subset of a universal set U, then $A \vee \sim A = U$, and $A \cdot \sim A = \varnothing$. This follows from the fact that every element of U is either in the set A or in the set $\sim A$, but not in both. Observe also that the negation of the universal set is the null set, and that the negation of the null set is the universal set. That is, $\sim U = \varnothing$ and $\sim \varnothing = U$.

EULER DIAGRAMS. The eighteenth-century mathematician, Leonhard Euler (pronounced "Oiler") employed diagrams to illustrate logical relationships. We have already seen that $S \subset P$ means that "All S is P," that is, that every element in S is also an element in P. In Euler diagrams, if the region representing S is contained in the region representing P, then the proposition "All S is P" is true; otherwise not. Below is an Euler diagram for the proposition "All Dogs are Mammals," or $D \subset M$. This diagram consists of three

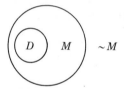

Figure 1

essential parts: (1) an area covered by both D and M, the inner circle, or the set $D \cdot M$, dogs; (2) an area covered by M alone, or the area between the inner and the outer circumferences, the set $M \cdot \sim D$, mammals that are not dogs, for example, lions, horses, whales; (3) an area outside the larger circle, or all nonmammals. In Euler diagrams, this set $\sim M$ is very indefinite and would include reptiles, fish, birds, chairs, fairies, and so on.

VENN DIAGRAMS. A Venn diagram for any two sets A and B consists of two overlapping circles *within a rectangle*, the rectangle representing the universal set.

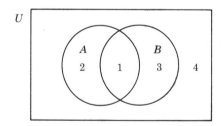

Figure 2

If we assume that each number in figure 2 represents the smallest area which contains it, then area $1 = A \cdot B$; $2 = A \cdot \sim B$; $3 = \sim A \cdot B$; and $4 = \sim A \cdot \sim B$; while $A =$ areas 1 and 2; $B =$ areas 1 and 3; $A \vee B =$ areas 1, 2, 3; and $U =$ areas 1, 2, 3, and 4.

Venn diagrams have two advantages over Euler diagrams. First, not only the sets A and B, but also their complements, $\sim A$ and $\sim B$, are clearly indicated. Second, it is never necessary to draw more than a single diagram, whether $A \subset B$, $A \subset \sim B$, $B \subset A$, $B \subset \sim A$, $\sim B \subset A$, $\sim B \subset \sim A$, $A = B$, $A = \sim B$, or $\sim A = \sim B$.

Even as Cartesian algebra made it possible to express Euclidean theorems as algebraic equations, so Boolean algebra (George Boole, 1815–64) made it possible to express logical relations as equations. Venn diagrams (John Venn, 1834–1923) are visual aids to help students better understand some of these relationships. Below are Venn diagrams and Boolean equations, for two such relations:

(1) All Dogs are Mammals,
$D \subset M$, or
No Dogs are non-Mammals,
$D \cdot \sim M = \varnothing$

(2) All Horses are non-Tigers,
$H \subset \sim T$, or
No Horses are Tigers,
$H \cdot T = \varnothing$

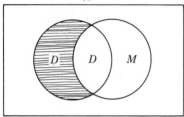

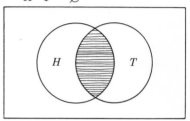

Boolean $D \cdot \sim M = \varnothing$
Equations: $D \cdot M \quad = D$
           $D \vee M \quad = M$

Figure 3

$H \cdot T \quad\ \ = \varnothing$
$H \cdot \sim T = H$
$H \vee \sim T = \sim T$

Figure 4

As used in this book, the shaded area in any Venn diagram represents the empty set. The shaded portion of a Venn diagram may be interpreted as though that portion of the diagram were nonexistent. In figure 3 the shaded portion is represented by the Boolean equation $D \cdot \sim M = \varnothing$; in figure 4, by $H \cdot T = \varnothing$.

Exercise 1.2C.   True-False Review

Directions: Let A and B be arbitrary sets. Determine which of the following statements are true and which are false. Circle T or F. Circle F unless the statement is *necessarily* true.

1. A is always contained in $A \vee B$.   1. T F
2. B is always contained in $A \vee B$.   2. T F
3. A is always contained in $A \cdot B$.   3. T F
4. B is always contained in $A \cdot B$.   4. T F
5. $A \vee B$ is always contained in A.   5. T F
6. $A \vee B$ is always contained in B.   6. T F
7. $A \cdot B$ is always contained in A.   7. T F
8. $A \cdot B$ is always contained in B.   8. T F
9. $A \subset B$ if and only if $A \cdot B = \varnothing$.   9. T F
10. $B \subset A$ if and only if $B \cdot \sim A = \varnothing$.   10. T F
11. $A \cdot B = \varnothing$ if and only if $A \subset \sim B$.   11. T F
12. If $A \vee B = \varnothing$ then $A = \varnothing$ and $B = \varnothing$. 12. T F
13. If $A \subset B$, then it always follows that $A \cdot B = A$.   13. T F
14. If $A \subset B$, then it always follows that $A \cdot B = B$.   14. T F
15. If $A \subset B$, then it always follows that $A \vee B = A$.   15. T F
16. If $A \subset B$, and if $B \subset C$, then $A \subset C$.   16. T F

PUNCTUATION: AUXILIARY SYMBOLS.   In ordinary English, punctuation is often necessary to avoid such ambiguities as are represented by the following pair of sentences:

What do you think? I am giving you a passing grade.
What? Do you think I am giving you a passing grade?

Analogously, in arithmetic: $4 \times (5 + 10) = 60$; whereas $(4 \times 5) + 10 = 30$.

"Punctuation" is also important in symbolic logic, where the mathematicians' rules concerning double negatives, use of parentheses, braces, brackets, and so forth, are adhered to. In the algebraic expression $(x - y)^2$, mathematicians speak of the letters x and y as variables, the minus sign $(-)$ and the exponent $(^2)$ as operations, and the parentheses as auxiliary symbols. Omission of the parentheses would change $(x - y)^2$ to an expression having a different meaning: $x - y^2$.

To reduce the number of parentheses ( ), brackets [ ], and braces { }, we adopt the following usages. The tilde $(\sim)$ refers to what follows immediately after it. Thus in "$\sim P \vee Q$" the tilde applies only to "P." In "$\sim (P \vee Q)$," the tilde applies to the entire expression, "$P \vee Q$." In "$\sim [(F \cdot G) \vee \sim K]$, the first tilde refers to the entire expression, "$[(F \cdot G) \vee \sim K]$," but the second tilde refers only to "K."

The equality sign $(=)$ implies a greater separation than the dot $(\cdot)$ or the wedge $(\vee)$. Hence "$A \cdot B = B \cdot A$" does not require parentheses. But parentheses are needed in $(A \cdot B = D) \vee F$ where the wedge $(\vee)$ is the expression's main connective. Similarly, parentheses are needed in "$(H \vee K = \sim M) \cdot W$," where the dot $(\cdot)$ is the major connective.

As for the arrangement of connectives, no student needs to be told that (1) $P \vee$; (2) $K \sim$; (3) $A \cdot \sim (\sim)$; and (4) $\vee P \sim$ are improper; whereas (5) $A \cdot B$; (6) $F \vee \sim G$; and (7) $(K \cdot \sim M) \vee \sim (\sim K \vee M) = K \cdot \sim M$ are well-formed formulae.

To simplify longer formulae, follow the usages of arithmetic. That is, "work from the inside out," thus:

$$- \{[-2\,(3 + 4)] + [3^2 + (-2)^3]\}$$
$$= - \{[-2\,(7)] + [9 + (-8)]\}$$
$$= - \{-14 + 1\}$$
$$= - \{-13\}$$
$$= 13$$

Exercise 1.2D.   Listing Elements of Sets

Comments. Below is a Venn diagram illustrating the placement of six elements into the following four sets: $U = \{a, b, c, x, y, z\}$; $A = \{a, x\}$; $B = \{b, y\}$; $C = \{c, a, b\}$.

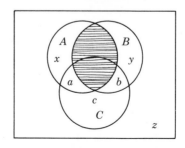

Figure 5

Directions: Let $A = \{a, x\}$; $B = \{b, y\}$; $C = \{c, a, b\}$; and $U = \{a, b, c, x, y, z\}$. Then list the elements in each of the following sets.

1. $\sim B = $ {   }
2. $\sim C = $ {   }
3. $B \cdot C = $ {   }
4. $\sim(B \cdot C) = $ {   }
5. $B \vee C = $ {   }
6. $\sim(B \vee C) = $ {   }
7. $A \cdot \sim B = $ {   }
8. $\sim(\sim B \cdot A) = $ {   }
9. $\sim A \cdot \sim B = $ {   }
10. $\sim(\sim B) = $ {   }

11. $\sim[\sim(B \cdot C)] = $ {   }
12. $\sim(A \vee B) = $ {   }
13. $\sim(A \cdot B) = $ {   }
14. $\sim A \vee \sim B = $ {   }
15. $\sim(A \cdot C) = $ {   }
16. $\sim B \vee \sim C = $ {   }
17. $\sim(B \cdot C) = $ {   }
18. $A \vee (A \cdot B) = $ {   }
19. $B \cdot \sim B = $ {   }
20. $(A \cdot C) \vee \sim(A \cdot C) = $ {   }

Exercise 1.2E.   Listing Members of Sets

In the Venn diagram below (figure 6), the rectangle signifies the universal set U. Within U are the two sets P and Q, and the four areas 1, 2, 3, and 4. These are conjoined so that $U = \{1, 2, 3, 4\}$; $P = \{1, 2\}$; $\sim P = \{3, 4\}$; $Q = \{1, 3\}$; $\sim Q = \{2, 4\}$; $P \cdot Q = \{1\}$; $\{P \cdot \sim Q\} = 2$; $\{\sim P \cdot Q\} = 3$; and $\sim P \cdot \sim Q = 4$.

$$U = \{1, 2, 3, 4\}$$

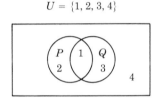

Figure 6

Directions: Using the numbers 1, 2, 3, 4 as answers, list the areas contained in each of the following sets.

1. $(P \cdot Q) \vee (P \cdot \sim Q) = $ {   }
2. $(P \cdot Q) \vee (\sim P \cdot Q) = $ {   }
3. $(\sim P \cdot Q) \vee (\sim P \cdot \sim Q) = $ {   }
4. $(\sim P \cdot \sim Q) \vee (\sim P \cdot Q) = $ {   }
5. $P \cdot \sim P = $ {   }
6. $P \vee \sim P = $ {   }
7. $(P \cdot Q) \vee \sim(P \cdot Q) = $ {   }
8. $(U \cdot P) \vee (P \cdot U) = $ {   }

9. $(U \vee P) \vee (P \vee U) = $ {   }
10. $(\varnothing \vee P) = $ {   }
11. $\varnothing \cdot P = $ {   }
12. $P \vee \sim Q = $ {   }
13. $(P \vee Q) \vee (\sim P \cdot \sim Q) = $ {   }
14. $(P \cdot Q) \vee (\sim P \cdot \sim Q) = $ {   }
15. $(P \cdot U) \vee (Q \cdot U) = $ {   }
16. $P \vee (\sim P \cdot \sim Q) = $ {   }

1.3   Seven Fundamental Laws of Mathematics and Logic

We now introduce, or review, seven basic laws of thought—laws emphasized in both mathematics and logic. Except for the DeMorgan laws, all of these were known and used long before the advent of modern logic.

We begin with four laws which should be familiar to anyone who has studied mathematics, the laws of *Double Negation, Commutation, Association*, and *Distribution*.

DN (*Double Negation, or Double Complementation*): $\sim(\sim A) = A$
Example from arithmetic: $-(-2) = 2$
Example from algebra: $-[-(xy)] = xy$
Example from ordinary English:
   "Fido is not a non-dog" = "Fido is a dog."

In the Venn diagram (figure 7), if D (the area in the circle) represents "Dogs," and $\sim D$ represents the remaining portion of the rectangle, then DN says that $\sim(\sim D) = D$.

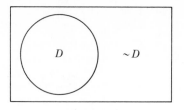

Figure 7

COM (*Commutation*): $A \vee B = B \vee A$; $A \cdot B = B \cdot A$
Examples from arithmetic: $2 + 3 = 3 + 2$; $5 \times 6 = 6 \times 5$
Examples from algebra: $x + y = y + x$; $ab = ba$
Examples from ordinary English:
  "Either Apples or Bananas" = "Either Bananas or Apples"
  "Apples that are Brown" = "Brown Apples"

ASSOC (*Association*): $A \vee (B \vee C) = (A \vee B) \vee C$;
$$A \cdot (B \cdot C) = (A \cdot B) \cdot C$$
Examples from arithmetic: $2 + (3 + 4) = (2 + 3) + 4$;
$$5 \times (6 \times 7) = (5 \times 6) \times 7$$
Examples from algebra: $a + (b + c) = (a + b) + c$; $a(bc) = (ab)c$
Examples from ordinary language:
  "Our grocer has apples, and he has bananas and carrots" =
  "Our grocer has apples and bananas, and he has carrots."
  "You can swim or play tennis, or you can play golf" =
  "You can swim, or you can play tennis or golf."

Although the laws of association are summarized in the above two formulas, throughout this book we shall interpret ASSOC broadly to mean "any series of sets conjoined entirely by dots can be rearranged at will," and "any series of sets combined exclusively by wedges can be arranged at will." This usage is common, as in:

$$1 + 2 + 3 + 4 + 5 + 6 + 7 + 8 + 9$$
$$= [(1 + 9) + (2 + 8) + (3 + 7) + (4 + 6)] + 5; \text{ or}$$
$$1 \times 2 \times 3 \times 4 \times 5 \times 10 \times 20$$
$$= [(1 \times 20) \times (2 \times 10) \times (4 \times 5)] \times 3$$

Adopting this usage, we shall let ASSOC include:

$$C \vee A \vee B \vee D \vee E \vee A \vee B \vee F$$
$$= [(A \vee B) \vee (A \vee B) \vee C \vee D \vee E \vee F;$$
$$C \cdot (G \cdot H) \cdot [D \cdot (H \cdot G) \cdot B] \cdot G \cdot A \cdot H$$
$$= [(G \cdot H) \cdot (G \cdot H) \cdot (G \cdot H)] \cdot (A \cdot B \cdot C \cdot D); \text{ and}$$
(Don and Ada) and (Fred and Bess) and (Ed and Clara)
= (Ada, Bess and Clara) and (Don, Ed and Fred).

DIST (*Distribution*): In arithmetic, multiplication is distributive over addition, but not vice versa:

$$2(3 + 4) = (2 \times 3) + (2 \times 4); \quad \text{but } 5 + (2 \times 6) \neq (5 + 2) \times (5 + 6)$$

But in set theory and logic, the dot is distributive over the wedge, and the wedge is also distributive over the dot. Here are the dual forms of the Distributive Laws:

$$A \vee (B \cdot C) = (A \vee B) \cdot (A \vee C); \quad A \cdot (B \vee C) = (A \cdot B) \vee (A \cdot C)$$

Exercise 1.3A.   Four Laws of Logic Used in Both
Traditional and Modern Algebra

Directions: Write abbreviations (COM; ASSOC; DIST; DN) to indicate which law is illustrated by each formula. Observe that problems 1–6 apply these four laws in arithmetic; problems 7–12 apply them in traditional algebra; problems 13–20 apply them in set theory; and problems 21–24 apply them in ordinary English.

_____   1. 50 percent of 80 percent = 80 percent of 50 percent.
_____   2. 100 thousands = 1000 hundreds.
_____   3. $97 \times 2 = 2 \times 97$.
_____   4. $(50 \times 97) + (50 \times 3) = 50 \times (97 + 3)$.
_____   5. $(2 + 3) + 7 = 2 + (3 + 7)$.
_____   6. $(4 \times 7.5) + (4 \times 2.5) = 4(7.5 + 2.5)$.
_____   7. $xy = yx$.
_____   8. $k(lm) = (kl)m$.
_____   9. $x(y + z) = xy + xz$.
_____ 10. $abc + axy = a(bc + xy)$.
_____ 11. $\sim(\sim a) = a$.
_____ 12. $a(bd + fg) = abd + afg$.
_____ 13. $P \vee Q = Q \vee P$.
_____ 14. $P \cdot (Q \cdot R) = (P \cdot Q) \cdot R$.
_____ 15. $\sim[\sim(\sim P)] = \sim P$.
_____ 16. $(P \cdot Q) \vee (P \cdot R) = P \cdot (Q \vee R)$.
_____ 17. $P \vee (Q \cdot R) = (P \vee Q) \cdot (P \vee R)$.
_____ 18. $A \cdot (\sim A \cdot B) = (A \cdot \sim A) \cdot B$.
_____ 19. $(A \cdot B \cdot C) \vee (A \cdot B \cdot \sim C) = [(A \cdot B) \cdot C] \vee [(A \cdot B) \cdot \sim C]$.
_____ 20. $[(A \cdot B) \cdot C] \vee [(A \cdot B) \cdot \sim C] = (A \cdot B) \cdot (C \vee \sim C)$.
_____ 21. A black truck is a truck that is black.
_____ 22. Any element that is not a non-metal is a metal.
_____ 23. "We will buy beans, or grapes, or peas, or pears, or onions" means that we will buy beans, or peas, or onions, or grapes, or pears.
_____ 24. "Ann is either sick or tired" means "Ann is either tired or sick."

TAUT (*Tautology*)—sometimes called *Idempotency* or *Redundancy*—is a modern version of Aristotle's Law of Identity: $A = A$. Expressed in terms of the wedge and the dot, this law takes two forms, and reads:

$$A \vee A = A; \quad A \cdot A = A$$

As the word "tautology" (or "redundancy") suggests, this law means that unnecessary repetition should be avoided. Also, in Latin "idem" means "the same" and "potency" means "value," hence, "idempotency" means "having the same value." Gertrude Stein's "A rose is a rose is a rose" is a famous line violating this law. Traditional logic affirmed this law, not only as Aristotle's Law of Identity ($A = A$), but also as Leibniz's Identity of Indiscernibles. Gottfried Leibniz's principle applies when, in listing members of a set, we do not count the same member twice. Thus:

$$\{1, 2, 1, 2, 1, 1, 2, 2, 1\} = \{1, 2\} \quad \text{and}$$
$$\{a, a, a, e, e, i, i, i, i, o, o, u, u, u\} = \{a, e, i, o, u\}$$

On a more fundamental level, the meaning of TAUT is: the world about us gives evidence of constancies and permanencies; and, recognizing these permanencies, we give them names, such as "1," "2," "a," "e," "i," "o," "u," "rose," "noise."

Some writers, notably Heraclitus (*d.* 485 B.C.?) and Hegel (1770–1831), unimpressed by nature's constancies, have emphasized the fact that "all things change." Certainly, there is a sense in which Heraclitus was correct when he declared, "A man cannot step into the same river twice." But do we understand the meaning of this statement by Heraclitus? If so, there must be *some* sense in which the words and concepts he used (namely "man," "cannot," "step," "into," "same," "river," "twice") are stable and definite. In short, we cannot say even that "all things change" without assuming some ideas that are constant.

Consider the following examples. We say "An acorn will grow into an oak"; and we can describe various stages of the growth, such as "acorn," "seedling," "sapling," "potential oak," "young oak," and "mature oak." Similarly we can describe various stages of growth from childhood to manhood. However "A child is a child" even though he is also a "potential man." "A man is a man" even though he was once a child.

From the viewpoint of set theory, we might speak of an individual man as the set of all of the man's changing manifestations as he moves from birth to death. But since these stages of growth are infinite in number, it becomes impossible to describe them. Hence we must satisfy ourselves with such relatively stable—though vaguely defined—words and ideas as "person," "embryo," "baby," "child," "adolescent," "youth," "adult," "senior citizen," "individual," and "John Doe."

The law of tautology (TAUT) is the bedrock upon which reason and logic are based. Viewed historically, TAUT is a modern reformulation of what Aristotle (384–322 B.C.) called The Law of Identity, and of what Leibniz (1646–1716) called The Identity of Indiscernibles.

ExM (*Excluded Middle*): The laws of Excluded Middle, in their dual forms, read:

$$A \lor \sim A = U; \qquad A \cdot \sim A = \varnothing$$

These laws also go back to Aristotle, except that they are now expressed in terms of the wedge ($\lor$), the dot ($\cdot$) and the tilde ($\sim$). Aristotle called the first one ($A \lor \sim A = U$) the law of Excluded Middle, and called the second one ($A \cdot \sim A = \varnothing$) the Law of Contradiction. But since their only difference is that one of them uses the wedge ($A \lor \sim A = U$) whereas the other uses the dot ($A \cdot \sim A = \varnothing$), we view them as dual forms of a single law which we call the Law of Excluded Middle.

Some twentieth century semanticists, notably Alfred Korzybski (1879–1950), have argued that modern science deals with change, and is itself everchanging; therefore it makes traditional logic's notion of fixed sets and complements of sets obsolete. The truth of the matter is that, by means of precise measurement, modern science makes it possible to *apply* the laws of Excluded Middle more precisely and more universally. Thus when clocks replaced sun dials and hour glasses as measures of time, it became possible to speak, not merely of "rapid" or "gradual" acceleration, but to measure acceleration in precise mathematical terms. It was this precision which made possible Galileo's and Newton's laws of motion. Likewise the prescientific world spoke vaguely of temperatures as "cold," "lukewarm," "quite hot," "hot," "hotter than blazes," and other terms that are extremely vague compared to the thermometric temperatures which range from $-273°C$ (Kelvin) to the theoretical temperatures of the stars. In ordinary life, we may now define bathwater as "hot" if it exceeds 60°C (140°F), and cold if, for example, it is below 10°C (50°F). Chemists determine the *precise* melting and boiling points of thousands of elements and compounds. The average citizen knows not merely that antifreeze will keep his car's radiator from freezing, but also that a certain amount of antifreeze will suffice to keep it from freezing at, say, 25°F, 10°F, -10°F, -30°F, or -60°F. Thus the logic of "This radiator will either freeze or not freeze" ($F \vee {\sim}F$) is not only used, but it is used with a knowledge and a precision that was utterly impossible before the days of precise scientific measurement. In short, Aristotle's law of Excluded Middle makes precise scientific measurement meaningful and useful.

DN (*Double Negation*): The law of Double Negation is well known in mathematics:

$$-1(-1) = +1; \qquad -[-(-x)] = -x$$

In set theory a somewhat similar (and somewhat unsimilar) law is properly called the Law of Double Complementation, but we here employ the more usual terminology and call it Double Negation. In figure 8 a single set A is represented by the circle, the universal set by the rectangle, and the complement of A, namely, ${\sim}A$, is represented by the area within U but not within A. The Law of Double Negation tells us that ${\sim}({\sim}A) = A$ and that ${\sim}[{\sim}({\sim}A)] = {\sim}A$.

U

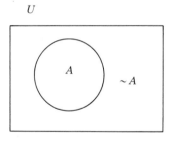

Figure 8

The same relationship holds for more complex sets. In the Venn diagram of figure 9, the universal set U consists of the four areas 1, 2, 3, and 4: $U = \{1, 2, 3, 4\}$; $P = \{1, 2\}$; ${\sim}P = \{3, 4\}$; $Q = \{1, 3\}$; ${\sim}Q = \{2, 4\}$.

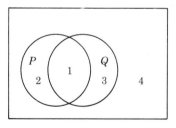

Figure 9

Note the following conjunctions, their negations (complementary sets) and their double negations:

$$
\begin{array}{lll}
(P \cdot Q) = \{1\}; & {\sim}(P \cdot Q) = \{2, 3, 4\}; & {\sim}[{\sim}(P \cdot Q)] = \{1\} \\
(P \cdot {\sim}Q) = \{2\}; & {\sim}(P \cdot {\sim}Q) = \{1, 3, 4\}; & {\sim}[{\sim}(P \cdot {\sim}Q)] = \{2\} \\
({\sim}P \cdot Q) = \{3\}; & {\sim}({\sim}P \cdot Q) = \{1, 2, 4\}; & {\sim}[{\sim}({\sim}P \cdot Q)] = \{3\} \\
({\sim}P \cdot {\sim}Q) = \{4\}; & {\sim}({\sim}P \cdot {\sim}Q) = \{1, 2, 3\}; & {\sim}[{\sim}({\sim}P \cdot {\sim}Q)] = \{4\}
\end{array}
$$

Compare the preceding conjunctions with the following disjunctions (alternations), their negations, and their double negations:

$$(P \vee Q) = \{1, 2, 3\}; \qquad \sim(P \vee Q) = \{4\}; \qquad \sim[\sim(P \vee Q)] = \{1, 2, 3\}$$
$$(P \vee \sim Q) = \{1, 2, 4\}; \qquad \sim(P \vee \sim Q) = \{3\}; \qquad \sim[\sim P \vee \sim Q)] = \{1, 2, 4\}$$
$$(\sim P \vee Q) = \{1, 3, 4\}; \qquad \sim(\sim P \vee Q) = \{2\}; \qquad \sim[\sim(\sim P \vee Q)] = \{1, 3, 4\}$$
$$(\sim P \vee \sim Q) = \{2, 3, 4\}; \quad \sim(\sim P \vee \sim Q) = \{1\}; \quad \sim[\sim(\sim P \vee \sim Q)] = \{2, 3, 4\}$$

Note finally that $(P \cdot Q) = \{1\} = \sim(\sim P \vee \sim Q)$,
and $(P \vee Q) = \{1, 2, 3\} = \sim(\sim P \cdot \sim Q)$.

This brings us to the DeMorgan laws [Augustus DeMorgan (1806–1871).]

DeM *(DeMorgan):* The DeMorgan Laws are among the most important laws in modern logic. They read as follows:

$$A \vee B = \sim(\sim A \cdot \sim B); \qquad A \cdot B = \sim(\sim A \vee \sim B)$$

For reasons which will become evident in chapter 2, let us now substitute P, $\sim P$, Q, and $\sim Q$ for A, $\sim A$, B, and $\sim B$. Then these DeMorgan laws will read:

$$P \vee Q = \sim(\sim P \cdot \sim Q); \qquad P \cdot Q = \sim(\sim P \vee \sim Q)$$

Applying various substitutions, these DeMorgan laws yield exactly eight forms, namely:

(1) $P \vee Q = \sim(\sim P \cdot \sim Q)$ $\{1, 2, 3\}$ (5) $\sim P \cdot \sim Q = \sim(P \vee Q)$ $\{4\}$
(2) $P \vee \sim Q = \sim(\sim P \cdot Q)$ $\{1, 2, 4\}$ (6) $\sim P \cdot Q = \sim(P \vee \sim Q)$ $\{3\}$
(3) $\sim P \vee Q = \sim(P \cdot \sim Q)$ $\{1, 3, 4\}$ (7) $P \cdot \sim Q = \sim(\sim P \vee Q)$ $\{2\}$
(4) $\sim P \vee \sim Q = \sim(P \cdot Q)$ $\{2, 3, 4\}$ (8) $P \cdot Q = \sim(\sim P \vee \sim Q)$ $\{1\}$

A study of these equations, and of those listed under DN, will show that the DeMorgan Laws may be viewed as a modern formulation of the laws of Double Negation and Excluded Middle. Observe that in Double Negation, two tildes are eliminated: no other change is required. But in the DeMorgan Laws changes are made in the tildes ($\sim$), the wedge ($\vee$), and the dot ($\cdot$).

Although the DeMorgan Laws are a part of the new math, of modern algebra and of set theory, they are not a part of traditional algebra or arithmetic. However, the DeMorgan Laws are implicit in language, as may be seen in the following two pairs of statements having equivalent meanings.

Either a person is a Male or that person is not a Bachelor. ($M \vee \sim B$)
It cannot be both that a person is not a Male and at the same time a Bachelor. $\sim(\sim M \cdot B)$

[This animal is] neither my Dog nor my Puppy. $\sim(D \vee P)$
[This animal is] not my Dog and it is not my Puppy. ($\sim D \cdot \sim P$)

Throughout this section we have emphasized the similarity of mathematics and logic with respect to their use of the seven laws: DN, COM, ASSOC, DIST, ExM, TAUT, and DeM. But a word of warning is in order concerning TAUT, DN, and DeM. In arithmetic, $(-1)(-1) = +1$, and in algebra, $(-a)(-b) = +ab$. But in set theory and in logic, $\sim A \cdot \sim A = \sim A$ (by TAUT), $\sim A \vee \sim A = \sim A$ (by TAUT); $\sim(\sim A \cdot B) = A \vee \sim B$ (by DeM), $\sim(\sim A \vee \sim B) = A \cdot B$ (by DeM); and $\sim(\sim A \cdot \sim A) = \sim(\sim A)$, by TAUT, although $\sim(\sim A) = A$ by DN.

SUMMARY.   These are the seven laws which have been explained, and which will be used in the following exercises:

COM (Commutation):
$$P \cdot Q = Q \cdot P$$
$$P \vee Q = Q \vee P$$

ASSOC (Association):
$$P \cdot (Q \cdot R) = (P \cdot Q) \cdot R$$
$$P \vee (Q \vee R) = (P \vee Q) \vee R$$

DIST (Distribution):
$$P \cdot (Q \vee R) = (P \cdot Q) \vee (P \cdot R)$$
$$P \vee (Q \cdot R) = (P \vee Q) \cdot (P \vee R)$$

DN (Double Negation, or Double Complementation): $\sim(\sim P) = P$

TAUT (Tautology):
$$P \cdot P = P$$
$$P \vee P = P$$

ExM (Excluded Middle):
$$P \cdot \sim P = \varnothing$$
$$P \vee \sim P = U$$

DeM (DeMorgan):
$$\sim(P \cdot Q) = \sim P \vee \sim Q$$
$$\sim(P \vee Q) = \sim P \cdot \sim Q$$

Exercise 1.3B.   Seven Fundamental Laws of Logic

Directions: In the answer blanks before each of the following, write in the name of the law which is used to effect the equality. (Write COM, ASSOC, DIST, TAUT, ExM, DN, or DeM.) If none of these seven laws are used, write "X" for an answer. The following Venn diagram (figure 10) may help you to visualize these relationships.

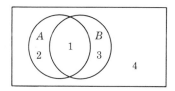

Figure 10

_____ 1. $A \vee A = A$

_____ 3. $A \cdot \sim A = \varnothing$

_____ 5. $A \cdot \sim B = \varnothing$

_____ 7. $(A \cdot B) \vee \sim B = \sim B \vee (A \cdot B)$

_____ 9. $B \cdot (A \cdot B) \cdot A = (A \cdot B) \cdot (A \cdot B)$

_____ 2. $A \vee \sim A = U$

_____ 4. $\sim A = \sim[\sim(\sim A)]$

_____ 6. $A \cdot B = B \vee A$

_____ 8. $\sim(A \cdot \sim B) = \sim A \cdot B$

_____ 10. $A \cdot (B \vee A) = (A \cdot B) \vee (A \cdot A)$

Note: Each of the remaining problems illustrates *two* laws of logic and requires *two* answers.

_____ and _____ 11 & 12. $(A \cdot B) \vee (B \cdot A) = A \cdot B$

_____ and _____ 13 & 14. $(A \vee \sim B) \cdot (A \vee \sim B) = \sim(\sim A \cdot B)$

_____ and _____ 15 & 16. $A \vee (B \cdot \sim A) = (A \vee B) \cdot U$

_____ and _____ 17 & 18. $(A \vee \sim A) \cdot (B \vee \sim B) = U$

_____ and _____ 19 & 20. $A \cdot (B \vee \sim A) = (A \cdot B) \vee \varnothing$

_____ and _____ 21 & 22. $\sim(\sim A \cdot \sim B) \vee B = A \vee (B \vee B)$

Exercise 1.3C.   Equivalent Expressions: Recognizing Laws of Logic

Directions: Each problem in this exercise expresses the same set in four or five different ways. In the answer blanks you are to write in the name of the law used to replace the formula on the previous line. Use abbreviations for the seven laws: COM, ASSOC, DIST, TAUT, ExM, DN, DeM.

(1) $\sim\{\sim[\sim(\sim Q \vee \sim Q)]\}$
$= \sim(\sim Q \vee \sim Q)$ _____
$= \sim(\sim Q)$ _____
$= Q$ _____

(2) $\sim[\sim(P \cdot Q) \cdot \sim(\sim P \vee \sim Q)]$
$= (P \cdot Q) \vee (\sim P \vee \sim Q)$ _____
$= (P \cdot Q) \vee \sim(P \cdot Q)$ _____
$= U$ _____

(3) $(P \vee P) \vee [(Q \cdot R) \cdot (R \cdot Q)]$
$= P \vee [(Q \cdot R) \cdot (R \cdot Q)]$ _____
$= P \vee [(Q \cdot R) \cdot (Q \cdot R)]$ _____
$= P \vee (Q \cdot R)$ _____

(4) $\sim\{\sim[\sim(\sim Q \vee P)]\} \cdot (Q \cdot \sim P)$
$= \sim(\sim Q \vee P) \cdot (Q \cdot \sim P)$ _____
$= (Q \cdot \sim P) \cdot (Q \cdot \sim P)$ _____
$= Q \cdot \sim P$ _____

(5) $\sim[\sim(\sim P \cdot \sim Q) \cdot \sim(P \vee Q)]$
  $= (\sim P \cdot \sim Q) \vee (P \vee Q)$ _____
  $= \sim(P \vee Q) \vee (P \vee Q)$ _____
  $= U$ _____

(6) $\sim(Q \vee P) \cdot Q$
  $= (\sim Q \cdot \sim P) \cdot Q$ _____
  $= \sim P \cdot (Q \cdot \sim Q)$ _____
  $= \sim P \cdot \varnothing$ _____

(7) $\sim[(\sim P \vee \sim Q) \cdot (\sim P \vee Q)]$
  $= \sim(\sim P \vee \sim Q) \vee \sim(\sim P \vee Q)$ ____
  $= (P \cdot Q) \vee (P \cdot \sim Q)$ _____
  $= P \cdot (Q \vee \sim Q)$ _____
  $= P \cdot U$ _____

(8) $\sim[(P \cdot Q) \cdot P]$
  $= \sim(P \cdot Q) \vee \sim P$ _____
  $= (\sim P \vee \sim Q) \vee \sim P$ _____
  $= (\sim P \vee \sim P) \vee \sim Q$ _____
  $= \sim P \vee \sim Q$ _____

(9) $(P \cdot Q \cdot \sim P \cdot R) \cdot (\sim Q \cdot P \cdot Q)$
  $= [(P \cdot \sim P) \cdot Q \cdot R] \cdot [(Q \cdot \sim Q) \cdot P]$
  $= [\varnothing \cdot Q \cdot R] \cdot (\varnothing \cdot P)$ _____
  $= P \cdot Q \cdot R \cdot (\varnothing \cdot \varnothing)$ _____
  $= P \cdot Q \cdot R \cdot \varnothing$ _____

(10) $[P \vee (P \vee \sim Q)] \cdot Q$
  $= [(P \vee P) \vee \sim Q] \cdot Q$ _____
  $= (P \vee \sim Q) \cdot Q$ _____
  $= (P \cdot Q) \vee (\sim Q \cdot Q)$ _____
  $= (P \cdot Q) \vee \varnothing$ _____

Answers for Chapter One

1.1A:

There are no answers given for this exercise.

1.1B:

1. "Tom is a cat" is true if and only if Tom is a cat.

3. It is true that the sentence, " 'The word *logic* contains five letters' contains exactly four words" is false.

5. In " 'John' is a name" the word in single quotes refers to a name and not to the bearer of that name.

7. "Smoke" and "the visible exhalation given off by a burning or smoldering substance, especially the gray, brown, or blackish mixture of gases and suspended carbon particles resulting from the combustion of wood, peat, coal, or other organic matter" are examples of *conventional symbols* used by English-speaking people; whereas real smoke is a *natural sign* on the basis of which men infer the existence of fire.

9. Problem 9 requires no change, for the algebraic equation stands out as a separate entity that is not confused with the rest of the sentence. This usage will be followed in this logic book; whenever possible, for the sake of brevity, quotation marks should be avoided. However, clarity is logic's primary aim. In logic clarity always takes precedence over brevity.

11. If "is" is not "is" and "is not" is not "is not," is not "is not" "is" and "is" "is not"?

1.1C:

1. F;   3. 0;   5. E;   7. M;   9. N;   11. B;   13. H;   15. J;   17. B;   19. E;
21. J;   23. H;   25. G.

1.2A:

Part A: 1. Textbooks, encyclopedias, dictionaries;   3. Freshmen, philosophy majors, coeds;   5. Roses, daisies, lilies.

Part B: 1. felines (or mammals, or vertebrates);   3. fish;   5. birds.

1.2B:

Part A: 1. Dogs;   3. $\varnothing$ (the empty set);   5. $\varnothing$;   7. Mammals;   9. Collies.

Part B: 1. Null;   3. Null;   5. Not null;   7. Null;   9. Null, if "oak" is defined to include only deciduous trees; but "not null" if "oak" is defined to include the evergreen called "live oak."   11. Not null.

1.2C:

1. T;   3. F;   5. F;   7. T;   9. F;   11. T;   13. T;   15. F.

1.2D:

1. $\sim\{b, y\} = \{a, c, x, z\}$;   3. $\{b, y\} \cdot \{a, b, c\} = \{b\}$;   5. $\{b, y\} \vee \{c, a, b\} = \{a, b, c, y\}$;
7. $\{a, x\} \cdot \{a, c, x, z\} = \{a, x\}$;   9. $\{b, c, y, z\} \cdot \{a, c, x, z\} = \{c, z\}$;

11. $\sim[\sim(\{b, y\} \cdot \{c, a, b\}) = \sim[\sim\{b\}] = \{b\}$;   13. $\sim(\{a, x\} \cdot \{b, y\} = \sim\{\} = \{a, b, c, x, y, z\}$;
15. $\sim(\{a, x\} \cdot \{c, a, b\}) = \sim\{a\} = \{b, c, x, y, z\}$;   17. $\sim(\{b, y\} \cdot \{c, a, b\}) = \sim\{b\} = \{a, c, x, y, z\}$;
19. $\{b, y\} \cdot \{a, c, x, z\} = \{\}$ or $\varnothing$.

1.2E:

1. $(P \cdot Q) \vee (P \cdot \sim Q) = \{1\} \vee \{2\} = \{1, 2\}$;   3. $(\sim P \cdot Q) \vee (\sim P \cdot \sim Q) = \{3\} \vee \{4\} = \{3, 4\}$;
5. $P \cdot \sim P = \{1, 2\} \cdot \{3, 4\} = \{\}$ or $\varnothing$;   7. $(P \cdot Q) \vee \sim(P \cdot Q) = \{1\} \vee \{2, 3, 4\} = \{1, 2, 3, 4\} = U$;
9. $(U \vee P) \vee (P \vee U) = P \vee U = U = \{1, 2, 3, 4\}$;   11. $\varnothing \cdot P = \varnothing = \{\}$;
13. $(P \vee Q) \vee (\sim P \cdot \sim Q) = \{1, 2, 3\} \vee \{4\} = \{1, 2, 3, 4\}$;
15. $(P \cdot U) \vee (Q \cdot U) = P \vee Q = \{1, 2\} \vee \{1, 3\} = \{1, 2, 3\}$.*

1.3A:

1. COM;   3. COM;   5. ASSOC;   7. COM;   9. DIST;   11. DN;   13. COM;
15. DN;   17. DIST;   19. ASSOC;   21. COM;   23. ASSOC.

1.3B:

1. TAUT;   3. ExM;   5. X;   7. COM;   9. ASSOC;   11 and 12. COM and TAUT;
15 and 16. DIST and ExM;   19 and 20. DIST and ExM.

1.3C:

1. DN; TAUT; DN;   3. TAUT; COM; TAUT;   5. DeM; DeM; ExM;
7. DeM; DeM (twice); DIST; ExM;   9. ASSOC (twice); ExM (twice); ASSOC; TAUT.

* Note to Instructor: In explaining solutions to the problems in exercises 1.2D and 1.2E, you should employ some of the laws to be explained in section 1.3. In this way exercises 1.2D and 1.2E will serve as a prelude to section 1.3, and students will more fully appreciate the *importance* of laws of logic.

chapter 2

MODERN LOGIC: THE STUDY OF TRUTH VALUES

2.1 Statements, Statement Forms, Connectives, and Truth Values

STATEMENTS (PROPOSITIONS). Logic's domain of discourse consists of statements or propositions, and we shall here use these terms synonymously.[1]

We define a proposition as a meaningful and unambiguous sentence which is either true or false, and not both. This means that we are not concerned with questions (for example, "Is it true?"), with commands ("Speak the truth"), or with exclamations ("How wonderfully true!"). Nor are we concerned with meaningless combinations of words such as "ruefully fiend not is" or "runs Jack is the"; or even with ambiguous declarations, such as "Amy told Bess that her sister liked her."

When we define a proposition as a well-formed statement that is either true or false, we do not say that we *know* whether it is true or whether it is false. *Logically*, the statement that "*pi* (3.14159 . . .) contains the series of numbers 1, 2, 3, 4, 5, 6, 7, 8, 9" is true or it is false—even though we may never *know* whether it is true or whether it is false. A similar analysis holds for modal or possible propositions, for example, "Next Monday *may* be a rainy day." We shall deal with these in chapter 7, where they will take the form, "There is x probability that the proposition 'Next Monday is a rainy day' is *true*." In summary, we shall employ the term "proposition" to mean any clear, meaningful declarative sentence that is either true or false, but not both.

SIMPLE AND COMPLEX PROPOSITIONS (OR STATEMENTS). We define a simple proposition as follows: a *simple* (or "atomic") proposition is one which has no parts which are themselves propositions. Thus "Birds chirp," "All birds are small," and "The child saw the bird" are simple propositions; whereas "Birds chirp and birds are small" and "Either the child saw the bird or birds are small" and "If the child did not see the bird then birds

---

[1] Some logicians distinguish *statements* and *propositions* as follows: when the context has to do with a sentence's meaning, they use the word "proposition," but when the context has to do only with the truth or falsity of a sentence, they use the word "statement." According to this usage, "It rains," "Il pleut," and "Es regnet" are three different statements, but only one proposition. We shall here use the terms "proposition" and "statement" synonymously, for, as we shall soon see, we are here considering statements, not with respect to their *meanings*, but only with respect to their *truth values*.

are small" are *complex* propositions. The relation between "atomic" and "molecular" propositions in logic is analogous to the relation between "atomic" elements (such as H and O) and "molecular compounds" (such as H_2O) in chemistry.[2]

OPERATORS OR CONNECTIVES.   As section 1.2 explained, set theory and modern logic have three common operators, or connectives, namely:

(1) Conjunction or Intersection [Symbol: the dot (·)]
(2) Disjunction, Alternation or Union [Symbol: the wedge (∨)]
(3) Negation or Complementation [Symbol: the tilde (∼)].

These three operations are basic to set theory and to modern algebra. We shall now see how modern logic applies these three operators to statements from ordinary language.

To represent a simple proposition, a single lower-case letter is used. For example, "Men are (m)ortal" would be symbolized by the single letter "*m*"; "Grass is (g)reen" by "*g*"; "Grass is not (g)reen by "∼*g*"; "Some girls are (d)ancers" by "*d*"; "It is false that some girls are (d)ancers" by "∼*d*." Throughout this book, in order that all students will employ the same letter to represent a given statement, we shall place parentheses around the letter to be used. Two simple statements may be conjoined into a complex statement "Men are (m)ortal and grass is (g)reen," and symbolized "*m* · *g*." In this conjunction, we are in no way conjoining their *meaning*. We are simply asserting that these two simple statements are both *true*.

Let us proceed with other examples. Suppose we have two simple statements: Joe has a (j)ob (*j*); Gladys is (g)lad (*g*). The *conjunction* of these two simple propositions would result in a *complex* proposition: Joe has a (j)ob *and* Gladys is (g)lad (*j* · *g*). The *alternation* or *disjunction* of the same two propositions would yield another *complex* proposition: Either Joe has a (j)ob *or* Gladys is (g)lad (*j* ∨ *g*). Combining *negation* with these results yields *complex* propositions such as the following:

Joe has a (j)ob *and* Gladys is (g)lad.   (*j* · *g*)
Joe has no job *and* Gladys is not (g)lad.   (∼*j* · ∼*g*)
Either Joe has a (j)ob or Gladys is not (g)lad.   (*j* ∨ ∼*g*)
Joe may or may not have a (j)ob, but Gladys is (g)lad.   [(*j* ∨ ∼*j*) · *g*]

Exercise 2.1A.   Symbolizing Conjunctions and Negations

Directions: Express the following propositions in symbolic form. First study the odds, and check your answers against the answers given at the end of the chapter.

1. This sentence is a (c)ategorical statement.   1. _____
2. This sentence is an (a)tomic type.   2. _____
3. This sentence is not a (c)ompound sentence.   3. _____
4. This sentence is not a (m)olecular type.   4. _____
5. It is false that this sentence is a (m)olecular proposition.   5. _____
6. It is true that this sentence is an (a)tomic proposition.   6. _____
7. This sentence is a (c)ompound sentence, and it consists of two simple
   (a)tomic components.   7. _____

---

[2] As we shall see in chap. 6, traditional logic carefully analyzed the component parts of simple statements into Subject, Predicate, Copula, and Quantifier, and distinguished such forms as "No dogs are (f)oxes," "All dogs are (m)ammals," "Lassie is a (d)og," and "Some dogs are (p)ets." But in this chapter we shall treat all such sentences as "atomic" or "simple," and shall represent them by the single letters "*f*," "*m*," "*d*" and "*p*."

8. A statement containing two or more atomic components is not an
   (a)tomic statement.   8. _____

Observe that the artificial language of logic, although simple and precise, is not
very expressive. Thus in problems 9–20 the dot (·) is employed, not only to replace
the conjunction "and," but also to replace words such as "but," "while," "although,"
or to replace a comma. It is obvious that some of the delicate nuances of meaning are
thereby lost. On the other hand, there is a gain in clarity because in logic "and" and
"or" are precisely defined.

9. Although some sentences do not contain the conjunction "(a)nd,"
   they are (c)onjunctions nevertheless.   9. _____
10. This sentence is (m)olecular, but it is not (l)ong.   10. _____
11. Some sentences are (a)ffirmative, but they contain (n)egative terms,
    and are (u)nambiguous.   11. _____
12. Columbus (d)iscovered a new world, but his (g)reatness lies in the
    fact that he searched for it on the faith of an opinion.   12. _____
13. The block of granite is an (o)bstacle in the pathway of the weak, but
    a (s)tepping stone in the pathway of the strong.   13. _____
14. Alexander undoubtedly (k)new the definition of fortitude, but he
    received more (d)irection of mind by the pattern of Achilles.   14. _____
15. Now good (d)igestion wait on appetite, and (h)ealth on both.
    (Shakespeare)   15. _____
16. Knowledge (c)omes, but wisdom (l)ingers.   (Tennyson)   16. _____
17. Dan (d)ozed and Dan (h)eard a noise.   17. _____
18. Dan was (d)ozing, Dan (h)eard a noise, and these two events occurred
    at the (s)ame moment.   18. _____
19. Dan (d)ozed, and *later* Dan (h)eard a noise.   19. _____
20. Dan (h)eard a noise, and *later* Dan (d)ozed.   20. _____
21. Dan (d)ozed and Dan (h)eard a noise, and he heard the noise (a)fter
    he had dozed.   21. _____
22. Dan (h)eard a noise and he heard it (b)efore he dozed, but he (d)ozed.   22. _____
23. Dan (h)eard a noise, and subsequently Dan did not (d)oze.   23. _____
24. Dan (h)eard a noise, and Dan did not (d)oze, and hearing the noise
    (e)xplained why Dan did not doze.   24. _____

The distinction between simple and complex statements is rather arbitrary.
For some purposes, the subtleties of ordinary language may be unimportant,
and may be glossed over in symbolizing a statement. But for other purposes
they are very important as in the temporal sequence of events in problems 18
to 24 of the preceding exercise. When this is the case, a statement should be
reanalyzed to include all of its essential meanings. A fond mother might
describe her son Tom in words like these: "Tom is (h)andsome, and Tom is
(d)ark-haired, and Tom is (m)y boy," $(h \cdot d \cdot m)$; or else might restate this
sentence to read "Tom is my handsome, dark-haired (b)oy"—symbolized by
the one letter "b." To take another example: the three sentences "The ugly
duckling was (a)wkward"; "This duckling (c)hanged into a swan"; and
"This swan was (b)eautiful" would be symbolized as the conjunction: $a \cdot c \cdot b$.
But the sentence might be rewritten "The ugly duckling (c)hanged into a
beautiful swan" and symbolized as a simple statement "c."

Sometimes it is advantageous to ignore the temporal sequence of events,
sometimes not. Thus we might say "On the average, in Yellowstone Park,
August has about twenty clear days and only eleven cloudy ones"—and the
specific time when these days occurred would not be important to that statement. Likewise, *if we ignore the temporal sequence of events*, "Dan and Dora

(d)ecided to get married, and they (h)ad five children" ($d \cdot h$) is logically equivalent to "Dan and Dora (h)ad five children and they (d)ecided to get married" ($h \cdot d$). However there are relatively few Dans and Doras who would be willing to ignore the temporal sequence of events in such statements. If a logician does not wish to ignore it, he is not compelled to do so; for he may add as another true statement "Dan and Dora got married (b)*efore* they had five children"; and this will remove the ambiguity.

Disjunction (Alternation, Union) is of two types: (1) Inclusive or Weak, and (2) Exclusive or Strong. *Inclusive (Weak) Disjunction* is symbolized by the wedge ($\vee$). As in set theory, the wedge is stipulated to signify the *weak* or *inclusive* sense, meaning "*either . . . or . . .* and *perhaps both.*" It means that *at least one, and perhaps all, of the alternatives are true.* "Or" in this inclusive sense is the "and/or" of legal terminology. Examples:

1. Good students either have natural (a)bility or they are (d)iligent. This is symbolized "$a \vee d$" and means "Either (a) or (d) or both (a) and (d)."
2. Either a football player is (h)eavy or he is (f)ast. This is symbolized "$h \vee f$" and means "Either (h) or (f) or perhaps both (h) and (f)."

Exclusive (Strong) Disjunction has the meaning "*either . . . or . . .* and *not both.*" Letting "b" signify "This baby is a (b)oy" and letting "g" signify "This baby is a (g)irl," here are the two ways in which exclusive disjunction is expressed:

Either b or g, but not both: $(b \vee g) \cdot \sim(b \cdot g)$.
Either b and not g, or g and not b: $(b \cdot \sim g) \vee (g \cdot \sim b)$.

In common speech the distinction between the exclusive and inclusive meanings of "or" may be difficult to detect. If a teacher says, "You may take (l)ogic or you may take (e)thics," does he mean that you may perhaps take both? ($l \vee e$)—meaning $[l \vee e \vee (l \cdot e)]$? Or does he mean that you may take one or the other, but not both $[(l \vee e) \cdot \sim(l \cdot e)]$? Confusion between these two meanings of "or" provides the humor in the following conversation between a bachelor and a college friend whom he had not seen for several years:

Bachelor: Are you (m)arried? Or do you still (c)ook your own breakfasts?
Married Man: Yes. [Meaning: $m \vee c$. This meaning includes ($m \cdot c$)].

In exercise 2.1B you will see that the context of the discourse *generally* makes it reasonably clear whether "or" is used in the weak, inclusive sense, or in the strong, exclusive sense.

Exercise 2.1B.   Symbolizing Weak and Strong Alternations

Remarks: This exercise provides drill in transforming alternations from ordinary language into symbols.

Directions: Express the following propositions in symbolic form.

1. It will (b)low or it will be (c)old, or perhaps both.   1. _____
2. Here we (e)at or we (d)rink.   2. _____
3. Either this medicine (c)ures your ailment or we gladly refund your (m)oney, but not both.   3. _____
4. My rich uncle is either (b)enevolent or (f)riendly.   4. _____
5. Either the word "or" means "(a)nd/or," or the two alternatives are mutually (e)xclusive.   5. _____
6. Dave is either a (d)entist or a (l)awyer, but not both.   6. _____
7. You may elect (h)istory or (a)nthropology, but not both.   7. _____

8. You may elect (h)istory or (g)eography or both history and geography.   8. _____
9. This baby either wants (f)ood or craves (a)ttention.   9. _____
10. John either (f)orgot his hat or doesn't (l)ike to wear it.   10. _____
11. Either he has a (l)ow I.Q., or he doesn't (a)pply himself.   11. _____
12. Either you have not (g)ained maturity, or you (r)ealize how little great men know.   12. _____
13. Wrong conclusions result from un(w)arranted assumptions or from in(v)alid inferences.   13. _____
14. Wrong conclusions result from (l)ack of factual data or (f)aulty reasoning.   14. _____
15. Either a college education challenges one's abilities (m)ore than a job, or it is of (l)ess value than a job.   15. _____
16. A person must either have the ability to (a)pply what he knows, or he does not have (g)enuine knowledge.   16. _____
17. Either you can correctly (s)ymbolize the statement you are now reading, or you do not (u)nderstand that "or" is sometimes used for exclusive alternation.   17. _____
18. A logic student must (r)ecognize the distinction between weak and strong disjunction, or he will have (t)rouble.   18. _____
19. Monthly payments on this mortgage loan may be made either by the (m)an or by his (d)aughter.   19. _____
20. You must either take the (h)ighway that turns left, or follow the (b)oulevard that goes straight ahead.   20. _____

As the concluding six problems of exercise 2.1B suggest, ordinary language quite frequently glosses over the precise distinction between inclusive (weak) and exclusive (strong) disjunction. Fortunately, as we shall see in section 2.5, the much used argument form called "The Disjunctive Syllogism" is a valid argument form whether its "either . . . or" premise is interpreted as an inclusive or as an exclusive disjunction.

Exercise 2.1C.   Symbolizing More Complex Statements

Listed below are four conjunctions of two statements:
A. Barkus is (a)ble and [Barkus is] (w)illing. $(a \cdot w)$
B. Barkus is (a)ble but not (w)illing. $(a \cdot \sim w)$
C. Barkus is not (a)ble, but he is (w)illing. $(\sim a \cdot w)$
D. Barkus is not (a)ble and he is not (w)illing. $(\sim a \cdot \sim w)$.

Directions: Following the usages in A, B, C, and D above (for symbolizing a, $\sim a$, w, and $\sim w$), "translate" the following symbolisms into ordinary English.

EXAMPLE: Problem 1: It is false that Barkus is either able or willing.

1. $\sim(a \vee w)$	5. $(\sim a \vee \sim w) \cdot \sim(\sim a \cdot \sim w)$	9. $(\sim a \vee \sim w) \cdot w$
2. $\sim a \vee w$	6. $(a \cdot \sim w) \vee (w \cdot \sim a)$	10. $(a \vee \sim a) \cdot w$
3. $(\sim a \cdot \sim w) \vee \sim w$	7. $(a \cdot w) \vee \sim(a \vee w)$	11. $(w \vee \sim w) \cdot a$
4. $\sim a \vee \sim w$	8. $(a \cdot w) \vee (\sim a \cdot \sim w)$	12. $\sim(a \cdot \sim a)$

STATEMENTS AND STATEMENT FORMS.   We have already defined a *statement* as any sentence that is either true or false. We now define a *statement form* as any logical formula—any string of symbols—that *becomes a statement* when its variables are replaced by specific statements.

Statement forms are of tremendous importance, because each variable in a statement form may be replaced by innumerable specific statements. For example, the statement form known as the law of double negation (or double complementation) is:

$$\sim(\sim p) = p$$

Suppose for p we substitute the statement "Apes are (a)nimals." Then, using this form, we know that the statement "It is false that apes are not animals" $[\sim(\sim a)]$ is truth-functionally equivalent (always has the same truth value as) "Apes are animals" (a). And, of course, thousands of other such substitutions might also be made.

A careful study of about thirty such statement forms constitutes the main subject matter of a modern book in introductory logic. In order better to understand the significance of statement forms, we must understand the significance of *truth values*.

TRUTH VALUES.   In ordinary life and in ordinary language, most of our attention is given, not to the *formal structure* of statements, but to their *meaning*. For example, we say simply "Apes are animals"; and not "The statement 'Apes are animals' is *true*." We say simply "Black is not blue"; and not "The statement 'Black is blue' is *false*." Ordinary language conjoins the meaning and the truth value of statements into one neat package; whereas formal logic has nothing to do with the initial judgment whether a statement is true or whether it is false. Formal logic deals with these propositions only *after* such judgment has been made. In short, ordinary language is used mainly to communicate about events immediate and present. It is seldom far removed from the "existential." Formal logic, on the other hand, disentangles itself from changing events in the world of space, time, and causality; moves to higher levels of abstraction; and concentrates entirely on truth values. In this respect, we may say of modern logic what Bertrand Russell (1872–1970) said about modern physics: "Physics is mathematical not because we know so much about the physical world, but because we know so little: It is only its mathematical properties that we can discover."[3] So it is in modern logic. In *formal logic* we deal, strictly speaking, not with *statements*, but only with the *truth values of statements*.

Even as arithmetic and algebra are built around the four connectives [plus ($+$), minus ($-$), multiplied by ($\times$), divided by ($\div$)] so modern algebra and symbolic logic are built around the three connectives [the dot ($\cdot$), the wedge ($\vee$), and the tilde ($\sim$)]. The impact of new symbols and of new connectives can be tremendous. On this point it may be well to recall the history of fourteenth and fifteenth century European arithmetic and algebra. Before Arabic numbers were introduced into Europe, zero was not a part of our number system; and before the development of algebra, irrational and negative numbers seemed not only unreal, but impossible. Accordingly, around 1500 A.D. the algebraic equations in Group I below were called "possible," whereas those in Group II were classified as "impossible."

$$\text{Group I: } A + 4 = 6 \qquad \text{Group II: } A + 6 = 4$$
$$2A = 8 \qquad\qquad\qquad 2A = 5$$
$$A^2 = 9 \qquad\qquad\qquad A^2 = 7$$

Since the empirical world is not made up of negatives, fractions, or irrationals, equations such as those in Group II were viewed by fifteenth century mathematicians as "meaningless" equations, or "impossibles" (like the null set discussed in chapter 1). But when one considers such equations from a purely algebraic point of view (when one studies the relations between *any* numbers X, A, B, and n with respect to "added to," "divided by," "the square

---

[3] Bertrand Russell, *An Outline of Philosophy* (London: Meridian, 1927), p. 163; cited in Arthur Koestler, *The Sleepwalkers* (London: Macmillan & Co., 1959), p. 533.

of," and so on) one sees that

$$X + B = A \text{ is equivalent to } X = A - B$$
$$BX = A \text{ is equivalent to } X = A/B$$
$$X^n = A \text{ is equivalent to } X = \sqrt[n]{A}, \text{ or } X = A^{1/n}$$

Once algebra was sufficiently advanced to provide such general, symbolic solutions to problems, it was freed from its previous connotations with positive integers—even as "2" is freed from the musical connotation of "duet," the baseball connotation of "double," or the childbirth connotation of "twin." Says Tobias Dantzig: "In vain, after this [the invention of algebraic symbolism], will one stipulate that the expression $A - B$ has a meaning only if A is greater than B, that A/B is meaningless when A is not a multiple of B, and that $\sqrt[n]{A}$ is not a number unless A is the perfect nth power."[4]

Even as algebra provided a new conceptual scheme for mathematicians of the post-sixteenth century era, so set theory, Boolean algebra, and symbolic logic provide new conceptual schemes for twentieth century mathematicians and logicians.

The strength of modern logic, like that of mathematics, derives from the fact that it is abstract: it is removed from the immediate world of language and experience. It is one step removed when, for example, we symbolize "Barkus is (a)ble and Barkus is (w)illing" by "$a \cdot b$"; it is two steps removed when, for *any* statement, $a \cdot b$, we substitute a *general statement form*, such as $p \cdot q$; and it is three steps removed because we deal with such statement forms only in terms of their *truth values*, not in terms of their meanings or their referents.

In brief, the strength of logic arises from its generality—its ability to ignore the temporal, spatial, and causal properties of events, and to consider statements *only* with respect to their truth or falsity. In this respect, logic is analogous to arithmetic, where "288 × 63 *sheep*" is the same problem as "288 × 63 *chairs*" or "288 × 63 *eggs*." In arithmetic, the problem becomes simply "288 × 63."

Even as we learn to substitute the number 2 for such words as "duet," "couple," "pair," "duo," or to substitute the number 3 for "trio," "triplet," "threesome," "triple," so we shall now substitute the letter T for "Statement _____ is *true*" and shall substitute the letter F for "Statement _____ is *false*." By such substitution, we move from the realm of categorical truth into the more abstract realm of truth values. Ultimately, as we shall see in later chapters, we return again to the realm of concrete experience and categorical truth. But, as an interim device for quick and accurate thinking, we will *for the time being* deal exclusively with the *truth values* of statements, and shall not be concerned about their meanings.

Here are *six rules for applying truth values* to Negation ($\sim$), Conjunction ($\cdot$), and Alternation ($\vee$).

Rules for Negation: (1) Replace "$\sim F$" by "T."
                        (2) Replace "$\sim T$" by "F."

Rules for Conjunction: (3) Each and every component of a conjunction is "T" if and only if that conjunction is "T."
                        (4) When one or more components of a conjunction

---

[4] Tobias Dantzig, *Number: The Language of Science* (New York: Macmillan Co., 1930), pp. 88–90. See also L. L. Conant, *The Number Concept* (New York: Macmillan Co., 1923).

has truth value "*F*," replace the conjunction by "*F*."

Rules for Alternation: (5) Each and every component of an alternation is "*F*" if and only if that alternation is "*F*."

(6) When one or more components of an alternation has truth value "*T*," replace that alternation by "*T*."

Examples: (A) $(T \cdot F) \vee (T \vee F)$ (B) $(T \cdot F) \cdot (T \vee F)$

Truth Value F $\vee$ T F $\cdot$ T

Replacements: T F

Examples: (C) $\sim(T \cdot F) \cdot \sim(T \vee F)$

Truth Value $\sim(\ \ F\ \ ) \cdot \sim(\ \ T\ \ )$

Replacements: T $\cdot$ F

F

Exercise 2.1D. Finding Truth Values of Complex Propositions (Conjunction, Disjunction, Negation)

Part A.   Directions: First substitute truth values T or F for the equations in parentheses; then determine the truth value of the complex statement. Write T or F in the answer blank which precedes each problem.

_____   1. $(2 + 1 = 3) \cdot (4 + 1 = 5)$
_____   2. $(2 + 1 = 3) \cdot (4 + 3 = 5)$
_____   3. $(2 + 1 = 3) \vee (4 + 1 = 5)$
_____   4. $\sim(2 + 1 = 6) \vee \sim(4 + 3 = 5)$
_____   5. $(2 + 1 = 3) \cdot (4 + 1 = 7)$
_____   6. $(2 + 1 = 3) \cdot (4 + 3 = 5)$
_____   7. $(2 + 1 = 6) \vee (4 + 3 = 5)$
_____   8. $(2 + 1 = 3) \cdot \sim(4 + 3 = 5)$
_____   9. $\sim[(2 + 1 = 3) \cdot (4 + 3 = 5)] \cdot (2 + 1 = 6)$
_____   10. $\sim(2 + 1 = 3) \vee \sim(4 + 1 = 5) \vee \sim(2 + 1 = 6)$

Part B.   Directions: Let the letters a and b symbolize the two *true* statements "Apes are (a)nimals" and "Buzzards are (b)irds"; and let g and h symbolize the two *false* statements "Goats are (g)eese" and "Horses are (h)ats." Then in the answer blank, write T or F to indicate the truth values for problems 11–16.

_____   11. [Apes are (a)nimals] $\cdot$ [Goats are (g)eese].
_____   12. [Horses are (h)ats] $\vee$ [Buzzards are (b)irds].
_____   13. [Goats are (g)eese] $\vee$ {$\sim$[Horses are (h)ats] $\vee$ [Buzzards are (b)irds]}.
_____   14. $\sim$[Goats are (g)eese] $\cdot$ $\sim${[Horses are (h)ats] $\vee$ [Buzzards are (b)irds]}.
_____   15. [Goats are (g)eese] $\cdot$ {[Horses are (h)ats] $\vee$ [Buzzards are (b)irds]}.
_____   16. $\sim$[Goats are (g)eese] $\cdot$ $\sim${$\sim$[Horses are (h)ats] $\vee$ $\sim$[Apes are (a)nimals]}.

Part C.   Directions: Let the letters a and b symbolize *true* statements, and let g and h symbolize *false* statements. Then determine the truth values of the statements in problems 17–24.

_____   17. $(a \cdot b) \vee h$ _____   21. $\sim(h \cdot \sim h) \vee \sim(b \vee \sim b)$
_____   18. $(\sim a \vee b) \vee \sim h$ _____   22. $(a \cdot \sim g) \vee h$
_____   19. $(a \cdot \sim b) \cdot \sim h$ _____   23. $(a \vee \sim a) \cdot \sim(b \cdot \sim b)$
_____   20. $b \vee \sim h \vee \sim(\sim g)$ _____   24. $[(a \vee \sim a) \vee h] \cdot \sim b$

The next exercise (2.1E) is intended to reemphasize the six rules given preceding exercise 2.1D. In addition substitution may sometimes be employed because the truth value (T or F) of any simple statement must be consistent throughout any complex statement in which it occurs.

Exercise 2.1E.   Truth Value Assignments for Conjunctions, Alternations, and Negations

Directions: Assuming the truth values that are given, and using only *necessary* inferences, complete the truth values of the following statements.

(1) $p \lor q$
    $F\ T$

(2) $d \cdot g$
    $T F$

(3) $\sim(m \lor w)$
    T

(4) $\sim(\sim h \lor \sim k)$
    T

(5) $\sim(\sim k \cdot \sim m)$
    F

(6) $(a \cdot b) \lor (b \lor d)$
    T F

(7) $(\sim p \cdot \sim q) \lor p$
             F

(8) $\sim[\sim p \cdot (\sim q \cdot r)]$
    F

(9) $a \cdot \sim[\sim b \lor \sim a]$
    T

(10) $\sim\{\sim h \cdot [g \lor \sim(g \cdot h)]\} \lor g$
                 F

(11) $k \cdot \sim[(k \cdot m) \lor \sim(\sim k \lor \sim m)]$
    T

(12) $p \cdot \sim[\sim p \lor \sim(q \lor \sim p)]$
    T

2.2   Truth Tables, Conditionals, and Contrapositives

TRUTH TABLES.   Truth tables are helpful because they show *every possible combination of truth values*. Before explaining truth tables, let us consider another example of combinations. Suppose we toss a single coin, say, a penny. There are two possible outcomes: A Head or a Tail (H or T; or H or $\sim H$). Suppose we toss two coins: a Penny and a Quarter. Now there are four possibilities—four possible ways in which these two coins can turn up:

1. Penny shows Heads *and* Quarter shows Heads. $Hp \cdot Hq$ or $p \cdot q$ or $H \cdot H$
2. Penny shows Heads *and* Quarter shows Tails. $Hp \cdot \sim Hq$ or $p \cdot \sim q$ or $H \cdot T$
3. Penny shows Tails *and* Quarter shows Heads. $\sim Hp \cdot Hq$ or $\sim p \cdot q$ or $T \cdot H$
4. Penny shows Tails *and* Quarter shows Tails. $\sim Hp \cdot \sim Hq$ or $\sim p \cdot \sim q$ or $T \cdot T$

In this symbolism (to be explained in chapter 6), "Hp" means "This penny shows Heads"; "$\sim Hp$" means "This penny does not show Heads" or "This penny shows Tails"; "Hq" means "This quarter shows Heads" and "$\sim Hq$" means "This quarter does not show Heads" or "This quarter shows Tails."

Similarly, given any two statements p and q, each of which may be either true or false, there are exactly *four possible conjunctions*, or four possible cases:

Truth Table Guide:

					Case	p	q
Case 1. p is True and q is True.	$Tp \cdot Tq$	or	$p \cdot q$	or	1	T	T
Case 2. p is True and q is False.	$Tp \cdot \sim Tq$	or	$p \cdot \sim q$	or	2	T	F
Case 3. p is False and q is True.	$\sim Tp \cdot Tq$	or	$\sim p \cdot q$	or	3	F	T
Case 4. p is False and q is False.	$\sim Tp \cdot \sim Tq$	or	$\sim p \cdot \sim q$	or	4	F	F

Using this Truth Table we can establish the truth value of any statement, however complex. Here are a few examples showing how this is done:

Guide:			*Examples:*				
Case	p	q	(A) $\sim p$	(B) $p \cdot q$	(C) $\sim p \cdot q$	(D) $(p \lor q)$	(E) $\sim p \lor \sim q$
1	T	T	$F\ T$	$T T T$	$F T F T$	$T\ T\ T$	$F T F F T$
2	T	F	$F\ T$	$T F F$	$F T F F$	$T\ T\ F$	$F T T T F$
3	F	T	$T\ F$	$F F T$	$T F T T$	$F\ T\ T$	$T F T F T$
4	F	F	$T\ F$	$F F F$	$T F F F$	$F\ F\ F$	$T F T T F$
		Steps:	2 1	1 2 1	2 1 3 1	1 2 1	2 1 3 2 1

We say that the statement form $\sim p$ has truth values $FFTT$; $p \cdot q$, $TFFF$; $\sim p \cdot q$, $FFTF$; $p \lor q$, $TTTF$; and $\sim p \lor \sim q$, $FTTT$.

Step 1 consists of copying the truth values of p and of q from the Guide. It is often better to do step 1 mentally, since this prevents cluttering:

(F) $(p \cdot q) \vee (\sim p \cdot \sim q)$

```
T   T F  FF
F   F F  FT
F   F T  FF
F   T T  TT

1 3 1  4  2 1 3  2 1
```

(G) $[(p \vee q) \cdot (\sim p \vee \sim q)] \vee (p \cdot \sim q)$

```
T   F F  F F    F  TFF
T   T F  T T    T  TTT
T   T T  T F    T  FFF
F   F T  T T    F  FFT

1 3 1 4 2   3 2    5  1 3 2 1
```

Exercise 2.2A.   Constructing Truth Tables

Remarks: The *answers* for the odd-numbered problems are given throughout this exercise.

Directions: Study carefully the truth tables for the odd-numbered problems. Then complete the truth tables for the even-numbered problems.

Guide

Case	p	q
1	T	T
2	T	F
3	F	T
4	F	F

(1A) $\sim q$ (1B) $\sim[\sim(\sim q)]$ (2A) p (2B) $\sim(\sim p)$

```
        F T        F T F
        T F        T F T
        F T        F T F
        T F        T F T

Steps:  2 1        4 3 2 1         1         3 2 1
```

(3A) $p \cdot \sim q$ (3B) $\sim q \cdot p$ (4A) $\sim p \vee q$ (4B) $q \vee \sim p$

```
        TFF        F  FT
        TTT        T  TT
        FFF        F  FF
        FFT        T  FF

Steps:  1 3 2 1    2 1 3 1        2 1 3 1       1 3 2 1
```

(5A) $\sim(p \cdot q)$ (5B) $\sim p \vee \sim q$ (6A) $\sim(p \vee \sim q)$ (6B) $\sim p \cdot q$

```
        F  T       F  F F
        T  F       F  T T
        T  F       T  T F
        T  F       T  T T

Steps:  3 1 2 1    2 1 3 2 1      4 1 3 2 1       2 1 3 1
```

(7A) $\sim[\sim(p \cdot q) \vee \sim p]$ (7B) $(p \cdot q) \cdot p$ (8A) $(p \vee q) \cdot q$ (8B) $\sim[\sim(p \vee q) \vee \sim q]$

```
        T F  T  F F           T  TT
        F T  F  T F           F  FT
        F T  F  T T           F  FF
        F T  F  T T           F  FF

Steps:  5 3 121 4 2 1         121 31        2   3        5 3   2   4 2
```

In exercise 2.2A observe that each pair of statement forms has the same set of truth values: (1A) and (1B) both have truth values *FTFT*; (2A) and (2B) have truth values *TTFF*; (3A) and (3B) have *FTFF*; (4A) and (4B) have *TFTT*; (5A) and (5B) have *FTTT*; (6A) and (6B) have *FFTF*; (7A) and (7B) have *TFFF*; and (8A) and (8B) have *TFTF*. Two statement forms whose truth values are identical are *equivalent*. Their equivalence is based on their equality of truth values. We shall use the equality sign (=) to represent this equality. In section 2.3 we shall define the equality sign more formally; and it shall signify a tautologous biconditional.

Three Laws of Logic:		*Equivalent Statement Forms:*	*Equality of Truth Values:*
DN	(Double Negation):	$\sim(\sim p) = p$	$TTFF = TTFF$
COM	(Commutation):	$p \cdot q = q \cdot p$	$TFFF = TFFF$
		$p \lor q = q \lor p$	$TTTF = TTTF$
DeM	(DeMorgan):	$\sim(p \cdot q) = \sim p \lor \sim q$	$FTTT = FTTT$
		$\sim(p \lor q) = \sim p \cdot \sim q$	$FFFT = FFFT$

What applies to DN, COM, and DeM, applies to all laws of logic: *Two statement forms are equivalent if and only if their truth values are equal.* Our definition of equality, and our usage of the equality sign (=) will be explained in section 2.3, when we deal with tautologous biconditionals.

Equality and *equivalence* are not synonymous. Suppose a farmer has a 20-pound turkey, a 180-pound pig, and an 800-pound cow. Their total weight is 20 + 180 + 800, or 1000 pounds. But, in combining the three *weights*, the farmer is not combining the three *animals*. Analogously, we must not confuse *equality of truth values* with *equivalence of meaning*.

Now compare the truth table guide for any two statements p and q (shown near the beginning of section 2.2) with the Venn diagram for any two sets P and Q (shown in exercise 1.3D). Note the one-to-one correspondence between Areas 1, 2, 3, 4 in the Venn diagram and Cases 1, 2, 3, 4 in the guide. In each instance $U = \{1, 2, 3, 4\}$. Areas $\{1, 2, 3, 4\}$ and Truth Value Cases $\{1, 2, 3, 4\}$ may also be expressed as *conjunctions*. Thus: for any two sets P and Q, $U = \{(P \cdot Q), (P \cdot \sim Q), (\sim P \cdot Q), (\sim P \cdot \sim Q)\}$; and for any two statements p and q, $U = \{(p \cdot q), (p \cdot \sim q), (\sim p \cdot q), (\sim p \cdot \sim q)\}$.

Since every four-element set has exactly 16 ($= 2^4$) subsets, there are exactly 16 combinations of truth values for any two statements p and q. These 16 combinations are also used in the Binary system of counting (where 0 and 1 replace F and T). We now list 16 subsets, each with two equivalent statement forms.

Arabic Numbers	*Binary Numbers*	*Truth Values*	*Examples of Equivalent Statement Forms*
0	0000	*FFFF*	$p \cdot \sim p = \sim(q \lor \sim q)$
1	0001	*FFFT*	$\sim p \cdot \sim q = \sim(p \lor q)$
2	0010	*FFTF*	$\sim\{\sim[\sim(p \lor \sim q)]\} = \sim p \cdot q$
3	0011	*FFTT*	$(\sim p \cdot q) \lor (\sim p \cdot \sim q) = \sim p$
4	0100	*FTFF*	$\sim(\sim p \lor q) = p \cdot \sim q$
5	0101	*FTFT*	$\sim q \lor (\sim q \cdot \sim q) = \sim q$
6	0110	*FTTF*	$\sim[\sim(p \cdot \sim q) \cdot \sim(q \cdot \sim p)] = (p \cdot \sim q) \lor (q \cdot \sim p)$
7	0111	*FTTT*	$\sim p \lor (p \cdot \sim q) = \sim p \lor \sim q$
8	1000	*TFFF*	$\sim(\sim q \lor \sim p) \lor (p \cdot q) = p \cdot q$
9	1001	*TFFT*	$\sim[\sim(p \cdot q) \cdot \sim(\sim p \cdot \sim q)] = (p \cdot q) \lor (\sim p \cdot \sim q)$
10	1010	*TFTF*	$(q \cdot p) \lor (q \cdot \sim p) = q$
11	1011	*TFTT*	$q \lor (\sim p \cdot \sim q) = \sim p \lor q$
12	1100	*TTFF*	$\sim(\sim p) \lor (p \cdot p \cdot p) = p$
13	1101	*TTFT*	$(p \cdot q) \lor (p \cdot \sim q) \lor (\sim p \cdot \sim q) = p \lor \sim q$
14	1110	*TTTF*	$p \lor (\sim p \cdot q) = p \lor q$
15	1111	*TTTT*	$(p \cdot q) \lor (p \cdot \sim q) \lor (\sim p \cdot q) \lor (\sim p \cdot \sim q) = p \lor \sim p$

The arabic and binary numbers may be ignored; but the preceding sixteen pairs of statement forms and their truth values should be studied carefully. A student will do well to construct truth tables to verify the equivalence of any pair of statements whose equivalence is not readily apparent.

THE CONDITIONAL.   We now introduce another connective, the conditional. This connective is not employed in Boolean algebra or set theory, but it is extremely important in logic. To symbolize the conditional, many logic books use the horseshoe ($\supset$); but because of its similarity to the sign generally used for "is a subset of" ($\subset$)—also called "the horseshoe"—we shall symbolize the conditional by the arrow ($\rightarrow$).

Conditional propositions are also known as hypothetical propositions, and are distinguished from categorical assertions. Much of our thinking deals directly with the real world about us. We give expression to such thinking by making categorical assertions about existent things, for example, "This paper is white"; or about the meanings of words, for example, "Beggars are poor (by definition)." But our thinking may also deal with the ideal: it may consider concepts that are merely imaginative, or logically possible, for example, "If wishes were horses, then beggars might ride," or "If this paper were gold leaf, it would be quite valuable." In such cases, we assume an ideal existence, speak about it in a conditional manner, and then, on the basis of consistency, proceed to evolve logical consequences. In brief, it is not categorical. It is hypothetical or conditional.

Propositions of the form "if p, then q" (symbolized: $p \rightarrow q$) are called conditional (also, "hypothetical," "implicative") propositions. The "if . . ." clause is called the *antecedent*, the "then . . ." clause the *consequent*. Thus in the conditional, "If you were in Berlin, then you were in Germany" ($b \rightarrow g$), "b" is the antecedent and "g" is the consequent.

CONDITIONAL EQUIVALENCE (CE).   We define the conditional $p \rightarrow q$ to have truth value T if and only if p has truth value F or q has truth value T. More briefly:

$$p \rightarrow q = \sim p \vee q; \qquad p \vee q = \sim p \rightarrow q$$

The above law (CE) defines the arrow ($\rightarrow$) in terms of the tilde ($\sim$) and the wedge ($\vee$). We may also define the arrow in terms of the dot ($\cdot$) and the tilde ($\sim$), thus: $p \rightarrow q = \sim (p \cdot \sim q)$. In words: any statement of the form $p \rightarrow q$ is *false* if and only if its antecedent p has truth value T and its consequent q has truth value F.

Let us now formalize the above two definitions, by giving them a name, and treating these definitions as added laws of logic:

CE (*Conditional Equivalence*): $p \rightarrow q = \sim p \vee q$
$$p \rightarrow q = \sim (p \cdot \sim q)$$

Because the DeMorgan laws make it very easy to change $\sim (p \cdot \sim q)$ to $\sim p \vee q$, we shall in this book use only the first of these two definitions. This definition may be called "CE" or "conditional equivalence" or "wedge-arrow" or "arrow-wedge." Observe that it involves (1) changing the wedge to the arrow (or changing the arrow to the wedge) and (2) at the same time changing the sign of negation preceding the left-hand symbol.

PUNCTUATION.   The following usages are all correct:

If a, then both b and d: $a \rightarrow b \cdot d$;
If either f or g, then neither k nor m: $f \vee g \rightarrow \sim (k \vee m)$;

"If p, then q" is false, but "w" is true: $\sim(p \to q) \cdot w$;
If a, then not b; and if b, then either f or g: $(a \to \sim b) \cdot (b \to f \vee g)$.

More will be said concerning punctuation on pages 45–46.

THE CONTRAPOSITIVE (COPO).   Every conditional is equivalent to another conditional called its contrapositive. For example:

If this creature is a (d)og, then it is a (m)ammal. $(d \to m)$
If this creature is not a (m)ammal, then it is not a dog. $(\sim m \to \sim d)$

Expressed in its most general form, the law of contraposition (COPO)—also known as the law of transposition—reads:

$$p \to q = \sim q \to \sim p^5$$

The contrapositive helps us understand why in $p \to q$ we call q the *necessary condition* for p. For by COPO, $p \to q = \sim q \to \sim p$. This means that, given $p \to q$, if q is *false*, p would necessarily be false also. In $p \to q$, then, we may say that q is a necessary condition for p, or that q is an attribute of p, or that property q is attributed to p, or predicated of p. On the other hand, in $p \to q$, we call p a *sufficient condition* for q. Thus in "If Prince is a (d)og, then Prince is a (m)ammal," d is a sufficient condition for m, even though other animals (e.g., horses, cows, foxes) would also constitute sufficient conditions for m. On the other hand, m is a necessary condition for d, since the absence of m necessitates the absence of d: $\sim m \to \sim d$.

Below are truth tables for (1) the conditional $p \to q$; (2) an equivalent statement form $\sim p \vee q$, which is equivalent to (1) by the rule CE (Conditional Equivalence); (3) a third equivalence, formed by using DeMorgan (DeM) on (2); and, finally, (4) an equivalent conditional, which is equivalent to (1) by COPO (Contraposition).

Guide			(1)	(2)	(3)	(4)
Case	p	q	$(p \to q)$	$(\sim p \vee q)$	$\sim(p \cdot \sim q)$	$(\sim q \to \sim p)$
1	T	T	T	T	T	F T F
2	T	F	F	F	F	T F F
3	F	T	T	T	T	F T T
4	F	F	T	T	T	T T T
Truth Values:			$TFTT$	$TFTT$	$TFTT$	$TFTT$
Subsets of U:			$\{1,3,4\}$	$\{1,3,4\}$	$\{1,3,4\}$	$\{1,3,4\}$

---

[5] COPO applies in set theory as well as in logic. In the Venn diagram (figure 11), $D \cdot \sim M = \emptyset$, $D \subset M$, and $\sim M \subset \sim D$. Viewed from the inside out, area 1 is a subset of areas 1 and 3: $\{1\} \subset \{1,3\}$; or $D \subset M$. Viewed from the outside in, area 4 is a subset of areas 4 and 3: $\{4\} \subset \{3,4\}$; or $\sim M \subset \sim D$.

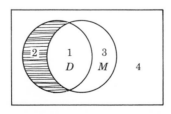

Figure 11

Cases 1 and 2 (for $p \rightarrow q$) are in general accord with the ordinary usage of "If p, then q." But cases 3 and 4 (for $p \rightarrow q$) may seem strange and paradoxical. The reason for this is quite easy to understand. We normally do not employ conditionals when the antecedent is known to be false. But symbolic logic defines $p \rightarrow q$ in a manner that is completely comprehensive and unambiguous for *all possible cases*. Accordingly, a truth value of T or F is given to *all* propositions of the form $p \rightarrow q$, including those in which the antecedent is false. The following example shows why, in accord with ordinary English usage, the proposition $p \rightarrow q$ has truth value T whenever p has truth value F.

Suppose your professor makes the following assertion to you: "If you pass the final examination, you will pass the course." Under what circumstances would you have reason to object to your grade in the course? That is, when should your professor's assertion be considered as false? If you pass the final, and also pass the course (case 1), there should be no objection. If you fail the final, then whether or not you fail the course, your professor's assertion should not be considered as false, since it was not in the agreement in the first place (cases 3 and 4). Only if you pass the final, and you fail the course (case 2), can you consider your professor's assertion as being false.

For another example of the correct definition, "A conditional is false if and only if its antecedent is true and its consequent is false," consider the following rule: "If x is divisible by 9, then x is divisible by 3." Here are three applications of this rule, illustrating cases 1, 3, and 4 where the conditional is true:

1. $(T \rightarrow T)$: "If 18 is divisible by 9, then 18 is divisible by 3."
3. $(F \rightarrow T)$: "If 15 is divisible by 9, then 15 is divisible by 3."
4. $(F \rightarrow F)$: "If 13 is divisible by 9, then 13 is divisible by 3."

In 1, 3, and 4 the total proposition was *true*. But now, as an example of case 2, let us begin with a false rule, namely: "If x is a single-digit number, then x^2 is a single-digit number." Here is an application of this false rule—a conditional proposition having a true antecedent and a false consequent:

2. $(T \rightarrow F)$ "If 4 is a single-digit number then 16 is a single-digit number."

This last example illustrates case 2, namely, that a conditional is *false* when its antecedent is true and its consequent is false.

Such examples show that the logician's definition of the conditional is in accord with the usage of ordinary language. However, not ordinary language, but the stipulated meanings of the basic operations of logic itself ($\vee$, $\cdot$, $\sim$, $\rightarrow$, and $\leftrightarrow$) are the final court of appeal. They cannot be justified in terms of anything more basic than themselves. In the words of Jan Lukasiewicz: "Our explanations concerning the intuitive sense of the primitive terms are in no way definitions of those terms. They are merely *comments* which make it easier to grasp the properties of the primitive terms."[6]

Exercise 2.2B. Symbolizing Statements Having Equivalent Meanings

This exercise requires the use of two new laws of logic (CE and COPO) plus two old laws (COM and DeM) which were explained in section 1.3, and in exercise 2.2A:

CE (Conditional Equivalence): $p \rightarrow q = \sim p \vee q$
COPO (Contraposition): $p \rightarrow q = \sim q \rightarrow \sim p$

---

[6] Jan Lukasiewicz, *Elements of Mathematical Logic*, trans. O. Wojtasiewicz (New York: Macmillan Co., 1963), p. 27. The examples from arithmetic are adapted from Lukasiewicz.

DeM (DeMorgan): $\sim p \vee q = \sim (p \cdot \sim q)$
COM (Commutation): $\sim p \vee q = q \vee \sim p.$

Directions: Below are five statements (A, B, C, D, and E), each followed by several equivalent statements. In the brackets after each statement: first, write in the appropriate symbolism for the statement; and second, using abbreviations, write in the name of the law whereby this statement is *equivalent to the one immediately above it.*

A.   We cannot be in (P)aris without also being in (F)rance. $[\sim (p \cdot \sim f)]$

_____   1. It is impossible for us not to be in (F)rance and [for us at the same time] to be in (P)aris.   [   ]
_____   2. Either we are in (F)rance or we are not in (P)aris.   [   ]
_____   3. Either we are not in (P)aris or we are in (F)rance.   [   ]
_____   4. If we are in (P)aris, then we are in (F)rance.   [   ]
_____   5. If we are not in (F)rance, then we are not in (P)aris.   [   ]

B.   It cannot be both that he is (g)uilty and also that he was not (p)resent at the scene of the crime. $[\sim (g \cdot \sim p)]$

_____   6. It cannot be both that he was not (p)resent at the scene of the crime and also that he is (g)uilty.   [   ]
_____   7. Either he was (p)resent at the scene of the crime, or he is not (g)uilty.   [   ]
_____   8. Either he is not (g)uilty, or he was (p)resent at the scene of the crime.   [   ]
_____   9. If he is (g)uilty, then he was (p)resent at the scene of the crime.   [   ]
_____ 10. If he was not (p)resent at the scene of the crime, he is not (g)uilty.   [   ]

C.   If a (t)heory is true, then the logical and experimental (c)onsequence of that theory will also be true. $[\ t \rightarrow c\ ]$

_____ 11. If the logical and experimental (c)onsequences of a theory are not true, then the (t)heory is not true either.   [   ]
_____ 12. Either the logical and experimental (c)onsequences of a theory are true, or the (t)heory is false (i.e., not true).   [   ]
_____ 13. Either a (t)heory is false (i.e., not true, or not tenable), or the logical and experimental (c)onsequences of that theory are true.   [   ]
_____ 14. It cannot be the case both that a (t)heory is true and that the logical and experimental (c)onsequences of that theory are untrue.   [   ]
_____ 15. It is unreasonable to hold [i.e., it cannot be the case] that the logical and experimental (c)onsequences of a theory are untrue, yet that the (t)heory itself is true.   [   ]

D.   If you are an avid (l)over of Gothic cathedrals, then [you may] (s)ee them in Paris, Rheims, Milan, or Seville. $[\ l \rightarrow s\ ]$

_____ 16. Either you are not an avid (l)over of Gothic cathedrals, or you will [stop to] (s)ee them in Paris, Rheims, Milan, or Seville.   [   ]
_____ 17. You cannot be an avid (l)over of Gothic cathedrals, and not [stop to] (s)ee one in Paris, Rheims, Milan, or Seville.   [   ]

E.   If you don't [manage to] see Gothic cathedrals in (M)ilan or in (S)eville, you [should take time to] see them in (P)aris or in (R)heims. $[\sim (m \vee s) \rightarrow (p \vee r)]$

_____ 18. If you don't [have time to] see Gothic cathedrals in (P)aris or in (R)heims, [you may still] see them in (M)ilan or in (S)eville.   [   ]
_____ 19. You may see Gothic cathedrals in (P)aris or in (R)heims, or you may see them in (M)ilan or in (S)eville.   [   ]
_____ 20. You may see Gothic cathedrals in (M)ilan or in (S)eville, or you may see them in (P)aris or in (R)heims.   [   ]

Exercise 2.2C.   Interpreting and Symbolizing Conditionals

Directions: In the answer blank before each problem, write *A*, *B*, *C*, or *D* to indicate whether that proposition is properly symbolized by:

A. $p \rightarrow q$ B. $\sim p \rightarrow q$ C. $p \rightarrow \sim q$ D. $\sim p \rightarrow \sim q$
    $\sim q \rightarrow \sim p$ $\sim q \rightarrow p$ $q \rightarrow \sim p$ $q \rightarrow p$

_____ 1. If p, then q.

_____ 2. p, provided that q.

_____ 3. Unless p, then not q.

_____ 4. p is a sufficient reason for q.

_____ 5. Not p, unless not q.

_____ 6. Unless $\sim q$, then not $\sim p$.

_____ 7. Granted that p is true, $\sim q$ follows.

_____ 8. Given that p is the antecedent, then q is the consequent.

_____ 9. On the hypothesis that q is false, p logically follows.

_____ 10. If we admit q, then we must also admit p.

_____ 11. q is a necessary condition for p.

_____ 12. q is a sufficient reason for p to happen.

_____ 13. q is an essential attribute of p [q is a necessary condition for p].

_____ 14. Without p, q can never occur.

_____ 15. Given that p, we must also grant $\sim q$.

_____ 16. If we do not grant p, then we also will not concede q.

_____ 17. Unless $\sim p$, then q.

_____ 18. q is a necessary attribute of p. [or q is necessarily predicated of p].

_____ 19. If anything is a p, then it is a q.

_____ 20. Each and every p is a q.

_____ 21. All p's are q's.

_____ 22. No p is a $\sim q$.

_____ 23. No $\sim q$ is a p.

_____ 24. No q is a $\sim p$.

_____ 25. There is no q that is not a p.

_____ 26. Anything that is a q is also a p.

_____ 27. Any $\sim q$ is a p.

_____ 28. Every q is a p.

_____ 29. No q's are $\sim p$'s.

_____ 30. All q's are p's.

Exercise 2.2D.   Symbolizing Statements

Directions: Symbolize each of the following statements.

1. Either she is not (b)eautiful or she is an (a)ctress.
2. It cannot be both that she is (b)eautiful and that she is not an (a)ctress.
3. That she is both (b)eautiful and not an (a)ctress is certainly true.
4. It is false to say either that she is not (b)eautiful or that she is an (a)ctress.
5. If she is not an (a)ctress then she is (b)eautiful.
6. It is not true that if she is not an (a)ctress then she is not (b)eautiful.
7. If she is not (b)eautiful, then she is not an (a)ctress.
8. She is (b)eautiful, but she is not a (b)eautiful (a)ctress.
9. It has been *said* that if she were (b)eautiful she would be an (a)ctress; but the *truth* is that she is (b)eautiful and she is not an (a)ctress.
10. If she is a (b)eautiful (a)ctress then she must be (b)eautiful.
11. Let us admit that if she were (b)eautiful she would be an (a)ctress; it remains true nevertheless that she is not (b)eautiful and she is not an (a)ctress.
12. She is either a (b)eautiful (a)ctress or she is a person who is not (b)eautiful and not an (a)ctress.
13. There are exactly two possibilities: Either she is not an (a)ctress but is (b)eautiful, or she is not (b)eautiful but is nevertheless an (a)ctress.
14. If she is an (a)ctress she is (b)eautiful, and, (if I may reemphasize my point) if she is not (b)eautiful then she is not an (a)ctress.
15. It is true both that if a girl is an (a)ctress she is (b)eautiful and also that if she is not (b)eautiful she is not an (a)ctress.
16. If you insist that it is *false* that she is not an (a)ctress, then you could just as well say that it is *true* that she is an (a)ctress.

When you are uncertain as to the precise meaning of any statement, it is generally helpful to reformulate that statement. Exercise 2.2E illustrates how this is done, using CE, COPO, and DeM.

Exercise 2.2E.   Reformulating Statements

Remarks: Logic should better enable us to reformulate statements so that the same thought is expressed in several different ways. In this exercise, it will be found that, by using DeM, COM, CE, or COPO, you can reformulate the four statements into conditionals, and thus more readily learn the answer.

Directions: Assume the following: John's four brothers each spoke honestly, and they gave him the information contained in the four statements below. Reformulate each of the four statements so you can clearly determine which of the four brothers told John where to find his pen. No answers are given for this exercise.   ·

ABE: Either you do not look behind the (d)esk, or you will not
       (f)ind your pen.   ABE: _____
BILL: If you don't fail to (f)ind your pen, it's because you have not
       looked in the (k)itchen.   BILL: _____
CARL: If you don't (f)ind your pen, it's because you have not looked
       in my coat (p)ocket.   CARL: _____
DICK: You can't both (f)ind your pen, and not fail to look in the
       (b)asement.   DICK: _____

                                                    Which brother? _____

Exercise 2.2F.   From Symbols to Statements

Remarks: This exercise is designed for students whose mathematical background is meager, and who therefore may have some difficulty interpreting the meanings contained in abstract statement forms. Below are four statement forms, each symbolized in six different, but equivalent, ways:

A. $p \to q$	B. $p \lor q$	C. $\sim(p \cdot q)$	D. $q \to p$
$\sim q \to \sim p$	$q \lor p$	$\sim(q \cdot p)$	$\sim p \to \sim q$
$q \lor \sim p$	$\sim(\sim q \cdot \sim p)$	$\sim q \lor \sim p$	$p \lor \sim q$
$\sim p \lor q$	$\sim(\sim p \cdot \sim q)$	$\sim p \lor \sim q$	$\sim q \lor p$
$\sim(p \cdot \sim q)$	$\sim p \to q$	$p \to \sim q$	$\sim(q \cdot \sim p)$
$\sim(\sim q \cdot p)$	$\sim q \to p$	$q \to \sim p$	$\sim(\sim p \cdot q)$

Directions: For each *statement form* substitute a specific *statement*. Thus:

For $p \to q$ in A, sub "If Fido is a (d)og, then Fido is a (m)ammal" $(d \to m)$.
For $\sim p \to q$ in B, sub "If it is not (w)ashable, then it must be (d)ry cleaned" $(\sim w \to d)$.
For $p \to \sim q$ in C, sub "If this is a (h)orse, it is not a (t)iger" $(h \to \sim t)$.
For $\sim p \to \sim q$ in D, sub "If he is not a (E)uropean, he is not a (S)wede" $(\sim e \to \sim s)$.

Now for each of these four *statements*, write (or simply speak) five other equivalent *statements*.

Exercise 2.2G.   Review of CE, COPO, DeM, and COM

Directions: Each problem in this exercise consists of a premise followed by three conclusions, *A*, *B*, and *C*. In the answer blank write, *A*, *B*, and/or *C* to indicate *valid* conclusions. You should lose points on this type of exercise (a) if you fail to list a *valid* conclusion, or (b) if you list as valid an answer which does not validly follow from the premise.

One of the best ways to do this exercise is to *first* list six equivalent expressions for each statement as was done in exercise 2.2F.

$$a \to \sim b = b \to \sim a = \sim b \lor \sim a = \sim a \lor \sim b = \sim(a \cdot b) = \sim(b \cdot a)$$

With this series before us, we see that *A*, and *A* alone, is the correct answer for problem 2 of this exercise.

It may also be helpful to "fill in" each statement form with some particular verbal statement, e.g., $(a \to \sim b)$ could become "If the creature is an (a)nt, then it is not a (b)ee."

1. $p \vee q$	A. $\sim p \to q$	B. $\sim q \to p$	C. $\sim(\sim p \cdot \sim q)$	1. _____
2. $a \to \sim b$	A. $\sim a \vee \sim b$	B. $b \vee a$	C. $b \to a$	2. _____
3. $\sim(f \cdot g)$	A. $\sim f \vee g$	B. $f \to g$	C. $\sim g \vee \sim f$	3. _____
4. $\sim(\sim k \cdot m)$	A. $k \vee \sim m$	B. $m \to k$	C. $\sim k \to \sim m$	4. _____
5. $x \vee \sim z$	A. $z \vee \sim x$	B. $\sim z \to x$	C. $x \to \sim z$	5. _____
6. $a \cdot \sim b$	A. $\sim(b \cdot a)$	B. $\sim(b \vee \sim a)$	C. $\sim(a \to b)$	6. _____
7. $f \vee k$	A. $k \vee \sim f$	B. $\sim k \to f$	C. $\sim(f \cdot k)$	7. _____
8. $g \vee \sim h$	A. $h \to g$	B. $\sim g \to \sim h$	C. $\sim(\sim g \cdot h)$	8. _____
9. $\sim(m \cdot w)$	A. $\sim m \vee w$	B. $\sim w \vee m$	C. $m \to \sim w$	9. _____
10. $a \cdot z$	A. $\sim(a \to \sim z)$	B. $\sim a \vee \sim z$	C. $a \cdot \sim z$	10. _____
11. $b \cdot \sim y$	A. $\sim(y \vee \sim b)$	B. $y \to \sim b$	C. $\sim y \vee \sim b$	11. _____
12. $d \to k$	A. $k \vee \sim d$	B. $\sim(d \cdot k)$	C. $\sim(d \cdot \sim k)$	12. _____

PUNCTUATION. A few remarks concerning punctuation may be needed before moving on to exercise 2.2H. The arrow ($\to$) signifies a stronger break than either the dot ($\cdot$) or the wedge ($\vee$). In examples (A), (B), (C), and (D) below, note the following: in (A) the first arrow is the major break, hence parentheses are placed around the remainder of the formula—the consequent. In (B) the second arrow is the major break, and the antecedent consists of the conjunction $(p \to q) \cdot p$. In (C) the dot is the major break. In (D) the first arrow is the major break, and the consequent is the negation (shown by the tilde) of the large expression to the right of the first arrow.

$$\text{(A) } p \to (\sim q \cdot p \to q) \qquad \text{(B) } (p \to \sim q) \cdot p \to q$$
$$\text{(C) } (p \to \sim q) \cdot (p \to q) \qquad \text{(D) } p \to \sim(q \cdot p \to q)$$

RULES FOR TRUTH-VALUE ASSIGNMENTS. If we know the truth values for some parts of a formula we can usually derive the remaining truth values. In the eight examples below, the number "1" is used to indicate the truth values originally given. All other truth values are logically derived. In order that each such derivation may be a *necessary* inference, keep in mind the following rules:

(1) The value assigned to any statement (e.g., that p has truth value T) must be the same wherever that statement reoccurs in the longer complex statement.

(2) The tilde ($\sim$) has the opposite truth value of whatever immediately follows it, e.g., If $(p \cdot q) \vee r \to k$ is true, then $\sim[(p \cdot q) \vee r \to k]$ is false.

(3) A conjunction $(p \cdot q)$ is *true* if and only if each of its conjuncts is true.

(4) A disjunction $(p \vee q)$ is *false* if and only if each of its alternants is false.

(5) A conditional $(p \to q)$ is *false* if and only if its antecedent (p) is true and its consequent (q) is false.

Using the above five rules, if we know the truth values of any statement's atomic components (indicated by step 1 in the following four examples), we can, by a series of inferences (indicated by steps 2, 3, 4, and 5), determine the truth value of that statement (step 5), thus:

(1) p is T, q is T:
$$p \to \sim(q \cdot p \to q)$$
$$T\ F\ F\ T\ T\ T\ \ T$$
$$1\ 5\ 4\ \ 1\ 2\ 1\ 3\ \ 1$$

(2) p is F, q is F:
$$p \to \sim(q \cdot p \to q)$$
$$F\ T\ F\ \ F\ F\ F\ T\ \ F$$
$$1\ 5\ 4\ \ 1\ 2\ 1\ 3\ \ 1$$

(3) p is T, q is F:
$$p \to \sim(q \cdot p \to q)$$
$$T\ F\ F\ \ F\ F\ T\ T\ \ F$$
$$1\ 5\ 4\ \ 1\ 2\ 1\ 3\ \ 1$$

(4) p is F, q is T:
$$p \to \sim(q \cdot p \to q)$$
$$F\ T\ F\ \ T\ F\ F\ T\ \ T$$
$$1\ 5\ 4\ \ 1\ 2\ 1\ 3\ \ 1$$

Using the same five rules, given the truth value of a complex statement, we can also derive the truth values of its component parts. In the following four examples only step 1 is initially given or assumed. The remaining steps in each example represent necessary inferences.

(A) $p \rightarrow (\sim q \cdot p \rightarrow q)$
   TF T FTTF F
    2 1 6 5 3 4 2 3

(B) $(p \rightarrow \sim q) \cdot p \rightarrow q$
   T T T FTTF F
    6 3 5 4 2 3 1 2

(C) $p \rightarrow \sim(q \cdot p \rightarrow q)$
     TF F TTTT T

   or   *FF   F*
        2 1 2 6 7 4 3 5

(D) $(p \rightarrow \sim q) \cdot (p \rightarrow q)$ or   (D) $(p \rightarrow \sim q) \cdot (p \rightarrow q)$
   TT T FT TF F   *TF F TF TT T*
    4 7 6 5 1 3 2 3   3 2 3 4 1 6 7 5

Exercise 2.2H.   Truth Value Assignments

Directions: Fill in the missing truth values for each of the following:

(1) $p \cdot q \rightarrow r$
     F

(2) $p \rightarrow q \cdot r$
    T T

(3) $\sim p \rightarrow q$
    T F

(4) $p \rightarrow \sim q$
   T T

(5) $(p \lor \sim q) \rightarrow q$
   F T

(6) $\sim p \rightarrow p$
    T

(7) $q \rightarrow \sim q$
    T

(8) $f \lor g \rightarrow g$
      F

(9) $(p \cdot q) \lor \sim p$
    F

(10) $[(m \lor w) \cdot (\sim m \rightarrow w)] \lor w$
       T   *F*

(11) $[(\sim p \lor \sim q) \cdot q] \rightarrow p$
          F

(12) $[(h \rightarrow k) \cdot (k \rightarrow m)] \rightarrow (m \rightarrow h)$
             F

(13) $a \rightarrow (\sim b \cdot a \rightarrow b)$
    F

(14) $(d \rightarrow \sim m) \cdot d \rightarrow m$
         F

(15) $(g \rightarrow \sim h) \cdot (g \rightarrow h)$
     F

(16) $k \rightarrow \sim(n \cdot k \rightarrow n)$
     F

2.3   Biconditionals, Strong Disjunction, and Review

THE BICONDITIONAL. The biconditional is symbolized $p \leftrightarrow q$; and is defined in two ways:

(1) $p \leftrightarrow q = (p \rightarrow q) \cdot (q \rightarrow p)$. This defined meaning is obvious from the symbols: for the double arrow ($\leftrightarrow$) points both ways, whereas the single arrows $(p \rightarrow q) \cdot (q \rightarrow p)$ each point only one way. Hence the biconditional is *commutative*, whereas the conditional is not.

(2) $p \leftrightarrow q = (p \cdot q) \lor (\sim p \cdot \sim q)$. In words: $p \leftrightarrow q$ has truth value *T* if and only if p and q have the *same* truth values: either p and q are both true, or p and q are both false.

We shall call these defined meanings "Biconditional Equivalence" (abbreviation: BE); and we now add BE to our rules, along with other laws of logic:

     BE (*Biconditional Equivalence*): $p \leftrightarrow q = (p \rightarrow q) \cdot (q \rightarrow p)$
                               $p \leftrightarrow q = (p \cdot q) \lor (\sim p \cdot \sim q)$

There are several ways to read "$p \leftrightarrow q$." One is "$p \rightarrow q$ and conversely." Another is "p has the same truth value as q." Or we may say "If and only if p, then q"; or "p if and only if q"; or "q if and only if p." Or we may substitute the word "iff" for "if and only if." We call "$\leftrightarrow$" the "double arrow" or the "biconditional."

PUNCTUATION. We give the equality sign ($=$) a greater strength of separation than either the arrow ($\rightarrow$) or the double arrow ($\leftrightarrow$); but the arrow and the double arrow have greater strength than the wedge ($\vee$) or the dot ($\cdot$). The following usages are all correct: (1) $p = \sim(\sim p)$; (2) $p \leftrightarrow q = q \leftrightarrow p$; (3) $p \leftrightarrow (p \cdot q) \vee (p \cdot \sim q)$; (4) $p \leftrightarrow q = (p \to q) \cdot (q \to p)$; (5) $(p \cdot q) \vee (\sim p \cdot \sim q) = p \leftrightarrow q$.

The use of the equality sign should help remind us that we are here dealing, not with the *meanings*, but with the *truth values* of statements. In this context, the equality sign cannot possibly connote quantitative or numerical equality. We define *the equality sign* to mean a *tautologous biconditional* (truth values: *TTTT*).

The laws of double negation (DN), or double complementation, apply to the biconditional. To see this more clearly, complete the following truth tables.

Guide					
p	q	$(p \leftrightarrow q) =$	$(\sim p \leftrightarrow \sim q) =$	$\sim(p \leftrightarrow \sim q) =$	$\sim(\sim p \leftrightarrow q)$
T	T	T T T	F $\quad$ T $\quad$ F	T $\quad$ TFFT	T $\quad$ FTFT
T	F	T F F	F $\quad\quad$ T	T $\quad$ T	F $\quad\quad$ F
F	T	F F T	T $\quad\quad$ F	F $\quad$ F	T $\quad\quad$ T
F	F	F T F	T $\quad\quad$ T	F $\quad$ T	T $\quad\quad$ F

The Venn diagram for $(P \cdot Q) \vee (\sim P \cdot \sim Q)$, or for $P = Q$, shows the set theory counterpart for the set of truth values $(p \cdot q) \vee (\sim p \cdot \sim q)$, or $p \leftrightarrow q$.

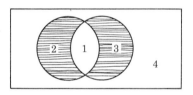

Figure 12

We will probably understand the biconditional most quickly if we use it in comparison and in contrast to the conditional. Exercise 2.3A is intended to help reinforce the following.

TRUTH VALUE RULES FOR CONDITIONALS AND BICONDITIONALS
Rules for the Conditional ($\to$):

1. When the antecedent of any conditional is "*F*," replace that conditional by truth value "*T*."

$$\text{Examples:} \quad F \to T; \quad F \to F$$
$$\text{Truth-value replacements:} \quad T \quad\quad T$$

2. When the consequent of any conditional is "*T*," replace that conditional by truth value "*T*."

$$\text{Examples:} \quad T \to T; \quad F \to T$$
$$\text{Truth-value replacements:} \quad T \quad\quad T$$

3. If and only if the antecedent of a conditional is "*T*" and the consequent of that conditional is "*F*," replace that conditional by truth value "*F*."

$$\text{Example:} \quad T \to F$$
$$\text{Truth-value replacement:} \quad F$$

Rules for the Biconditional ($\leftrightarrow$):

4. When the two components of a biconditional have the *same* truth value, replace that biconditional by "*T*."

Examples: $T \leftrightarrow T$; $F \leftrightarrow F$
Truth-value replacements: T T

5. When the two components of a biconditional have opposite truth values, replace that biconditional by "*F*."

Examples: $T \leftrightarrow F$; $F \leftrightarrow T$
Truth-value replacements: F F

Exercise 2.3A.   Finding Truth Values of Conditionals and Biconditionals

Part A.   Directions: Substitute *T* or *F* for the truth value of the equations in parentheses, then determine the truth value for each of the following complex statements.

_____ 1. $(2 + 1 = 3) \rightarrow (2 + 1 = 6)$ _____ 2. $(2 + 1 = 3) \rightarrow (4 + 1 = 5)$
_____ 3. $(2 + 1 = 6) \rightarrow (4 + 3 = 5)$ _____ 4. $(2 + 1 = 6) \rightarrow (4 + 1 = 5)$
_____ 5. $(2 + 1 = 3) \leftrightarrow (2 + 1 = 6)$ _____ 6. $(2 + 1 = 3) \leftrightarrow (4 + 1 = 5)$
_____ 7. $(2 + 1 = 6) \leftrightarrow (4 + 3 = 5)$ _____ 8. $(2 + 1 = 6) \leftrightarrow (4 + 1 = 5)$
_____ 9. $\sim(2 + 1 = 6) \rightarrow [(2 + 1 = 3) \leftrightarrow (4 + 1 = 5)]$
_____ 10. $\sim(2 + 1 = 6) \leftrightarrow [(2 + 1 = 3) \rightarrow (4 + 1 = 5)]$
_____ 11. $\sim(2 + 1 = 3) \rightarrow [(4 + 3 = 5) \leftrightarrow (2 + 1 = 6)]$
_____ 12. $\sim(2 + 1 = 3) \leftrightarrow [(4 + 3 = 5) \rightarrow (2 + 1 = 3)]$

Part B.   Directions: Let *a* and *b* signify the two *true* statements "Apes are (a)nimals" and "Buzzards are (b)irds." Let *g* and *h* signify the two *false* statements "Goats are (g)eese" and "Horses are (h)ats." Then determine the truth values of each of the following:

_____ 13. $a \rightarrow (h \rightarrow b)$ _____ 14. $\sim a \rightarrow (h \leftrightarrow b)$
_____ 15. $(\sim a \leftrightarrow h) \leftrightarrow b$ _____ 16. $(a \leftrightarrow h) \rightarrow \sim b$
_____ 17. $h \cdot \sim h \rightarrow b \cdot g$ _____ 18. $(h \vee \sim h) \rightarrow \sim(g \cdot h)$
_____ 19. $(h \vee g) \cdot \sim b \rightarrow g$ _____ 20. $(h \vee g \vee b) \rightarrow g$

Part C.   Directions: Express in words problems 14, 16, 18, and 20. You should first study the *answers* in part C for problems 13, 15, 17, and 19.

Exercise 2.3B.   Finding Necessary Truth Value Assignments

Remarks: This exercise will be quite easy if you begin with forms whose truth values make other truth values necessary, for example,

$p \rightarrow q$; $p \vee q$; $p \cdot q$; p; $\sim q$
F F T T T

On the other hand, you should delay filling in the values of such forms as these:

$p \rightarrow q$; $p \vee q$; $p \cdot q$
T T F

because none of these three admits of three possible answers.

Directions: Complete the following truth value assignments. Assign necessary truth values first. This means that the *sequence* of assignments is important.

(1) $(d \vee f) \leftrightarrow (f \leftrightarrow d)$ (2) $(k \vee m) \leftrightarrow (m \rightarrow k)$
     T T F F

(3) $(p \leftrightarrow q) \rightarrow (p \cdot q)$ (4) $(w \rightarrow z) \leftrightarrow (z \cdot w)$
          F T

Note: Problems (4), (7), and (8) each have two answers.

(5) $(g \cdot h) \rightarrow [(h \rightarrow k) \vee (g \leftrightarrow m)]$ (6) $(a \rightarrow b) \leftrightarrow (b \leftrightarrow a)$
          F F

(7) $(d \leftrightarrow m) \leftrightarrow (\sim m \rightarrow d)$ (8) $k \cdot [(m \leftrightarrow w) \leftrightarrow (k \cdot w)]$
          F T

EXCLUSIVE DISJUNCTION (STRONG ALTERNATION). In section 2.1, when explaining the meaning of the wedge ($\vee$), two meanings of the English word "or" were distinguished:

(1) "Either p or q (and perhaps both)" ($p \vee q$)

This defined meaning of the wedge is called *inclusive disjunction* or *weak alternation*. Its truth values are *TTTF*; hence, by CE, $p \vee q = {\sim}p \rightarrow q$. In English usage, the phrase "and perhaps both" is generally implied without being explicitly stated.

(2) "Either p or q (but not both)" ($p \vee q$) $\cdot$ ${\sim}(p \cdot q)$

This usage of the word "or" is called *exclusive disjunction* or *strong alternation*. The phrase "but not both" explicitly asserts that exclusive disjunction does *not* have truth value T in case 1. Rather, its truth values are *FTTF*. Here are other ways of symbolizing *FTTF*:

$$(p \vee q) \cdot {\sim}(p \cdot q) = (p \cdot {\sim}q) \vee (q \cdot {\sim}p) = p \leftrightarrow {\sim}q$$

Observe that truth values *FTTF* (for exclusive disjunction) are complementary to *TFFT*—the truth values for the biconditional. Hence, even as the biconditional was symbolized four ways [for *TFFT*]:

(1) $p \leftrightarrow q$ (2) ${\sim}p \leftrightarrow {\sim}q$ (3) ${\sim}({\sim}p \leftrightarrow q)$ (4) ${\sim}(p \leftrightarrow {\sim}q)$

so exclusive disjunction may be symbolized four ways [for *FTTF*]:

(1A) ${\sim}(p \leftrightarrow q)$ (2A) ${\sim}({\sim}p \leftrightarrow {\sim}q)$ (3A) ${\sim}p \leftrightarrow q$ (4A) $p \leftrightarrow {\sim}q$

The symbolisms for (1), (2), (3), and (4) show that the biconditional has either no tildes or two. The symbolisms of (1A), (2A), (3A), and (4A) show that exclusive disjunction (expressed with the double arrow) has either one tilde or three. What we have just said may also be expressed by saying that DN (*double negation*) *applies to the double arrow*. We might have added the following special definition:

EDE (*Exclusive Disjunctive Equivalence*): $(p \vee q) \cdot {\sim}(p \cdot q) = p \leftrightarrow {\sim}q$

However, since "either p or q and not both" $(p \vee q) \cdot {\sim}(p \cdot q)$ may also be expressed either as "either p and not q, or q and not p" $(p \cdot {\sim}q) \vee (q \cdot {\sim}p)$, or as "$p$ if and only if not q" $(p \leftrightarrow {\sim}q)$, the use of one added tilde makes it possible to adapt biconditional equivalence (BE) to exclusive disjunctive equivalence (EDE). Hence we will *not* include EDE among our laws of logic. We thus let the defined meaning of biconditional equivalence (BE) include:

biconditional equivalence (BE): $p \leftrightarrow q = (p \rightarrow q) \cdot (q \rightarrow p)$
$p \leftrightarrow q = (p \cdot q) \vee ({\sim}p \cdot {\sim}q)$
(and by substitution): $(p \rightarrow {\sim}q) \cdot ({\sim}q \rightarrow p) = (p \leftrightarrow {\sim}q)$
$(p \cdot {\sim}q) \vee (q \cdot {\sim}p) = (p \leftrightarrow {\sim}q)$
$(p \vee q) \cdot {\sim}(p \cdot q) = (p \leftrightarrow {\sim}q)$

Exercise 2.3C.   Symbolizing Conditionals and Biconditionals

Directions: Below are twelve statements and twelve symbols of statements. In the answer blank before each statement, write in the *letter* representing the symbols which correctly represent that statement. If none of the twelve symbols (*A* through *L*) represent the statement, write "*X*."

In all statements, let "*a*" symbolize "John is ambitious."
Let "*s*" symbolize "John is smart" and let "${\sim}s$" symbolize "John is dumb."
Let "*i*" symbolize "John is industrious," and let "${\sim}i$" symbolize "John is lazy."

You will probably find it easiest first to symbolize each statement, then to compare your symbolisms with the twelve symbolisms given from *A* through *L*.

Symbols:
  A. $a \to \sim(s \cdot i)$
  B. $\sim(s \vee i) \to a$
  C. $\sim i \cdot s \to \sim(i \vee \sim s)$
  D. $(s \cdot i) \to \sim a$
  E. $s \to (i \to a)$
  F. $s \cdot a \to i$
  G. $\sim(\sim s) \to i \cdot a$

  H. $(\sim i \cdot \sim s) \to \sim(i \vee s)$
  I. $s \to \sim i \vee \sim a$
  J. $\sim s \leftrightarrow \sim s$, or $s \leftrightarrow s$
  K. $\sim i \cdot a \leftrightarrow a \cdot \sim i$
  L. $s \leftrightarrow \sim i$; or $\sim(\sim s \leftrightarrow \sim i)$; or $\sim(s \leftrightarrow i)$;
  or $(\sim s \vee \sim i) \cdot \sim(\sim s \cdot \sim i)$; or
  $(s \cdot \sim i) \vee (\sim s \cdot i)$

_____ 1. If John is smart and industrious, then he must not be ambitious.
_____ 2. If John is smart, then if he is industrious he must be ambitious.
_____ 3. John is dumb if and only if he's not smart.
_____ 4. If it is true that John is ambitious, then it is false that he is both smart and industrious.
_____ 5. Either John is dumb or he is lazy, but John is not both dumb and lazy.
_____ 6. If John is both lazy and smart then he is neither industrious nor dumb.
_____ 7. Unless John is either smart or industrious, he is ambitious.
_____ 8. John is industrious and ambitious unless he is not smart.
_____ 9. If John is neither smart nor industrious then he is ambitious.
_____ 10. John is smart and ambitious if and only if he is industrious.
_____ 11. Either John is smart but not industrious, or he's industrious but not smart.
_____ 12. If John is smart then John is either lazy or he is lacking in ambition.

Exercise 2.3D.   Symbolizing Statements from Ordinary Language

Remarks: Below are several different statement forms, *A—F*, representing the following six truth values:

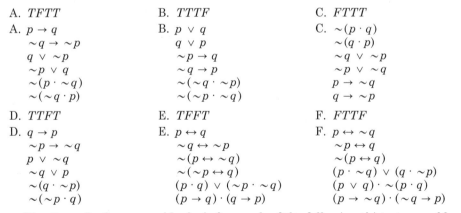

A. *TFTT*
A. $p \to q$
  $\sim q \to \sim p$
  $q \vee \sim p$
  $\sim p \vee q$
  $\sim(p \cdot \sim q)$
  $\sim(\sim q \cdot p)$

B. *TTTF*
B. $p \vee q$
  $q \vee p$
  $\sim p \to q$
  $\sim q \to p$
  $\sim(\sim q \cdot \sim p)$
  $\sim(\sim p \cdot \sim q)$

C. *FTTT*
C. $\sim(p \cdot q)$
  $\sim(q \cdot p)$
  $\sim q \vee \sim p$
  $\sim p \vee \sim q$
  $p \to \sim q$
  $q \to \sim p$

D. *TTFT*
D. $q \to p$
  $\sim p \to \sim q$
  $p \vee \sim q$
  $\sim q \vee p$
  $\sim(q \cdot \sim p)$
  $\sim(\sim p \cdot q)$

E. *TFFT*
E. $p \leftrightarrow q$
  $\sim q \leftrightarrow \sim p$
  $\sim(p \leftrightarrow \sim q)$
  $\sim(\sim p \leftrightarrow q)$
  $(p \cdot q) \vee (\sim p \cdot \sim q)$
  $(p \to q) \cdot (q \to p)$

F. *FTTF*
F. $p \leftrightarrow \sim q$
  $\sim p \leftrightarrow q$
  $\sim(p \leftrightarrow q)$
  $(p \cdot \sim q) \vee (q \cdot \sim p)$
  $(p \vee q) \cdot \sim(p \cdot q)$
  $(p \to \sim q) \cdot (\sim q \to p)$

Directions: In the answer blanks before each of the following thirty-two problems, indicate by letter (*A, B, C, D, E, F*) which of the above six statement forms is exemplified. If none of the six is exemplified, write *X*.

_____ 1. All *p*'s are *q*'s.
_____ 3. Every *p* is a $\sim q$.
_____ 5. *p* is false, but $\sim p$ is true.

_____ 2. If *p*, then not *q*.
_____ 4. Each and every *p* is a *q*.
_____ 6. It is false to say that $\sim p$ is true if and only if $\sim q$ is also true.

_____ 7. *p* is false and so is *q*.
_____ 9. There is not a single *p* that is also a *q*.
_____ 11. *q* is a necessary condition of *p*.

_____ 8. *q* is predicated of *p*.
_____ 10. Every $\sim p$ is a $\sim q$.
_____ 12. $\sim q$ is a necessary condition for $\sim p$.

_____ 13. p is a sufficient condition for q.

_____ 14. $\sim p$ is a sufficient condition for $\sim q$.

_____ 15. If $\sim p$ occurs, so will $\sim q$.

_____ 16. It is false either that p or that q.

_____ 17. If $\sim p$, then q.

_____ 18. p if and only if q.

_____ 19. Unless p, then q.

_____ 20. $\sim q$ if and only if $\sim p$.

_____ 21. q unless p.

_____ 22. If p, q; and if q, p.

_____ 23. Unless $\sim p$ is false, then q.

_____ 24. Either both p and q or both $\sim p$ and $\sim q$.

_____ 25. Neither p nor q is true.

_____ 26. p if and only if $\sim q$.

_____ 27. Both $\sim p$ and $\sim q$ are true.

_____ 28. No p is a q.

_____ 29. p is true, but q is false.

_____ 30. Either p and $\sim q$ or else q and $\sim p$.

_____ 31. Unless p, then $\sim q$.

_____ 32. Either p or q, but not both.

As an optional assignment to be turned in: write a statement in ordinary language illustrating any twelve of the above expressions.

Exercise 2.3E.   Conditionals, Biconditionals, and Exclusive Alternations in Ordinary English

Directions: In the blank space at the left of each of the following twenty statements, symbolize that statement as it now reads. Then, on separate paper, perhaps as an assignment to be turned in, write at least two other equivalent expressions in symbolic form.

_____ 1. These creatures are (a)nts and they are (b)eautiful.

_____ 2. These creatures are not (a)nts and they are not (b)ees.

_____ 3. These creatures are neither (a)nts nor (b)ees.

_____ 4. Either I'm (a)iling or these creatures are not (b)eautiful.

_____ 5. If this is a (b)ee then it's not an (a)nt; and if it's an (a)nt, then it is not a (b)ee.

_____ 6. This is an (a)piary if and only if it is a place where (b)ees are kept.

_____ 7. It cannot be that this is an (a)piary and that it is not a place where (b)ees are kept.

_____ 8. If and only if this is (a)le is it a good (b)everage.

_____ 9. If and only if this does not make me "(a)il," is it a good (b)everage.

_____ 10. It this is (a)le, then it is what I am supposed to (b)uy, and if it is not (a)le then I'm not supposed to (b)uy it.

_____ 11. If this is not a (b)everage it cannot be (a)le.

_____ 12. To say "a is the antecedent of non-b and b is the antecedent of non-a" is to speak truly.

_____ 13. To say "a is the consequent of b and b is the consequent of a" is to speak falsely.

_____ 14. If and only if non-a is true will non-b be false.

_____ 15. If and only if non-b is false will a be true.

_____ 16. [You may purchase] either (a)pples or (b)ananas.

_____ 17. If this is an (a)pple then it is not a (b)anana.

_____ 18. Nothing is both an (a)pple and a (b)anana.

_____ 19. Either these creatures are (a)nts or they are (b)ees, but they are not both.

_____ 20. The person we are talking about is either a (b)achelor and an (a)scetic or he is neither a (b)achelor nor an (a)scetic.

Exercise 2.3F.   Transforming Statements via Laws of Logic

Directions: Below are twenty pairs of statements. The two members of each pair have the same meaning. You are to (A) express each statement symbolically, and (B) state the law of logic which makes the statements in each pair alike. The laws used are:

DN: Double Negation: $\sim(\sim p) = p$; or $(p \leftrightarrow q) = \sim(p \leftrightarrow \sim q) = (\sim p \leftrightarrow \sim q)$

COM: Commutation: $p \vee q = q \vee p$; or $p \cdot q = q \cdot p$; or $p \leftrightarrow q = q \leftrightarrow p$

COPO: Contraposition: $p \rightarrow q = \sim q \rightarrow \sim p$
DeM: DeMorgan: $\sim(p \vee q) = \sim p \cdot \sim q;$ or $\sim(p \cdot q) = \sim p \vee \sim q$
CE: Conditional Equivalence: $\sim p \vee q = p \rightarrow q$
BE: Biconditional Equivalence: $(p \leftrightarrow q) = (p \rightarrow q) \cdot (q \rightarrow p)$
$\qquad\qquad\qquad\qquad\qquad\qquad (p \leftrightarrow q) = (p \cdot q) \vee (\sim p \cdot \sim q)$
$\qquad$ (and by substitution): $(p \leftrightarrow \sim q) = (p \rightarrow \sim q) \cdot (\sim q \rightarrow p)$
$\qquad\qquad\qquad\qquad\qquad\qquad (p \leftrightarrow \sim q) = (p \cdot \sim q) \vee (q \cdot \sim p)$
$\qquad\qquad\qquad\qquad\qquad\qquad (p \leftrightarrow \sim q) = (p \vee q) \cdot \sim(p \cdot q)$

		a	
EXAMPLE:	A. You must (a)ttend class.		
	B. You must not be excused from (a)ttending class.	$\sim(\sim a)$	DN
1A.	The ambulance was (c)alled.	____	
1B.	It is not the case that the ambulance was not (c)alled.	____	____
2A.	If Ed is a (f)reshman he will be required to take either (h)istory or (g)eography.	____	
2B.	Either Ed is not a (f)reshman, or he will be required to take either (h)istory or (g)eography.	____	____
3A.	Either this proposition is (f)alse, or it is (d)oubtful.	____	
3B.	Either this proposition is (d)oubtful, or it is (f)alse.	____	____
4A.	If the soup is (h)ot, then it is not (f)rozen.	____	
4B.	If the soup is (f)rozen, then it isn't hot.	____	____
5A.	If the weather is (f)avorable, then we will either take a hike or play (b)aseball.	____	
5B.	Unless the weather is not (f)avorable, we will take a (h)ike or we'll play (b)aseball.	____	____
6A.	Joe either inherited lots of (m)oney, or he is now in (d)ebt.	____	
6B.	Either Joe is in (d)ebt, or he inherited lots of (m)oney.	____	____
7A.	If we don't win this (g)ame, then we'll lose the (c)onference.	____	
7B.	If we are not to lose the (c)onference, then we must win this (g)ame.	____	____
8A.	Either Mary is (m)erry or Jane is not (j)olly.	____	
8B.	To say both that Mary is not (m)erry and that Jane is (j)olly is false.	____	____
9A.	It simply can't be the case both that Tom has a (l)ow I.Q. and also that he doesn't study (d)iligently.	____	
9B.	Either Tom doesn't have a (l)ow I.Q. or he studies (d)iligently.	____	____
10A.	If you can't find God at the end of a (t)elescope, neither should you expect to find Him at the end of a (s)yllogism.	____	
10B.	If you expect to find God at the end of a (s)yllogism, then you should also expect to find Him at the end of a (t)elescope.	____	____
11A.	If you don't take this course in (m)ath, you won't get your (d)egree.	____	
11B.	Either you take this course in (m)ath, or you won't get your (d)egree.	____	____
12A.	Vitamin pills are (i)nexpensive, and they either (h)elp or they don't (h)elp.	____	
12B.	Vitamin pills may or may not (h)elp, but they are (i)nexpensive.	____	____
13A.	Either this man is lacking in (a)mbition or he is in(c)ompetent.	____	
13B.	This man cannot be both (a)mbitious and (c)ompetent. [It cannot be both that this man is (a)mbitious and also that he is (c)ompetent.]	____	____
14A.	This is a (q)uadrangle if and only if it has (f)our sides.	____	
14B.	If this is a (q)uadrangle then it has (f)our sides; and if it has (f)our sides then it is a (q)uadrangle.	____	____
15A.	This man is a (b)achelor if and only if he is not (m)arried.	____	
15B.	This man is either a (b)achelor who is un(m)arried, or he is (m)arried but not a (b)achelor.	____	____

16A. I'm going to buy either a (b)oat or a (c)ar, but not both. _____
16B. I'm going to buy a (b)oat if and only if I don't buy a (c)ar. _____ _____
17A. Either John is a (p)ro halfback and he is not a (g)irl, or he is a (g)irl who is not a (p)ro halfback. _____
17B. John is a (p)ro halfback if and only if he is not a (g)irl. _____ _____
18A. A present is a "Greek (g)ift" if and only if there is some (h)idden motive for giving it. _____
18B. A present is either a "Greek (g)ift" with some (h)idden motive for giving it, or it is not a "Greek (g)ift" and there is no (h)idden motive for giving it. _____ _____
19A. The man is either George (W)ashington who was our (F)irst President, or he is not George (W)ashington and he was not our (F)irst President. _____
19B. If and only if the man was George (W)ashington was he our (F)irst President. _____ _____
20A. To say that Joe is not (d)eaf is false. _____
20B. Joe is (d)eaf. _____
21A. This triangle has equal (s)ides if and only if it has equal (a)ngles. _____
21B. This triangle has equal (a)ngles if and only if it has equal (s)ides. _____ _____
22A. This is a (s)quare if and only if it has (f)our equal angles and sides. _____
22B. This is not a (s)quare if and only if it does not have (f)our equal angles and sides. _____ _____

SUMMARY: THE SIX MAJOR CONNECTIVES OF LOGIC. Below are definitions of, and truth tables for, the six logical operations whereby simple propositions are combined to form complex propositions.

Note: The words in brackets are redundant [they could be omitted].

1. *Negation.* Any proposition of the form "$\sim p$" is true *iff* its constituent proposition is false [and false *iff* its constituent proposition is true.]

2. *Alternation (Union).* Any proposition of the form "$p \vee q$" is true *iff* at least one of its constituent statements is true [and false *iff* both of its constituent propositions are false].

3. *Conjunction.* Any proposition of the form "$p \cdot q$" is true *iff* both of its constituent propositions are true [and false *iff* at least one of its constituent propositions is false].

4. *The Conditional.* Any proposition of the form "$p \rightarrow q$" is true *iff* the first of these statements (the antecedent) is false or the second (the consequent) is true [and false *iff* the first of its constituent propositions is true and the second false].

5. *The Biconditional.* Any statement of the form "$p \leftrightarrow q$" is true *iff* its constituent propositions are either both true or both false [and false *iff* one of them is true and the other false].

6. *The Equality Sign.* By definition, a tautologous biconditional. [The equality sign ($=$) signifies a biconditional which has truth values *TTTT*].

Here are these same six definitions expressed as a truth table:

Guide		Negation		Alternation (or Union)	Conjunction	Conditional	Biconditional	Tautologous Biconditional
p	q	$\sim p$	$\sim q$	$(p \vee q)$	$(p \cdot q)$	$p \rightarrow q$	$p \leftrightarrow q$	$p = p \cdot p$
T	T	F	F	T	T	T	T	T T T
T	F	F	T	T	F	F	F	T T T
F	T	T	F	T	F	T	F	F T F
F	F	T	T	F	F	T	T	F T F

It should be realized that the above six connectives or operators are analogous to the operators used in arithmetic (addition, subtraction, multiplication, division). They are the means—the tools—by which logical operations are performed.

Although logic includes the arrow ($\rightarrow$) and the double arrow ($\leftrightarrow$), these connectives can be defined in terms of the wedge ($\vee$), the dot ($\cdot$), and the tilde ($\sim$). Indeed, it is because of such "translation" that the modern computer is able to perform logical operations.

Guide (for two statements, p and q)			
Case	p	q	
1.	T	T	or $(p \cdot q)$
2.	T	F	or $(p \cdot \sim q)$
3.	F	T	or $(\sim p \cdot q)$
4.	F	F	or $(\sim p \cdot \sim q)$

Venn Diagram (for two sets, P and Q)

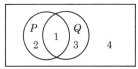

Figure 13

Exercise 2.3G.   Review of Sections 2.1, 2.2, and 2.3

Remarks: Given any four-membered set, there are exactly sixteen ($= 2^4$) combinations of these four elements. Here are the sixteen ($= 2^4$) possible combinations of the set of truth values containing the four members $\{(p \cdot q), (p \cdot \sim q), (\sim p \cdot q), (\sim p \cdot \sim q)\}$. These are listed below, first as truth values, then as sets (where we "count" T, but do not count F). Following each of these sixteen possible combinations are several different statement forms which have those truth values.

A. $TTTT$ $\{1, 2, 3, 4\}$ $p \vee \sim p = \sim(\sim q \cdot q) = (p \cdot q) \vee (p \cdot \sim q) \vee (\sim p \cdot q) \vee (\sim p \cdot \sim q)$
B. $TTTF$ $\{1, 2, 3\}$ $p \vee q = (p \cdot q) \vee (p \cdot \sim q) \vee (\sim p \cdot q) = \sim p \rightarrow q$
C. $TTFT$ $\{1, 2, 4\}$ $p \vee \sim q = (p \cdot q) \vee (p \cdot \sim q) \vee (\sim p \cdot \sim q) = \sim(\sim p \cdot q) = q \rightarrow p$
D. $TFTT$ $\{1, 3, 4\}$ $\sim p \vee q = p \rightarrow q = \sim(p \cdot \sim q) = q \vee (\sim p \cdot \sim q)$
E. $FTTT$ $\{2, 3, 4\}$ $p \rightarrow \sim q = \sim p \vee \sim q = \sim(p \cdot q) = (p \cdot \sim q) \vee \sim p$
F. $TTFF$ $\{1, 2\}$ $p = \sim(\sim p) = (p \cdot q) \vee (p \cdot \sim q) = (p \vee q) \cdot (p \vee \sim q)$
G. $TFTF$ $\{1, 3\}$ $q = (p \cdot q) \vee (\sim p \cdot q) = (p \vee q) \cdot (\sim p \vee q) = \sim q \rightarrow q$
H. $TFFT$ $\{1, 4\}$ $p \leftrightarrow q = \sim(p \leftrightarrow \sim q) = (p \cdot q) \vee (\sim p \cdot \sim q) = (\sim p \vee q) \cdot \sim(\sim p \cdot q)$
I. $FTTF$ $\{2, 3\}$ $\sim(p \leftrightarrow q) = p \leftrightarrow \sim q = (p \cdot \sim q) \vee (\sim p \cdot q) = (p \vee q) \cdot \sim(p \cdot q)$
J. $FTFT$ $\{2, 4\}$ $\sim q = (p \cdot \sim q) \vee (\sim p \cdot \sim q) = \sim q \vee \sim q = q \rightarrow \sim q$
K. $FFTT$ $\{3, 4\}$ $\sim p = \sim p \cdot \sim p = (\sim p \vee \sim p) \cdot \sim(p \cdot p \cdot p)$
L. $TFFF$ $\{1\}$ $p \cdot q = \sim(\sim p \vee \sim q) = \sim(p \rightarrow \sim q) = \sim(q \rightarrow \sim p)$
M. $FTFF$ $\{2\}$ $p \cdot \sim q = \sim(q \vee \sim p) = \sim(p \rightarrow q) = p \cdot p \cdot \sim q \cdot p$
N. $FFTF$ $\{3\}$ $\sim p \cdot q = \sim(p \vee \sim q) = \sim(\sim p \rightarrow \sim q) = \sim(q \rightarrow p)$
O. $FFFT$ $\{4\}$ $\sim p \cdot \sim q = \sim(p \vee q) = \sim(\sim p \rightarrow q) \cdot \sim(\sim q \rightarrow p)$
P. $FFFF$ $\{\ \}$ $p \cdot \sim p = q \cdot \sim q = p \cdot (q \cdot \sim q) = (p \vee q) \cdot (\sim p \cdot \sim q)$

Directions: In the answer blanks before each problem, write in the letter (A to P) indicating the proper set of truth values. For example, the answer to problem 1 is A, the answer to problem 2 is B, the answer to problem 3 is H.

_____ 1. $p \vee \sim p$ _____ 2. $p \vee q$
_____ 3. $(p \cdot q) \vee (\sim p \cdot \sim q)$ _____ 4. $\sim q$

_____	5. $\sim p$	_____	6. $\sim(p \vee q)$
_____	7. $\sim(q \cdot p)$	_____	8. $(p \cdot \sim q) \vee (q \cdot \sim p)$
_____	9. $p \cdot (p \cdot \sim q)$	_____	10. $q \vee (p \cdot \sim q)$
_____	11. $\sim p \vee (p \cdot \sim q)$	_____	12. $(q \cdot \sim p) \vee (\sim p \cdot q)$
_____	13. $(p \cdot q) \vee (\sim p \cdot q)$	_____	14. $(\sim p \cdot \sim q) \cdot \sim p$
_____	15. $(\sim q \vee p) \vee \sim q$	_____	16. $(p \vee \sim q) \vee p$
_____	17. $(p \to q) \vee (q \vee \sim p)$	_____	18. $(\sim q \to \sim p) \cdot (p \to q)$
_____	19. $(\sim q \vee \sim p) \vee \sim(p \cdot q)$	_____	20. $\sim(\sim q \cdot p) \vee (\sim p \vee q)$
_____	21. $(p \leftrightarrow q) \cdot (\sim q \leftrightarrow \sim p)$	_____	22. $\sim(p \leftrightarrow \sim q)$
_____	23. $(\sim p \to \sim q) \cdot (p \to q)$	_____	24. $(\sim q \cdot p) \vee (\sim p \cdot q)$

2.4   Tautologous Conditionals, Valid Arguments, MP, and MT

TAUTOLOGIES.   Some molecular propositions, by the very way in which they are composed, have truth value T in all possible cases. Such propositions, or propositional forms, which are true purely on logical grounds, are called *tautologies.*

One of the simplest examples of a tautology is the proposition "Either apes are (a)nimals or apes are not (a)nimals," ($a \vee \sim a$). This proposition is modeled after the propositional form "$p \vee \sim p$," which always has truth value T: the truth table for "$p \vee \sim p$" will consist of a column composed entirely of T's.

Here are other tautologous forms which are analytically true, that is, true whether or not their component elements, p and q, are true or false—though we must assume that in any complex proposition the truth value of any simple component p will remain consistently true or consistently false throughout the entire statement.

$$(p \to q) \to \sim p \vee q \qquad (\sim p \vee q) \to (p \to q)$$
$$p \cdot q \to q \cdot p \qquad p \vee q \to \sim(\sim p \cdot \sim q)$$
$$p \to q \vee \sim q \qquad p \cdot \sim p \to q$$

Each of these forms has truth value T in all possible cases. No matter what truth values (T or F) are substituted for the variables, the total proposition will always have truth value T. That is, each of the above forms has truth value T regardless of the truth values of its component parts. Each is true solely because of its form.

INCONSISTENT OR SELF-CONTRADICTORY PROPOSITIONS.   Some molecular propositions, by the very manner in which they are formed, will have truth values F in all possible cases. Such propositions (or propositional forms), which are false on purely logical grounds, are said to be *self-contradictory* or *inconsistent.* Consider "$p \cdot \sim p$." If any proposition p has truth value T, then its negation $\sim p$ has truth value F; also, if p has truth value F, then its negation $\sim p$ has truth value T. Since T and F exhaust the entire range of truth values, and since $T \cdot F = F$, the statement form "$p \cdot \sim p$" is self-contradictory. Truth tables will show that "$p \cdot \sim p$" always has truth value F.

Here are some other examples of self-contradictory propositional forms:

$$(p \cdot q) \cdot \sim(p \cdot q) \qquad q \cdot (p \cdot \sim p)$$
$$(p \to q) \cdot (p \cdot \sim q) \qquad \sim(p \to \sim q) \cdot (q \to \sim p)$$
$$(p \to \sim p) \cdot (\sim p \to p) \qquad \sim p \vee p \to p \cdot \sim p$$

Again, these propositions are always false solely because of their *form*; their truth values are independent of the truth values of the individual ("atomic") component propositions.

CONTINGENT PROPOSITIONS (OR PROPOSITIONAL FORMS). Most of the forms we have been studying, for example, p, $\sim p$, $p \vee q$, $p \cdot q$, $p \to q$, and $p \leftrightarrow q$, are contingent propositions, or contingent propositional forms. Contingent propositions are propositions whose truth values are sometimes true (T) and sometimes false (F); and whose associated sets are neither U nor $\varnothing$.

To summarize, propositions are of three types: (1) tautologous—logically true propositions—all of whose cases have truth value T; (2) self-contradictory—logically false propositions whose components are inconsistent or incompatible—all of whose cases have truth value F; and (3) contingent—propositions whose truth values are mixed—some T and some F.

Truth tables are helpful in showing all possible truth value assignments. Below are six tautologous conditionals. Truth tables have been completed for 1, 3, and 5. You are to complete 2, 4, and 6. The valid argument forms to be studied in sections 2.4 and 2.5 are valid because their related conditionals (shown below in exercise 2.4A) are tautologous.

Exercise 2.4A. Truth Tables for Tautologous Conditionals

Related Argument Forms: Guide   **(1.) Affirming the Antecedent (MP: *Modus Ponens*)**   **(2.) Denying the Consequent (MT: *Modus Tollens*)**

Case	p	q	$[(p \to q) \cdot p]$	→	q	$[(p \to q) \cdot \sim q]$	→	~p
1	T	T	T T T Ⓣ T	T	Ⓣ			
2	T	F	T F F F T	T	F			
3	F	T	F T T F F	T	Ⓣ			
4	F	F	F T F F F	T	F			
Steps: 1 1			2 3 2 4 2	5	2	2 3 2 4 3 2	5	3 2

Truth Values: Subsets of $\{1, 2, 3, 4\}$: $TFFF \to TFTF$ $\{1\} \subset \{1, 3\}$

Related Argument Forms: Guide   **(3.) DS: Disjunctive Syllogism Eliminating one Alternant**   **(4.) Affirming one Conjunct in the Negation of a Conjunction**

Case	p	q	$[(p \vee q) \cdot \sim p]$	→	q	$[\sim(p \cdot q) \cdot p]$	→	~q
1	T	T	T F F	T	Ⓣ			
2	T	F	T F F	T	F			
3	F	T	T Ⓣ T	T	Ⓣ			
4	F	F	F F T	T	F			
Steps 1 1			2 4 2 5 3 2	6	2	4 2 3 2 5 2	6	3 2

Truth Values: Subsets: $FFTF \quad TFTF$ $\{3\} \subset \{1, 3\}$

Related Argument Forms: Guide   **(5.) HS: Hypothetical Syllogism (Transitivity)**   **(6.) HS: Hypothetical Syllogism (Transitivity)**

Case	p	q	r	$[(q \to r) \cdot (p \to q)]$	→	$(p \to r)$	$[(p \to q) \cdot (q \to r)]$	→	$(p \to r)$
1	T	T	T	T T T Ⓣ T T T	T	T Ⓣ T			
2	T	T	F	T F F F T T T	T	T F F			
3	T	F	T	F T T F T F F	T	T Ⓣ T			
4	T	F	F	F T F F T F F	T	T F F			
5	F	T	T	T T T Ⓣ F T T	T	F Ⓣ T			
6	F	T	F	T F F F F T T	T	F Ⓣ F			
7	F	F	T	F T T Ⓣ F T F	T	F Ⓣ T			
8	F	F	F	F T F Ⓣ F T F	T	F Ⓣ F			
Steps: 1 1 1				2 3 2 4 2 3 2	5	2 3 2	2 3 2 4 2 3 2	5	2 3 2

Truth Values: Subsets: $TFFFTFTT \quad TFTFTTTT$ $\{1, 5, 7, 8\} \subset \{1, 3, 5, 6, 7, 8\}$

TAUTOLOGOUS STATEMENT FORMS AND VALID ARGUMENT FORMS. Since tautologous propositions are the basis for all laws of logic, and since laws of logic provide the foundation for every type of formal argument, it is well to be clear as to their meaning. On this point we quote from Stephen F. Barker: " . . . laws of logic are necessary truth about sentences and arguments, which hold true in virtue of the ways words are used and which we grasp through mastering our language."[7]

The ordinary meaning of the word *tautological* becomes obvious when we consider a statement such as the following: "This is a (d)esk, and either it is made of (m)etal or it is not made of (m)etal $[d \cdot (m \vee \sim m)]$." Obviously, the only portion of this statement which gives us specific information is "This is a (d)esk." The "$(m \vee \sim m)$" portion of the statement is tautologous, or trivial. Any statement d conjoined to a tautology, as in "$d \cdot (m \vee \sim m)$," says no more than "d" by itself.

The meaning of a tautologous proposition may perhaps be more clearly understood if compared with a contingent proposition. Consider the empirical proposition "This is a desk," which we may symbolize by "d." Then the following propositions are all analytically true, or tautologous. They are true whether "This is a desk" is true or false:

Either this is a desk, or this is not a desk. $(d \vee \sim d)$
If this is a desk, then this is a desk. $(d \rightarrow d)$
If this is not a desk, then this is not a desk. $(\sim d \rightarrow \sim d)$
It cannot be both that this is a desk, and also that this is not a desk. $\sim(d \cdot \sim d)$

Observe that the above statements are *tautologous propositions*, but they are *not arguments*.

Now consider a conditional proposition which contains two factual (categorical) propositions, call them d and m:

If this is a (d)esk, then it is made of (m)etal. $(d \rightarrow m)$

Obviously "$d \rightarrow m$" is a contingent proposition: its truth is not established merely by examining its *form*.

But contingent propositions may be combined with other contingent propositions to produce *larger forms*, and some of these larger forms are tautological. Here is a tautologous conditional—one which we shall soon examine in greater detail:

$$[(p \rightarrow q) \cdot p] \rightarrow q$$

---

[7] S. F. Barker, *The Elements of Logic*, rev. ed., (New York: McGraw-Hill, 1974), p. 301. Read also Ilham Dilman, *Induction and Deduction: A Study in Wittgenstein*, (New York: Barnes & Noble, 1973), esp. chap. 11, "Logical Necessity." Consider also the following statement by Michael Foucault, *The Order of Things: An Archeology of the Human Sciences* (a translation of *Les Mots et les Choses*, Paris, 1966) (New York: Pantheon Books, 1971), p. 297:

> [In the 19th century there began] a search for a logic independent of grammars, vocabularies, synthetic forms, and words; a logic that could clarify and utilize the universal implications of thought while protecting them from the singularities of a constituted language in which they might be obscured. It was inevitable that a symbolic logic should come into being, with Boole, at precisely that period when languages were becoming philological objects; for, despite some superficial resemblances and a few technical analogies, it was not a question . . . of constituting a universal language, but of representing the forms and connections of thought outside all language. And since language was becoming an object of science, a language had to be invented that would be a symbolism rather than a language, and would for that reason be transparent to thought in the very movement that permits it to know.

Here is a substitutional instance of this conditional:

$$[(d \to m) \cdot d] \to m$$

Here is the way these brief symbols might be expressed in ordinary language: "Assuming (1) that if this object is a (d)esk this object is made of (m)etal, and assuming (2) that this object is a (d)esk, then, granting these two assumptions, it necessarily follows that this object is made of (m)etal."

Rather than form sentences into such long and awkward combinations, logic has traditionally treated statements under one category and arguments under an entirely different category. In most argument forms, the premises are presented as separate and distinct from the conclusion, thus:

Premises: 1. If this object is a (d)esk, it is made of (m)etal. $d \to m$
              2. This object is a (d)esk. d

Conclusion: Therefore, this object is made of (m)etal. $\therefore m$

The advantages of separating premises from conclusion are obvious: not only are the propositions simpler, but it is easier to examine each premise separately to see whether or not it is true. Moreover, the conclusion is clearly seen to be the terminal point of the inference.

Nevertheless, there is a very important relationship between statement forms and argument forms, namely: an argument form based on a tautologous conditional is a valid form of argument; an argument form based on a contingent (or on a self-contradictory) conditional is an invalid argument form. Here, for example, is an argument form based on the contingent conditional $[(d \to m) \cdot {\sim} d] \to {\sim} m$, whose truth values are *TTFT*. Hence this is *not* a valid argument form:

Premises: 1. If this object is a (d)esk, it is made of (m)etal. $d \to m$
              2. This object is not a (d)esk. ${\sim} d$

Conclusion: Therefore, this object is not made of (m)etal. $\therefore {\sim} m$

In a conditional proposition, we distinguish the antecedent (the "if" clause) from the consequent (the "then" clause). In arguments we distinguish the premise(s) from the conclusion. Since every argument takes the general form "If these premises are true, then this conclusion follows," argument forms are closely related to conditional statement forms.

We define a valid argument as one in which the premise(s) logically imply the conclusion, or one in which the conclusion necessarily follows from the premise(s). How can we tell whether or not an argument is valid? The answer is quite simple: *any argument form is valid if and only if it is based on a correlative tautologous conditional.*

Here are four forms of argument we will be using shortly. Each argument form (shown on the right) is valid precisely because its related statement form (shown on the left) is a tautologous conditional:

Four Tautologous Conditionals   *Four Related Argument Forms*

1a. $[(p \to q) \cdot p] \to q$ MP   1b. $(p \to q) \cdot p \mathbin{/} \therefore q$
2a. $[(p \to q) \cdot {\sim} q] \to {\sim} p$ MT   2b. $(p \to q) \cdot {\sim} q \mathbin{/} \therefore {\sim} p$
3a. $[(p \lor q) \cdot {\sim} q] \to p$ DS   3b. $(p \lor q) \cdot {\sim} q \mathbin{/} \therefore p$
4a. $[(p \to q) \cdot (q \to r)] \to (p \to r)$ HS   4b. $(p \to q) \cdot (q \to r) \mathbin{/} \therefore p \to r$

The order in which the antecedents of these conditionals, or in which the premises of MP, MT, DS, and HS appear, is unimportant. So they might also read:

1c. $[p \cdot (p \to q)] \to q$ MP   1d. $p \cdot (p \to q) \mid \therefore q$
2c. $\sim q \cdot (p \to q) \to \sim p$ MT   2d. $\sim q \cdot (p \to q) \mid \therefore \sim p$
3c. $[\sim p \cdot (p \vee q)] \to q$ DS   3d. $\sim p \cdot (p \vee q) \mid \therefore q$
4c. $[(q \to r) \cdot (p \to q)] \to (p \to r)$ HS   4d. $(q \to r) \cdot (p \to q) \mid \therefore p \to r$

Argument forms may also be structured vertically, with a separate number assigned to each premise. The three dots ($\therefore$) preceding each conclusion mean "therefore." Sometimes the conclusion is separated from the premises by a line, as in 1e, 2e, 3e, and 4e.

(1e) 1. $p \to q$ (2e) 1. $p \to q$ (3e) 1. $p \vee q$ (4e) 1. $p \to q$
     2. p 2. $\sim q$ 2. $\sim q$ 2. $q \to r$
   ∴ q ∴ $\sim p$ ∴ p ∴ $p \to r$

A modification of this method places the conclusion immediately after the concluding premise. This usage is especially convenient in extended arguments, and will be used later in this book. Here are four examples:

(1f) 1. $p \to q$ (2f) $p \to q$ (3f) 1. $p \vee q$ (4f) 1. $p \to q$
     2. $p \mid \therefore q$ 2. $\sim q \mid \therefore \sim p$ 2. $\sim q \mid \therefore p$ 2. $q \to r \mid \therefore p \to r$

In sum, a valid argument is more than a tautologous proposition: it is a tautologous conditional such that, when a portion of this tautologous form (the premise, or premises) is *asserted*, then the remainder of this tautologous form (the conclusion) *necessarily follows*. The distinction between premise(s) and conclusion is essential to every form of argument. Hence, although tautologous conditionals form the *basis* for valid argument forms, conditional statements are not arguments. Conditionals are statements, not arguments: in any conditional, antecedent and consequent are joined to form a single proposition. But in an argument the premises are separate and distinct from the conclusion.

Most of the argument forms to be studied during the remainder of this chapter are built around conditionals. However, since the "if" of a conditional is sometimes mistaken to mean the "if and only if" of a biconditional, it may be well to begin with an argument form based on the biconditional.

The easiest of all inferences are those built around biconditionals, for they involve nothing more than simple substitution. Given the biconditional $p \leftrightarrow q$ as *true*, then: when p is true, q is true; when p is false, q is false; when q is true, p is true; and when q is false, p is false. Exercise 2.4B illustrates this form of argument.

Exercise 2.4B.   Arguments Employing Biconditionals (Substitution)

Directions: In the answer column, write V or I to indicate whether the argument is valid or invalid.

A.   *Major Premise:* This animal is (s)afe if and only if it is (t)ame. $(s \leftrightarrow t)$

Minor Premises:	*Conclusions:*	
1. But it is tame.	So it is not safe.	1. _____
2. But it is not safe.	So it is tame.	2. _____
3. But it is not tame.	So it is safe.	3. _____
4. But it is safe.	So it is not tame.	4. _____
5. But it is tame.	So it is safe.	5. _____
6. But it is not safe.	So it is not tame.	6. _____
7. But it is not tame.	So it is not safe.	7. _____
8. But it is safe.	So it is tame.	8. _____

B. Either this triangle is both equi(a)ngular and equi(l)ateral, or it is neither equi(a)ngular nor equi(l)ateral. ($a \leftrightarrow l$)

9. But it is equiangular.	So it is not equilateral.	9. _____
10. But it is not equiangular.	So it is equilateral.	10. _____
11. But it is not equiangular.	So it is not equilateral.	11. _____
12. But it is equiangular.	So it is equilateral.	12. _____
13. But it is equilateral.	So it is equiangular.	13. _____
14. But it is equilateral.	So it is not equiangular.	14. _____
15. But it is not equilateral.	So it is equiangular.	15. _____
16. But it is not equilateral.	So it is not equiangular.	16. _____

AFFIRMING THE ANTECEDENT (MODUS PONENS: MP) AND DENYING THE CONSEQUENT (MODUS TOLLENS: MT). We turn now to two forms of argument widely used in both traditional and modern logic.

Each of the following argument forms contains as its premises two propositions: (1) a conditional, called the *major premise*; and (2) a simple statement, called the *minor premise*. This minor premise either (a) "affirms the antecedent" of the major premise, or (b) "denies the consequent" of the major premise, thus:

Argument Forms

1. Affirming the antecedent (MP)
    Symbols:
    $(p \to q) \cdot p$ / $\therefore$ q; or
    $(f \to s) \cdot f$ / $\therefore$ s

Examples

If x is a fish, then x can swim. (major premise)
But x is a fish. (minor premise)
Therefore, x can swim. (conclusion)
—*valid*: affirming the antecedent

2. Denying the consequent (MT)
    Symbols:
    $(p \to q) \cdot \sim q$ / $\therefore$ $\sim p$; or
    $(d \to m) \cdot \sim m$ / $\therefore$ $\sim d$

If x is a dog, then x is a mammal. (major premise)
But x is not a mammal. (minor premise)
Therefore, x is not a dog. (conclusion)
—*valid*: denying the consequent

Let us note a further relationship between these two forms of conditional arguments. First, recall the law of logic: $(p \to q) = (\sim q \to \sim p)$. Applying contraposition to the major premise, we may rewrite the above arguments as follows, so that (1) affirming the antecedent becomes (1a) denying the consequent, and (2) denying the consequent becomes (2a) affirming the antecedent. All are *valid* forms. *Note*: $\sim(\sim p) = p$.

1a. Denying the consequent (MT)
    Symbols:
    $(\sim q \to \sim p) \cdot p$ / $\therefore$ q; or
    $(\sim s \to \sim f) \cdot f$ / $\therefore$ s

If x cannot swim, then x is not a fish. (major premise)
But x is a fish. (minor premise)
Therefore, x can swim. (conclusion)
—*valid*: denying the consequent

2a. Affirming the antecedent (MP)
    Symbols:
    $(\sim q \to \sim p) \cdot \sim q$ / $\therefore$ $\sim p$; or
    $(\sim m \to \sim d) \cdot \sim m$ / $\therefore$ $\sim d$

If x is not a mammal, then x is not a dog. (major premise)
But x is not a mammal. (minor premise)
Therefore, x is not a dog. (conclusion)
—*valid*: affirming the antecedent

These examples show how a *modus tollens* (MT) (denying the consequent) may be changed into a *modus ponens* (MP) (affirming the antecedent) and vice versa. In spite of their similarity, MP and MT have traditionally been treated as separate forms, and we shall treat them that way here. Using MP for *modus ponens* (affirming the antecedent) and MT for *modus tollens* (denying the consequent), we formalize these two argument forms thus:

$$\text{MP } (\textit{Modus Ponens}): \quad (p \to q) \cdot p \mid \therefore q$$
$$\text{MT } (\textit{Modus Tollens}): \quad (p \to q) \cdot {\sim}q \mid \therefore {\sim}p$$

Observe that we "deny the consequent" either by adding a tilde, or by subtracting a tilde. Thus $[(p \to {\sim}q) \cdot q \mid \therefore {\sim}p]$ and $[({\sim}p \to {\sim}q) \cdot q \mid \therefore p]$ are interpreted as forms of MT, and the use of double negation (DN) seems too obvious to deserve more than passing mention.

Exercise 2.4C. Arguments Which Affirm the Antecedent (MP) or Deny the Consequent (MT)

Directions: In the answer space before each problem, write V or I to indicate whether the argument is valid or invalid. In problems 11 to 24 check your answers by restating them in symbolic form.

_____ 1. $(a \to b) \cdot b \mid \therefore a$

_____ 2. $({\sim}f \to {\sim}q) \cdot q \mid \therefore f$

_____ 3. $({\sim}c \to d) \cdot c \mid \therefore d$

_____ 4. $(k \to {\sim}l) \cdot k \mid \therefore l$

_____ 5. $(r \to s) \cdot {\sim}s \mid \therefore r$

_____ 6. $(w \to {\sim}x) \cdot {\sim}w \mid \therefore {\sim}x$

_____ 7. $({\sim}y \to {\sim}z) \cdot {\sim}y \mid \therefore {\sim}z$

_____ 8. $({\sim}p \to {\sim}q) \cdot q \mid \therefore p$

_____ 9. $[(w \cdot k) \to x] \cdot {\sim}x \mid \therefore {\sim}(w \cdot k)$

_____ 10. $[m \to (f \to g)] \cdot (f \to g) \mid \therefore m$

_____ 11. If air is composed (e)xclusively of hydrogen and nitrogen, then, when all the hydrogen and nitrogen have been (r)emoved by being chemically combined with other elements, the total weight of air should be (a)ccounted for. But such is not the case. Therefore, air is not composed (e)xclusively of hydrogen and nitrogen.

_____ 12. [Shortly after learning that the heart had valves, and after learning the approximate amount of blood moved by each heart beat, Harvey argued as follows:] If the blood pumped by the heart does not (c)irculate, then within less than an hour's time, the amount of blood going from the heart to the body's extremities would (e)xceed the total weight of the body. But this is impossible. Therefore, the blood pumped by the heart does (c)irculate.

_____ 13. The (i)gnition is on, so the (e)ngine should run; for the mechanic said that if the (i)gnition is off, then the (e)ngine won't run.

_____ 14. If this man is (t)elling the truth, I'll (e)at my hat. But you know I don't intend to (e)at my hat. So, you should know [I think] he is not (t)elling the truth.

Note: As problem 14 suggests, MP and MT are such easy and obvious forms of argument that we sometimes employ them in preference to more direct statements.

_____ 15. If it (r)ained, the (p)icnic was to have been called off. But it has not (r)ained. So, there'll be a (p)icnic for sure.

_____ 16. If the ignition is not (o)n, the car radio won't (p)lay. But the ignition is (o)n, [otherwise, the car wouldn't be running]. So, the radio will (p)lay.

_____ 17. This patient must have (m)alaria; because we know that if a patient has (m)alaria, he will have a (f)ever; and this patient certainly has a (f)ever.

_____ 18. If I (i)nterpret "if" to mean "if and only if," then I'll get (w)rong answers on most of these problems. But I am not (i)nterpreting "if" to mean "if and only if." Therefore, my answers will be right.

_____ 19. If light rays are lacking in (m)ass, they will not be (d)eflected by gravitational attraction toward the sun when passing by the sun. They are so (d)eflected. Hence, they are not lacking in (m)ass.

_____ 20. He is always the (l)ast one to finish an exam, unless it is a (t)rue-false exam. But today's exam was a (t)rue-false exam. So, we may be sure he won't be the (l)ast one done. (*Note:* "Unless" = "if not.")

_____ 21. The clutch must be (o)ut; for unless the clutch is (o)ut, the wheels will not (t)urn, and the wheels are (t)urning.

_____ 22. Unless we can (c)ontrol "the population bomb," all qualitative advances resulting from modern science and technology will soon be (n)ullified. But this must not be allowed to happen. Therefore, we must somehow (c)ontrol the population bomb.

_____ 23. If this new scientific theory is (t)rue, then these experimental consequences should (f)ollow. But many experiments verify the fact that such consequences do (f)ollow. Therefore, this new scientific theory is (t)rue.

_____ 24. If the traditional scientific theory is (t)rue, then these experimental consequences should (f)ollow. But many experiments have verified the fact that such consequences do not (f)ollow. Therefore, the traditional scientific theory is false.

We conclude this section by reviewing six laws of logic—laws that will be used over and over again in this book. It should be noted that MP and MT were based on tautologous conditionals, and were therefore not commutative. In contrast, the following six laws are based on tautologous biconditionals, and are commutative. The equality sign indicates that the two sides of the equation each have the same set of truth values.

Exercise 2.4D.   Transforming Statements

This exercise is intended to review your knowledge of the following laws:

ASSOC (Association): $p \cdot (q \cdot r) = (p \cdot q) \cdot r$; $p \vee (q \vee r) = (p \vee q) \vee r$
CE (Conditional Equivalence): $p \vee q = \sim p \rightarrow q$
COM (Commutation): $p \vee q = q \vee p$; $p \cdot q = q \cdot p$
COPO (Contraposition): $p \rightarrow q = \sim q \rightarrow \sim p$
DeM (DeMorgan): $\sim(p \cdot q) = \sim p \vee \sim q$; $\sim(p \vee q) = \sim p \cdot \sim q$
DN (Double Negation): $\sim(\sim p) = p$; $\sim(p \leftrightarrow \sim q) = p \leftrightarrow q$

Directions: In the answer blank before each problem, write ASSOC, CE, COM, COPO, DeM, or DN, to indicate which of the above six laws of logic is exemplified. If none of the above laws is used, write X.

_____ 1. $f \vee (g \vee h) = (f \vee g) \vee h$
_____ 2. $w \rightarrow \sim z = z \rightarrow \sim w$
_____ 3. $\sim(\sim f \vee g) = f \cdot \sim g$
_____ 4. $p \vee (q \cdot r) = (q \cdot r) \vee p$
_____ 5. $p \vee \sim(\sim q \cdot r) = p \vee q \vee \sim r$
_____ 6. $\sim(\sim a \cdot b) = a \cdot b$

_____ 7. $\sim m \vee w = m \rightarrow w$
_____ 8. $h \cdot [(m \vee k) \cdot j] = h \cdot j \cdot (m \vee k)$
_____ 9. $\sim[(f \cdot g) \vee \sim h] = \sim(f \cdot g) \cdot h$
_____ 10. $\sim\{\sim[(a \cdot b) \vee d]\} = (a \cdot b) \vee d$
_____ 11. $d \cdot (f \vee g) = (d \cdot f) \vee g$
_____ 12. $\sim k \cdot \sim w = \sim(k \cdot w)$

Note: Each of the remaining six problems requires the use of *two* laws of logic.

_____ _____ 13 & 15. $\sim\{[(f \vee g)] \cdot k\} = (\sim f \cdot \sim g) \vee \sim k$
_____ _____ 14 & 16. $\sim(h \vee w) \rightarrow f = \sim f \rightarrow (\sim h \rightarrow w)$
_____ _____ 17 & 19. $k \rightarrow \sim(b \vee d) = (\sim b \rightarrow d) \rightarrow \sim k$
_____ _____ 18 & 20. $\sim\{\sim[f \cdot (g \cdot b)]\} = b \cdot g \cdot f$
_____ _____ 21 & 23. $\sim\{\sim[(a \cdot b) \vee f]\} = a \vee b \vee \sim f$
_____ _____ 22 & 24. $(m \cdot \sim k) \rightarrow \sim d = d \rightarrow \sim m \vee k$

2.5   Truth, Validity, and Soundness; DS; and HS

TRUTH, VALIDITY, AND SOUNDNESS.   The conclusion of an argument is a logically proven consequent of other assertions (the premises) which have already been explicitly stated or implicitly assumed. Whether or not the premises of an argument are factually true is a problem outside the domain of formal logic, and more properly belongs within the domain of the empirical sciences.

EMPIRICAL TRUTH.   A proposition is empirically true if it is factually correct—if it is in accord with a state of affairs which could be used as evidence to verify it. Examples: "Africa is larger than Europe," "Water freezes at approximately 0°C." The truth or falsity of a factual proposition cannot be established merely by examining the words or language used; it can be established only on the basis of nonlinguistic evidence.

ANALYTICAL TRUTH. A proposition is analytically true if it is a tautology, that is, if it is patterned after a statement form which is necessarily true. Every law of logic is analytically true, for example, the seven laws studied in section 1.3; the six laws reviewed in the concluding exercise of section 2.4; or MP and MT.

The overall soundness of any argument depends both on the truth of the premises and on the validity of the argument's form. There are four possible combinations of true-false premises and of valid-invalid inferences:

Premises	Validity	Soundness
1. True	Valid	Sound
2. True	Invalid	Unsound
3. False	Valid	Unsound
4. False	Invalid	Unsound

The meaning of this chart may also be expressed as follows: an argument is (s)ound if and only if the argument is expressed in a (v)alid argument form, and all of the argument's premises are (t)rue ($s \leftrightarrow v \cdot t$).

The distinction between truth and validity is shown in the following examples:

A. *True premise:* All cows are mammals.
   Valid inference; sound conclusion: No cows are nonmammals.
B. *True premise:* All cows are mammals.
   Invalid inference; unsound conclusion: All mammals are cows.
C. *False premise:* No cows are mammals.
   Valid inference; unsound conclusion: No mammals are cows.
D. *False premise:* No cows are mammals.
   Invalid inference; unsound conclusion: All cows have hoofs.

Each of the following four arguments is formally *valid*, but the conclusions cannot be said to be *sound*, because they rest on premises which are doubtful or ambiguous:

A. Any institution over a century old (is worthy of veneration and) should not be changed. Our system of government is over a century old. Therefore, our system of government should not be changed.
B. All institutions more than a century old (are out of date and) should be changed. Our system of government is an institution that is more than a century old. Therefore, it should be changed.
C. All moral maxims are man-made rules. The golden rule is a moral maxim. Therefore, the golden rule is a man-made rule.
D. A perfect maxim (that is, all perfect maxims) must have a supernatural source. The golden rule is a perfect moral maxim. Therefore, the golden rule must have a supernatural source.

Two chapters of this book deal with problems of truth: chapter 3, "Informal Logic," and chapter 5, "Logic and Science." The other chapters are concerned almost exclusively with *validity*. However, exercise 2.5A is an exception. In this exercise you are expected to draw upon your general knowledge to decide whether or not the premises are true or false.

Exercise 2.5A. Judging Validity and Soundness of Arguments

Directions: On the right-hand side of each problem are three choices:

$\sim V$: The argument is formally invalid.

$V \cdot \sim S$: The argument is formally valid but unsound, i.e., based on a premise that is untrue.

$V \cdot S$: The argument is both valid and sound.

Circle the appropriate choice for each problem.

1. If this creature is a (b)at, it is a (m)ammal. But it is a (b)at. Therefore, it is a (m)ammal. $\qquad\qquad \sim V \quad V \cdot \sim S \quad V \cdot S$
2. If bats are (m)ammals, then they cannot (f)ly. But bats can (f)ly. Therefore, bats are not (m)ammals. $\qquad\qquad \sim V \quad V \cdot \sim S \quad V \cdot S$
3. If this creature is a (b)at, it belongs to the order (C)hiroptera (the order of flying mammals that have membranous wings that extend from the forelimbs to the hind limbs or tail). But this creature is a (C)hiroptera (for it has membranous wings that extend from the forelimbs to its rear end). Therefore, this creature is a (b)at. $\qquad\qquad \sim V \quad V \cdot \sim S \quad V \cdot S$
4. If any creatures cannot (f)ly, they are not (b)irds. But these creatures (ostriches and penguins) cannot fly. Therefore, they are not birds. $\qquad \sim V \quad V \cdot \sim S \quad V \cdot S$
5. If (u)p is up and down is down (i.e., if the earth is stationary, and if all heavy objects fall from "up" to "down"), then there can be no (a)ntipodes living on the opposite side of the earth. But (u)p is up, and down is down. So, there can be no (a)ntipodes living on the opposite side of the earth. $\qquad\qquad \sim V \quad V \cdot \sim S \quad V \cdot S$
6. If any substance is a (m)etal, then it will (c)onduct electricity. But this substance will not (c)onduct electricity. Therefore, this substance is not a (m)etal. $\qquad\qquad \sim V \quad V \cdot \sim S \quad V \cdot S$
7. If any substance is a (m)etal, then it is a (s)olid. But this substance (i.e., mercury) is not a (s)olid. Therefore, this substance (i.e., mercury) is not a (m)etal. $\qquad\qquad \sim V \quad V \cdot \sim S \quad V \cdot S$
8. If any animal has (h)ipbones, it uses its legs for (l)ocomotion. This animal (which is a whale) has (h)ipbones. Therefore, this animal (i.e., this whale) uses its legs for (l)ocomotion. $\qquad\qquad \sim V \quad V \cdot \sim S \quad V \cdot S$
9. If sponges fall within the (p)hylum Porifera (having pores), then sponges are (z)oological species (which, as animals, have the power of locomotion). But, sponges do fall within the phylum Porifera. Therefore, sponges are (z)oological species. $\qquad\qquad \sim V \quad V \cdot \sim S \quad V \cdot S$
10. If a platypus lays (e)ggs, it cannot be a (m)ammal. But the platypus is a (m)ammal. Therefore, a platypus does not lay (e)ggs. $\qquad\qquad \sim V \quad V \cdot \sim S \quad V \cdot S$

We turn now to a form of argument widely used in traditional logic—a form very similar to MP and MT, as studied in section 2.4.

THE DISJUNCTIVE SYLLOGISM (DS). This ancient argument form consists of the elimination of one disjunct, or the *elimination of one alternative.* In the truth tables below, note that the wedge is true when *both p* and *q* are true (case 1). Hence, given that the wedge ($\vee$) is true, it is only when one of the conjuncts is false that the other conjunct is *necessarily* true (case 2 or case 3).

	$[(p \vee q) \cdot \sim q] \to p$		$[(p \vee q) \cdot \sim p] \to q$	
1	$T\ T\ T\ F\ F$	$T\ T$	$T\ T\ T\ F\ F$	$T\ T$
2	$T\ T\ F\ T\ T$	$T\ T$	$T\ T\ F\ F\ F$	$T\ F$
3	$F\ T\ T\ F\ F$	$T\ F$	$F\ T\ T\ T\ T$	$T\ T$
4	$F\ F\ F\ F\ F$	$T\ F$	$F\ F\ F\ F\ T$	$T\ F$

Here, then, are the two valid forms for DS:

$$(p \lor q) \cdot \sim p \mid \therefore q; \quad \text{and} \quad (p \lor q) \cdot \sim q \mid \therefore p$$

Applying various substitutions, six other forms are valid, for example:

$$(p \lor \sim q) \cdot q \mid \therefore p; \quad \text{and} \quad (\sim p \lor \sim q) \cdot p \mid \therefore \sim q$$

DS is such an easy argument form that around 225 B.C. the Stoic logician Chrysippus (282–208 B.C.) declared that dogs use it! Chrysippus told of a dog which was chasing a rabbit. During the chase they came to two forks or paths, which will be called paths A and B. After scenting path A (and then "inferring" that the rabbit had not followed path A), the dog *immediately* (i.e., without further scenting) followed path B in pursuit of the rabbit. Had the dog been able to speak about its logical processes, the dog might have explained its reasoning as follows:

> The rabbit followed either path A or path B.
> But (by scenting the dog knew) the rabbit did *not* follow path A.
> Therefore (the dog inferred) the rabbit followed path B.

Had the dog learned how to employ logical symbols, he might have written:

$$(a \lor b) \cdot \sim a \mid \therefore b$$

At this point we will not discuss the extent to which Chrysippus verified these statements, nor will we comment further about animal intelligence. However, we will insist that the elimination of an alternative is an extremely easy form of inference. We shall give it its traditional name, the *Disjunctive Syllogism* (DS), although it might perhaps better be called "The Elimination of one Disjunct." We make no distinction as to whether it is the first or the second disjunct which is eliminated. Here, then, are the two forms:

DS (Disjunctive Syllogism): $(p \lor q) \cdot \sim p \mid \therefore q; \quad$ and
$\qquad\qquad\qquad\qquad\qquad\quad (p \lor q) \cdot \sim q \mid \therefore p$

Since by CE, $p \lor q = \sim p \to q$, and by COPO, $\sim p \to q = \sim q \to p$, DS is only one step removed from modus ponens (MP) and modus tollens (MT):

DS: 1. $p \lor q$ MP: 1. $\sim p \to q$ MT: 1. $\sim q \to p$
      2. $\sim p \mid \therefore q$ 2. $\sim p \mid \therefore q$ 2. $\sim p \mid \therefore q$

There is only one real problem in applying DS. It is the problem of distinguishing weak (inclusive) from strong (exclusive) alternation. Suppose the major premise of an argument were a strong disjunction, as in

  (A) Today is either (T)uesday or (W)ednesday; or
  (B) This creature is either a (t)iger or a (w)olf.

For either of these two statements, the proper symbolism is:

$$(t \cdot \sim w) \lor (w \cdot \sim t); \text{ or } (t \lor w) \cdot \sim (t \cdot w); \text{ or } t \leftrightarrow \sim w$$

If a disjunctive syllogism (DS) has as its major premise an exclusive disjunction—a strong alternation meaning "either . . . or, but not both"—the DS argument form involves nothing more than substitution. For, given $p \leftrightarrow \sim q$, when p is true, q is false; when p is false, q is true; when q is true, p is false; and when q is false, p is true. We insert exercise 2.5B to emphasize this point, and to remind students that, unless a major premise is explicitly indicated as an exclusive disjunction, it should be interpreted as a weak or inclusive disjunction.

Exercise 2.5B.   Arguments Employing Exclusive Disjunctions

Directions: In the answer column, write V or I to indicate whether the argument is valid or invalid.

A.   *Major Premise:* Either we (r)ide to school, or we (w)alk to school, but not both $[(r \lor w) \cdot \sim(r \cdot w)]$; or we (r)ide to school if and only if we do not (w)alk $(r \leftrightarrow \sim w)$.

Minor Premises	*Conclusions*	
1. But we are riding.	Therefore, we are not walking.	1. _____
2. But we are riding.	Therefore, we are walking.	2. _____
3. But we are walking.	Therefore, we are not riding.	3. _____
4. But we are walking.	Therefore, we are riding.	4. _____
5. But we are not riding.	Therefore, we are walking.	5. _____
6. But we are not riding.	Therefore, we are not walking.	6. _____
7. But we are not walking.	Therefore, we are riding.	7. _____
8. But we are not walking.	Therefore, we are not riding.	8. _____

B.   *Major Premise:* If and only if he is a (b)achelor, he is un(m)arried. $(b \leftrightarrow \sim m)$

9. But he is a bachelor.	So, he must be unmarried.	9. _____
10. But he is not a bachelor.	So, he must be unmarried.	10. _____
11. But he is a bachelor.	So, he is married.	11. _____
12. But he is not a bachelor.	So, he is married.	12. _____
13. But he is unmarried.	So, he is not a bachelor.	13. _____
14. But he is unmarried.	So, he is a bachelor.	14. _____
15. But he is married.	So, he is not a bachelor.	15. _____
16. But he is married.	So, he is a bachelor.	16. _____

ARGUMENT WHOSE MAJOR PREMISE IS A NEGATION OF A CONJUNCTION.   This type of argument takes this form: $\sim(p \cdot q) \cdot q \mathbin{/} \therefore \sim p$; and is valid if and only if the minor premise *affirms* one of the conjuncts in the major premise.

In this book, however, we recommend that the DeMorgan laws be applied to the major premise, changing the above argument to: $(\sim p \lor \sim q) \cdot q \mathbin{/} \therefore \sim p$. This recommendation entails an extra step because DeM must be used, but it avoids learning another argument form, one which some students find quite confusing.

Before beginning exercise 2.5C keep in mind the following truth about DS. In either exclusive or inclusive disjunction, the *denial* (i.e., the elimination) of one disjunct means that the other disjunct remains; hence whether "either . . . or" is taken in the weak or strong sense, the *denial* of one disjunct is a *valid* form of argument.

On the other hand, the *affirmation* of one disjunct is an *invalid* form of argument whenever the disjunction is weak or inclusive because, since $p \lor q$ has truth values *TTTF*, case 1 allows the possibility that *both p and q may be true.*

Exercise 2.5C.   Arguments Whose Major Premises are Disjunctions or Negations of Conjunctions

In the first twelve problems of exercise 2.5C, the major premise is a weak alternation. In problems 13–24 the major premise is a negation of a conjunction, and will require the use of the DeMorgan laws to transform it into a weak alternation. Problems 25–40 represent a mixture of the two types.

Directions: In the answer blanks, write V or I to indicate whether the argument is valid or invalid. Symbolize arguments now expressed only in verbal terms. Also, symbolize all arguments whose major premise is a negation of a conjunction, and use DeMorgan to change this major premise to an alternation.

_____ 1. $(a \lor b) \cdot \sim a \mathbin{/} \therefore b$

_____ 2. $(\sim c \lor \sim d) \cdot \sim c \mathbin{/} \therefore \sim d$

_____ 3. $(f \lor g) \cdot f \mathbin{/} \therefore g$

_____ 4. $(\sim k \lor l) \cdot k \mathbin{/} \therefore l$

_____ 5. $(\sim p \lor q) \cdot \sim q \mathbin{/} \therefore p$

_____ 6. $(r \lor s) \cdot s \mathbin{/} \therefore r$

_____ 7. $(\sim w \lor x) \cdot x \mathbin{/} \therefore \sim w$

_____ 8. $(\sim y \lor \sim s) \cdot s \mathbin{/} \therefore \sim y$

Note: In the verbal problems, interpret "or" to mean "either . . . or, and perhaps both."

_____ 9. Either the premises are (f)alse or the deduction is (i)nvalid. But the deduction is (i)nvalid. Therefore, the premises are true.

_____ 10. Either his assumptions are in(c)orrect, or his reasoning is (f)allacious. But his assumptions are (c)orrect. Therefore, his reasoning is (f)allacious.

_____ 11. Either he is suffering a (r)elapse, or he has picked up some new (d)isease. The doctors insist that he does not have a (r)elapse. So he must have picked up some new (d)isease.

_____ 12. Either Bill is (o)ut of town, or his (p)hone is out of order. But I just learned that Bill is in town. So, his (p)hone is out of order.

_____ 13. $\sim(a \cdot b) \cdot b \mathbin{/} \therefore \sim a$

_____ 14. $\sim(c \cdot \sim d) \cdot c \mathbin{/} \therefore d$

_____ 15. $\sim(f \cdot g) \cdot \sim f \mathbin{/} \therefore \sim g$

_____ 16. $\sim(\sim j \cdot \sim k) \cdot j \mathbin{/} \therefore k$

_____ 17. $\sim(p \cdot q) \cdot q \mathbin{/} \therefore p$

_____ 18. $\sim(r \cdot \sim s) \cdot s \mathbin{/} \therefore r$

_____ 19. $\sim(\sim t \cdot w) \cdot w \mathbin{/} \therefore t$

_____ 20. $\sim(\sim x \cdot \sim y) \cdot \sim y \mathbin{/} \therefore x$

_____ 21. It cannot be both that students help (g)overn this college and also that its outdated curriculum has not been (m)odified. But everyone agrees that many important (m)odifications have been made in its curriculum. Therefore, students now help (g)overn this college.

_____ 22. It is impossible for this number to (e)nd in zero, and for it not to be (d)ivisible by five. But it does (e)nd in zero. So, it must be (d)ivisible by five.

_____ 23. No honor student can both have a (l)ow I.Q. and also (s)kip his homework. But this honor student certainly (s)kips his homework. So he must not have a (l)ow I.Q.

_____ 24. It cannot be the case both that my watch is (r)ight and that we are late. But we are not (l)ate. So, my watch must be right.

_____ 25. This coin will (f)all *either* heads or tails, *or* it will (s)tand on its side. Well, it won't (s)tand on its side. So, it will (f)all either heads or tails.

_____ 26. Rufus was either a (b)aseball hero or a (f)ootball star. But his school annual says here that he was a (b)aseball hero. So, he was not a (f)ootball star.

_____ 27. It is impossible for a good athlete to be (b)oth tall and fast, and also not good (m)aterial for the basketball squad. But no one can deny that John is a good athlete who is (b)oth tall and fast. So, John is good (m)aterial for the basketball squad.

_____ 28. A person cannot (p)ass every exam and also (f)ail the course. But Jane did not (f)ail the course. So, she must have (p)assed every exam.

_____ 29. Maud must either (m)ake an A on the final exam or (f)ail the course. But she cannot (m)ake an A on the final. Surely, then, she cannot pass the course.

_____ 30. Jane either had to (p)ass the exam or (f)ail the course. So, she must have (p)assed the exam, for the records show that she didn't (f)ail the course.

_____ 31. It cannot be the case both that I (u)nderstand these argument forms well and also that I am unable to complete these problems with (s)peed and (e)ase. But I do (u)nderstand these argument forms well. Therefore, I am able to complete these problems with (s)peed and (e)ase.

_____ 32. It is impossible for the (f)irst witness and the (s)econd witness both to be telling the truth. But the (f)irst witness is obviously not telling the truth. Therefore, the (s)econd witness is telling the truth.

_____ 33. Bob either (f)lunked the exam or failed to (t)urn in some assignments. But he passed the exam. So he must not have (t)urned in some assignments.

_____ 34. He's either dis(h)onest or in(c)ompetent. He is (h)onest. So he's not (c)ompetent.

_____ 35. Either I (u)nderstand this section of the book [and hence can do these problems very quickly] or I (n)eed the practice which these problems provide. But I do (u)nderstand this section of the book. Therefore, I do not (n)eed the practice which these problems require.

_____ 36. It cannot be that the (a)ntecedent of a conditional is false and that the (c)onditional considered as a whole is also false. But this (c)onditional considered as a whole is true. Therefore, its (a)ntecedent must be false.

HS: THE HYPOTHETICAL SYLLOGISM.   One of the oldest and most used of all argument forms, the syllogism is now seen to be one application among many of the principle of *transitivity*.

Long before studying either logic or mathematics, one employs transitivity in reasoning such as the following: "If Art is taller than Bill, and if Bill is taller than Carol, then Art is taller than Carol." "If a pound is heavier than an ounce, and if an ounce is heavier than a gram, then a pound is heavier than a gram." If $1 + 2 = 1 + (1 + 1)$, and if $1 + (1 + 1) = 3$, then $1 + 2 = 3$. Relations such as "is taller than," "is heavier than," "is lighter than," and "is equal to" are called *transitive* relations.

It should be obvious that the relation "is a subset of" ($\subset$) of set theory, and the relation "if ... then ... " ($\rightarrow$) of propositional logic, are both transitive relations. Hence, although they employ different symbols, the following argument forms all apply the same principle of transitivity.

1. If $2 < 3$ and if $3 < 4$, then $2 < 4$.
2. All Swedes are Men. All Men are Primates. So, all Swedes are Primates.
3. If $(S \subset M)$ and if $(M \subset P)$, then $(S \subset P)$.
4. If John is a (S)wede, then John is a (m)an; and if John is a (m)an, then John is a (p)rimate; hence, if John is a (S)wede, then John is a (p)rimate. In symbols:

$$(s \rightarrow m) \cdot (m \rightarrow p) / \therefore (s \rightarrow p)$$

Using s, p, and m to represent any three statements, here are the two valid argument forms of the *Hypothetical Syllogism* (HS):

$$(s \rightarrow m) \cdot (m \rightarrow p) / \therefore (s \rightarrow p)$$
$$(m \rightarrow p) \cdot (s \rightarrow m) / \therefore (s \rightarrow p)$$

Since commutation (COM) transforms the second of these forms into the first, we might say that there is but one form for HS:

$$(s \rightarrow m) \cdot (m \rightarrow p) / \therefore s \rightarrow p.$$

By substitution, the following are also valid syllogistic arguments:

5. If x is an S, then x is an M. If x is an M, then x is not a P. Therefore, if x is an S, then x is not a P. $(s \rightarrow m) \cdot (m \rightarrow \sim p) / \therefore s \rightarrow \sim p$

5A. All (S)wedes are (m)en. No (m)en are (p)orpoises. So, no (S)wedes are porpoises. $(s \rightarrow m) \cdot (m \rightarrow \sim p / \therefore s \rightarrow \sim p$

Three simple rules suffice to tell us whether or not any argument fits into one of these valid forms:

1. In analyzing any argument, the first step is to spot the conclusion. As we shall see in section 6.1, traditional logic called the subject of the conclusion the subject term of the syllogism (S), and called the predicate of the conclusion the predicate term (P) of the entire syllogism. In modern logic S would be

called the conclusion's *antecedent*, and P the conclusion's *consequent*. Note that the middle term (M) appears in each premise but does not appear in the conclusion.

2. For the conclusion to be valid, it is necessary in the *premises* that the *subject* of the conclusion (S) appear on the *left* of one arrow, and that the *predicate* of the conclusion (P) appear on the *right* side of the other arrow. Only thus can the principle of transitivity apply.

3. The entire syllogism must contain exactly three simple propositions, which we have indicated above as s, p, and m; but which might also be symbolized by the three other letters for statement *forms*, p, q, and r. To meet this third requirement, it is often necessary, but very easy, to contrapose one or more of the statements. Consider, for example, the following argument:

$$(p \to q) \cdot (\sim r \to \sim q) \mid \therefore p \to r$$

By COPO, this becomes: $(p \to q) \cdot (q \to r) \mid \therefore p \to r$

Or, using COPO twice, it becomes: $(\sim q \to \sim p) \cdot (\sim r \to \sim q) \mid \therefore \sim r \to \sim p$

If it is impossible to make the argument conform to the pattern of a valid hypothetical syllogism, the argument is invalid. Here is an example of an HS which is *invalid*, even though it is symbolized in three equivalent ways:

$$(\sim m \to p) \cdot (\sim m \to \sim s) \mid \therefore s \to p$$
$$(\sim p \to m) \cdot (\sim m \to \sim s) \mid \therefore \sim p \to \sim s$$
$$(\sim p \to m) \cdot (s \to m) \mid \therefore s \to p$$

Exercise 2.5D.   The Hypothetical Syllogism (HS)

Directions: Symbolize each of the following arguments. Then, in the answer blanks write V or I to indicate whether the argument is valid or invalid.

_____ 1. If x is a (f)ish then x can (s)wim. If x is a (p)orpoise, then x can (s)wim. Hence, if x is a (p)orpoise, x is a (f)ish.

_____ 2. If anyone makes a great deal of (m)oney, he should become (r)ich. If any businessman is (s)uccessful, he should make a great deal of (m)oney. So, if any businessman is (s)uccessful, he should become (r)ich.

_____ 3. If a plant is a (m)um then it is a (f)lower. If a plant is a (s)edum, it is not a (m)um. So, if a plant is a (s)edum, it is not a (f)lower.

_____ 4. If any nation is (m)ilitaristic, it is a (t)hreat to its neighbors. Hence, if any nation spends (b)illions for munitions, it is a (t)hreat to its neighbors; because, if any nation spends (b)illions for munitions, it is (m)ilitaristic.

_____ 5. If any animal is a (b)eaver, it is not a non(r)odent. If any animal is a (r)odent, it is not an (u)ngulate. So, if any animal is a (b)eaver, it is not an (u)ngulate.

_____ 6. If this creature is a (m)ammal, then it doesn't have (f)eathers; but if it is a (b)ird, then it does have (f)eathers. Therefore, if this creature is a (b)ird, then it is not a (m)ammal.

_____ 7. If anything is a (w)ombat, it is not a (b)ird. But if any creature is a (b)ird, it is a (v)ertebrate. Therefore, if anything is a (w)ombat, it is not a (v)ertebrate.

_____ 8. If anyone is a (n)aturalist, he is not [likely to be] a (m)ystic. But if anyone is a (y)ogi, he is [almost sure to be] a (m)ystic. So, if anyone is a (n)aturalist, [you can bet] he's not a (y)ogi.

_____ 9. If any man is a (p)olitician, then he's not a (m)artyr; because, if any man is a (p)olitician, he's not an (i)dealist; and if anyone is a (m)artyr, then he has to be an (i)dealist.

_____ 10. If any primitive people is (c)annibalistic, it is a (s)avage culture. But if any primitive people is from Central (A)ustralia, you can be sure it is a (s)avage culture. Therefore, if any primitives are from Central (A)ustralia, they must be (c)annibalistic.

_____ 11. If any creature is a (m)arsupial, then it is not a (d)og. So, if any creature is a (d)og, it cannot be a (k)angaroo; because, if any creature is a (k)angaroo, it is a (m)arsupial.

_____ 12. If any democracy gets embroiled in (r)acial conflicts, it cannot long (s)urvive. Furthermore, if any democracy has an overly (a)pathetic citizenry, that democracy cannot long (s)urvive. Hence, if a democracy gets embroiled in (r)acial conflicts, it will not have an overly (a)pathetic citizenry.

Note: The remaining problems of this exercise will include the forms "All *p* are *q*" ($p \to q$) and "No *p* are *q*" ($p \to \sim q$). These are included among the basic statement forms of traditional logic, and will be studied in detail in chapter 6. Their similarity to the conditional may be seen by noting that problems 13a and 13b (also problems 14a and 14b) have the same meanings.

_____13a. All (a)ffluent people are (w)ealthy. No (p)aupers are (w)ealthy. Therefore, no (a)ffluent people are (p)aupers.

_____13b. If anyone is (a)ffluent, he is (w)ealthy; and if anyone is a (p)auper, he is not (w)ealthy. Hence, if anyone is (a)ffluent, he is not a (p)auper.

_____14a. No (h)uman beings are perfectly (c)ontented. Every (f)reshman is a (h)uman being. Therefore, no (f)reshmen are perfectly (c)ontented.

_____14b. If these people are (h)uman beings, they are not perfectly (c)ontented. Now [you'll have to give a freshman this much credit, that] if he is a (f)reshman, he is [at least] a (h)uman being. Therefore, if any person is a (f)reshman, he is not perfectly (c)ontented.

_____ 15. No (I)rishmen are (c)orruptible. Now, in our town, if anyone is a member of the (p)olice force, he is an (I)rishman. Therefore, if any man is a member of our (p)olice force, he is not (c)orruptible.

_____ 16. If any syllogism is (v)alid, it exemplifies the principle of (t)ransitivity; and if it exemplifies the principle of (t)ransitivity, it exemplifies a (r)ule of logic. Therefore, every (v)alid syllogism exemplifies a (r)ule of logic.

_____ 17. Every (g)iraffe is an (u)ngulate, and no (c)amels are (g)iraffes. Hence, no (c)amels are (u)ngulates.

_____ 18. All (a)nthropoidae have (o)pposable thumbs. Any creature that is either a (m)onkey or a (g)ibbon is an (a)nthropoidae. Therefore, if any creature does not have (o)pposable thumbs, it is neither a (m)onkey nor a (g)ibbon.

_____ 19. Any worker who is (f)airly treated received a (m)inimum living wage. No (s)laves are treated (f)airly. Therefore, if a person is a (s)lave, he does not receive a (m)inimum living wage.

_____ 20. No workers who are treated un(f)airly receive (j)ust treatment. All (s)laves receive un(j)ust treatment. Therefore, no (s)laves are treated (f)airly.

Exercise 2.5E.   Review of MP, MT, DS, and HS

Directions: (a) Symbolize each of the following arguments, (b) In the answer blank before each problem, write V or I to indicate whether the argument is valid or invalid.

_____ 1. If George had (g)raduated, he would have taken a (t)rip to Europe. So, since he didn't go to Europe, he must not have (g)raduated.

_____ 2. Either (n)ature tells us what's natural, or (m)an himself declares what is natural. Now surely (n)ature does not say what is natural. Therefore, it is (m)an who decides whether or not something is natural.

_____ 3. It is never the case both that it is (s)nowing and that (v)isibility is good. So, (v)isibility must be good today, for it certainly is not (s)nowing.

_____ 4. It is impossible for this animal to be a (w)olf and not have (e)yeteeth. But it does have (e)yeteeth. Therefore, it is a (w)olf.

_____ 5. If there are nonsyllogistic propositional forms which yield (t)ruth values *T* in all possible cases, then these nonsyllogistic forms are (l)ogically valid forms of argument. But truth tables show that there exist many such nonsyllogistic forms. Hence, there exist many nonsyllogistic forms which are (l)ogically valid forms of argument.

_____ 6. If a system of logic is able to (c)ombine several forms of argument into a lengthy proof, that system of logic is quite (f)lexible. But, if traditional logic used but (o)ne form of argument at a time, traditional logic was not able to (c)ombine several forms of argument into a lengthy proof. Therefore, if traditional logic used but (o)ne form of argument at a time, it was in(f)lexible.

_____ 7. If the law of (u)niformitarianism is not true, geology is not a very highly (d)eveloped science. But, as all geology books state in bold print, the law of (u)niformitarianism is true. So, geology must be a highly (d)eveloped science.

_____ 8. If this ore is (g)old, then its (m)elting point is 1,064°C. But if this ore is (p)yrite, its (m)elting point is much less than 1,064°C. Therefore, if this ore is (p)yrite, it is not (g)old.

_____ 9. If any ore is (g)old, it is (h)ard, (y)ellowish, and (f)airly heavy. If any ore is (p)yrite, it is (h)ard, (y)ellowish, and (f)airly heavy. Hence, if any ore is (p)yrite, it is (g)old.

_____ 10. Either the team will (w)in at least half of its games, or the coach will be (f)ired. Well, the team won all but one of its long season of games. So, the coach was not (f)ired.

_____ 11. Either Sam is not (f)rugal, or he (s)aves his money. But Sam certainly (s)aves his money. So, he must not be (f)rugal.

_____ 12. If anything is a coal (t)ar derivative, then it is not a (n)ourishing food, because all (a)rtificial dyes are coal tar derivatives, and no artificial dyes are nourishing foods.

_____ 13. If we are willing to admit (p)robable knowledge as a legitimate part of knowledge, then (r)ules of probable reasoning should be a part of logic. But surely (p)robable knowledge is legitimate and useful to man. Therefore, (r)ules concerning probable reasoning should be a part of logic.

_____ 14. If the worthy (k)new that worthiness is worthless, then they would not (r)emain worthlessly worthy. But the worthy do (r)emain worthlessly worthy. Therefore, the worthy do not (k)now that worthiness is worthless.

_____ 15. It cannot be both that the (s)enate investigation will continue and that Americans will remain (i)gnorant about these affairs. Well, the (s)enate investigation has been going on now for two months. So, it surely cannot be claimed that Americans are (i)gnorant of these affairs.

_____ 16. If any physical body were freed (that is, completely isolated) from all external (f)orces, then it would continue (u)nchanged in the state of rest or motion in a straight line and at the same speed. But no physical body is in such a state of perfect rest or of (u)nchanging motion. Therefore, no physical body is free from all external (f)orces.

_____ 17. [Hume argued]: Either laws of nature which operate without exception in our own age were not (o)perating in the past when miracles occurred, or reports about some miracles are un(r)eliable. But it is unreasonable to suppose that laws of nature did not (o)perate in the past as they do today. Therefore, it is reasonable to believe that some reports about miracles are un(r)eliable.

_____ 18. Either Sam and Sue are the (s)ame age, or Orville is (o)lder than Orton. But Sam is four years older than Sue. Hence, Orville is (o)lder than Orton.

_____ 19. It is impossible for Columbus to have (c)ircumnavigated the globe and also for the earth to be (f)lat. So, since Columbus did not (c)ircumnavigate the globe, the earth must not be (f)lat.

_____ 20. Either women are approximately as (i)ntelligent as men, or a large proportion of women should be (d)iscouraged about continuing their higher education. But a large proportion of women are so (d)iscouraged. So, women are less (i)ntelligent than men.

_____ 21. If Columbus had not (d)iscovered the new world, Americus Vespucius would not have written his (b)ook about the new continent. And if Americus

Vespucius had not written his (b)ook, our continent would not now be called (A)merica. Hence, if Columbus had not (d)iscovered the new world, it would not be called (A)merica.

_____ 22. It cannot be both that there are (s)atellites (or moons) going around the planet Jupiter, and also that the earth is the (o)nly center in the universe. Observations through telescopes reveal such (s)atellites of Jupiter. So, the earth is not the (o)nly center in the universe.

_____ 23. If anyone employs a (c)ontrary-to-fact conditional, he is implicitly affirming that the antecedent is (f)alse. But anyone who says "If this antecedent is true, then I'll eat my (h)at" is employing a (c)ontrafactual conditional. Therefore, anyone who argues "If this antecedent is true, then I'll eat my (h)at," is implicitly affirming that the antecedent is false.

_____ 24. If the antecedent of a conditional is (a)bsurd, it must also be (f)alse. But if the antecedent of a conditional is (f)alse, then that conditional considered as a whole must have (t)ruth-value T. Hence, if the antecedent of any conditional is not (a)bsurd, then that conditional considered as a whole will not have (t)ruth-value T.

_____ 25. No (q)uails are (b)irds, because all (p)eacocks are (b)irds, and no (q)uails are (p)eacocks.

_____ 26. If any animal chews its (c)ud it is a (r)uminant. No (r)uminants are (m)arsupials. Therefore, no (c)ud-chewing animals are (m)arsupials.

_____ 27. No (b)ovines are (m)arsupials. No (o)xen are (m)arsupials. Therefore, no (o)xen are (b)ovines.

_____ 28. No (m)arsupials are (u)ngulates. Every (k)angaroo is a (m)arsupial. Therefore, if any animal is an (u)ngulate, it is not a (k)angaroo.

_____ 29. Every female (k)angaroo has an abdominal (p)ouch to shelter and nurse its young. Every (o)pposum has a similar (p)ouch. Therefore, if this creature is an (o)pposum it must be some kind of a (k)angaroo.

_____ 30. Every (i)nnovator (s)ees old things in new ways. Hence, if anyone is an (i)nnovator he must be (e)ccentric, since every eccentric sees old things in new ways.

The four argument forms we have just studied (MP, MT, DS, and HS) are so basic that it might even be argued that babies employ them before they can speak. Perhaps in some nonvocal manner a baby learning to walk "reasons" thus:

"If I am not to (f)all down [this time], I must (l)ift my feet. But I am [determined] not to fall down. So [this time] I'll (l)ift my feet." [$(\sim f \rightarrow l) \cdot \sim f \mid \therefore l$]

Whether on a verbal or nonverbal level, the four argument forms we have been studying are employed by each of us thousands of times every day. For example, while reading a book, we reason (consciously or subconsciously): "If I wish to continue (r)eading I must (t)urn the page. I do wish to continue reading. So I turn the page" [$(r \rightarrow t) \cdot r \mid \therefore t$]. Again, "For dessert, I'll have either (c)ake or (i)ce cream. There is no cake here today. So, I'll have ice cream." [$(c \vee i) \cdot \sim c \mid \therefore i$]. "If I am to (m)ove from this room to the next, I must (w)alk. If I am to (w)alk, I must (s)tand up and (m)ove my legs. So, if I am to (m)ove from this room to the next, I must (s)tand up and (m)ove my legs." [$(m \rightarrow w) \cdot (w \rightarrow s \cdot m) \mid \therefore m \rightarrow s \cdot m$]. "If I don't (w)atch where I'm going, I'll (b)ump into something. But I am [determined] not to (b)ump into something. So, I'll (w)atch where I'm going. [$(\sim w \rightarrow b) \cdot \sim b \mid \therefore w$].

However, although MP, MT, DS, and HS are fundamental to human thought and action, the fact remains that incorrect and invalid forms are frequently mistaken for valid ones. It is imperative that students of logic know the difference.

MP, MT, DS, and HS are employed so frequently, and their meaning is so readily understood, that abbreviated arguments are more common than formally structured ones. For example, a lawyer might say, "This culprit should be (p)unished, for he committed a (c)rime"—a condensed form for "Any person who (c)ommits a crime should be (p)unished. This culprit committed a crime. Therefore, he should be punished" [$(c \rightarrow p) \cdot c$ / $\therefore p$]. Again, you might reason to yourself, "Joe must be taking (l)ogic, because he's in the logic (c)lass"—an abbreviation for "If Joe is in the logic (c)lass, Joe must be taking (l)ogic. Joe is in the (l)ogic class. So, Joe must be taking (l)ogic." [$(c \rightarrow l) \cdot c$ / $\therefore l$].

Exercise 2.5F. Formalizing Abbreviated Syllogisms

Part A. Directions: Add the missing premise which will change what is now an informal, abbreviated syllogism into a formal valid syllogism.

1. Since one of its premises is (m)issing, this argument may be called an (e)nthymeme.
2. This magazine is (p)oorly bound, so it is not a (f)irst-rate magazine.
3. Some disputes are purely (v)erbal, since they are based entirely on the (m)eanings of the words used.
4. (L)ions do not make good (p)ets, for they are (w)ild and (f)erocious.
5. This statement means "All B is A" because it reads "Only A is B."
6. No college graduate who has not learned to (q)uestion his inherited beliefs is genuinely (e)ducated. Therefore, many college (g)raduates are not genuinely (e)ducated.
7. Traditional logic (a)ssumed that every well formed proposition was a categorical statement about existing events. Hence, traditional logic allowed no place for assertions which might refer to the (e)mpty set.
8. This exercise must have some (v)alue, because it was (a)ssigned to us by our teacher.

Part B. Directions: Problems 1–8 asked you to supply missing *premises*. Problems 9–12 ask you to supply missing *conclusions*.

9. No knowledge is truly humanizing unless it is cumulative and progressive. Science is the only type of knowledge that is cumulative and progressive. Therefore, . . .
10. If most students who study a subject make the Honor Roll, then that subject has great educational value. But every student in our high school who studied Latin made the Honor Roll. Therefore, . . .
11. This term can be given two different interpretations, both within the same context; and any term that can be given two different interpretations, both within the same context, is ambiguous. Therefore, . . .
12. No person who does not try to see things as they really are is a genuine scientist. No reformer tries to see things as they really are (since the reforms he advocates would make things different than they are). Hence, . . .

Answers for Chapter Two

2.1A:

1. c;   3. $\sim c$;   5. $\sim m$;   7. $c \cdot a$;   9. $\sim a \cdot c$;   11. $a \cdot n \cdot u$;   13. $o \cdot s$;
15. $d \cdot h$ *Note:* Is the sentence in problem 15 a *statement*? Can it be said to be *true*? (or *false*?) Or is it a command, a request, an invitation? To make it into a *statement*, we would have to interpret it somewhat as follows: "Now [let us assume that] good digestion [will] wait on appetite, and health on both."
17. $d \cdot h$;   19. $d \cdot h$;   21. $d \cdot h \cdot a$;
23. $h \cdot \sim d$ *Note:* In problem 17, the temporal sequence of events is not included in the statement; but the temporal sequence is included in the statements in problems 18–24.

2.1B:

1. $b \lor c$;   3. $(c \lor m) \cdot \sim(c \cdot m)$; also $(c \cdot \sim m) \lor (\sim c \cdot m)$;
5. $(a \lor e) \cdot \sim(a \cdot e)$; also $(a \cdot \sim e) \lor (e \cdot \sim a)$;   7. $(h \lor a) \cdot \sim(h \cdot a)$; also $(h \cdot \sim a) \lor (a \cdot \sim h)$;

9. $f \lor a$;   11. $l \lor \sim a$;   13. $\sim w \lor \sim v$;
15. $(m \lor l) \cdot \sim(m \cdot l)$; also $(m \cdot \sim l) \lor (l \cdot \sim m)$; problem 15 might also be interpreted $m \lor l$;
17. Again without knowledge of the context, problem 17 could be either $s \lor \sim u$; or it could be $(s \lor \sim u) \cdot \sim(s \cdot \sim u)$;
19. Statement 19 is ambiguous. Assuming that "Monthly payment" means "*total* monthly payment," then, for a given month, payment would be made by the man, or by his daughter, but not by both $(m \cdot \sim d) \lor (d \cdot \sim m)$. But in a series of payments, one month's payment might be made by the man, the next month by the daughter, etc., and the statement would be symbolized $m \lor d$.

2.1C:

1. Barkus is neither able nor willing.
3. Either Barkus is unable and unwilling, or he's simply unwilling.
5. Barkus is unable, or Barkus is unwilling, but he is not both.
7. Either Barkus is both able and willing, or it is false that he is either able or willing.
9. Barkus is either not able or he's not willing, and [I feel quite sure that] he is willing.
11. Barkus may or may not be willing, but he is able.

2.1D:

1. $T \cdot T = T$;   3. $T \lor T = T$;   5. $T \cdot F = F$;   7. $F \lor F = F$;
9. $\sim(T \cdot F) \cdot F = \sim(F) \cdot F = T \cdot F = F$;   11. $T \cdot F = F$;   13. $F \lor \{\sim F \lor T\} = F \lor T = T$;
15. $F \cdot (F \lor T) = F \cdot T = F$;   17. $(T \cdot T) \lor F = T \lor F = T$;
19. $(T \cdot \sim T) \cdot \sim F = (T \cdot F) \cdot T = F \cdot T = F$;
21. $\sim(F \cdot \sim F) \lor \sim(T \lor \sim T) = \sim(F \cdot T) \lor \sim(T \lor F) = \sim F \lor \sim T = T \lor F = T$;
23. $(T \lor \sim T) \cdot \sim(T \cdot \sim T) = (T \lor F) \cdot \sim(T \cdot F) = T \cdot \sim F = T \cdot T = T$.

2.1E:

(1) $p \lor q$	(3) $\sim(m \lor w)$	(5) $\sim(\sim k \cdot \sim m)$	(7) $(\sim p \cdot \sim q) \lor p$
$F\ T\ T$	$T\ F\ F\ F$	$F\ T\ F\ T\ T\ F$	$T\ F\ F\ F\ T\ \ F\ \ F$
$1\ 1\ 2$	$1\ \ 3\ 2\ \ 4$	$1\ \ 3\ 5\ 2\ 4\ 6$	$4\ 3\ 2\ 5\ 6\ \ 1\ \ 2$

For most problems, various "orders of steps" are possible. The student should observe these numbered orders if he is puzzled as to how solutions have been obtained.

(9) $a \cdot \sim(\sim b \lor \sim a)$	(11) $k \cdot \sim[(k \cdot m) \lor \sim(\sim k \lor \sim m)]$
$T\ T\ T\ \ F\ T\ F\ \ F\ T$	$T\ T\ T\ \ T\ F\ F\ \ F\ \ F\ F\ T\ T\ \ T\ \ T\ F$
$2\ 1\ 2\ \ 4\ 5\ 3\ \ 6\ 7$	$2\ 1\ 2\ \ 5\ 4\ 6\ \ 3\ \ 4\ 7\ 7\ 9\ \ 8\ 8$
or $2\ 1\ 2\ \ 4\ 6\ 3\ \ 5\ 7$	or $2\ 1\ 2\ \ 3\ 5\ 6\ \ 4\ \ 5\ 3\ 3\ 8\ \ 7\ 7$
or $2\ 1\ 2\ \ 6\ 7\ 5\ \ 4\ 3$	or $2\ 1\ 2\ \ 6\ 4\ 9\ \ 3\ \ 4\ 7\ 7\ 5\ \ 8\ 8$

In these answers, the numbers indicate the order of the steps used in reasoning. As the answers for problems (9) and (11) indicate, various orders of step sequences are sometimes possible. Be sure each step represents a *necessary* inference.

To save space, we shall throughout this book use the above method of numbering to indicate the step-by-step processes of reasoning. However, for this initial exercise, it may be helpful to also present another way of visualizing the step-by-step processes of reasoning. This method is shown below for problems (3), (5), and (7):

2.1E:

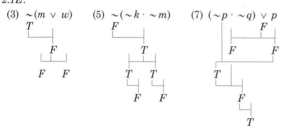

(3) $\sim(m \lor w)$ (5) $\sim(\sim k \cdot \sim m)$ (7) $(\sim p \cdot \sim q) \lor p$

2.2A:
Answers are given in the exercise itself.

2.2B:

1. $\sim(\sim f \cdot p)$, COM;   3. $\sim p \lor f$, COM;   5. $\sim f \to \sim p$, COPO;   7. $p \lor \sim g$, DeM;
9. $g \to p$, CE;   11. $\sim c \to \sim t$, COPO;   13. $\sim t \lor c$, COM;   15. $\sim(\sim c \cdot t)$, COM;
17. $\sim(l \cdot \sim s)$, DeM;   19. $(p \lor r) \lor (m \lor s)$, CE.

2.2C:

1. *A*; 3. *D* (*Note:* "unless" = "if . . . not"); 5. *C*; 7. *C*; 9. *B*; 11. *A*;
13. *A*; 15. *C*; 17. *A*; 19. *A*; 21. *A*; 23. *A*; 25. *D*; 27. *B*; 29. *D*.

2.2D:

1. $\sim b \vee a$; 3. $b \cdot \sim a$; 5. $\sim a \to b$; 7. $\sim b \to \sim a$;
9. $[b \to a] \cdot b \cdot \sim a$ is incorrect; for we want what is *true* to be symbolized. Note that $b \to a =$ $\sim b \vee a = \sim(b \cdot \sim a)$—and that $\sim(b \cdot \sim a)$ contradicts the *true* statement $b \cdot \sim a$. Hence the *truth* contained in this statement would be symbolized simply $b \cdot \sim a$. However, it would be better to restructure the sentence thus: "It has been (s)aid that if she were beautiful she would be an actress; but the truth is that she is (b)eautiful and she is not an (a)ctress." Then the correct symbolism would be $s \cdot b \cdot \sim a$.
11. $(b \to a) \cdot \sim b \cdot \sim a$; 13. $(\sim a \cdot b) \vee (\sim b \cdot a)$; 15. $(a \to b) \cdot (\sim b \to \sim a)$.

2.2E:

No answers are given for this exercise.

2.2F:

(*A* only): If Fido is a dog, Fido is a mammal; If Fido is not a mammal, Fido is not a dog; Either Fido is a mammal, or Fido is not a dog; Either Fido is not a dog, or Fido is a mammal; It cannot be both that Fido is a dog and that Fido is not a mammal; Fido can't be a non-mammal and also be a dog. (*Note:* The statement "Fido is either not a dog, or Fido is a mammal" is contrary to good English usage, because such usage requires that in a disjunction, the first disjunct should be the more general term, so as to provide the *context* for the entire statement.)

To the above six equivalent statements, the following might also be added: All dogs are mammals. All non-mammals are non-dogs; No non-mammals are dogs; No dogs are non-mammals. Such subject-predicate statements will be emphasized in chapter 6.

2.2G:

1. *A, B, C*; 3. *C*; 5. None; 7. *B*; 9. *C*; 11. *A*.

2.2H:

(1) $p \cdot q \to r$
TTTFF
3 2 3 1 2

(3) $\sim p \to q$
F T T F
2 3 1 1

(5) $(p \vee \sim q) \to q$
F T T F F F
1 1 2 3 5 4

(7) $q \to \sim q$
F T T F
4 1 2 3
or 2 1 4 3

(9) $(p \cdot q) \vee \sim p$
TFF F FT
4 2 5 1 2 3

(11) $[(\sim p \vee \sim q) \cdot q] \to p$
TF TFTTT F F
4 4 3 5 6 2 3 1 2
or 3 3 5 6 6 4 5 1 2

(13) $a \to (\sim b \cdot a \to b)$
TF TFTTF F
2 1 5 5 3 4 2 3

(15) $(g \to \sim h) \cdot (g \to h)$
TF FTFTT T
TT TFF TF T
or 2 1 2

2.3A:

Part A. 1. $T \to F = F$; 3. $F \to F = T$; 5. $T \leftrightarrow F = F$; 7. $F \leftrightarrow F = T$;
9. $\sim(F) \to [T \leftrightarrow T] = T \to T = T$; 11. $\sim(T) \to (F \leftrightarrow F) = F \to T = T$;
Part B. 13. $T \to (F \to T) = T \to T = T$; 15. $(\sim T \leftrightarrow F) \leftrightarrow T = (F \leftrightarrow F) \leftrightarrow T = T \leftrightarrow T = T$;
17. $F \cdot \sim F \to T \cdot F = F \cdot T \to F = F \to F = T$; 19. $(F \vee F) \cdot \sim T \to F = F \cdot F \to F = F \to F = T$.

Part C. 13. If apes are (a)nimals, then, if horses are (h)ats, black is (b)eautiful.
15. "Apes are not (a)nimals if and only if horses are (h)ats" has the same truth value as the statement "Black is (b)eautiful."
17. If horses are both (h)ats and not (h)ats, then it is true both that Black is (b)eautiful and that Goats are (g)eese.
19. If either Horses are (h)ats or Goats are (g)eese and if Black is not (b)eautiful, then Goats are (g)eese.

2.3B:

(1) $(d \vee f) \leftrightarrow (f \leftrightarrow d)$
TTT TTT
1 2 6 1 5 3 4

(3) $(p \leftrightarrow q) \to (p \cdot q)$
FTF F FFF
4 2 5 1 3 2 6

(5) $(g \cdot h) \to [(h \to k) \vee (g \leftrightarrow m)]$
TTT F TFF F TFF
3 2 3 1 4 5 6 2 4 5 7
or 6 2 5 1 4 3 4 2 7 3 8

(7) $(d \leftrightarrow m) \leftrightarrow (\sim m \to d)$
TFF F TFTT
or FTF F TFFF
2 1 2

2.3C:

1. *D*; 3. *J*; 5. *L*; 7. *B*; 9. *B*; 11. *L*.

2.3D:

1. A;   3. C;   5. X;   7. X;   9. C;   11. A;   13. A;   15. D;   17. B;
19. B;   21. B;   23. B;   25. X;   27. X;   29. X;   31. D.

2.3E:

1. $a \cdot b = \sim[\sim(a \cdot b)] = \sim(\sim a \vee \sim b) = \sim(a \rightarrow \sim b) = b \cdot a$;
3. $\sim(a \vee b) = \sim(b \vee a) = \sim b \cdot \sim a = \sim a \cdot \sim b = \sim(\sim a \rightarrow b) = \sim(\sim b \rightarrow a)$;
5. $(b \rightarrow \sim a) \cdot (a \rightarrow \sim b) = (\sim b \vee \sim a) \cdot (\sim a \vee \sim b) = (a \rightarrow \sim b) \cdot (b \rightarrow \sim a)$. *Note:* In section 4.2
   we will introduce the law of Tautology (TAUT) whereby this statement becomes simply
   $(b \rightarrow \sim a)$, or $(\sim b \vee \sim a)$, or $(a \rightarrow \sim b)$.
7. $\sim(a \cdot \sim b) = \sim(\sim b \cdot a) = b \vee \sim a = \sim b \rightarrow \sim a = a \rightarrow b$;
9. $\sim a \leftrightarrow b = b \leftrightarrow \sim a = (\sim a \cdot b) \vee (a \cdot \sim b) = (a \vee b) \cdot \sim(a \cdot b)$;
11. $\sim b \rightarrow \sim a = b \vee \sim a = \sim(a \cdot \sim b) = a \rightarrow b$;
13. $\sim[(b \rightarrow a) \cdot (a \rightarrow b)] = \sim(a \leftrightarrow b) = a \leftrightarrow \sim b = (a \cdot \sim b) \vee (b \cdot \sim a) = (a \vee b) \cdot \sim(a \cdot b)$;
15. $\sim(\sim b) \leftrightarrow a = b \leftrightarrow a = a \leftrightarrow b = (a \cdot b) \vee (\sim a \cdot \sim b)$;
17. $a \rightarrow \sim b = b \rightarrow \sim a = \sim a \vee \sim b = \sim(a \cdot b)$;
19. $(a \vee b) \cdot \sim(a \cdot b) = (a \cdot \sim b) \vee (b \cdot \sim a) = a \leftrightarrow \sim b = \sim(a \leftrightarrow b) = \sim a \leftrightarrow b$.

2.3F:

1A. c.   1B. $\sim(\sim c)$; DN;   3A. $f \vee d$;   3B. $d \vee f$; COM;   5A. $f \rightarrow h \vee b$;
5B. $\sim(\sim f) \rightarrow h \vee b$; DN;   7A. $\sim g \rightarrow c$;   7B. $\sim c \rightarrow g$; COPO;   9A. $\sim(l \cdot \sim d)$;
9B. $\sim l \vee d$; DeM;   11A. $\sim m \rightarrow \sim d$;   11B. $m \vee \sim d$; CE;   13A. $\sim a \vee \sim c$;
13B. $\sim(a \cdot c)$; DeM;   15A. $b \leftrightarrow \sim m$;   15B. $(b \cdot \sim m) \vee (m \cdot \sim b)$; BE;
17A. $(p \cdot \sim g) \vee (g \cdot \sim p)$;   17B. $p \leftrightarrow \sim g$; BE;   19A. $(w \cdot f) \vee (\sim w \cdot \sim f)$;
19B. $w \leftrightarrow f$; BE;   21A. $s \leftrightarrow a$;   21B. $a \leftrightarrow s$; COM.

2.3G:

1. A;   3. H;   5. K;   7. E;   9. M;   11. E;   13. G;   15. C;   17. D;
19. E;   21. H;   23. H.

2.4A:

Answers to odd-numbered problems are given in exercise 2.4A.

2.4B:

1. I;   3. I;   5. V;   7. V;   9. I;   11. V;   13. V;   15. I.

2.4C:

1. I;   3. I;   5. I;   7. V;   9. V;   11. V; $[e \rightarrow (r \rightarrow a)] \cdot \sim(r \rightarrow a) / \therefore \sim e$;
13. I; $[(\sim i \rightarrow \sim e) \cdot i] / \therefore e$;   15. I; $[(r \rightarrow \sim p) \cdot \sim r] / \therefore p$;   17. I; $[(m \rightarrow f) \cdot f] / \therefore m$;
19. V; $[(\sim m \rightarrow \sim d) \cdot d] / \therefore m$;   21. V; $[(\sim o \rightarrow \sim t) \cdot t] / \therefore o$;   23. I; $[(t \rightarrow f) \cdot f] / \therefore t$.

2.4D:

1. ASSOC;   3. DeM;   5. DeM;   7. CE;   9. DeM;   11. X;   13 & 15. DeM, DeM;
17 & 19. COPO, CE;   21 & 23. X.

2.5A:

1. $V \cdot S$;   3. $\sim V$;   5. $V \cdot \sim S$;   7. $V \cdot \sim S$;   9. $V \cdot S$.

2.5B:

1. V;   3. V;   5. V;   7. V;   9. V;   11. I;   13. I;   15. V.

2.5C:

1. V;   3. I;   5. I;   7. I;   9. I; $[(f \vee i) \cdot i / \therefore \sim f]$ 11. V; $[(r \vee d) \cdot \sim r / \therefore d]$;
13. V; By DeM, it becomes $(\sim a \vee \sim b) \cdot b / \therefore \sim a$
15. I; By DeM, it becomes $(\sim f \vee \sim g) \cdot \sim f / \therefore \sim g$
17. I; By DeM, it becomes $(\sim p \vee \sim q) \cdot q / \therefore p$ 19. V; By DeM, it becomes $(t \vee \sim w) \cdot w / \therefore t$
21. I; $\sim(g \cdot \sim m) \cdot m / \therefore g$. By DeM, no. 21 becomes $(\sim g \vee m) \cdot m / \therefore g$
23. V; $\sim(l \cdot s) \cdot s / \therefore \sim l$. By DeM, no. 23 becomes $(\sim l \vee \sim s) \cdot s / \therefore \sim l$
25. V; $(f \vee s) \cdot \sim s / \therefore f$
27. V; $\sim(b \cdot \sim m) \cdot b / \therefore m$. By DeM, no. 27 becomes $(\sim b \vee m) \cdot b / \therefore m$
29. V; $(m \vee f) \cdot \sim m / \therefore f$
31. V; $\sim[u \cdot \sim(s \cdot e)] \cdot u / \therefore s \cdot e$. By DeM, no. 31 becomes $[\sim u \vee (s \cdot e)] \cdot u / \therefore s \cdot e$
33. V; $(f \vee \sim t) \cdot \sim f / \therefore \sim t$ 35. I; $(u \vee n) \cdot u / \therefore \sim n$.

2.5D:

1. $(f \rightarrow s) \cdot (p \rightarrow s) / \therefore (p \rightarrow f)$. Invalid. In both premises S is at the tip of the arrow.

3. $(m \to f) \cdot (s \to \sim m) \mid \therefore s \to \sim f$. Before the rule of transitivity can be applied, the number of terms must be reduced from 5 $(m, \sim m, s, f, \sim f)$ to 3. This can be done by employing contraposition (COPO) to give these premises: $(m \to f) \cdot (m \to \sim s) \mid \therefore$?, or these: $(\sim f \to \sim m) \cdot (s \to \sim m) \mid \therefore$?. But in each of these cases, the middle term is *not* on the left-hand side of the arrow in one premise, and on the right-hand side in the other. Therefore, this argument is not structured as it must be if it is to apply the rule of transitivity, and thus be a valid syllogism. Invalid.

5. $[b \to \sim(\sim r)] \cdot (r \to \sim u) \mid \therefore (b \to \sim u)$. Using DN (double negation) this becomes $(b \to r) \cdot (r \to \sim u) \mid \therefore (b \to \sim u)$. Valid.

7. $(w \to \sim b) \cdot (b \to v) \mid \therefore (w \to \sim v)$. These premises contain four terms, namely w, $\sim b$, b, and v. By employing contraposition, we may restructure the premises to contain exactly three terms, thus: $(w \to \sim b) \cdot (\sim v \to \sim b) \mid \therefore$?, or thus: $(b \to \sim w) \cdot (b \to v) \mid \therefore$?. But neither pair of premises accord with the rule concerning transitivity (see explanation in problem 3 above). Invalid.

9. $(p \to \sim i) \cdot (m \to i) \mid \therefore (p \to \sim m)$. In its present form, this contains five terms $(p, \sim i, i, m, \sim m)$. But by contraposition, it becomes: $(p \to \sim i) \cdot (\sim i \to \sim m) \mid \therefore (p \to \sim m)$. Valid. The premises could also be contraposed thus: $(i \to \sim p) \cdot (m \to i) \mid \therefore (m \to \sim p)$. And this conclusion $(m \to \sim p)$ may then be contraposed to give $(p \to \sim m)$. Valid.

11. $(m \to \sim d) \cdot (k \to m) \mid \therefore (d \to \sim k)$. Observe that the conclusion did *not* appear *last*, as the argument was originally stated. The conclusion $(d \to \sim k)$ is equivalent to its contrapositive $(k \to \sim d)$; hence, the argument is valid.

13. $(a \to w) \cdot (p \to \sim w) \mid \therefore (a \to \sim p)$. Contraposing the second premise yields: $(a \to w) \cdot (w \to \sim p) \mid \therefore (a \to \sim p)$. Valid. If the first premise were contraposed, the conclusion would have to be contraposed also: $(\sim w \to \sim a) \cdot (p \to \sim w) \mid \therefore (p \to \sim a)$; and $\therefore (a \to \sim p)$. Valid.

15. $(i \to \sim c) \cdot (p \to i) \mid \therefore (p \to \sim c)$. Valid.

17. $(g \to u) \cdot (c \to \sim g) \mid \therefore c \to \sim u$. Change to $(\sim u \to \sim g) \cdot (c \to \sim g) \mid \therefore c \to \sim u$. Invalid. The middle term "$\sim g$" is on the right side of the arrow in each of the two premises.

19. $(f \to m) \cdot (s \to \sim f) \mid \therefore s \to \sim m$. By COPO this may be made to have three terms: $(\sim m \to \sim f) \cdot (s \to \sim f) \mid \therefore s \to \sim m$; but it is invalid, because the middle term "$\sim f$" is on the right side of the arrow in both premises.

2.5E:

1. (a) $(g \to t) \cdot \sim t \mid \therefore \sim g$; (b) Valid.
3. (a) $\sim(s \cdot v) \cdot \sim s \mid \therefore v$; (b) Invalid.
5. (a) $(t \to l) \cdot t \mid \therefore l$; (b) Valid.
7. (a) $(\sim u \to \sim d) \cdot u \mid \therefore d$; (b) Invalid.
9. (a) $(g \to h \cdot y \cdot f) \cdot (p \to h \cdot y \cdot f) \mid \therefore p \to g$; (b) Invalid.
11. (a) $(\sim f \vee s) \cdot s \mid \therefore \sim f$; (b) Invalid.
13. (a) $(p \to r) \cdot p \mid \therefore r$; (b) Valid.
15. (a) $\sim(s \cdot i) \cdot s \mid \therefore \sim i$; (b) Valid.
17. (a) $(\sim o \vee \sim r) \cdot \sim(\sim o) \mid \therefore \sim r$; (b) Valid.
19. (a) $\sim(c \cdot f) \cdot \sim c \mid \therefore \sim f$; (b) Invalid.
21. (a) $(\sim d \to \sim b) \cdot (\sim b \to \sim a) \mid \therefore \sim d \to \sim a$; (b) Valid.
23. (a) $(c \to f) \cdot (h \to c) \mid \therefore h \to f$; (b) Valid.
25. (a) $(p \to b) \cdot (q \to \sim p) \mid \therefore q \to \sim b$. By COPO, this becomes:
    (a) $(\sim b \to \sim p) \cdot (q \to \sim p) \mid \therefore q \to \sim b$; (b) Invalid.
27. (a) $(b \to \sim m) \cdot (o \to \sim m) \mid \therefore o \to \sim b$; (b) Invalid.
29. (a) $(k \to p) \cdot (o \to p) \mid \therefore o \to k$; (b) Invalid.

2.5F: (Missing premise italicized.)

1. *If a premise of an argument is (m)issing, that argument may be called an (e)nthymeme.* One of the premises of this argument is (m)issing. Therefore, this argument may be called an (e)nthymeme.

3. *If a dispute is based entirely on the (m)eanings of the words used, that dispute is purely (v)erbal.* Some disputes are based entirely on the (m)eanings of the words used. Therefore, some disputes are entirely (v)erbal.

5. *If any statement reads "Only A is B" it has the meaning "All B is A."* This statement reads "Only A is B." So, this statement means "All B is A."

7. *If traditional logic (a)ssumed that every well formed proposition was a categorical statement about existing events, then traditional logic allowed no place for assertions which might refer to the (e)mpty set.* But traditional logic did make this assumption. Therefore, traditional logic allowed no place for assertions which might refer to the (e)mpty set.

9. All cumulative and progressive knowledge is scientific knowledge. All truly humanizing knowledge is cumulative and progressive knowledge. Hence, *all truly humanizing knowledge is scientific knowledge.* (*Note:* George Sarton defended this thesis).

11. (Premises not restated). Therefore, *this term is ambiguous.*

chapter 3

INFORMAL LOGIC

3.1 Assumptions and Creativity

In their search for truth, science and philosophy are alike in one important respect: both represent man's response to the inadequacies of his inherited beliefs. "The trouble with learning," Bill Nye once said, "is that so much of what we learn ain't so." Anyone seriously dedicated to the search for truth soon discovers that the so-called "wisdom of our ancestors" includes "the foolishness of our ancestors" as well; that many of our inherited beliefs will not stand up under careful scrutiny; and that many generalizations which we had thoughtlessly accepted as true turn out to be over-generalizations and half-truths.

Why is it reasonable to assume that the "heritage of the ages" contains mistaken beliefs? To answer this question, consider the simple statement, "Water freezes at 0°C." This seemingly incontrovertible proposition assumes a host—indeed, it assumes an infinity—of conditions. Under what atmospheric pressure? How many impurities does the water have? What kinds of impurities? Must the water be completely still? If so, would that mean that the earth must be completely still? Do the phases of the moon have any effect? To most of us, such questions will seem to be irrelevant. But the history of science shows that we can never be sure what is relevant and what is not. Putting antifreeze in water so that its freezing point is lower than 0°C, or placing water under different atmospheric pressure so that its boiling point is less than 100°C, are cases in point.

Granting that aimless wandering gets us nowhere, the question arises: how can the criteria of relevance be determined in *advance* of actual experience— or of controlled experiment? For it would be circular to argue that a conclusion is true in terms of a set of assumptions, when these assumptions are justified if and only if the conclusion *is* true. Therefore, in order to possess any beliefs at all, we are compelled to cut off this infinite regress of assumptions and conditions, and to proceed on the meager knowledge that we have, namely, that "water *probably* will freeze at about 0°C." Or, as we sometimes say, "Under *normal* circumstances, water will freeze at about 0°C."

As we look back at our ancestors—even the greatest of them—we sometimes feel toward them as we feel toward the pigeon in *Alice in Wonderland*. In that story, one may recall, Alice had eaten something which made her neck extremely long. From this observed fact, the pigeon accused Alice of being a serpent, and they argued as follows:

> "But I'm not a serpent, I tell you," said Alice. "I'm a . . . I'm . . . "
>
> "Well *what* are you?" said the pigeon, "I can see you are trying to invent something."
>
> "I—I'm a little girl," said Alice, rather doubtfully, as she remembered the number of changes she had gone through that day.
>
> "A likely story indeed," said the pigeon, in a tone of deepest contempt. "I've seen a good many girls in my time, but never one with such a neck as that. No. No. You're a serpent. There's no use denying it. I suppose you'll be telling me next that you've never tasted an egg."
>
> "I *have* tasted eggs, certainly," said Alice, who was a very truthful child, "but little girls eat eggs quite as much as serpents do, you know."
>
> "I don't believe it," said the pigeon, "but if they do, then they're a kind of serpent, that's all I can say."[1]

As we read this story we ask, "Why didn't the pigeon *test* his theory about Alice being a serpent?" Surely even a pigeon would know that all humans are warm-blooded and that no serpents are warm-blooded. But, of course, it was precisely because he did not take into account such "truths"—such "relevant data"—that the pigeon made his hasty generalization.

The pigeon's thinking is more typical than we like to believe. For example, let us suppose we had asked Aristotle to define gold. He would probably have told us that gold is a precious metal, that it does not tarnish, that it may be pounded out to form gold leaf, and that it is heavy. A century or so later Archimedes could have told us that the specific gravity of gold is 19.2. Medieval alchemists would have added that gold dissolves in *aqua regia*. Nineteenth century chemists would have informed us that its atomic number is 79.

Each of the above discoveries represented *new* knowledge about gold. All of them provided important and highly relevant information pertaining to gold. However, *before* such discoveries were made, it would have been quite uncharitable to say that Aristotle and other scientists of ancient times "neglected relevant data" or committed the "fallacy of hasty generalization." Rather, it should be stated that the prevailing views of every generation of men contain errors as well as truths, and that the advance of science consists of a series of successive approximations to the truth. "Relevant data" refers to much more than a mere collection of raw facts, for "facts" are always understood in terms of some conceptual scheme—in terms of a set of assumptions—available at a particular era of history. Even as our sense perceptions have limitations which can be partially overcome, though never completely eliminated, by such inventions as the microscope, telescope, or pendular clock, so, too, our powers of rational understanding, though always limited, are nevertheless greatly enhanced by new conceptual schemes.

To better appreciate this last point, consider the following very carefully executed experiment—almost a model of "inductive reasoning"—designed to establish from what source plants derive food for growth. Remember that this experiment by Jan Baptista Van Helmont (1577–1644) was performed many generations before Pascal, Torricelli, and others discovered that we live in a "sea of air," and before Dalton, Lavoisier, and others learned that

---

[1] Lewis Carroll, *Alice's Adventures in Wonderland* (New York: Watts, 1962), chap. 5, p. 72.

this "sea of air" is composed of some of the same elements that are also to be found in "fire," "earth," and "water."

> [Van Helmont's] reasons for the belief that water can be changed into all other forms of matter, except air, are based upon his own experiments and observations. ... Van Helmont calls attention to the fact that a great number of substances, mineral, animal, and vegetable, yield water on distillation or ignition, and he assumes that they are partly converted into water. His widely cited experiment upon the willow tree was his most impressive argument.
>
> Van Helmont placed two hundred pounds of carefully dried earth in an earthen pot, and planted in it a five-pound willow. The pot was covered with a perforated plate of tinned iron to guard against loss or gain of weight by dust, etc. The pot was supplied with nothing but water, either rain water or distilled water. After five years, he removed the willow, weighed it again, finding one hundred sixty-nine pounds and three ounces. The earth was dried and again weighed and found to have lost but two ounces. Van Helmont concluded that one hundred and sixty-four pounds of willow tree had been produced from pure water.[2]

Exercise 3.1A.   Changing Assumptions; New Hypotheses

Directions: Below are several theories, once widely believed, but now generally abandoned. Choose *one* of the topics listed below, preferably in a field in which you have some familiarity,[3] and explain (a) why the hypothesis was once believed, and (b) why it was later abandoned.

(1) (Physics, Astronomy, Geography) the belief that the earth stands still, and that the sun, moon, and planets move in circular orbits around the earth.
(2) (Chemistry) the pholgiston theory of combustion.
(3) (Biology, Geology) the belief in fixed species in pre-Darwinian biology.
(4) (Theology) the belief that the first five books of the Bible were written by (or dictated by) God to Moses.
(5) (History, Anthropology, Economics, Political Science) belief in the divine right of kings, and/or in primogeniture.

[Lest anyone suppose such changes occur only in the scientific and scholarly disciplines, we add the following more down-to-earth topics.]

(6) Changes between 1870 and 1970 in the ways in which farmers thought food should be raised.
(7) Changes during the past century in the methods in which retailers (e.g., grocery stores, dry goods stores, drug stores) operate.
(8) Changes in the past 150 years in the manner in which doctors, lawyers, and other professional people were educated and admitted to their professions.
(9) Any other topic of your own choosing to illustrate a radical change of outlook.

Exercise 3.1B.   Locating Hidden Assumptions

Part A.   Directions: In each of the following eight problems, explain the assumption (a dubious one) which would make the argument valid.

1. Why should I look out for posterity? What has posterity ever done for me?
2. As both fascists and communists know, any pretense that people are ruled by persuasion rather than by force is an illusion. Hence, the men in Washington, whether Republicans or Democrats, are nothing more than the paid lackeys of Wall Street.

---

[2] John M. Stillman, *The Story of Early Chemistry* (New York and London: D. Appleton and Co., 1924), p. 382.

[3] Readable accounts of transitions in thinking that occurred in various branches of physics, chemistry, geology, and biology may be found in James B. Conant, *Science and Common Sense* (New Haven: Yale University Press, 1951); and in A. D. White, *The Warfare of Science with Theology* (New York: Braziller, 1955). There are numerous more detailed histories of the various fields of knowledge. There are also numerous references for question (4), but we would call special attention to an old book, *Introduction to Reflective Thinking*, by the Columbia Associates in Philosophy (New York: Columbia University Press, 1923), chap. 8.

3. If A, B, and C all have properties f, g, and h, and also have properties k and m, then D, which has properties f, g, and h, will also have properties k and m.
4. Right now the temperature outside is 32°F while inside it is 64°F. Therefore, the temperature inside is presently twice as warm as the temperature outside.
5. Since all knowledge is based on experience, such truths as "2 + 2 = 4" and "$p \vee \sim p$ is always true" must ultimately come to us by way of sense experience.
6. There is a high correlation between I.Q. test scores and success in college. Therefore, high I.Q. scores are the cause of success in college.
7. Today, a man twenty years old has twice the likelihood of living to be sixty than a twenty-year-old man would have had in 1800, because the average life span has doubled since 1800.
8. A person driving during a holiday weekend is about three times as likely to have a fatal accident, for the records show that there are about three times as many fatal accidents per day on holiday weekends as there are on other days.

Part B.   Remarks: Problems 9–16 are built around the following situation: Jim Lee, a black high school student in a small New Jersey town, broke into his high school, damaging windows and furniture in the break in, and stole $60 from the school safe. His only alibi was, "I did it just for kicks."[4]

Directions: Read each of the following statements. Then supply the missing assumptions which would change each statement into a meaningful valid argument.

9. *Judge:*   Society must protect itself against people like this. The boy is sentenced to two years in a reformatory.
10. *Psychologist:*   This is a beautiful example of the Freudian principle: "Inability to sublimate unconscious drives leads to aggressive and resentful attitudes."
11. *School Counselor:*   No one defends stealing. But every youth must find some way to assert himself and to show his individuality.
12. *Policeman:*   This is an example of modern permissiveness. The schools must give greater emphasis to the need for law and order.
13. *Reverend White:*   Until religion is taught in our schools, this sort of thing will go on.
14. *Racist:*   This is another example of the way in which blacks are ruining our schools and our society.
15. *Citizen A:*   The parents should be made accountable. There's always a delinquent parent behind a delinquent child.
16. *Citizen B:*   That's the way the ball bounces. Some get caught. Others go scot free.

CONCLUSION.   When Charles F. Kettering said, "Beware of logic. It is an organized way of going wrong with confidence," he was emphasizing the point that *valid* arguments are not always *sound* ones.[5] The conclusion of an argument may validly follow from the premises, but the premises themselves may be wrong. A. N. Whitehead once wrote that "by the aid of symbolism we can make transitions in reason almost mechanically . . . which otherwise would call into play the higher faculties of the brain."[6] The very fact that

---

[4] Part B of exercise 5.2C is adapted from Charles G. Martin, *The Tangle of the Mind* (London and New York: Longmans, 1968), pp. 21–23.

[5] Charles F. Kettering, cited by Warren Weaver, in *Science: Meaning and Method*, ed. Samuel Rapport and Helen Wright (New York: Washington Square Press, 1964), p. 27. See also the opening paragraphs of sec. 2.5 in this book.

[6] A. N. Whitehead, *An Introduction to Mathematics* (New York: Oxford, 1911), p. 42. In *The Logic of Modern Physics* (New York: Macmillan, 1927), chap. 2, P. W. Bridgman pointed out the difficulties which arise when facility in handling familiar symbols, and reliance on habitual patterns of thought, become a substitute for genuine empirical inquiry:
The structure of our mathematics is such that we are almost forced, whether we want to or not, to talk about the inside of an electron, although physically we cannot assign any meaning to such statements. As presently constructed, mathematics reminds one of the loquacious and not always coherent orator, who was said to be able to set his mouth going and go off and leave it.

our logical symbolism is so precise, our deductions so easy, and our conceptual scheme so neat, may lead us to forget that *our basic assumptions*—the premises of our argument—*need reexamination.*

3.2 Ambiguity, Definition, and Vagueness

An Australian logician, A. E. Mander, once summarized the two most fundamental principles of reasoning in two simple rules: "Speak the same language" and "Stick to the point."[7]

Mander's first rule, "Speak the same language," is the subject of this section. If Mr. E speaks only English, if Mr. F speaks only French, and if Mr. G speaks only German, then everyone knows that E, F, and G cannot communicate because they do not "speak the same language." However, if E, F, and G all speak English, but employ English words to mean different things, E, F, and G cannot communicate either—until they learn to use the same words to mean the same things.

A horse is "fast" if it is tied to a hitching post. The same horse is "fast" if it breaks loose and gallops away. In the 1920s a woman was "fast" if she smoked cigarettes. The colors in a dress are "fast" if they do not fade. Ascetics "fast" to renounce their bodies. Dietiers "fast" to keep slender and thus to glorify their bodies. Since there are thousands of words with such varied meanings, until speaker and hearer, or writer and reader, attach the same meanings to the same words, communication is impossible.

CONTEXT.   Unless the viewpoints, or mind sets, of speaker and hearer are quite similar, the same words may call forth quite different meanings. "Play" means different things to a musician, an actor, a gambler, or a football player. "Pipe" calls up different ideas to a smoker, a plumber, or an organist. "Pitcher, plate, and batter" call up different meanings to a cook than to a baseball fan. To a card player, "set" suggests an unearned bid; to a poultryman, it calls to mind a hen and eggs; to a logician, it means a class of objects or ideas; to a psychologist, it suggests "mind set," a mind's prejudice or outlook.

Suppose one overhears two friends, A and B, saying:

A: "Jeet?"
B: "No. Jew?"

If it is known that these two people often eat lunch together, this noonday conversation may be interpreted to mean:

---

[7] A. E. Mander, *Logic for the Millions* (New York: Philosophical Library, 1947), chap. 1. To Mander's "two simple rules" we would add two more: (3) "Analyze the assumptions which underlie the reasoning" and/or (4) "Be wary of hasty generalizations."

But Mander is certainly correct in calling "Speak the same language" one of logic's most fundamental principles, and much more time and reading could easily be devoted to this topic than is to be found in sec. 3.2. We therefore recommend supplementary reading and/or lectures based on books such as the following: Stuart Chase, *Power of Words* (New York: Harcourt, Brace, Jovanovich, 1953); Stuart Chase, *The Tyranny of Words* (New York: Harcourt, Brace, Jovanovich, 1938); S. I. Hayakawa, *Language in Thought and Action*, 3rd ed. (New York: Harcourt, Brace, Jovanovich, 1972); S. I. Hayakawa, ed., *Language, Meaning and Maturity* and *Our Language and Our World* (Greenwich, Conn.: Fawcett, 1961); Louis B. Salomon, *Semantics and Common Sense* (New York: Holt, Rinehart and Winston, 1966); Hugh Walpole, *Semantics: The Nature of Words and Their Meanings* (New York: Norton, 1941); Nicholas Capaldi, *The Art of Deception* (a book about Fallacies) (New York: Prometheus Books, 1971); Edwin Newman, *Strictly Speaking* (New York: Bobbs-Merrill, 1974).

A: "Did you eat?"
B: "No. Did you?"

Suppose, in a noisy room, one hears a simple statement, which might be:

A lot of peas.   Al ought to please.
All out of peas.   Al's auto please.
All out to please. Paul's auto please.

Context will generally enable us to choose the sentence having the proper meaning, even when all that is said is not clearly heard. Considering that each of the above six sentences takes only a second to utter, we may realize how rapidly we interpret and reinterpret what we "hear" by fitting the separate sounds into meaningful patterns.

The meaning we ascribe to a symbol is greatly affected by mind set or "atmosphere effect." For example: *polk* is pronounced *poke* with the *l* silent, and *folk* is pronounced *foke* with the *l* silent. How is the word for the white of an egg pronounced? It is a rare subject who will respond that the white of the egg is not the yolk, but albumen.

But when communication is successful, language bridges the gap between various human organisms, gives each individual the ability to understand vicariously (and to use) the experience of his fellows, and makes possible a minute division of labor and a high specialization of individual ability. By virtue of his ability to use language, man enters a new world. He sees the value of using names to represent absent objects; he learns to reflect on the past and to imagine the future; he increases his independence and mastery of the natural environment; and he gains access to the realm of reason.

However communication is not always successful, so we are often compelled to find alternative, nearly equivalent, ways of saying the same thing. Thus if a guide says, "Our college has a pretty little girls' gym," the hearer may be confused until he decides that "pretty" modifies "little" rather than "girls" or "gym"; and that "little" modifies "gym" rather than "girls." And he may ask, "Do you mean that our college's girls' gym is pretty little?"

Such "translation" occurs in almost every moment of conversation, and it occupies a major portion of every logic book. Here are three examples of "translation" (or "equivalence") from mathematics, two from logic: "X exceeds Y by 5" has the same meaning as "$X - Y = 5$"; "75 percent of \$20" has exactly the same value as "20 percent of \$75"; "$3 \times 23 \times 71$" = "69×71" = "$70^2 - 1^2$" = "4899"; "All dogs are mammals" means the same as "If anything is a dog, then it is a mammal"; "Either Paris is in Europe, or Paris is not in France" means the same as "If Paris is not in Europe, then Paris is not in France."

A major purpose of any course in logic is to increase the student's ability to make such translations, to express the same ideas in many different ways, and to replace ambiguous statements with clear ones. To appreciate the necessity of such "translation" consider the data assembled by Irvin J. Lorge in *The Semantic Account of 570 Commonest English Words*.[8] In his book, Lorge states that these 570 most-used English words average twelve different meanings per word. Of these twelve meanings, let us suppose that six are obsolete, and that three are rare. This still leaves three distinct and different meanings for each word. Now suppose we speak a short sentence, four of whose words each have

---

[8] Teachers College, Columbia University, New York, 1938.

three different meanings. This four-word sentence could, in theory, be interpreted in 81 (= 3^4) different ways. A little reflection on this point should make us stop asking, "Why are we sometimes *misunderstood?*" Instead, we should ask, "How is it possible that we are *ever* able to be *understood?*"

Here it may be noted that the Jains, a maverick Hindu sect, answered, "We can't be understood! We can never really understand one another." This Jain doctrine of "Viewpoints" emphasized the "manysidedness" of human experience, and of human discourse. It was illustrated by the Indian parable of the blind men describing an elephant. Since each blind man experienced the elephant in a different way—one touched the elephant's ear, another the trunk, another the tail, another the legs, another the body, another the tusks—the six blind men found nothing in common in their experience of "the elephant."[9]

Is it possible to escape from such relativity? Is it possible to communicate? The answer is, "Yes—with an important proviso." The proviso is this: that the speaker and listener (the writer and reader) view the same subject from the *same perspective*, and that they interpret the meanings of words in the *same context*. In the context of *color*, a white horse, a white lily, and a white snowflake are all alike: they are all white, in spite of the fact that they differ in other respects. Similarly, if we understand "horse" to mean a "domesticated riding animal," then a white horse, a black horse, and a spotted horse are all alike, i.e., "alike" with respect to the fact that they are domesticated riding animals.

To more fully appreciate the importance of context, let us return to the Jain story of the blind men and the elephant. A blind man who said, "Elephants exist," would be less clear than one who said, "Some (h)erbivorous (a)nimals are (e)lephants." "For all x, x is (s)oft and (f)lexible" is less clear than "All (e)lephant (t)runks are (s)oft and (f)lexible." "For all x, x is (h)ard and (r)ocklike" is less clear and meaningful than "If this is part of an (e)lephant, and if it is (h)ard and (r)ocklike, then it is the elephant's (t)usk" ($e \cdot h \cdot r \rightarrow e \cdot t$). We shall return to this point in section 6.3.

Etymologically, "define" (*de fino*) means "to place within limits." Whether we think of every element of a *subset* as also a member of a *set*, or of every member of a *species* as also a member of a *genus*, clarity is increased when we are able to place any class of objects within some larger class. The most comprehensive of all classes, such as Aristotle's ten categories (Substance, Relation, Time, Space, and so on), are the most difficult concepts of philosophy. If we go beyond such categories and say, for example, that "by definition" the word "God" refers to a Being that "cannot be placed within limits"—hence a concept not to be counted among the most general categories of thought—then debates about "the existence of God" or "the validity of rational proofs for the existence of God" are usually profitless. However, an exception is in raising this further question: "Should (or should not) man's total conceptual scheme allow any place for words or concepts such as 'God'; 'what is beyond human comprehension'; or 'what cannot be defined'?" If we believe that there *should* be a place for such words or concepts in our total conceptual scheme, we should nevertheless admit that such concepts cannot be defined, and therefore cannot be argued about in a rational manner.

---

[9] Concerning the Jain "Manysidedness" doctrine, read W. T. DeBary, ed., *Sources of Indian Tradition* (New York: Columbia University Press, 1958), pp. 73–75. In ancient Greek philosophy, Zeno the Eleatic argued that "motion" was impossible, because things move relative to other things, which are not alike. Ancient China also had its sophists, such as Kung-sung Lung (c. 340 B.C.) who is said to have argued that "a white horse is not a horse."

However very few words are like that. The words which give us trouble, day after day, are words which have different meanings in different contexts, e.g., "set" in the contexts of (1) playing cards, (2) raising chickens, or (3) modern algebra. Exercise 3.2A illustrates this point with the two words, "law" and "education."

Exercise 3.2A.   Which Meaning Does a Word Have?

Directions: In statements A and B below, the word "law" is used in two different ways. In the answer blanks before each of the numbered statements, write A or B to indicate which of the two meanings seems to be intended.

A. This *law* is unjust and should be repealed.
B. *Laws* of nature are generalizations concerning the sequences of events in nature.

_____ 1. Avagadro's law states that equal volumes of different gases (pressures and temperatures remaining constant) contain the same number of molecules.
_____ 2. Justinian's code of law is a milestone in the history of civilization.
_____ 3. Laws grind the poor, and rich men rule the law.   (Goldsmith)
_____ 4. A scientific law is a theoretical principle deduced from particular facts, applicable to a definite group or class of phenomena, and stating that a particular phenomenon always occurs if certain conditions are present.
_____ 5. Happy the man, who, studying nature's laws,
Through known effects can trace the secret cause.   (Dryden)
_____ 6. The law of England compels no man to be his own accuser.
_____ 7. The Ten Commandments are laws of God and should be obeyed.
_____ 8. The law of gravity is universal and cannot be disobeyed.
_____ 9. Senator Sorghum proposed that a law be *enacted* decreeing that the schools should teach that pi (π) is exactly 3—with no fractions or decimals added thereto.
_____ 10. Boyle's law states that the volume of an enclosed gas varies inversely as the pressure exerted upon it.

Directions: Apply the same directions, using the word "education":

A. One's *education* is measured by the number of years he has spent in school.
B. You are *educated* if you are open-minded, competent, and of service to society.

_____ 11. If our schools merely make students conform; if they crush individual initiative and creativity, then they are no longer instruments of education.
_____ 12. *Teacher:* "You are educated if you keep working and learning the rest of your life."
_____ 13. Heifitz cannot be very well educated in music, for he has no Ph.D. degree.
_____ 14. With all of his talent, it's too bad that Thomas Edison lacked an education.
_____ 15. The true measure of a man's education cannot be made when the man is twenty or thirty years old, but only when he is sixty or seventy.
_____ 16. By "education" many people mean "college bred"—a four year loaf.

Both the pronunciations and the meanings of words are in constant flux. An easy way to note such changes of usage is to compare old and new translations of the Bible. Below are pairs of words or phrases showing the change in English usage in less than 350 years in Protestant (left-hand column) and Catholic (right-hand column) translations:

King James (1611). . .*Rev. Standard* (1952)	*Douay* (1610). . . . . *Knox* (1948)
virgin. . . . . . . .young woman (Isaiah 7:14)	tempt . . . . test (Mark 10:2)
wealth . . . . .well-being (I Cor. 10:24)	libertines. . . . . freedmen (Acts 6:9)
advertise. . . . . notify (Ruth 4:4)	communicate . . . . share (Phil. 4:15)
sincere. . . . . pure (I Peter 2:2)	seed . . . . race (Gen. 15:5)
lunatic. . . . . .epileptic (Matt. 4:24)	bloody flux . . . . dysentery (Acts 28:8)

mortify............put to death (Col. 3:5)	evil.............. diseased (Luke 11:34)
take no thought.......................	gave up the ghost....... died (Acts 5:10)
be not anxious (Matt. 6:25)	feeble-minded..........................
forever.......as long as I live (Psalm 23:6)	faint-hearted (I Thess. 5:14)
corn.................. grain (Luke 6:1)	conversation.......behavior (I Tim. 4:12)

We enjoy giving old words new meanings, as when the *hands* of our bodies become the *hands* of a clock. But after a time, in different contexts, we no longer even think of them as having a common origin. This is illustrated in the following doublets:

bench..... bank	parson..... person	fabric....... forge
core...... heart	zero....... cipher	musket..... mosquito
label...... lapel	word....... verb	rover....... robber
outer..... utter	name...... noun	zealous..... jealous

With doublets, where the two words, as well as their two meanings, are quite distinct, there is no danger of confusion. But when words remain unchanged, even though, in different contexts, their meanings have become quite distinct, ambiguities occur. In exercise 3.2B, since their contexts have not been made explicit, some problems may lend themselves to different interpretations. In spite of this difficulty, the ability to do the type of analysis required in exercise 3.2B is one of the most important abilities anyone can acquire.

Exercise 3.2B.   Clarifying Ambiguities

Directions: On separate paper, indicate the two meanings of the italicized word(s) or phrase(s) which give rise to the following ambiguities. Make these two meanings precise and distinct. Answer the odd numbers first, and compare your answers with those given. Then do the evens.

1. The man who is walking away from me does not grow smaller. But *what I see* grows smaller. Therefore, *what I see* is not the man.
2. Told to "stop making *that noise*," a school boy replied, "I am not making *that noise*. I am making another noise just like it."
3. American public schools are *secular*. Hence, no religious person should allow his child to attend these godless institutions.
4. The Bible is the *Word* of God. The Bible is in English. Therefore, English is the language of God.
5. *No* cat has nine tails. One cat has one more tail than *no* cat. Therefore, one cat has ten tails.
6. A crust of bread is better than *nothing*. *Nothing* is better than true love. Therefore, a crust of bread is better than true love.
7. Whoever obeys *laws* submits himself to a governing will. Nature obeys *laws*. Therefore, nature submits itself to a governing will.
8. The numerator and the denominator of the fraction $\frac{3}{5}$ are both odd numbers. But $\frac{6}{10}$ is *the same as* $\frac{3}{5}$. So, the numerator and denominator of $\frac{6}{10}$ are odd numbers.
9. *Improbable* events happen every day. Events which happen every day are *probable* events. Therefore, *improbable* events are *probable* events.
10. As a thing is generally sold for more than it is *worth*, or for less, one of the parties in a transaction is a loser.
11. Every event has a cause. *Nature* is an event. Therefore, *nature* has a cause.
12. Tired of helping his child with mathematics, a state legislator proposed that a *law* be passed changing the value of pi from 3.14159 . . . to exactly 3.
13. Mathematics is a type of logic because mathematics and logic both employ *variables*.
14. A hunter goes *around* a tree onto which a squirrel clings. But the squirrel always

moves so as to keep the trunk of the tree between itself and the hunter. Does the hunter go *around* the squirrel? (from *Pragmatism*, by W. James, chapter 1).

15. Deductive logic deals with a type of truth that is rigorous and logical; hence, is not concerned with probability which is concerned only with the *probable*.

16. The child of Themistocles *governed* his mother; she *governed* her husband; he *governed* Athens, Greece; and Greece, the world. So, the child of Themistocles *governed* the world.

17. He who acts from necessity is *determined*. But in making a so-called free choice, you necessarily choose one alternative or another. Therefore, your so-called free choice is not really free, but is *determined*.

18. Our state legislature should *represent* all groups within the state. There are nudists and vegetarians in our state. Therefore, some of the *representatives* in our state legislature should be nudists and vegetarians.

19. No man should attempt to change the beliefs of his church; for if he *believes* in these doctrines, he will not want to change them; and if he doesn't *believe* in them, he should not remain in that church.

20. *Old age* is wiser than youth. Therefore, it is only reasonable that we should follow the traditions of our ancestors.

21. A vacuum is impossible; for if there is *nothing* between two bodies, the two bodies must be in contact.

22. All *criminal actions* should be punishable by law. Murder trials are *criminal actions*. Therefore, murder trials should be punishable by law.

23. Food is either animal or vegetable. But animal food may be *dispensed with* (as vegetarians do), and vegetable food may also be *dispensed with* (as native Eskimos sometimes do). Hence, all food may be *dispensed with*.

24. *Persons who thrust a knife into other persons* are guilty of murder. Surgeons who perform major operations often *thrust knives into other persons*. So, surgeons who perform major operations often are guilty of murder.

DEFINITION. To deal intelligently with words, we must know how to make their meanings clear. To do this, we must specify the membership of a class, the individuals to which any word refers. The membership of any class, or set, may be specified in two ways:

(1) *Listing:* List the members of a group; enumerate the elements of a set. This method is sometimes called the *roster* method. Somewhat related to the roster method is the method of "incomplete listing," usually called "definition by example." Here a few representative members of a set are used to exemplify the entire set.

(2) *Definition:* Explain the general and specific traits which determine membership in a set.

Here are three examples of these two methods:

Listing	*Definition*
{1, 2, 3, 4, 5, 6, 7, 8, 9}	"the set of single-digit natural numbers"
{2, 4, 6, 8}	"the set of single-digit even natural numbers"
"This shoe and that shoe" (accompanied by pointing)	"the pair of shoes I now am wearing."

These two methods are often used in combination, as in "positive even numbers" are "numbers such as 2, 4, or 10 which, when divided by two, result in whole numbers."

To see how these two types of definition are actually employed, consider an example from botany. Most of us know the meaning of "rose," "tulip," "onion," "potato," and other common plants long before we study botany. The typical amateur gardener may be surprised when he first discovers that single families of plants comprise such varied species as the following: *Liliaceae*—lily, tulip, hyacinth, trillium, asparagus, onion; *Rosaceae*—rose, spirea, apple, almond, blackberry, strawberry, hawthorn; *Solanaceae*—potato, tomato, pepper, tobacco.

The gardener may have thought of these plants only in terms of such categories as "large," "small," "tree," "vegetable," "fruit," "flower"; and, until he studies botany, may remain quite ignorant of their structural similarities: *Liliaceae*—the embryo plant within the seed contains only a single seed leaf; flowers have 3 sepals and 3 petals, all alike; 6 stamens and a pistil of 3 parts. *Rosaceae*—have 2 seed leaves; have 5 sepals; 5 petals, always free from one another; usually have many stamens, and one to several pistils. *Solanaceae*— have 2 seed leaves; calyx and corolla are both 5-parted tubes resulting from fusion of sepals and petals; 5 stamens and a pistil of 2 parts.

Genuine understanding requires both types of knowledge. Exemplification provides acquaintance with individual plants. Definition and classification show the relationships of one species to another. A gardener does not truly understand these plants until he has both first-hand experience of specific plants and theoretical understanding of the ways in which plants are defined and classified.

Any object or event may be related to other objects or events in many different ways. Thus the capsule that I swallow before dinner may be called "food," "medicine," "vitamins," "small," "spherical," "expensive," "edible," "annoying," "habit forming," etc. If I use my index finger to point to "this" thing before me, different observers may interpret "this" to mean "index finger," "the act of pointing," "table," "book on table," "table top," "oak," "tan colored object," "flat surface," and so on. Any individual perception (any individual thing) may be related to a great variety of other perceptions (or things).

If individual events are related in so many different ways, how is it possible for a speaker to make his listener know just what meaning he intends to convey?

FORMAL DEFINITION.   Generally we make clear the meaning of a word by relating it to other words whose meanings are (presumed to be) more familiar. For example, "synonyms" may be defined as "words whose meaning is the same"; "breakfast" as "morning meal." Observe, in each of these two examples, that one portion of the definition (the *genus*) placed that word within a broad, general set, and the other portion (the *species*, or the *subset*) specified just what part of the general set the word belongs in. In the definition of "synonym," "words" was the *genus*, and "whose meanings are the same" was the *species*. In the definition of "breakfast," "meal" was the *genus*, and "morning" was the *species*. A formal definition, then, designates or limits the meaning of a word by naming a *genus* (general class or set) and a *species* (a subclass or *species* whose difference from other members within the general class is made explicit).

DEFINITION BY STIPULATION.   Since many words have several different meanings (each meaning appropriate within a particular context) it may be necessary to *stipulate* which meaning is to be employed within a given body of discourse. Thus, a gardener might stipulate that, in his speaking or writing, he classifies a tomato as a vegetable, and not as a fruit. The Department of Health, Education, and Welfare may stipulate that all women over sixty-two years of age are eligible for Medicare. In this book it is stipulated that the terms "statement" and "proposition" have the same meaning.

ACCIDENTAL PROPERTIES.   Many of the properties of any object or event are extremely transient, and, from the standpoint of definition, unimportant. Thus, the fact that "word" has exactly four letters, or that "word" appears in this sentence, would, in most contexts, be classified as accidental properties.

Humorous definitions are the result of a deliberate emphasis of some accidental quality. It is much less dramatic to say "American universities over-emphasize athletics" than to say "An American university may be *defined* as a vast athletic association where, however, some studies are maintained for the benefit of the feeble-bodied." We have all enjoyed "definitions" such as the following: "An honest politician is one who, when bought, stays bought." "An atheist is a man who has no invisible means of support." "Education is what remains after you have forgotten all you learned." "Knowledge is that small part of ignorance which we define and classify."

DEFINITION BY EXAMPLE.   For many sets, a complete listing of all a set's members is impossible; so, as an alternative, we resort to incomplete listing, or "definition by example." This method has the virtue of relating the set to specific members of that set, and thus of making our ideas pertinent to experience. It is difficult, for instance, to point to specific instances of ghosts or ogres except in myths and fairy tales. However, definition by example has several major disadvantages. First, it confines us to things present. It will not help to explain what is meant by Antarctica; the inside of an atom; a distant galaxy of stars; or a past event. Second, definition by example tends to be partial rather than complete. For example, to define "bird" as "a creature like a robin, sparrow, or crow" might restrict the meaning of "bird" to "land bird." Third, definition by example does not help us to widen our boundaries of knowledge, whereas formal definition does. Thus when we formally define the species *dogs*, *wolves*, and *foxes* as members of the genus *canines*, we also relate dogs, wolves, and foxes to vertebrates, to carnivorous creatures, and to many other zoological species. Finally, except in sets having only a very few members, definition by example is an extremely unwieldy device; whereas formal definition is neat and concise.

Exercise 3.2C.   Types of Definition

Directions: After each numbered statement below, indicate by letter (E, F, B, H, or S) which of these five types of definition is represented.

E. Exemplification: definition by example: incomplete listing.
F. Formal: genus-species (or set-subset) definition.
B. Both E and F; or partly E and partly F.
H. Humorous definition: exaggeration of some accidental trait.
S. Stipulation: Asserting and insisting on a specified usage.

_____ 1. *Long:* An inch is short, a mile is long. A year is a long time.
_____ 2. *Long:* Having a certain measure from end to end in space or time; measuring much from end to end; having a great range; taking much time or space.
_____ 3. *And:* Conjunction meaning "in addition to," used for connection of words or statements, as in "go and see," "two and two," "Do that, and I will go."
_____ 4. *Air:* Birds fly in the air. We are always breathing air.
_____ 5. *Air:* The mixed gas breathed by land animals.
_____ 6. *Monologue:* A conversation between a man and his wife.
_____ 7. *Diplomat:* A man who always remembers a woman's birthday, but never remembers her age.
_____ 8. *Lame Duck:* A president whose goose is cooked.
_____ 9. *Transitivity:* A relation involving three or more entities, such that, if *A*

_____ 10. *Transitivity:* A relation of the type "is less than," "is greater than," "is a subset of," "is included in," "includes," "implies," "is taller than."

_____ 11. In this course, the grade of *A* shall mean one based on an average test score of at least 90.

_____ 12. By "short" a pro basketball coach means anyone under six feet.

_____ 13. *Logic:* The study of forms of valid inference; a study of methods whereby conclusions are derived from premises, inferences from assumptions, and information is extracted from linguistic formulations.

_____ 14. *Logic:* The study of the most economical methods of formulating and storing information in language, where the term "language" is broadly interpreted to include symbolic languages and the axiomatic systems of mathematics.

_____ 15. *Kind:* What kind of cake would you prefer? All kinds of animals were in the ark.

_____ 16. *If:* Conjunction. On condition that, as in "Come if you can."

_____ 17. *Because:* Conjunction meaning "for the reason that."

_____ 18. In this book, the word "conjunction" signifies a logic connective having the meaning "and/or."

_____ 19. In this book, we shall define "inclusive disjunction" or "weak alternation" to mean "either . . . or, and perhaps both"; and we shall define "exclusive disjunction" or "strong alternation" to mean "either . . . or, and not both."

_____ 20. By a "poor family" we shall mean any family of four or more persons whose total annual income is less than $4,000.

_____ 21. *Complement:* Either of two parts that complete the whole or mutually complement each other.

_____ 22. *Negative:* A thing or concept considered to be the counterpart of something positive, as " -2 is the negative of the positive number 2."

_____ 23. *Expression:* In mathematics and logic, a designation of any symbolic form, such as an equation, as in $x \cdot y = y \cdot x$.

_____ 24. *Formula:* A mathematical statement, especially an equation, of a rule, principle, answer, or other logical relation.

VAGUENESS. "Ambiguous" and "vague" are not synonymous terms. Terms are ambiguous when, viewed in different contexts, they have different meanings. Terms are vague when, viewed along some scale, such as long–short, heavy–light, young–old, light–dark, we are not sure as to what point along the scale the vague term refers. In the sentence, "This book is hard," the word *hard* is ambiguous; for it may mean that the book is firm, rigid and inflexible, as in "Stones are hard"; or it may mean that the book is difficult, that it requires much effort to be understood, as in "Calculus is hard." The word *hard* may also be vague, as in "This crust of bread is *hard*" or "Basalt is a *hard* rock." "Wood is harder than bread, but not as hard as basalt."

To represent *degrees* of hardness, and thus to reduce vagueness, ordinary language employs adverbs or analogies, as in "very hard," "extremely soft," "hard as a rock," or "soft as a pillow." In geology, the Mohs Hardness Scale, based on scratching, ranks hardness on a scale ranging from 0 to 10, with the following substances used for the ten numbers.

1. talc	2. gypsum	3. calcite	4. flourite	5. apatite
6. orthoclase	7. quartz	8. topaz	9. corundum	10. diamond

On this scale the hardness of fingernails is about 2.5; a copper penny, about 3; a knife blade, about 5; glass, about 5.5; a steel file, about 6.5. But on such a scale it would be completely wrong to say that, e.g., topaz is twice as hard as flourite and four times as hard as gypsum. For similar reasons it would be wrong in psychology to say that an I.Q. of 140 represents intellectual ability *twice* as great as an I.Q. of 70. If brief, caution must be used when dealing with numbers which represent nonadditive properties.

However, the use of numbers in place of emotionally laden adverbs often may help to free thinking from prejudice. For example, if John were to assert that Irishmen are hot-tempered, and Mary were to respond, "I suppose that 50 to 60 percent of all Irishmen really are hot-tempered," Mary would have agreed with John in suggesting that the majority of Irishmen are hot-tempered, but she would also have lifted the discussion to a different plane. For no one can think in terms of amounts and percentages and, at the same time, be completely captivated by emotionally laden slogans or clichés. Thus using numbers to represent amounts and degrees not only reduces vagueness, it also helps to free thinking from emotional prejudice. More will be said about vagueness in section 5.1 when studying "the quantitative principle" of science.

3.3 Propaganda and Prejudice

SOME NONLOGICAL USES OF LANGUAGE. Words are used for purposes other than to describe facts or to argue from premises to conclusions. They are also used to express feelings, to convey attitudes, and to control the thoughts and actions of other men.[10] The full gamut of human behavior includes wishful thinking as well as scientific proof; ideologies as well as ideals; rationalization as well as the unprejudiced weighing of evidence; day-dreaming as well as concentrated thought. Logic does not require that we remove, or even that we reduce, the nonrational aspects of language. But if language is to be an aid and not an impediment to thought, we must at least be able to *distinguish* the rational from the emotional, volitional, and other facets of language.

The feeling that seems to exercise the most powerful influence on our thinking is our love of ease and comfort, and a consequent dislike of anything that threatens to disturb them. Hence the general prejudice against change and innovation, or, for a person committed to some utopian cause, the prejudice against idea that goes contrary to *his* prejudices.

---

[10] The art of persuasion, first developed by the Greek sophists around 400 B.C., included both logic and rhetoric. Their main concerns were public speaking, skill in debating, and ability to plead a case before an assembly of fellow citizens. With his adversary constantly in mind, the rhetorician's chief purpose was to drive his opponent into a corner out outsmart him. Thus during most of the ancient Greek and Roman era, logic was an aid to rhetoric, and both were viewed as means of winning arguments, rather than as means for attaining truth.

During the Middle Ages logic gradually became disassociated from rhetoric. R. W. Southern contrasts logic and rhetoric as follows:

> Rhetoric is static; logic dynamic. The one aims at making old truths palatable, the other at searching out new, even unpalatable truths. . . . Rhetoric is persuasive, logic compulsive. The former smooths away divisions, the latter brings them into the open. The one is a healing art, an art of government; the other is surgical, and challenges the foundations of conduct and belief.

From R. W. Southern, *The Making of the Middle Ages* (New Haven: Yale University Press, 1953), p. 176.

In medieval Europe, the monks in isolated monasteries were not only freed from worldly concerns, they were also freed from active work in propagating the Christian faith. In spite of what most moderns would consider a drab and uninteresting style of life, these monks found logic an exciting study because, unlike rhetoric and propaganda, the inferences of logic led to *new* ideas. Thus it happened that deductive logic became the cornerstone of scholasticism. Later, during the Renaissance, this deductive logic was conjoined with empirical observation, giving birth to Western science.

Because we pick up prejudices as quickly as we pick up knowledge, because feelings and emotional bias are as much a part of human nature as are thoughts and inferences, it is important to understand some of the difficulties which obstruct the quest for truth. The following facetious story from the British humor magazine, *Punch*, dramatizes the futility of logic and of reason when dealing with someone obsessed with a fixed idea.

The Unbeliever

I met a man about a week ago who took a very firm line about badgers. He said they didn't exist. "Somehow or other," he said, "the idea has grown up that people wish to be told stories about this preposterous animal, and letters are written to the *Times* and to *Country Life* about it. But there aren't any. If there were, I should have seen them—and I haven't."

I said I had.

"Where?"

"In a wood."

"Pure hallucination. A lot of people have told me that they have seen ghosts. But I don't believe it. I've seen none myself. What was this thing doing?"

"Moving about."

"Was it eating anything?"

"Not that I noticed."

"Did it emit any groans?"

"No."

"Did it carry its head in its hand?"

I was thoroughly annoyed. . . . "There were badgers," I said, "in Kenwood at Hampstead quite recently. They came into people's gardens."

"Did you see them there?"

"They came at night, and left their traces."

"You're sure you don't mean burglars?"

"Look here," I said, "there is a badger at the Zoo."

"Probably a small panda."

"How do you know there is a panda at the Zoo?"

"Because there aren't any badgers."

"When I tell you I know farmers who give a guilder a year to badger-digging parties, because they say badgers eat their young lambs, when I say that you can see the traces of badgers at any time in hundreds of places, when I assure you that books have been written about the lives and loves of badgers, photographs reproduced of badgers and their young—"

"Ectoplasm," he said.

"Badgers make admirable pets. There are people writing to the papers who honour and cherish them. These people sit down to tea with their badgers and drink milk with them. Badgers are very tidy. They live in setts, and are drawn by dogs—"

"Like the Eskimos."

"They are plantigrades. They bring out their beds to be aired. They are obstinate. They bite. They eat roots, beetles, worms, rabbits. The shriek of a badger at night is a very terrible thing."

"So is the shriek of a ghost."

"Probably many of the stories about ghosts originate from the cry of a badger."

"You might just as well say that many of the stories about badgers originate from the cry of a ghost."

"Possibly the trolls and gnomes were badgers."

"Possibly the badgers were gnolls and tromes."

"Badger-baiting was one of the most popular sports of our ancestors."

"So was killing dragons."

"Well," (I asked), "What do you *really* believe about badgers?"

"In an excessively urbanized country it is found necessary to invent stories of glamour and mystery about the countryside, and the wild creatures of the wood. . . . There may have been badgers long ago, just as there were dragons and griffins. But they are gone."

"Do you deny the whole testimony of natural history books, encyclopedias and ecologists?"

"Paid propaganda."

The man was becoming tiresome. "Just because you've never seen a badger," I said, "you say there aren't any. Very well. Do you often go through Trafalgar Square?"

"Almost never."

"Can you believe there's a haystack in it?"

"No."

"I thought so. Just because you don't pass by Trafalgar Square every day on a bus as I do . . . you suppose I'm a liar when I say there's a haystack in it."

"Yes, I do."

"Very well. Come and see then."

We went. There wasn't. Some idiot had burned it down.

"Don't ever talk to me about badgers again," said the man.

I shall not.[11]

Having once adopted an opinion, our pride makes us loathe to admit that this opinion may be wrong. When objections are made to our views, we are more concerned with discovering how to combat the objections to these views than we are to learn how much truth and how much falsehood is to be found in them. In short, we go to great pains searching for fresh support for the views we entertain, and we tend to ignore evidence which appears to contradict them.[12]

In section 3.2 it was noted that different contexts give words different meanings. Here it should also be noted that different words may denote the same referents, yet connote different meanings and attitudes, as in "Venus" and "evening star" or "wife" and "ball and chain." A Southern gentleman said that he was seventy years old before he learned that "damned Yankee" was two words! In any cultural group, most of the words learned are tinged with emotion, so that things are seldom viewed as they really are, but, rather, as people react to them. Thus attitudes as well as meanings are conveyed by words, and they rub off from one speaker to another, and from one generation to the next.

There is nothing unreasonable or unnatural about having emotional attitudes or in employing words to convey such attitudes. However we should be constantly aware of the fact that language is employed for nonlogical as well as for logical purposes. As the muscles of the diaphragm are used for

---

[11] "The Unbeliever" by Evoe, London: *Punch* Magazine, 206 (May 17, 1944): 410. Reproduced by permission of *Punch*. For another humorous account illustrating some of the difficulties involved in securing factual evidence, read A. L. Sharp, "Turtle Eggs for Agassiz," in *A Treasury of Science*, ed. Harlow Shapley, Samuel Rapport and Helen Wright (New York: Harper & Row, 1946). A briefer version of this Shapley-Rapport-Wright anthology is the inexpensive paperback, edited by Samuel Rapport and Helen Wright, *Science: Method and Meaning* (New York: Washington Square Press, 1963). Also see James B. Conant, *Two Modes of Thought* (New York: Pocket Books, 1964).

[12] J. H. Robinson, in *The Mind in the Making* (New York: Harpers, 1921), declared that we can always find a dozen *"good* reasons" to support our prejudices, without once suspecting that the *"real* reason" is pride and our unwillingness to lose face. For an excellent analysis of the manner in which language can be a substitute, rather than an aid, to thinking, read George Orwell, "Politics and the English Language," in *Shooting an Elephant and Other Essays* (New York: Harcourt, 1950).

lifting weights as well as for breathing, and as the muscles around the larynx are used for swallowing as well as for speaking and singing, so, too, language is used for numerous purposes, many of which obstruct rather than aid rational thought.

THE "CONJUGATION" OF EMOTIONAL WORDS AND PHRASES. Attitudes are so deeply embedded in language that Bertrand Russell facetiously called them forms of "conjugation"; for example, "I am firm; you are obstinate; he is a pig-headed fool." Here "I" is associated with a laudatory term, "you" with a neutral term, and "he" with a disparaging word or phrase. Below are some illustrations of "conjugation" on the basis of emotional attitude:

> I am a teacher.   You exercise thought control. He brainwashes.
> I am a student. You work for grades. He is a bookworm.
> I drink beverages. You drink liquor. He drinks booze.
> I am prudent. You are cautious. He is cowardly.
> I am logical. You are unemotional.   He is a cold fish.
> I offer trenchant criticism.   You embarrass the speaker.   He is abusive and insulting.

Language provides ready-made tools to help reinforce prejudices. The same man who says "You can't teach an old dog new tricks" when he is resisting a change, will say "It's never too late to learn" when he is encouraging change. An innovation that one *favors* is "progressive" but an innovation that is *disfavored* is a "dangerous experiment." When a member of the majority, one rests his case upon "the wisdom of the people"; but when a member of the minority, "the ignorance of the masses" is looked upon with scorn.

Exercise 3.3A.   Development Awareness of Prejudice and Propaganda

Part A.   Directions: Give at least one illustration of what Russell called "emotional conjugation," i.e., the use of different words or phrases to promote favorable, neutral, or unfavorable attitudes. *Example:*

> I am a creative thinker.   You have some queer ideas.   He is a crackpot.

Part B.   Directions: Is education a form of propaganda? As a springboard for the discussion of this question, consider the following two statements:
  (1) Education is an institutionalized means of influencing thought and opinion; hence, education is a form of propaganda.
  (2) Education is genuine only if it cultivates self-reliance and independence of judgment; hence, education is an attempt to gain freedom from emotional bias and from irrational propaganda.

Part C.   Directions: From newspaper, magazine, radio, or television advertising, or from personal experience, give one or two examples showing specific ways in which emotions and attitudes are influenced by the use of emotionally charged words or by other nonrational appeals.

3.4   Fallacies

The road to unambiguous communication and valid reasoning is straight and narrow, but the ways to ambiguous statements and fallacious arguments are legion. Fallacies may be divided into three general types: (a) Formal Fallacies, (b) Fallacies of Ambiguity, and (c) Informal Fallacies.

FORMAL FALLACIES.   These consist of deviations from valid forms of inference, e.g., from MP, MT, DS, and HS studied in sections 2.4 and 2.5. Many of the exercises in chapters 2, 4, and 6 consist of arguments which are either "valid" or "invalid." All "invalid arguments" are "formal fallacies." Here is an example of what traditional logic called "the fallacy of false conversion"— an argument which violates the rule that conditionals are noncommutative:

Because (h)oly men (b)ow their heads in prayer and say "Lord, Lord," therefore those who (b)ow their heads in prayer and say "Lord, Lord" are (h)oly men. $[h \to b \ / \ \therefore \ b \to h]$

FALLACIES OF AMBIGUITY. These were discussed in section 3.2. Here we should reemphasize the point that ability to clearly differentiate the two or more meanings which give rise to misunderstanding, is indispensable to communication and to rational thought. We may also call attention to the fact that "the quantitative principle" of science discussed in chapter 5, and all of chapter 7 (Probability), may be viewed as a method of reducing vagueness and, therefore, of diminishing ambiguity.

INFORMAL FALLACIES (POPULAR FALLACIES, MATERIAL FALLA-CIES). Such fallacies are of many different types, and so varied that any classification of them necessarily involves overlapping categories. We begin with three types or clusters:

(1) fallacies of irrelevance, including various forms of *argumentum ad hominem*;
(2) various types of hasty generalization or special pleading; and
(3) circular reasoning, with which we here include the fallacy of reification.

(1) *Fallacies of Irrelevance.* This cluster of fallacies violates a basic principle of disciplined thinking: *stick to the point.* To reason effectively, we must concentrate. Like a skillful woodsman using an axe, we must confine our efforts to a small area. To solve any problem, we must focus our attention on that problem; we must not let our minds ramble, or give way to daydreaming or to idle reverie.

This type of fallacy takes a variety of forms, and, over the centuries, a variety of names, such as *appeal to force, appeal to authority, appeal to pity, smearing, scapegoating, poisoning the wells,* and its most widely used form, *argumentum ad hominem*—arguing "to the person" rather than to the point at issue.

As an example of the appeal to force (*argumentum ad baculum*): suppose a student asks his teacher, "Why should I study about fallacies?" and the teacher replies, "Because you'll flunk this course if you don't." The reply is not a responsible answer to a reasonable question; it is an appeal to force.

Suppose the teacher replies, "Because Aristotle considered fallacies to be a part of logic." This is an appeal to authority, but it does not provide the student with *reasons* why he should study fallacies.

Or suppose the teacher replies, "Why should I listen to your question? You were on probation last year, and your I.Q. test score was very low." Here attention is directed to the person, rather than to the point at issue, and the teacher is employing an argumentum ad hominem.

Or suppose the teacher replies, "I just received a telegram saying my mother has died. How can you expect me to respond to your question?" This reply will undoubtedly silence the student, but it will not be an answer to his question. Rather, it exemplifies the appeal to pity (*argumentum ad misericordiam*)— another method of evading the issue. Usually the appeal to pity is couched in highly emotional language. For example, when Thomas I. Kidd, general secretary of the Amalgamated Woodworkers' International Union, was indicted on a charge of criminal conspiracy, Clarence Darrow, attorney for the defense, argued thus:

> I appeal to you not for Thomas Kidd, but I appeal to you for the long line—the long, long line reaching back through the ages and forward to the years to come—the long line of despoiled and downtrodden people of the earth. I appeal to you for those men who rise in the morning before daylight comes and who go home at night when the light has faded from the sky and give their life, their strength, their toil to make others rich and great. I appeal to you in the name of those women who are offering up their lives to this modern god of gold, and I appeal to you in the name of those little children, the living and the unborn.[13]

Is Thomas Kidd guilty as charged? Although nothing relevant to this issue was said by Darrow, the effect on the jury was nonetheless powerful.

The ad hominem occurs in many forms, including "smearing," "scapegoating," and "poisoning the wells." The term "scapegoating" derives from primitive times, when, plagued with some disease, a community would sacrifice a goat to appease the gods. Although few people now believe that scapegoating is relevant to the curing of disease, many communities still revert to this fallacy. When Hitler made a scapegoat of the Jews and when Americans blamed their ills on the Communists, scapegoating was being employed.

The phrase "poisoning the wells" goes back to medieval times when anti-Jewish prejudice was extreme. If a plague struck a community, the people would blame it on the Jews, saying they had "poisoned the wells." These people did not prove that the wells actually were contaminated or that the Jews caused the contamination. They simply avoided intelligent thinking about their problem, by resorting to emotional diatribes against the suffering Jew—who provided them with a "scapegoat," and who thus provided them with an occasion for committing an argumentum ad hominem.

Ad hominem arguments frequently occur as *question-begging epithets*, i.e., as forms of *name calling*. Here is an example: "Why should the hard-working, civilized, efficient American spend his hard-earned tax dollar to subside these lazy, ignorant, unappreciative foreigners?"

(2) The second cluster of fallacies is also known by many different names. Particular emphasis should be given to *neglect of relevant data* and *hasty generalization*. However, the following related fallacies are also included within this second cluster: *overgeneralization, oversimplification, post hoc ergo propter hoc*, the *genetic fallacy*, the *imperfect analogy*, the *non sequitor, special pleading, card stacking, quoting out of context, half-truths*, and *cliché thinking*.

Neglect of relevant data (card stacking, special pleading) occurs whenever we present only those facts which support our own case and ignore or conceal any facts which might disprove our case. This fallacy is common practice in courtrooms, where opposing lawyers cite precedents favorable to their clients' cases, but ignore or belittle equally cogent precedents which might weaken their clients' cases.

Special pleading, or card stacking, signifies the tendency to represent things as we would wish them to be—to stress facts favorable to our own interests,

---

[13] Example taken from W. H. Werkmeister, *An Introduction to Critical Thinking* (Lincoln, Nebraska: Johnsen, 1957), rev. ed., p. 52. This book devotes over 100 pages to "Fallacies" and "Propaganda."

and to ignore facts which contravert them. This fallacy is illustrated in one of Aesop's fables:

> A man and a lion were discussing the relative strength of men and lions. The man contended that he and his fellows were stronger than lions and, to prove his point, he took the lion into the public garden and showed him a statue of Hercules overcoming a lion and tearing the lion's mouth in two.
>
> "That is all very well," said the lion, "but it proves nothing, for it was a man who made the statue."
>
> *Moral:* We can easily represent things as we wish them to be.

Quoting out of context is a form of special pleading. If someone says "Fascism is an excellent form of government—if you don't value freedom," he would be quoted out of context if he were cited as saying merely that "Fascism is an excellent form of government."

How often have we heard only one or two of Kipling's lines:

> Oh East is East and West is West, and never the twain shall meet,
> Till Earth and Sky stand presently at God's great Judgment Seat.

even though the next two lines in Kipling's poem read:

> But there is neither East nor West, Border, nor Breed, nor Birth,
> When two strong men stand face to face, tho' they come from the ends of the earth.

The phrase "beautiful but dumb" is not only quoted, but actually believed, not because there is a negative correlation between beauty and intelligence, but simply because women of unusual beauty are more noted (more "noticed") for their beauty than for their intelligence.

The neglect of relevant data seems to be based on the psychological truth that we all tend to take note of those facts or events which corroborate our preconceptions, and to ignore facts which might compel us to abandon our pet beliefs. To a very large extent, scientific method consists of ways of avoiding this fallacy.

Hasty generalization (overgeneralization, oversimplification, post hoc ergo propter hoc, half-truths, cliché thinking, the argumentative leap or non sequitor, the imperfect analogy, the fallacy of accident, and the converse fallacy of accident) also belongs to this second cluster of fallacies. Hasty generalization occurs whenever conclusions go further than the evidence warrants. It is easy to understand why hasty generalizations and half-truths are widespread. When we learn a language, we memorize numerous words and phrases, and thus accept uncritically many clichés and overgeneralizations. It is only with great difficulty that we later free ourselves from their grip.

Suppose we have been brought up to believe that "Scotsmen are miserly" or that "blacks are dirty." Later, when we come face to face with a Scotsman or a black, we will probably not see the individual as he really is. We will see only the definition of him that we have learned to expect. We "pre-judge," i.e., we are "prejudiced."

Half-truths and cliché thinking are perhaps better classified as *causes* of fallacies, rather than fallacies as such—assuming we define "fallacy" to mean a fallacious *argument*. But since they are frequently classified as fallacies, we include them here. We should realize that prejudices are studiously reinforced. The world is full of sloganeers—men who have simple remedies for the most complex problems, men with patent medicines to cure all diseases, men whose discourse is full of tidy half-truths and misleading analogies. Indeed, in order to form "desired attitudes," the leaders of most social groups practice sloganeering of one type or another. Communist dictators and American capitalists have this much in common: both employ skilled psychologists to help produce irrationally held beliefs. Both "sell the sizzle instead of the steak." Both know that most listeners believe what they hear repeated over and over again, and fall into the groove of prefabricated ideas.

People in every age and in every culture are pressured by colored terms, by heart-rending phrases, by panaceas of every description. It is difficult to resist their spell. But in our better moments, at least, we can raise our mental guards by asking questions such as, "What facts does he produce as evidence?" "Are they distorted?" "What are his arguments?" "Are they valid?" "What are his underlying assumptions?" "Are they tenable?" A free society requires that more and more citizens learn to ask such questions. Lincoln's aphorism, "You can fool some of the people all of the time, and you can fool all of the people some of the time, but you can't fool all of the people all of the time," is based on confidence in the mature and independent judgment of at least some of democracy's citizens.

The discussion of this second cluster of fallacies concludes with several examples. Each example is given a name, sometimes two names, but in most cases, some other name in the second cluster might have been used quite as well. However, giving the proper *name* to a fallacy is much less important than the ability to analyze a particular argument in terms of its questionable assumptions; its vague or ambiguous terms; its emotionally charged words; or its neglect of relevant data.

Oversimplification: During wars some people make immense profits. There-fore, wars are caused by profiteers.

Post hoc ergo propter hoc: (Because event *A* comes before event *B*, event *A* is the cause of event *B*): this patient developed a high fever, then became extremely sick. Therefore, the high fever is the cause of his sickness.

The *genetic fallacy:* (The contemporary state of affairs may be best explained by noting its origins or its earlier antecedents. Therefore,): since men have descended from hairy apes, men *are* hairy apes.

The *imperfect analogy*, or *false analogy:* The earth and Mars are both planets. Therefore, since the earth has a satellite (the moon), Mars must also have a satellite.

The *non sequitor*, or *argumentative leap:* Congresses, parliaments, and other legislative bodies are strong on talk, weak on action. Therefore, more power should go to the executive branch.

Fallacy of Accident: All citizens have a right to vote. Therefore, these citizens in the insane asylum have a right to vote.

Converse Fallacy of Accident: Since the government may draft men in times of war, the government may draft men in times of peace as well.

Before discussing a third cluster of fallacies, let us review. The first group of fallacies simply ignores evidence, and argues "to the person" rather than to the relevant evidence. The second group, although presenting factual evidence to support a case, presents only such evidence as is favorable to the desired outcome, and ignores other evidence even though that evidence is relevant. Finally, the third group of fallacies is quite different:

(3) *Circular Reasoning.* In *arguing in a circle* a premise is used to establish a conclusion, and later this conclusion is used to establish the original premise. Circular reasoning occurs when we prove *A* by *B* and then later prove *B* by *A*. This type of fallacy would be easily detected were it not for the fact that

the same meanings are often expressed by different words. Consider the statement, "suicide is justified, because anyone has a right to take one's own life." If we analyze this sentence, we see that "suicide" means "to take one's own life," and that "is justified" means "anyone has a right to." Thus the "argument" consists of the replacement of one set of words by another set of synonomous *words*. Obviously, since the two sets of words have the same meaning, the conclusion is equivalent to its premise—and is formally *valid*. But to *prove* or to *establish* a conclusion, something more is expected than mere repetition.

To better explain the above example—sometimes called the *fallacy of reification*, or the *fallacy of misplaced concreteness*—we must refer to "the empirical principle" of science, the most basic principle of induction, a topic to be discussed at some length in section 5.1. The empirical principle insists that the words and concepts used in any causal explanation must connect, directly or indirectly, with empirical reality. It will not suffice merely to replace one set of *words* with another set of *words*. Consider the following series of questions and replies:

Question: Why does turning on the switch make the light bulb glow?
Reply: Because the switch thus connects the light bulb with the source of power.
Question: What is the source of power?
Reply: The source of power is the electric generating plant.
Question: What is the electric generating plant?
Reply: The electric generating plant is the place where the chemical energy of coal, the kinetic energy of water, or atomic energy, is transformed into electric energy.

Obviously such replies could go on and on. Circular reasoning would not occur unless the response became "because the light bulb glows."
But now, by way of contrast, consider the following two examples:

Question: Why does opium put people to sleep?
Reply: Because of its soporific powers.
Question: What is meant by "soporific powers"?
Reply: This means the power to put people to sleep.
Civilian: Why do men go to war and kill one another?
General: Because they have warlike instincts.
Civilian: But how can you be sure they have warlike instincts?
General: Because, as history shows, men go to war and kill one another.

Certainly there is nothing wrong with substituting synonyms for synonyms, e.g., substituting "soporific powers" for "the power to put people to sleep." But we should realize that words alone, when lacking in empirically based referents, are not explanations; hence such verbal substitutions do not produce *sound* arguments.

When we prove *A* by *B* and then prove *B* by *A* circular reasoning is easy to detect, provided it is not concealed by an ambiguity. But if we prove *A* by *B*, *B* by *C*, and *C* by *D*; and then, several chapters later, prove *D* by *A*, circular reasoning may be very difficult to detect.

Because it generally involves the confusion of words with objective reality, circular reasoning and the fallacy of reification occur most frequently in arguments dealing with social and moral issues, where factual data and objective evidence is less clearly recognizable than in the natural sciences; for example, where an all-too-human ideology is mistaken for a divinely inspired natural law, or where a self-seeking rationalization is falsely assumed to be an unassailable truth.

Exercise 3.4A.   Three Types of Fallacies

Directions: Label each of the following as A, B, or C where:

A = fallacies of irrelevance (scapegoating; argumentum ad hominem; etc.);
B = hasty generalization (special pleading; neglect of relevant data; etc.);
C = circular reasoning, or fallacy of reification.

Each problem in this exercise is quite brief, and, therefore, the context or the unstated assumptions of the problem may be unclear. Hence it will sometimes be possible to classify an argument in two different ways; and the "right answer" refers to the fallacy which (in the author's judgment) is *most conspicuously* committed.

_____ 1. Since I learned that this symphony was a favorite of Hitler's, I can no longer enjoy it.

_____ 2. Under the capitalistic system there are many poor people, there is waste of men and materials, cutthroat competition, a glorification of the acquisitive instinct, depressions on the one hand and inflation on the other. This proves that the system is thoroughly bad and should be discarded.

_____ 3. A lawyer for the defense handed his brief to his colleague with the added note: "We have a very poor case. You better poke fun at the prosecuting attorney."

_____ 4. Modern art is greater than traditional art because all the best critics say so. Who are the best critics? You can easily identify them by the fact that they prefer modern art to traditional art.

_____ 5. Religion brought intolerance into the world, denied freedom of thought, and retarded scientific progress. So, religion has done more harm than good.

_____ 6. I love Mary because she is beautiful. She is beautiful because she is lovely. She is lovely because she is lovable. She is lovable because I love her.

_____ 7. Since democracy is admittedly an imperfect form of government, it follows that we should abandon it for totalitarianism.

_____ 8. This law should not be passed because it is being advocated by men who are radicals, troublemakers, and in some instances even subversives.

_____ 9. We all know that there is no significant difference between men and women with respect to mental capacity. All arguments against coeducation, therefore, fall to the ground.

_____ 10. My church is God's church. How do I know it is God's church? Because it was founded by divinely appointed prophets. How do I know they are divinely appointed? Because the Holy Scriptures say so. How do I know they are Holy Scriptures? Because my church, which is God's church, assured me that such is the case.

_____ 11. Heard at a PTA Meeting: "That woman's arguments cannot be sound; for she is a veritable nobody. She has no social standing, and her manners are rude."

_____ 12. Sugar diabetic to his nondiabetic doctor: "But Doctor, surely your advice that I should not eat candy cannot be sound advice, for you yourself often eat candy."

_____ 13. *Censor:* This book should be withdrawn from circulation. Its author spent ten years in Sing Sing, and he was in a communist cell.

_____ 14. *Muggs:* The new school bell is louder than the old one.
Buggs: How do you figure that?
Muggs: Because the old one didn't make as much noise.

_____ 15. It is the trained people who make the gravest mistakes. For example, it is the trained lawyer who gives bad legal advice, and it is the professional doctor who makes a wrong diagnosis which may have injurious and even fatal results. To avoid such grave mistakes, therefore, it is best to consult with untrained people.

_____ 16. The downfall of France resulted from her lack of spirit. This was a result of the weakening of her moral fiber due to the impact of secularism. By secularism we mean the forsaking of moral absolutes, and this comes about because of lack of spirit.

_____ 17. The early Christian Church was a model of a perfect society; and in that church, as the Bible relates in chapters IV and V of the Book of Acts, all property was held in common. Private ownership, therefore, is morally wrong.

_____ 18. "He talks with angels," the man declared. "How do you know?" I asked. "He said he did," the man replied. "But suppose that he lied?" I suggested. "O, perish the thought!" he responded angrily, "How could any man lie who is capable of talking with angels?"

_____ 19. When we examine the courses studied by students who ranked high scholastically, we find that all math majors ranked high. This proves that the study of math improves the mind.

_____ 20. *A:* Why is Bill such a friendly, outgoing person?
B: Because he is an extrovert.
A: Why is Bill an extrovert?
B: Because he is a friendly, outgoing person.

_____ 21. Francis Bacon was referring to which fallacy when he wrote (in *Novum Organum*, Aphorism 45): "And therefore it was a good answer that was made by one who, when they showed him hanging in a temple a picture of those who had paid their vows as having escaped shipwreck, and would have him acknowledge whether he did not now admit the power of the gods: 'Aye,' asked he again, 'But where are they painted that were drowned after their vows? . . .'"

_____ 22. *Bank cashier:* You will need to be identified, Madam.
Lady: My friend here will identify me.
Bank cashier: But I don't know her.
Lady: Oh! Then I'll introduce you to her.

_____ 23. The meat you ate today was the same meat you bought yesterday. The meat you bought yesterday was raw meat. Therefore, the meat you ate today was raw meat.

_____ 24. *Communist:* Why debate the merits of capitalism? Those who defend it are either bloated plutocrats or paid lackeys of Wall Street.

Exercise 3.4A illustrates only three of the many types of fallacies. Here are some other well known types:

(4) *The Black and White Fallacy* and *The Fallacy of the Beard*. The black and white fallacy occurs very frequently because the use of contrast is such an effective rhetorical device. In our weaker moments at least, all of us tend to classify people as "friends or enemies," "saints or devils," "rich and poor," "capitalists and communists," and, in our lighter moments, we enjoy the nursery rhyme telling about the little girl who "when she was good, was very, very good, but when she was bad, she was horrid."

This fallacy is easy to analyze. Instead of employing the law of excluded middle to divide colors into "black" and "nonblack," the division is into "black" and "white"—thus ignoring the many shades of gray between.

Following is an example of the black and white fallacy—also known as the *fallacy of bifurcation*, or as *false bifurcation*: "Every society must choose between freedom and security. Americans have chosen freedom. Therefore, Americans cannot expect to have security."

The converse of the black and white fallacy is the fallacy of the beard. This fallacy derives its name from the difficulty of deciding exactly how many whiskers it takes to make a beard. Surely ten whiskers is not enough. Then how about 20? 30? 50? 100? 200? Suppose we were to settle on 300. Then how about 299? Or 301? Since the dividing point is sure to be arbitrary—a form of "definition by *stipulation*"—the conclusion is drawn that there is *no real basis for any dividing point,* hence that there is no real difference between having and not having a beard.

The argument of the beard is illustrated by the gourmet who argues: "Surely this one tiny piece of candy won't make me fat or hurt my health." It is also committed by the health faddist who says, "If I eat too many sweets, I will become unhealthy, perhaps diabetic; therefore, I dare not eat one tiny piece of candy."

(5) *Fallacies of Composition and Division.* These two fallacies confuse the part with the whole. The fallacy of composition assumes that what is true of the composite parts is also true of the whole, e.g., "Each flower in this bouquet is beautiful; therefore, it must be a beautiful bouquet." The fallacy of division argues from the whole to the part, e.g., "This is a beautiful bouquet; therefore, each flower in the bouquet must be beautiful."

Here are two additional examples:

Fallacy of composition: Each grain in the bushel of wheat weighs less than an ounce. Therefore, the bushel of wheat weighs less than an ounce.

Fallacy of division: This rhubarb pie is delicious. Therefore, rhubarb is delicious, flour is delicious, and shortening is delicious.

(6) *Fallacies Involving Unwarranted Assumptions.* Because these fallacies are so pervasive, all of section 3.1 was devoted to "Assumptions." Here we present only two of the many types of arguments involving unwarranted assumptions: the *Appeal to Ignorance* and the *Complex Question.*

Appeal to ignorance (argumentum ad ignorantiam) is a way to avoid presenting factual evidence or logical proof. Suppose an atheist argues, "There is no God because you cannot prove that there is," and a theist replies, "There is a God because you cannot prove that there isn't." Each of these men has based his argument on an "appeal to ignorance."

Appeal to ignorance forms the basis of a delightful legend concerning a medieval miracle. On Good Friday of each year, while the congregation was bowed in prayer, it was affirmed that the statue on the church altar would shed real tears. However, if even one member of that congregation looked up from his prayers (to see the tears), the miracle would not occur; for it occurred only when all members of the congregation exhibited complete faith.

Complex question. Consider the question, "When did you stop beating your wife?" This is called a complex question for two reasons. First, it assumes what probably needs to be proved, namely, that you *did* beat your wife. (For this reason, some logicians classify the complex question as a form of *petitio principii,* or begging the question.) Second, because the argument implies that you did beat your wife, it is a case of "smearing"—an example of argumentum ad hominem. Although sometimes done in jest, this form of argument is also used by people who quite innocently (or who quite deliberately) assume the very thing that needs to be established.

Exercise 3.4B.   Four Informal Fallacies

Directions: Label each of the following as A, B, C, or D, where:
A = black and white fallacy, or the fallacy of the beard.
B = fallacy of composition, or fallacy of division.
C = two forms of the fallacy of unwarranted assumption
D = fallacy of ambiguity (a review and a reminder of section 3.2)

_____ 1. Einstein was famous. Einstein was a violinist. Therefore, Einstein was a famous violinist.

_____ 2. How long did you contemplate murdering the victim before actually carrying out the vile deed?

_____ 3. One plus two times three is seven. Also, one plus two times three is nine. Therefore, seven is nine.

_____ 4. The London Symphony is a world famous orchestra. Therefore, Joe Doe, who plays violin in the London Symphony, is a world famous violinist.

_____ 5. Student trying to enroll in an over-filled class: "Just one more student in the class surely won't make any real difference."

_____ 6. Amy loves Bob. Bob loves Carol. Therefore, Amy loves Carol.

_____ 7. Why are women more interested in religion than men?

_____ 8. According to some historians, for twenty years after World War II, U.S. foreign policy was based on the following reasoning:
   If we do not give aid to the countries adjacent to communist Russia and China, these countries will become communized. Then these countries, in turn, will communize the countries adjacent to them; and so on and on, until finally Russia and China will be at our own doorstep.

_____ 9. If we match them position by position, the players on the All-Star team are better than those on the Giants. Therefore, the All-Stars are a better team than the Giants.

_____ 10. Since aspirin, quinine, and citric acid all have medicinal value, the combination of the three should make an excellent all-purpose medicine.

_____ 11. Teacher to Pupil: "Since you cannot show me the essay you claim to have handed in last month, and which you say was returned to you by me, I am justified in assuming that you never handed it in in the first place."

_____ 12. How long will our newspapers continue to be slaves to big business?

_____ 13. Client to Architect: "Since I want the best house in town, let your design include the best features of the colonial, the Georgian and the ranch house styles.

_____ 14. Ireland is a poor nation. Therefore, these Irish emigrants must be poor.

_____ 15. Since carbon monoxide (CO) is poisonous, carbon (C) must also be poisonous.

_____ 16. You cannot serve two masters. Either you serve God or you serve Satan.

_____ 17. High prices for farm products help farmers. High wages help the laboring man. High profits help the capitalist. High prices for retail goods help the retailer. Therefore, high prices help the nation.

_____ 18. Why is there more dishonesty in government than there is in industry?

_____ 19. Hunter: "There are millions of ducks shot down each year. So, it surely cannot make any real difference if I kill two or three before the season opens."

_____ 20. The whole crew could lift the boat. Therefore, Pete, who is a member of the crew, could lift the boat.

_____ 21. Why are college graduates less happy than uneducated people?

_____ 22. Opium is a poison. But physicians advise some patients to take opium. Therefore, physicians advise some patients to take poison.

_____ 23. A wholesaler sued a retailer for $500, claiming that he had shipped that amount of goods, and had not been paid for them. The retailer claimed that he had paid the bill. The wholesaler stated that he had no record of the payment. The retailer then said that, since the plaintiff could not disprove his claim that he (the retailer) had paid the bill, the court should dismiss the case.

_____ 24. All abstract subjects are difficult. If anything is difficult it is a stumbling block. Therefore, all abstract subjects are stumbling blocks.

The fallacies studied in exercises 3.4A and 3.4B are not the only types. Indeed, new types of fallacies, or new words for old fallacies, appear with each oncoming generation. For example, in 1971 Neil H. Jacoby listed "four modern

fallacies" which, in his opinion, are widely committed by contemporary uto-
pians and social reformers. He called them the "Nirvana," the "other grass is
greener," the "free lunch," and the "people could be different" fallacies:

Four Modern Fallacies:

The "Nirvana" approach to social policy presents a choice between a theoretical
ideal never approached in man's history and existing conditions. The vast distance
between the two naturally creates a social "crisis." The true choice, however, lies
between existing conditions and others that are feasible in the sense of being
capable of attainment. Because the expectation-reality gap in the latter case is
usually small, the "crisis" is reduced to a manageable problem.

The "other grass is greener" illusion credits an alternative social condition,
usually in some foreign country, with great virtues said to be lacking in American
society. Thus atmospheric pollution is said to be the product of capitalistic enterprise, and its cure is to adopt state socialism. This idea is repeated by social critics
who have not taken the trouble to ascertain that pollution levels in socialist
countries have risen, along with their G.N.P.'s, even faster than in capitalist
countries.

The "free lunch" fallacy is that there are costless remedies for social ills. Since
unemployment is an evil, say the critics, abolish it and reduce the unemployment
ratio to zero. They choose to ignore the heavy social costs of such a policy in the
form of restrictions on individual freedom, lowered productivity, and price inflation. Every decision that produces public benefits imposes costs, and the problem
is to weigh both and determine the balance.

The "people could be different" fallacy is that the Good Society can be attained
by radical changes in the moral and ethical behavior of people. Thus the "new
communist man," imbued with a totally altruistic concern for the public welfare,
was seen by the older Marxists as the condition for the ultimate transformation of
socialism into true communism. Unfortunately, he has not yet appeared in sufficient
numbers to make this possible; and he shows no sign of doing so. While moderate
changes in men's values and behavior can occur over time (indeed, changes are
essential if our society is to improve) sharp mutations in human nature are a
fantasy. In reforming our society, we are wise to take human nature as a datum,
and to design structures and processes for imperfect men and women rather than
for saints and philosophers. . . . [14]

Exercise 3.4C. Four Modern Fallacies

Remarks: It should be obvious that Jacoby's "Four Modern Fallacies," might also
have been classified as examples of the *fallacy of unwarranted assumption.*

Directions: First, clearly state the assumption(s) which form the basis of each of the
above "Four Modern Fallacies" by Jacoby. Then, defend or criticize those assumptions
of "utopian liberals" as "warranted" (i.e., as "not fallacious"—the utopian liberal's
view) or as "unwarranted" (i.e., as "fallacious"—Jacoby's view).

3.5 The Dilemma

Like MP, MT, DS, and HS, the dilemma is one of the important forms of argument inherited from traditional logic. However, we shall now argue (1) that
"the" dilemma is not *one* form of argument, but a whole cluster of argument
forms; (2) that it is more important to rhetoric than to logic; and (3) that it is
notorious for its use of the black and white fallacy.

---

[14] Neil H. Jacoby, "What is a Social Problem?", *The Center Magazine*, July–August, 1971.
Reprinted with permission of *The Center Magazine*, a publication of the Center for the Study of
Democratic Institutions, Santa Barbara, California.

Structurally, the dilemma combines one "either . . . or" premise with two "if . . . then" premises. These three premises may be combined in numerous ways, such as:

(A) If p, then w. If q, then w.   But either p or q. Therefore, w.
(B) If p, then q. If $\sim p$, then $\sim w$.   But either $\sim q$ or w. Therefore, p.
(C) If p, then w. If q, then w.   But not w. Therefore, neither p nor q.
(D) If p, then w. If q, then y.   But either p or q. Therefore, either w or y.
(E) If p, then w. If q, then y.   But either p or $\sim y$. Hence, either w or $\sim q$.

The effectiveness of the dilemma *as a rhetorical device* may be explained on psychological grounds. The listener becomes so intrigued by (and entangled in) the argument's complex *form* that he gives little thought to its *content*. He listens open-mouthed, and becomes so fully occupied by the argument's intricacies that he does not attend to its logical weaknesses.

From a logical point of view, however, a dilemma is no stronger than its weakest link. Since the dilemma contains three distinct links, the critical listener will generally find at least one of them to be vulnerable.

ANSWERING A DILEMMA.   There are three ways to answer a dilemma:

1. To *escape between the horns of the dilemma* is to show that there is another alternative—to show that the opponent's "either . . . or" is not exhaustive. A little ingenuity will usually uncover some alternative not mentioned in the "either . . . or" bifurcation. Consider the following dilemma, which is said to have been used by the Caliph Omar when he ordered the destruction of the library at Alexandria: "If these books contain the same doctrines as those of the Koran, they are unnecessary. If they contradict the doctrines of the Koran, they are pernicious. But they must do one or the other. Therefore, in either case, they should be destroyed."

To escape between the horns of this dilemma, one would point out that the "either . . . or" is not exhaustive, by showing that there are books which do not contradict the doctrines of the Koran, yet whose contents are not contained in the Koran. For example, Euclid's geometry is neither "moral" nor "immoral"; it is "amoral"—its contents do not relate to problems of religion and morality. By pointing out that there is a third alternative—books which are "amoral"—one would escape between the horns of the dilemma!

Division by two is the easiest form of division, and most people are overly impressed by "either . . . or" logic. Comfort and even survival have taught men to classify foods as nutritious or poisonous—yet more accurate knowledge reveals degrees of more or less. We commonly classify men as friends or enemies; yet, when we give the matter a little thought, we realize that there are many types and degrees of friendship and enmity. We are all inclined to commit the black and white fallacy even though we know that there are a thousand shades of gray.

Let us note the reason for this persistent tendency to "divide by two." Each day we make hundreds of decisions on the basis of *two* alternatives: "Shall I drink coffee this noon, or some other drink?" "Shall I use one spoonful of sugar, or more?" "Shall I stay at school, or leave?" "Shall I continue studying, or quit?" Such choices between two options are repeated hundreds of times each day. But a moment's thought will reveal that there are, in most cases, more than two alternatives. In answering a dilemma, if we can show that the "either . . . or" is an oversimplification of the alternatives available, we have escaped between the horns of the dilemma.

2. To *take the dilemma by the horns* means to take one of the alternatives (one of the charging bull's "horns") and show that the consequent does not necessarily follow. For example, Zeno the Eleatic argued that motion was impossible. Thus:

> If a body moves, it must move either where it is, or where it is not.
> But it cannot *move* in the place where it is; and it cannot move in a place where it is not.
> Therefore, motion is impossible.

Plato took one horn of this dilemma and said "But a body *can* move in the place where it is. Witness a spinning top." This is only one of several answers to this dilemma.

We may also take a dilemma by the horns by showing that one of its alternatives is based on a false assumption, on a hasty generalization, or on some other fallacy of the type discussed in section 3.3.

To take a dilemma by the horns, then, is simply to deny one of the alternatives, and to demonstrate that *one* of the proposed "if . . . thens" is untrue.

3. To *rebut* a dilemma is to construct another *counterdilemma* with a contradictory conclusion. The following is adapted from an example by E. A. Burtt.[15]

> If a woman is good-looking, higher education is superfluous; if she is not good-looking, higher education is inadequate.
> But a woman is either good-looking or not.
> Therefore, higher education for women is either superfluous, or inadequate.

The following is a *rebuttal* or *counterdilemma*:

> If a woman is good-looking, higher education provides her with good "contacts" for a future husband.
> If a woman is not good-looking, higher education provides her with an alternative means of livelihood.
> Therefore, whether or not a woman is good-looking, higher education is of value.

Observe that the counterdilemma refutes *both* horns: it shows that something desirable results from each alternative.

Although most dilemmas are more specious than real, it would be a mistake to assume that every dilemma admits of a good reply. During the Lincoln-Douglas debates, Lincoln asked Douglas this question: "Shall the federal government restrict the extension of slavery in new territories?" If Douglas replied "Yes," he would please his Illinois constituents in the senatorial race, but displease Southern voters in the coming presidential election. If Douglas replied "No," he would displease his Illinois constituents (and thus lose the senatorial race against Lincoln) while pleasing Southerners who looked to him as a likely presidential candidate.

On logical and constitutional grounds, Douglas's reply was quite reasonable: he proposed that the decision be left to the majority vote of the residents in the new territories. But with the rising tide of sentiment in favor of abolition, his evasive reply proved to be politically unsatisfactory—and he was indeed caught in the horns of a dilemma.

Exercise 3.5A.   Answering a Dilemma

Directions: On separate paper, answer any ten of the following dilemmas, using one or more of the following methods: (1) take by the horns, (2) escape between the horns, (3) rebuttal or counterdilemma. No answers are given for this exercise.

Remember that this chapter deals with *informal* logic. Accordingly, although every dilemma in this exercise is *formally valid*, each of these dilemmas, with the possible

---

[15] E. A. Burtt, *Right Thinking* (New York: Harper, 1946), p. 146.

exception of problem 16, admits of an answer—an answer not based on formal logic, but on common sense.

1. Either you (k)now how to spell a word, or you don't. If you (k)now how, there is no need to consult a (d)ictionary. If you don't (k)now how, a (d)ictionary won't help you, since you can't find in it a word you cannot spell. In either case, a (d)ictionary is useless.

2. If a minority group (s)peaks up against the majority, the minority will be (r)epressed; and if a minority group does not (s)peak up, it will be (r)epressed. But a minority group must either (s)peak up or not (s)peak up. Therefore, regardless of which policy it pursued, a minority group is sure to be (r)epressed.

3. Every person is either an (e)goist or an (a)ltruist. If an (e)goist, by definition, he always looks out for his own (s)elf-interest. And if an (a)ltruist, he works for the good of others only because in the long run he knows this will be to his own (s)elf-interest. Whichever way a man behaves, then, his actions must therefore be motivated by (s)elf-interest.

4. If the nations of the world keep their (p)eace, the U.N. is un(n)ecessary. If the nations decide to go to (w)ar, the U.N. will be (h)elpless in its attempts to prevent war. But either the nations will keep their (p)eace or go to (w)ar. So the U.N. will prove to be either un(n)ecessary or (h)elpless.

5. [Epicurus argued:] Either God (c)an or cannot prevent evil. If God (c)an prevent evil (and does not prevent it) then God is (m)alevolent; and if God cannot prevent evil, then God is not (o)mnipotent. Hence, either God is (m)alevolent or God is not (o)mnipotent.

6. If a nation (a)dopts universal military training it is preparing for (w)ar; and if it does not, it is inviting (i)nvasion by an aggressor. But either a nation (a)dopts universal military training or it does not. Therefore, a nation is either preparing for (w)ar or is inviting (i)nvasion by an aggressor.

7. If (J)ames is right, Abraham attained (s)alvation by works, and if (P)aul is right, Abraham attained (s)alvation by faith. But surely one of these two apostles is right. So, we may rest assured that Abraham attained (s)alvation.

8. Either logical inferences are (f)allacious or they are not. If (f)allacious, they are obviously (w)orthless. But even when they are not (f)allacious, since they bring nothing new to light, they are also (w)orthless. So, logical inferences are worthless.

Note: The remaining dilemmas are either abbreviated, or extended beyond the simple forms we have set forth. Try to restate them in strict form, and then answer them.

9. If a dictator is benevolent, he provides the best type of government; if he is despotic, it is better to have one blunderer rather than many at the head of the government. Either way you look at it, dictatorship is the best form of government.

10. No man can serve two masters: For either he will hate the one, and love the other; or else he will hold to the one, and despise the other. Ye cannot serve God and mammon. (Matt. 6:24, King James translation).

11. [Here is a proof justifying Emerson's saying that "A foolish consistency is the hobgoblin of little minds"]: If we admit that our (f)ormer views were wrong, then we are (i)nconsistent with our own beliefs. But if (in a changing world) we do not admit we were wrong, our beliefs are (i)nconsistent with the (n)ew truths recognized as such by all civilized men. On either alternative, we cannot avoid inconsistency.

12. [From a novel]: "If I am (g)uilty, I am unworthy of (y)ou; and if I am innocent, you are unworthy of (m)e (because you were suspicious of me). In either case, we should be (d)ivorced."

13. [On July 4, 1861, Lincoln posed the following question, which is an abbreviated dilemma:] "Must a government of necessity be too strong for the liberties of its own people, or too weak to maintain its own existence?"

14. Ancient Greek Sophists asked: "How is education possible? For if you know to begin with, there is nothing to learn. And if you do not know to begin with, how can you recognize knowledge, if perchance you should meet it?" (Compare Pascal: "We would not seek God if we did not already know Him.")

15. The following is a *trilemma*, taken from Marcus Aurelius (*Meditations* XII, pp. 14–15):

There are three alternatives: Either the universe is governed by a foreordained destiny, or by a merciful providence, or operates entirely by chance and in chaos. If we accept the first alternative, where the universe is governed by inexorable fate, reason tells us not to struggle against our foreordained destiny. If we choose the second alternative, and a merciful providence watches over all, again reason speaks up and says to render oneself worthy of celestial aid. Finally, even if we assume that the physical universe is a chaotic flux of atoms in motion, we are nevertheless fortified by the thought that reason is able to rule the thoughts of our own mind.

16. The Greek Sophist Protagoras is reported to have made an agreement with a pupil Euathlus, to teach him the art of pleading at law, on condition that one-half the fee was to be paid when the instruction was completed, the other half when Euathlus had won his first case in court. Euathlus paid the first half, but put off beginning practice. Protagoras finally brought suit for the remainder of the fee, offering this dilemma to justify his position:

> If Euathlus loses this case he must pay me, because that will be the judgment of the court; if he wins he must pay me as the contract provides.
> But he must either lose or win.
> Therefore in any case he must pay the fee.

Euathlus countered with the following dilemma:

> If I win the case in court, I will not have to pay, for such will be the judge's decision; if I lose it, according to the contract I will not yet have to pay.
> But I must win or lose.
> Therefore in any case I will not have to pay.[16]

SUMMARY. This chapter has considered four impediments to rational thinking: mistaken assumptions acquired as part of our cultural heritage—a type of mistake which Francis Bacon called "idols of the tribe" (3.1); mistakes in communication caused by vague or ambiguous words and phrases—which Bacon called "idols of the market place" (3.2); mistakes caused by our tendency to justify our pet prejudices—which Bacon called "idols of the cave," and "idols of the theatre"—caused by becoming enslaved by emotionally laden language and by highly persuasive and propagandistic rhetoric (3.3; 3.5); and, finally, by fallacious reasoning (3.4).

Exercise 3.5B.   Review: Take-Home Written Assignment

Directions: This exercise is intended to encourage you to analyze arguments and discussions, whether in newspapers, magazines and books, TV panels, or in private conversations. Write a brief account of at least one of the following:

(A) Describe some situation in which ambiguity occurred, causing communication to break down, or causing meaningful discussion to come to an end. Your description should explain the two meanings of the word or phrase which gave rise to the difficulty.

(B) Give an example of the way in which emotionally laden words or phrases were used to distort, rather than to present clearly, the truth.

(C) Give an example of fallacious reasoning.

Answers for Chapter Three

3.1A:

No answers are given for this exercise.

3.1B:

1. Assumption: that no one should be of service to anyone who has not helped, or who is not likely to be of help to the person doing the service.

---

[16] Problem 16 is mentioned in sec. 6.3 as an example of a self-referential paradox.

3. In a single formula, this problem summarizes what are variously known as (A) "reasoning from experience," "Aristotle's 'inductive leap,'" "learning by induction," and "argument by analogy." But this same formula also summarizes (B) "hasty generalization," "neglect of relevant data," "the fallacy of unwarranted assumption," and "false analogy." In this problem it would be an "unwarranted assumption" either to think only of (A) and to disregard (B), or to think only of (B) and to disregard (A).

5. Assumption: that there is no "experience" except sense experience. This point will come up again when we discuss Mill's methods.

7. The "average life span" statistics include infants and young children, and it is only in these age brackets where the loss of life has been very significantly reduced.

9. Sending boys to reformatories will (a) protect society from the individual (for two years) and/or (b) teach the boy never to do anything like this again.

11. Our schools and our society are not now doing enough to help young people assert themselves and to show individuality.

13. The teaching of religion will assure the absence of crime.

15. Citizen A's second sentence represents his major assumption. Another assumption would seem to be that parents are the *only* significant causal factor with respect to delinquency.

3.2A:

1. B;   3. A;   5. B;   7. A;   9. A;   11. B;   13. A;   15. B.

3.2B:

1. What I see: (a) the perceptual image; (b) the conceptual (interpretation of that image or) idea.

3. Secular: (a) nonsectarian; administered by the state, not by the church; (b) antireligious, opposed to religious; atheistic.

5. No: (a) there exists no cat that . . . ; (b) No—zero; one less than "one."

7. Laws: (a) edicts, commands; (b) regularities, uniformities. For example, if a man jumps off a skyscraper, he may violate a law (that is, an ordinance) prohibiting such behavior; but he merely illustrates Newton's law of gravitation.

9. Improbable: (a) improbable with respect to a small number, for example, that 1 in 50 shall die this hour; (b) probable with respect to a large number, for example, that 1 in 100,000,000 shall die.

11. Event: (a) phenomena or events *within* the totality of events; (b) Nature viewed as the totality of such events. This may also be analyzed as a confusion between the "distributive" and "collective" use of terms; or between "efficient" and "final" causes.

13. E. We may illustrate the ambiguity in problem 13 by considering a simple formula: "The area of a rectangle is equal to the base multiplied by the height." ($A = bh$). In this formula, not only can "b" and "h" be *replaced* by a great variety of different numbers, (a property which logic and mathematics have in common) but also (what is not the case with logic) these numbers represent *measurable quantities* of length, and are *additive*, and hence also amenable to the rules of arithmetic (addition, subtraction, multiplication, and division). In this latter sense, logic is *not* a form of mathematics.

15. Probable: (a) uncaused, accidental, uncertain, fortuitous, pure chance; (b) likely, reasonable, plausible, well-grounded, logical.

17. Determined: (a) determined by someone or something external to oneself; (b) self-determined, assuming that human behavior inevitably involves choosing between alternatives. Using this distinction, "freedom" is defined as "self-determination."

19. Believes: (a) without reservations; (b) with qualifications or reservations.

21. Nothing: (a) no space; (b) no physical object.

23. "Dispensed with" is what A. E. Mander would call an "unfinished term," for, in this context, it would mean "dispensed with when no other food is available."

3.2C:

1. E;   3. B;

5. F or B (*Note:* For children, this might be rated F; for adults, it might be classified as B);

7. H;

9. F (In this definition, the first 7 words constitute the "genus," the last 27 constitute the "species.");

11. S;   13. F;   15. E;   17. F;   19. S;   21. F;   23. B.

3.3A:

No answers are given for this exercise.

3.4A:

1. A;   3. A;   5. B;   7. B;   9. B;   11. A;   13. A;   15. B;   17. B;
19. B;   21. B;

23. B. (In scholastic logic, problem 23 would have been called a "fallacy of accident" because it emphasized such nonessential properties as the fact that the meat was cooked or uncooked.)

3.4B:

 1. D;   3. D;   5. A;   7. C;   9. B;   11. C;   13. B;   15. B;   17. B;
19. A;   21. C;   23. C.

3.4C:

No answers are given for this exercise.

3.5A and *3.5B:*

No answers are given for these two exercises.

chapter 4

TRUTH-VALUE LOGIC FORMALIZED

4.1 Discursive Reasoning, SIMP, ADD, and CONJ

DISCURSIVE REASONING.   By "discursive reasoning" we mean a step-by-step procedure where, on the basis of premise p, we prove q; then, on the basis of p and q, we prove r; then, on the basis of p, q, and r, we prove s; and so on. This procedure is employed in Euclidean geometry when, once any theorem has been demonstrated, that theorem may thereafter be used to help demonstrate other theorems.

In applying this method to logic, it is helpful if each new conclusion (each new "theorem") is written on a separate line. This procedure makes it possible to check and to double check each step of any proof. It also makes it possible to conjoin the newly established conclusion to premises already assumed, or already proved.

In traditional logic, the nearest thing to discursive reasoning is the polysyllogism (chain argument, sorites), illustrated by the following example:

All (b)loodhounds are (d)ogs. All (d)ogs are (c)anines. All (c)anines are (m)ammals. All (m)ammals are (v)ertebrates. Therefore, all (b)loodhounds are (v)ertebrates.

In symbols: $(b \to d) \cdot (d \to c) \cdot (c \to m) \cdot (m \to v) \mid \therefore b \to v$

Use of the polysyllogism means that we do *not* need to break this argument up into:

$$(b \to d) \cdot (d \to c) \mid \therefore b \to c; \qquad (b \to c) \cdot (c \to m) \mid \therefore b \to m;$$
$$(b \to m) \cdot (m \to v) \mid \therefore b \to v$$

Suppose to the above four premises, we add the following additional premise: No (w)orms are (v)ertebrates; and wish to test the validity of the following conclusion: No (w)orms are (b)loodhounds. Applying COPO to the original premises, and placing the new premise at the beginning, would yield the following valid chain argument:

$$(w \to \sim v) \cdot (\sim v \to \sim m) \cdot (\sim m \to \sim c) \cdot (\sim c \to \sim d) \cdot (\sim d \to \sim b) \mid \therefore w \to \sim v$$

Exercise 4.1A.   Chain Arguments

Directions: (A) Express each of the following arguments in symbolic form, and (B) indicate whether the argument is valid or invalid.

1. If a logic textbook is to be (r)elevant to students of the 1970s it must be of (s)ignificance in [the contemporary world, sometimes called] "the age of the computer." To be (s)ignificant to "the age of the computer," it should provide basic understanding about (c)omputers. But if it is to give students basic understanding about (c)omputers, logic must deal with (m)odern algebra or set theory, at least in its elementary phases. Therefore, any logic text which does not deal with (m)odern algebra and set theory, at least in its elementary stages, is not (r)elevant to students of the 1970s.

2. If you finish (h)igh school, you may enter (c)ollege. In (c)ollege (that is, "If you enter college") you may study (b)iology. If you study (b)iology, then you are prepared to study (m)edicine. If you study (m)edicine, you may become a (p)hysician. Finally, if you are a (p)hysician, you may become a (s)urgeon. So, if you don't finish (h)igh school, you'll never become a (s)urgeon.

3. If a person is (h)appy, he does not (c)omplain. Anyone with (i)ndigestion (c)omplains. Whoever (e)ats too many rich chocolates has (i)ndigestion. All (b)ug-eating African natives are (h)appy people. Therefore, no one who (e)ats too many rich chocolates is a (b)ug-eating African native. (Adapted from Lewis Carroll, *Symbolic Logic*. Ten other Lewis Carroll polysyllogisms may be found near the end of section 6.1).

4. For want of a (n)ail the (s)hoe was lost; for want of a (s)hoe the (h)orse was lost; for want of a (h)orse the (b)attle was lost; and for the loss of the (b)attle the (k)ingdom was lost. Hence, for want of a (n)ail the (k)ingdom was lost.

5. If a man is (w)ise, he is (t)emperate.
   If he is (t)emperate, he is (c)onstant.
   If he is (c)onstant, he is (i)mperturbable; and,
   If he is (i)mperturbable, then he is without (s)orrow.
   But, if any man is without (s)orrow, then he is never extremely (e)lated. Therefore, if a man is (w)ise then he is without (s)orrow; but, at the same time, if a man is (w)ise, then he is never extremely (e)lated.

6. All (a)nimals are (z)oological creatures [*or* If any creature is an (a)nimal, then it is a (z)oological creature].
   All (v)ertebrates are (a)nimals.
   All (m)ammals are (v)ertebrates.
   All (u)ngulates are (m)ammals.
   All (h)orses are (u)ngulates.
   All (r)ace horses are (h)orses.
   Therefore, all (r)ace horses are (z)oological creatures.

7. If a logic teacher completed high school (b)efore the 1960s, and if he has not taken courses in or otherwise kept abreast with "the new (m)ath," then he will probably not be (f)amiliar with set theory. But anyone who is un(f)amiliar with set theory will feel un(p)repared to teach from *Logic: Modern and Traditional*. But anyone who feels thus un(p)repared will not (a)dopt *Logic: Modern and Traditional* as a textbook. Therefore, if any teacher (a)dopts *Logic: Modern and Traditional* as a textbook, that teacher will probably be someone who did not complete high school (b)efore the 1960s or someone who has kept abreast with "the new (m)ath."

8. The human (s)oul is a thing whose activity is (t)hinking. A thing whose activity is (t)hinking is one whose activity is (i)mmediately apprehended, and without any representation of parts therein. A thing whose activity is (i)mmediately apprehended without any representation of parts therein is a thing whose activity does not contain (p)arts. A thing whose activity does not contain (p)arts is not a (b)ody. What is not a (b)ody is not in (sp)ace. What is not in (sp)ace is not affected by (m)otion. What is not affected by (m)otion is (w)ithout beginning or end. What is (w)ithout beginning or end is (im)mortal. Therefore, the human (s)oul is (im)mortal. (Adapted and abbreviated from Leibniz, *Monadology*, 1714.)

It should be noted that the eight chain arguments in exercise 4.1A merely represent an extension of the hypothetical syllogism. In contrast, as we shall soon explain, the extended arguments of modern logic combine a variety of argument forms into a single extended argument.

Among the laws most used in modern logic are a few which were never formally stated as laws of logic until the nineteenth century, after the wedge ($\vee$), the dot ($\cdot$), and the tilde ($\sim$) became part of mathematics and logic. Stated as formal rules or laws, SIMP (Simplification) and ADD (Addition) make usable what are contained in the meanings of the dot and the wedge. SIMP states that the dot is contractive. ADD states that the wedge is expansive.

Two New Laws of Logic:	*Simplification*	*Addition*
	SIMP: $p \cdot q \mid \therefore p$	ADD: $p \mid \therefore p \vee q$
Related tautologous conditionals:		
Truth Values:	$p \cdot q \to p$ $TFFF \ \ TTFF$	$p \to p \vee q$ $TTFF \ \ \ \ TTTF$
Associated Sets:	$P \cdot Q \subset P$	$P \subset P \vee Q$

(For a Venn Diagram, see figure 12 at the beginning of section 2.3)

These two laws are so obviously tautological that they are seldom heard in ordinary speech. Who would say "All Brown Apples are Brown" or "If this object is (b)rown and if it is an (a)pple, then it is (b)rown" ($b \cdot a \to b$)? And who would say "All Apples are either Apples or Bananas" or "If this is an Apple, then it is either an Apple or a Banana" ($a \to a \vee b$)? Nevertheless, these two tautologous conditionals are extremely important in modern logic. Here are their truth tables:

Rules of Inference:		1. ADD (Addition)			2. SIMP (Simplification)					
Related Tautological Conditionals:										
Guide										
Case p q		p	$\to$	$(p \vee q)$	2A. $(p \cdot q)$	$\to$	p	2B. $(p \leftrightarrow q)$	$\to$	$(p \to q)$
1	T T	T	T	T	T	T	T	T	T	T
2	T F	T	T	T	F	T	T	F	T	F
3	F T	F	T	T	F	T	F	F	T	T
4	F F	F	T	F	F	T	F	T	T	T
Steps: 1	1	2	4	3	3	4	2	3	4	3
Truth Values:		$TTFF$	$\to$	$TTTF$	$TFFF$	$\to$	$TTFF$	$TFTF$	$\to$	$TFTT$

A third law, *Conjunction* (abbreviation: CONJ), says this: given a premise p as *true*, and given another premise q as *true*, then the two premises may be conjoined to form $p \cdot q$, which will also be *true*. It should be remembered that the premises of any complex argument consist of the conjunction of the several individual premises. Conjunction (CONJ) merely states this fact as a *law*.

Even as modern chemistry breaks down various compounds into their component elements, and then recombines them in new and varied ways, so modern logic uses Simplification to break down conjunctions, and then uses Conjunction and Addition to construct new and varied logical compounds. Thus these three laws are very important in discursive reasoning.

In order to use discursive reasoning, it is necessary to introduce a new format—a new way of structuring extended arguments. This format consists of a vertical series of steps of proof.

For example, suppose we are given the single premise $p \to q$; and are to decide whether or not the conclusion $\sim(p \cdot \sim q)$ may validly be derived from that premise. Listed below, on the left side of the page, is a series of steps of proof. To the right of each step is an explanation of what the symbols mean.

1. $p \to q \mid \therefore \ \sim(p \cdot \sim q)$ *Meaning.* On the left, "1" means that this is the first step, and that "$p \to q$" is the initial premise. In the middle, "/" shows that this is the last premise

of this argument. To the right, "∴" signifies "therefore," and ~(p · ~q) is the conclusion we are to try to prove.

2. ~p ∨ q   1, CE   *Meaning.* To the far left, "2. ~p ∨ q" is the second step in our reasoning. Moving to the right, "1, CE" means "From premise 1, using CE (the definition of conditional equivalence)," we may validly derive "~p ∨ q." Since we are thus assured that "~p ∨ q" is true, we may use "~p ∨ q" in later steps of the proof.

3. ~(p · ~q) 2, DeM   *Meaning.* "3. ~(p · ~q)" says that we have derived "~(p · ~q)." How? "2, DeM" indicates that we derived it from the second premise "2" by using a DeMorgan law "DeM."
                             Since "~(p · ~q)" was the formula sought in "/ ∴ ~(p · ~q)," our proof is now completed.

One cannot learn to swim without getting into the water, nor can one learn to employ discursive reasoning without working on specific problems. Nevertheless, the following general suggestions may be helpful.

First, locate the conclusion of the argument.

Next, analyze the argument to see in which premise or premises this conclusion is to be found.

Finally, devise a plan, even though only a tentative one, for "unlocking" the elements required in the conclusion.

Here are three examples:

Example A:
1. (a ∨ b) · (f → g)
2. (~b → ~g) · (a · k) | ∴ f → b
3. f → g   1, SIMP   Since f is in the conclusion, we separate "f → g" from premise 1.

4. ~b → ~g   2, SIMP   Since b is in the conclusion we now separate ~b → ~g from premise 2.

5. g → b   4, COPO   This transformation of premise 4 changes ~b to b and ~g to g, and makes step 6 possible.

6. f → b   3, 5, HS   "3, 5, HS" means "Apply the law of HS to premises 3 and 5." This completes the proof.

Example B:
1. ~(k · ~m)
2. ~m ∨ w | ∴ k → w   First, note that the conclusion "k → w" requires that we use both premises.

3. ~k ∨ m   1, DeM   The form ~(k · ~m) is not usable, until unlocked by the use of DeM.

4. k → m   3, CE   In the hope that HS may be possible, we apply CE to premise 3.

5. m → w   2, CE   Similarly with premise 2.
6. k → w   4, 5, HS   Now apply HS to the conjunction of premises 4 and 5, and we have reached our goal.

Example C:
1. ~a → a
2. ~b → ~a | ∴ b   *Plan:* To get at b, we'll first need some way to get at "a" in premise 2.
3. a ∨ a   1, CE   Since a is in premise 1, we begin here.

4. a	3, TAUT	Now we have the single element a.
5. b	2, 4, MT	We can now deny the consequent of premise 2 by conjoining it to premise 4.

Exercise 4.1B.   Elementary Discursive Reasoning

Directions: Every problem in this exercise is a valid argument. You are to fill in the blank spaces needed to complete the proofs. *Note:* Problems 1–4 use only three laws: SIMP: $p \cdot q \mid \therefore p$; ADD: $p \mid \therefore p \lor q$; and CONJ: Give p as a premise, and given q as another, p and q may be conjoined to form $p \cdot q$.

(1) 1. $p \cdot q \mid \therefore p \lor q$
    2. p 1, _____
    3. $p \lor q$ 2, _____

(2) 1. $a \cdot b \mid \therefore b \cdot a$
    2. a 1, _____
    3. b 1, _____
    4. $b \cdot a$ 2, 3, _____

(3) 1. $d \cdot f \mid \therefore (d \lor g) \cdot f$
    2. d 1, _____
    3. $d \lor g$ 2, _____
    4. f 1, _____
    5. $(d \lor g) \cdot f$ 3, 4, _____

(4) 1. $m \cdot (k \cdot w) \mid \therefore k \cdot (m \cdot w)$
    2. $k \cdot w$ 1, _____
    3. k 2, _____
    4. m 1, _____
    5. w 2, _____
    6. $(m \cdot w)$ 4, 5, _____
    7. $k \cdot (m \cdot w)$ 3, 6, _____

Note: In addition to SIMP, ADD, and CONJ, problems 5–12 employ:
   MP (Modus Ponens: affirming the antecedent): $(p \to q) \cdot p \mid \therefore q$;
   MT (Modus Tollens: denying the consequent): $(p \to q) \cdot {\sim}q \mid \therefore {\sim}p$; and
   DS (Disjunctive Syllogism: eliminating one alternant): $(p \lor q) \cdot {\sim}p \mid \therefore q$
The remaining problems each have two or more premises.

(5) 1. $p \cdot q$
    2. $(p \lor r) \to x \mid \therefore x$
    3. p 1, _____
    4. $p \lor r$ 3, _____
    5. x 2, 4, _____

(6) 1. $a \to b$
    2. ${\sim}b \cdot f \mid \therefore {\sim}a \lor g$
    3. ${\sim}b$ _____, SIMP
    4. ${\sim}a$ 1, 3, _____
    5. ${\sim}a \lor g$ _____, ADD

(7) 1. $h \to m$
    2. $r \lor {\sim}m$
    3. $h \cdot k \mid \therefore r \lor w$
    4. h _____, SIMP
    5. m _____, _____, MP
    6. r 2,   5, _____
    7. $r \lor w$ 6, _____

(8) 1. $(w \lor x) \cdot (y \lor z) \cdot (w \to z)$
    2. $w \to y$
    3. ${\sim}y \mid \therefore x$
    4. ${\sim}w$ _____, _____, MT
    5. $w \lor x$ _____, SIMP
    6. x _____, _____, DS

(9) 1. $b \to {\sim}f$
    2. $b \cdot a \cdot g \cdot (g \to {\sim}k)$
    3. $({\sim}f \cdot {\sim}k) \to m \mid \therefore {\sim}f \cdot {\sim}k$
    4. b 2, _____
    5. _____   1, 4, MP
    6. $g \cdot (g \to {\sim}k)$ 2, _____
    7. _____   6, MP
    8. ${\sim}f \cdot {\sim}k$ 5, 7, _____

(10) 1. $m \lor w \to x$
    2. $x \lor m \to [{\sim}m \lor (y \cdot z)]$
    3. $m \mid \therefore y \cdot z$
    4. $m \lor w$ 3, _____,
    5. _____   1, 4, MP
    6. $x \lor m$ _____, _____
    7. ${\sim}m \lor (y \cdot z)$ _____, _____, _____
    8. $y \cdot z$ _____, _____, _____

(11) 1. $h \to (k \to m)$
    2. ${\sim}m \cdot h \mid \therefore {\sim}k$
    3. h _____, _____
    4. _____   1, 3, MP
    5. ${\sim}m$ _____, _____
    6. _____   4, 5, _____

(12) 1. $p \to q$
    2. ${\sim}q \lor z$
    3. ${\sim}z \mid \therefore {\sim}p$
    4. ${\sim}q$ _____, _____, _____
    5. _____   _____, _____, _____

Suggestion: Before continuing with this exercise, read the directions for part II of exercise 4.1D, then apply those directions to problems 5–12 of this exercise.
Note: In addition to SIMP, ADD, CONJ, MP, MT, and DS, problems 13–20 use:
HS (Hypothetical Syllogism): $(p \to q) \cdot (q \to r) \mid \therefore p \to r$
COM (Commutation): $p \lor q = q \lor p$; $p \cdot q = q \cdot p$
ASSOC (Association): $p \lor (q \lor r) = (p \lor q) \lor r$; $p \cdot (q \cdot r) = (p \cdot q) \cdot r$

CE (Conditional Equivalence): $p \to q = \sim p \lor q$
DeM (DeMorgan): $\sim(p \lor q) = \sim p \cdot \sim q$; $\quad \sim(p \cdot q) = \sim p \lor \sim q$
COPO (Contraposition): $p \to q = \sim q \to \sim p$
TAUT (Tautology): $p \lor p = p$; $\quad p \cdot p = p$.

(13) 1. $a \lor (d \to f)$
  2. $\sim(a \lor f) \mid \therefore \sim d \lor m$
  3. _____   2, DeM
  4. _____   3, SIMP
  5. $d \to f$ ____, ____, ____
  6. $\sim f$ 3, _____
  7. _____   5, 6, _____
  8. $\sim d \lor m$ ____, _____

(14) 1. $x \to y$
  2. $(\sim y \lor z) \cdot (y \to w)$
  3. $\sim z \mid \therefore x \to p$
  4. $\sim y \lor z$ _____, _____
  5. _____   ____, ____, ____
  6. $\sim x$ 1, 5, _____
  7. _____   6, ADD
  8. $x \to p$ 7, CE

(15) 1. $w \to [(y \cdot \sim z) \cdot x]$
  2. $m \cdot w \mid \therefore m \cdot \sim z$
  3. m ____, ____
  4. w ____, ____
  5. _____   ____, ____, MP
  6. $(x \cdot y) \cdot \sim z$ ____, ____
  7. _____   _____, ____
  8. _____   _____, ____

(16) 1. $(k \lor m) \to p$
  2. $\sim(p \cdot q)$
  3. $q \mid \therefore \sim k$
  4. _____   2, DeM
  5. _____   3, 4, _____
  6. _____   1, 5, MT
  7. $\sim k \cdot \sim m$ ____, _____
  8. $\sim k$ ____, _____

(17) 1. $p \to q$
  2. $\sim(r \cdot s)$
  3. $p \lor s$
  4. $\sim q \mid \therefore \sim k \to \sim r$
  5. _____   1, 4, _____
  6. s 3, ___, _____
  7. _____   2, _____
  8. $\sim r$ 6, 7, _____
  9. $\sim r \lor k$ ____, _____
  10. $k \lor \sim r$ ____, _____
  11. $\sim k \to \sim r$ ____, _____

(18) 1. $a \to \sim d$
  2. $\sim b \to f$
  3. $(f \cdot g) \to d$
  4. $\sim(\sim a \lor b) \mid \therefore g \to \sim f$
  5. _____   4, _____
  6. a 5, _____
  7. $\sim d$ ____, _____
  8. $\sim(f \cdot g)$ 3, 7, _____
  9. _____   8, _____
  10. $f \to \sim g$ 9, _____
  11. $g \to \sim f$ 10, _____

(19) 1. $k \to \sim k$
  2. $\sim b \to b$
  3. $\sim f \lor k \mid \therefore \sim f \cdot b$
  4. $b \lor b$ ____, _____
  5. _____   4, TAUT
  6. _____   1, _____
  7. $\sim k$ 6, _____
  8. $\sim f$ ___, ___, _____
  9. _____   ___, ___, _____

(20) 1. $(g \lor k) \cdot \sim(m \cdot w)$
  2. $\sim h \lor m$
  3. $w \mid \therefore \sim h \cdot (h \to k)$
  4. $\sim(m \cdot w)$ ____, ____
  5. _____   4, ____
  6. $\sim m$ ____, ____, DS
  7. _____   2, ____, DS
  8. $\sim h \lor k$ ____, ____, _____
  9. _____   _____, ____
  10. _____   _____, ____

Exercise 4.1C. Some Techniques of Discursive Reasoning

Directions: In the answer blanks, fill in (a) the number of the line (or numbers of the two lines) which furnish the basis of the inference (e.g., 1; 1, 2; 1, 3; 2, 3); and (b) the law of logic (rule of inference) used. In each problem, the last three lines are left entirely to the student.

Remarks: Problems (1), (2), and (3) review SIMP, ADD, CONJ, MP, MT, and DS.

(1) 1. $a \to b$
  2. $f \cdot \sim b \mid \therefore (f \cdot \sim a) \lor k$
  3. $\sim b$ ____, _____
  4. $\sim a$ ___, ___, _____
  5.   ___, ___, _____
  6.   ____, _____
  7.   ____, _____

(2) 1. $(h \to x) \cdot g$
  2. $\sim g \lor h \mid \therefore (x \cdot h) \lor m$
  3. g ____, _____
  4. h ___, ___, _____
  5. $h \to x$ ___, ___, _____
  6.   ____, _____
  7.   ____, _____
  8.   ____, _____

Note: Problems (3) and (4) also require the use of DeM and CE.

(3) 1. $a \lor b \to f$
    2. $f \to \sim k$
    3. $\sim k \lor \sim q \to w$
    4. $\sim w \mid \therefore \sim a \cdot \sim b$
    5. $\sim(\sim k \lor \sim q)$ —, —, —
    6. $k \cdot q$ —, —
    7. k —, —
    8. ————
    9. ————
    10. ——

(4) 1. $\sim(s \to \sim m) \to p$
    2. $(\sim p \to q) \to k$
    3. $s \cdot m \mid \therefore k$
    4. $\sim(\sim s \lor \sim m)$ —, —
    5. $\sim(s \to \sim m)$ —, —
    6. p —, —, —
    7. ————
    8. ————
    9. ————

Note: Problems (5) and (6) also require the use of TAUT, ASSOC, HS, and COPO. These and other laws are listed on the back inside cover of this book.

(5) 1. $f \to g$
    2. $\sim(h \cdot f)$
    3. $\sim g \lor h \mid \therefore f \to k$
    4. $g \to h$ —, —
    5. $f \to h$ —, —, —
    6. $\sim h \lor \sim f$ —, —
    7. $h \to \sim f$ —, —
    8. $f \to \sim f$ —, —, —
    9. $\sim f \lor \sim f$ —, —
    10. ————
    11. ————
    12. ————

(6) 1. $\sim p \lor (g \lor d)$
    2. $(\sim k \to g) \to m$
    3. $\sim d \cdot p \mid \therefore m \cdot g$
    4. $\sim(d \lor \sim p)$ —, —
    5. $(d \lor \sim p) \lor g$ —, —
    6. g —, —, —
    7. $g \lor k$ —, —
    8. $\sim g \to k$ —, —
    9. ————
    10. ————
    11. ————

Note: Problems (7) and (8) also require the use of DIST and BE.

(7) 1. $(y \cdot z) \lor k$
    2. $\sim z \cdot m \mid \therefore k \cdot m$
    3. $(y \lor k) \cdot (z \lor k)$ —, —
    4. $z \lor k$ —, —
    5. $\sim z$ —, —
    6. k —, —
    7. ————
    8. ————

(8) 1. $f \leftrightarrow g$
    2. $h \to \sim g \mid \therefore \sim(f \cdot h)$
    3. $(f \to g) \cdot (g \to f)$ —, —
    4. $f \to g$ —, —
    5. $g \to \sim h$ —, —
    6. ————
    7. ————
    8. ————

Exercise 4.1D.   Recognizing Logical Implications

Part I.   Directions: The thirty problems of this exercise consist of the thirty conclusions, listed as (1) through (30). Conclusions (1), (2), and (3) are to be derived, if possible, from premise (A), conclusions (4), (5), and (6) from premise (B), and so on. In the answer column circle only those numbers whose conclusions are valid.

Try to solve each problem mentally; but, if in doubt, copy the premise and its one conclusion as a separate problem, and then solve in the manner shown in exercise 4.1B.

Premises:	Conclusions:			Answers:		
(A) $\sim(a \lor \sim b) \mid \therefore$	(1) $a \cdot b$	(2) $\sim b$	(3) $k \lor b$	(1)	(2)	(3)
(B) $f \cdot (g \to \sim f) \mid \therefore$	(4) $\sim g \lor h$	(5) $\sim f \to h$	(6) $f \cdot \sim g$	(4)	(5)	(6)
(C) $k \leftrightarrow m \mid \therefore$	(7) $\sim m \to \sim k$	(8) $m \lor k$	(9) $m \lor \sim k$	(7)	(8)	(9)
(D) $(p \lor q) \cdot \sim(p \cdot q) \mid \therefore$	(10) $p \leftrightarrow \sim q$	(11) $\sim p \lor \sim q$	(12) $\sim(p \to q)$	(10)	(11)	(12)
(E) $w \lor (y \cdot z) \mid \therefore$	(13) $w \lor z$	(14) $y \cdot z$	(15) w	(13)	(14)	(15)
(F) 1. $a \to b$						
2. $a \to \sim b \mid \therefore$	(16) $\sim a \to a$	(17) $a \to \sim a$	(18) $b \to \sim b$	(16)	(17)	(18)
(G) 1. $f \to g$						
2. $\sim(g \cdot f) \mid \therefore$	(19) $g \to \sim f$	(20) $f \to \sim f$	(21) $\sim(\sim f)$	(19)	(20)	(21)
(H) 1. $h \cdot (k \lor m)$						
2. $\sim m \mid \therefore$	(22) $h \cdot m$	(23) $\sim m \lor \sim h$	(24) $h \cdot k$	(22)	(23)	(24)
(I) 1. $(p \cdot q) \lor (w \cdot y)$						
2. $\sim p \mid \therefore$	(25) q	(26) $\sim q \lor \sim p$	(27) $y \cdot w$	(25)	(26)	(27)
(J) 1. $a \lor b \to \sim f \cdot g$						
2. $g \to f \mid \therefore$	(28) f	(29) $\sim a \cdot \sim b$	(30) $\sim[\sim(\sim b)]$	(28)	(29)	(30)

Part II.   Directions: On separate paper, copy a minimum of twelve problems from exercises 4.1B and/or 4.1C, in each case stopping where the conclusion first appears. Then "on your own" solve each problem. In some cases, your proof may differ from the one given in the text.

Part II of exercise 4.1D is the most difficult and the most important exercise in chapter 4. It is recommended that the student first apply these directions to problems 5–12 of exercise 4.1B on page 115; then move on to the more difficult problems on pages 116 and 117.

Exercise 4.1E.   Applying Rules of Inference to Verbal Arguments

Directions: The directions for this exercise are the same as for 4.1B except that (a) each argument should first be put into symbolic form, and (b) the last three arguments are invalid. *Note:* It is possible to solve some of these problems in more than one way.

1. If he uses (w)orms, then, if perch are (b)iting, he will get a (s)tringer of fish. He uses (w)orms, but he does not get a (s)tringer of fish. Therefore, the perch are not (b)iting.
2. If either (E)verett or (M)arvin go on the picnic then (D)onald will go. If (E)verett stays at home (that is, doesn't go), then (M)arvin will definitely go. Therefore, (D)onald will surely go on the picnic.
3. If Pete does not (p)rotest, Arch will be (a)dmitted into the fraternity. If Arch is (a)dmitted, then Milton will not be the (m)aster of ceremonies at the homecoming banquet. But [everyone agrees that] either Milton will be the (m)aster of ceremonies at that banquet, or the annual homecoming banquet will be (b)elow standard. Well, we attended that banquet, and nothing about it was (b)elow standard. So, Pete must have (p)rotested.
4. If thought is based on (s)ensation, then it is not completely understandable in terms of (i)ntrospection. But all thought is based on (e)xperience. And anything based on (e)xperience is also based on (s)ensation. Therefore, thought is not completely understandable in terms of (i)ntrospection.
5. Either both (G)ary and (L)en like tea, or (W)illiam and (T)om both like milk. But (G)ary does not like tea. Therefore, (T)om likes milk.
6. It cannot be the case either that this student has a (h)igh I.Q. or that he (w)orks hard. But if he is (a)lert, he (w)orks hard. So, he is not (a)lert.
7. Either Jim holds onto his (j)ob, or he won't (b)uy the car. But if he either (r)eturns home or doesn't (b)uy the car, he would surely have (p)aid this bill. Now we know this bill has not been (p)aid. Therefore, Jim must be holding onto his (j)ob.
8. Either Sam will get a (r)aise in salary or he won't (b)uy the Buick. But if his company makes no (p)rofit, Sam won't get a (r)aise in salary. But his company is not making a (p)rofit. Therefore, Sam won't (b)uy the Buick.
9. If Jim studied (p)sychology he would have become (a)ntisocial, and if he had studied (m)ath he would have become (b)ored. If he is either (a)ntisocial or (b)ored, he would not be a (f)raternity officer. Well, he is not a (f)raternity officer. Therefore, he did not study either (p)sychology or (m)ath.
10. If Sam is a (s)urgeon, then he must be a (d)octor. Furthermore, if he's a (s)urgeon, he must have (p)assed his state examinations. But he never (p)assed these examinations. So, he cannot be either a (s)urgeon or a (d)octor.

4.2   Logic as a Form of Boolean Algebra

The distinctive feature of modern logic is that it concentrates on the truth values of statements. Only indirectly, as we shall see in chapter 6, does it deal with categorical statements about events in the world of everyday experience. "Logic as a Form of Boolean Algebra," then, refers only to truth-value logic. Hence, to structure such a logic, we must formalize some basic *truth value rules.* We do this by adapting patterns developed by Cantor, Frege, Whitehead,

Russell, Hilbert, and many others who have built systems of logic around the three connectives: Disjunction ($\vee$), Conjunction ($\cdot$), and Complementation ($\sim$). If we let A signify any set; U the universal set; and $\varnothing$ the null set, then the meanings of the wedge ($\vee$), the dot ($\cdot$) and the tilde ($\sim$) are formalized in the following *rules of set theory*:

$$\sim\varnothing = U; \quad A \vee U = U; \quad A \vee \varnothing = A; \quad U \vee \varnothing = U;$$
$$\sim U = \varnothing; \quad A \cdot U = A; \quad A \cdot \varnothing = \varnothing; \quad U \cdot \varnothing = \varnothing.$$

Note the isomorphism of the above rules with (i.e., note the one-to-one correspondence of the several elements of) the following *Truth Value Rules*:

$$\sim F = T; \quad p \vee T = T; \quad p \vee F = p; \quad T \vee F = T;$$
$$\sim T = F; \quad p \cdot T = p; \quad p \cdot F = F; \quad T \cdot T = F.$$

Since we are here dealing exclusively with *statement forms*, we use T to signify any statement which is true because of its *form*. In this formal context, T signifies any tautologous statement form. Similarly, we use F to signify any statement which is necessarily false because of its *form*, i.e., any self-contradictory form. The advantages of including these TV rules among our laws of logic will become evident as we proceed.

LOGIC AS A SYSTEM. Every demonstration necessarily rests on unde-monstrable principles, otherwise the steps of demonstration would be endless. Hence every axiomatic system must begin with a few rules of procedure; some undefined terms; plus a few definitions and *axioms* (postulates). From these, following the model of Euclidean geometry, other *theorems* are demonstrated.

Below are the four most basic axioms of the Hilbert-Ackermann system,[1] which is a modification of the five axioms used in the *Principia Mathematica* of Russell and Whitehead. Note that each of these axioms may be stated in more than one way, depending upon which operators are taken to be primitive or undefined. Axioms IA—IVA express these four axioms in terms of the wedge ($\vee$) and the arrow ($\rightarrow$); axioms IB—IVB express the same four axioms but use the wedge ($\vee$) and the tilde ($\sim$) as undefined primitive operators:

IA. $p \vee p \rightarrow p$
IIA. $p \rightarrow p \vee q$
IIIA. $p \vee q \rightarrow q \vee p$
IVA. $(p \rightarrow q) \rightarrow [(r \vee p) \rightarrow (r \vee q)]$
IB. $\sim(p \vee p) \vee p$
IIB. $\sim p \vee p \vee q$
IIIB. $\sim(p \vee q) \vee q \vee p$
IVB. $\sim(\sim p \vee q) \vee \sim(r \vee p) \vee (r \vee q)$

It will be seen that Axiom I is the law of TAUTology; II is the law of ADDition; and III is the law of COMmutation. The fourth axiom is suffi-ciently complex to permit numerous substitutions (hence to permit numerous

[1] David Hilbert and W. Ackermann, *Principles of Mathematical Logic* (German editions, 1928 and 1938), trans. R. E. Luce et al. (New York: Chelsea, 1950), p. 27. Slightly adapted. For an excellent account of the historical development of modern logic, read Howard DeLong, *A Profile of Mathematical Logic* (Reading, Mass.: Addison-Wesley, 1970).

Although the study of axiomatic systems is generally introduced later in a logic course, we introduce it here because the proofs in sec. 4.2 review and thus help students understand the laws studied in sec. 4.1.

derivations). Thus the seeming "simplicity" gained by having only four, rather than more, basic axioms is achieved by including an axiom which is far less simple than several of the laws of logic employed in set theory. It becomes a matter of taste, therefore, as to whether one prefers an axiomatic system having a very small number of primitive axioms, some of which (e.g., IV above) are relatively complex; or whether one prefers a system having a larger number of primitive axioms, all of which are relatively simple.

The second option is employed in the following five axioms of Boolean algebra by Sikorski.[2] These five axioms consist of five laws that are familiar to every student of elementary set theory. The expression of these five axioms in symbolic form assumes a knowledge of the three connectives ($\vee$, $\cdot$, and $\sim$), the symbols A, B, C, U, ( ), and $=$, and the various rules of punctuation.

Sikorski:

Axioms	Dual Form of Axiom	Name of Law
A1: $A \vee B = B \vee A$	$A \cdot B = B \cdot A$	COMmutation
A2: $A \vee (B \vee C)$	$A \cdot (B \cdot C)$	
$\quad = (A \vee B) \vee C$	$\quad = (A \cdot B) \cdot C$	ASSOCiation
A3: $A \cdot (B \vee C)$	$A \vee (B \cdot C)$	
$\quad = (A \cdot B) \vee (A \cdot C)$	$\quad = (A \vee B) \cdot (A \vee C)$	DISTribution
A4: $(A \cdot B) \vee B = B$	$(A \vee B) \cdot B = B$	ABSorption
A5: $(A \cdot \sim A) \vee B = B$	$(A \vee \sim A) \cdot B = B$	Rules for using the wedge ($\vee$), the dot ($\cdot$), and the tilde ($\sim$).

In this book, we adapt these five Sikorski axioms for Boolean algebra to fit the needs of truth-value logic. Our first three axioms are the same as the first three of Sikorski. However, for Sikorski's fourth and fifth axioms, we shall substitute the following:

Our fourth axiom consists of the Law of Excluded Middle (ExM). This axiom and its dual form were discussed in section 1.2.

Our fifth axiom consists of a group of rules regulating the use of, or defining the meaning of T, F, p, q, r, $\vee$, $\cdot$, and $\sim$.

It will be noted that our fifth axiom substitutes T for Sikorski's $(A \vee \sim A)$; substitutes F for Sikorski's $(A \cdot \sim A)$; and includes what in some systems are listed, not as axioms, but as rules of procedure.

Here, then, are the *Five Basic Axioms* of our system. Note that each of these axioms has a dual form, and that all ten of them are usable laws of logic.

Truth-Value Logic

Five Axioms	Dual Form of Axiom	Name of Law
A1: $p \vee q = q \vee p$	$p \cdot q = q \cdot p$	COM (Commutation)
A2: $p \vee (q \vee r)$	$p \cdot (q \cdot r)$	
$\quad = (p \vee q) \vee r$	$\quad = (p \cdot q) \cdot r$	ASSOC (Association)
A3: $p \cdot (q \vee r)$	$p \vee (q \cdot r)$	
$\quad = (p \cdot q) \vee (p \cdot r)$	$\quad = (p \vee q) \cdot (p \vee r)$	DIST (Distribution)

---

[2] Slightly adapted from Roman Sikorski, *Boolean Algebras*, 3rd ed. (Berlin and New York: Springer-Verlag, 1971), p. 1. For a relatively easy explanation of the nature of axiomatic systems, read J. G. Brennan, *A Handbook of Logic* (New York: Harper & Row, 1957, 1961), pp. 126–72. For more advanced treatments, read Benson Mates, *Elementary Logic* (New York: Oxford University Press, 1971), chap. 11; or Hughes Leblanc and William A. Wisdom, *Deductive Logic* (Boston: Allyn and Bacon, 1972), pp. 239–344.

For a brief and clearly written exposition of the view that the basic axioms of formal logic ultimately rest on experience, and not on some completely nonempirical "intuition," read N. A. Court, "Plane Geometry and Plain Logic," *Scientific Monthly* 83 (July 1956): 28–34.

A4: $p \lor \sim p = T$ $p \cdot \sim p = F$ ExM (Excluded Middle)
A5: $T \lor F = T;$ $T \cdot F = F;$ TV (Truth Value Rules)
     $p \lor T = T;$ $p \cdot T = p;$ $\sim T = F$
     $p \lor F = p;$ $p \cdot F = F;$ $\sim F = T$

From these five axioms, as we shall now see, all the other laws of truth-value logic may be derived. Once derived, each new law—or if using Euclidean terminology, each new theorem—may be used as an additional law. This process could go on interminably, but in exercise 4.2A we shall derive only those laws that are used in this book. In this next exercise students are to enter into the game of deriving theorems from axioms. The game progresses as we employ these newly derived theorems to derive still other theorems. When the game has ended, we will have derived all of the theorems, i.e., all of the laws of truth-value logic, that are used in this book.

Exercise 4.2A. Deriving Theorems of Logic

Directions: This exercise consists of the step-by-step derivation of the most basic laws of logic. Answers are given for the odd-numbered problems—which should be studied carefully. You are to fill in the laws of logic used in the proofs for the even-numbered problems. Note that the first two proofs use only the five basic axioms—the five laws of logic listed above, namely, COM, ASSOC, DIST, ExM, and TV.

(6) and (7): TAUT (Tautology—sometimes called Idempotency, or Redundancy)

(6) $p \lor p = p$
   1. $p \lor p \mid \therefore p$
   2. $(p \lor p) \cdot T$ 1, _____
   3. $(p \lor p) \cdot (p \lor \sim p)$ 2, _____
   4. $p \lor (p \cdot \sim p)$ 3, _____
   5. $p \lor F$ 4, _____
   6. p 5, _____

(7) $p \cdot p = p$
   1. $p \cdot p \mid \therefore p$
   2. $(p \cdot p) \lor F$ 1, TV
   3. $(p \cdot p) \lor (p \cdot \sim p)$ 2, ExM
   4. $p \cdot (p \lor \sim p)$ 3, DIST
   5. $p \cdot T$ 4, ExM
   6. p 5, TV

In (6) and (7) we have established the dual forms of the law of Tautology (TAUT). So now we add TAUT to COM, ASSOC, DIST, ExM, and TV as an added "tool of reasoning" and we are free to employ TAUT in the proofs which follow.

Observe that in modern logic TAUT is stated in terms of the wedge and the dot; but that, except for the manner in which it is expressed, it is a reaffirmation of what Aristotle called the Law of Identity ($A = A$). In defense of Aristotle, it should be realized that the law of identity (or the laws of tautology), although not *explicitly* stated as an axiom, was *implicit* in the above five axioms. If this were not so, we could not say that Axiom 1 (COMmutation) was the same COM we studied earlier in chapters 1 and 2; and we could not say that TAUT as expressed here is the "same" as TAUT on other pages of this book—or of other books.

The Laws of Absorption. These laws are an integral part of Boolean algebra, and since our five basic postulates are a modification of those used in Sikorski's *Boolean Algebras*, we include them here. However, because some logic books give the name "absorption" to an altogether different law—one we will explain on page 138—we will not employ the laws of absorption in this book.

ABS: *The Laws of Absorption*
   (8) $p \lor (p \cdot q) = p$
     1. $p \lor (p \cdot q) \mid \therefore p$
     2. $(p \cdot T) \lor (p \cdot q)$ 1, _____

ABS (*Dual Form*):
   (9) $p \cdot (p \lor q) = p$
     1. $p \cdot (p \lor q) \mid \therefore p$
     2. $(p \lor F) \cdot (p \lor q)$ 1, TV

3. $[p \cdot (q \vee \sim q)] \vee (p \cdot q)$ 2, _____
4. $[(p \cdot q) \vee (p \cdot \sim q)] \vee$
   $(p \cdot q)$ 3, _____
5. $[(p \cdot q) \vee (p \cdot q)] \vee$
   $(p \cdot \sim q)$ 4, _____
6. $(p \cdot q) \vee (p \cdot \sim q)$ 5, _____
7. $p \cdot (q \vee \sim q)$ 6, _____
8. $p \cdot T$ 7, _____
9. p 8, _____

3. $[p \vee (q \cdot \sim q)] \cdot (p \vee q)$ 2, ExM
4. $[(p \vee q) \cdot (p \vee \sim q)] \cdot$
   $(p \vee q)$ 3, DIST
5. $[(p \vee q) \cdot (p \vee q)] \cdot$
   $(p \vee \sim q)$ 4, ASSOC
6. $(p \vee q) \cdot (p \vee \sim q)$ 5, TAUT
7. $p \vee (q \cdot \sim q)$ 6, DIST
8. $p \vee F$ 7, ExM
9. p 8, TV

DeM: The DeMorgan Laws

Problems (10) and (11) constitute the proof of the DeMorgan laws—perhaps the most important laws of modern logic. Problem (10) is part A, and problem (11) is part B of what combines to form a single proof. Since part A shows that $(p \cdot q) \cdot (\sim p \vee \sim q) = F$, and part B shows that $(p \cdot q) \vee (\sim p \vee \sim q) = T$, and since F and T have complementary sets of truth values, the DeMorgan laws follow immediately, namely, that:

$$(p \cdot q) = \sim(\sim p \vee \sim q), \text{ and, by substitution, that}$$
$$(p \vee q) = \sim(\sim p \cdot \sim q)$$

(10) DeMorgan (Part A of proof)

1. $(p \cdot q) \cdot (\sim p \vee \sim q) \;/\; \therefore \; F$
2. $[(p \cdot q) \cdot \sim p] \vee [(p \cdot q) \cdot \sim q]$ 1, _____
3. $[\sim p \cdot (p \cdot q)] \vee [(p \cdot q) \cdot \sim q]$ 2, _____
4. $[(\sim p \cdot p) \cdot q] \vee [p \cdot (q \cdot \sim q)]$ 3, _____
5. $[F \cdot q] \vee [p \cdot F]$ 4, _____
6. $F \vee F$ 5, _____
7. F 6, _____

(11) DeMorgan (Part B of proof)

1. $(p \cdot q) \vee (\sim p \vee \sim q) \;/\; \therefore \; T$
2. $[p \vee (\sim p \vee \sim q)] \cdot [q \vee (\sim p \vee \sim q)]$ 1, DIST
3. $[(p \vee \sim p) \vee \sim q] \cdot [q \vee (\sim q \vee \sim p)]$ 2, COM, ASSOC
4. $[(p \vee \sim p) \vee \sim q] \cdot [(q \vee \sim q) \vee \sim p]$ 3, ASSOC
5. $[T \vee \sim q] \cdot [T \vee \sim p]$ 4, ExM (twice)
6. $T \cdot T$ 5, TV (twice)
7. T 6, TAUT

Each step in every proof for problems 6–11 was based on a tautologous biconditional. Since biconditionals are commutative, this means that every proof in problems 6–11 could be done in reverse order. Problems (12) and (13) illustrate how this is done.

DN (*Double Negation*). Observe that only two laws (DeM and TAUT) are needed for these proofs.

(12) $p = \sim(\sim p)$
   1. $p \;/\; \therefore \; \sim(\sim p)$
   2. $p \cdot p$ 1, _____
   3. $\sim(\sim p \vee \sim p)$ 2, _____
   4. $\sim(\sim p)$ 3, _____

(13) $\sim(\sim p) = p$
   1. $\sim(\sim p) \;/\; \therefore \; p$
   2. $\sim(\sim p \cdot \sim p)$ 1, TAUT
   3. $p \vee p$ 2, DeM
   4. p 3, TAUT

Unlike mathematical forms of Boolean algebra, logic requires rules for transforming the "if . . . then" ($\rightarrow$) and the "if and only if . . . then" ($\leftrightarrow$) of ordinary language into the wedge, the dot and the tilde—the three basic operations of set theory and Boolean algebra. Since conditionals and biconditionals occur in the remaining laws of logic, we now introduce their definitions. Note the use of the equality sign in definitions: every definition is to be treated as a tautological biconditional. These definitions [(14), (15), and (16)] may now be added to our usable kit of "tools for thinking."

Definitions:
(14) CE (Conditional Equivalence): $p \rightarrow q = \sim p \vee q$
(15) BE (Biconditional Equivalence): $p \leftrightarrow q = (p \rightarrow q) \cdot (q \rightarrow p)$
(16) BE (Second Definition): $p \leftrightarrow q = (p \cdot q) \vee (\sim p \cdot \sim q)$

By substitution, BE also serves to symbolize Exclusive Disjunctive equivalence, thus:

$$(p \leftrightarrow \sim q) = (p \rightarrow \sim q) \cdot (\sim q \rightarrow p)$$
$$(p \leftrightarrow \sim q) = (p \cdot \sim q) \cdot [\sim p \cdot \sim(\sim q)]$$

Having defined conditional equivalence (CE) and biconditional equivalence (BE), proofs (17) and (18) employ these definitions to establish two theorems concerning exclusive disjunctive equivalence, or concerning the negation of biconditional equivalence.

(17) Negation of BE

$(p \cdot \sim q) \vee (q \cdot \sim p) = \sim(p \leftrightarrow q)$
1. $(p \cdot \sim q) \vee (q \cdot \sim p) \mid \therefore \sim(p \leftrightarrow q)$
2. $\sim(\sim p \vee q) \vee \sim(\sim q \vee p)$ 1, DeM (twice)
3. $\sim(p \rightarrow q) \vee \sim(q \rightarrow p)$ 2, CE   (twice)
4. $\sim[(p \rightarrow q) \cdot (q \rightarrow p)]$ 3, DeM
5. $\sim(p \leftrightarrow q)$ 4, BE

(18) Exclusive Disjunctive Equivalence

$(p \leftrightarrow \sim q) = (p \vee q) \cdot \sim(p \cdot q)$
1. $p \leftrightarrow \sim q \mid \therefore (p \vee q) \cdot \sim(p \cdot q)$
2. $(p \rightarrow \sim q) \cdot (\sim q \rightarrow p)$ 1, _____
3. $(\sim p \vee \sim q) \cdot (q \vee p)$ 2, _____
4. $\sim(p \cdot q) \cdot (q \vee p)$ 3, _____
5. $(p \vee q) \cdot \sim(p \cdot q)$ 4, _____

Proofs (19), (20), and (21) prove three laws that will be stressed in section 4.3.

(19) CP: (Conditional Proof)
(*or:* The Law of Exportation)

$[(p \cdot q) \rightarrow r] = [p \rightarrow (q \rightarrow r)]$
1. $p \cdot q \rightarrow r \mid \therefore p \rightarrow (q \rightarrow r)$
2. $\sim(p \cdot q) \vee r$ 1, CE
3. $\sim p \vee \sim q \vee r$ 2, DeM
4. $\sim p \vee (\sim q \vee r)$ 3, ASSOC
5. $p \rightarrow (\sim q \vee r)$ 4, CE
6. $p \rightarrow (q \rightarrow r)$ 5, CE

(20) RAA: (Reductio ad Absurdum):
First Form:

$\sim p \rightarrow p = p$
1. $\sim p \rightarrow p \mid \therefore p$
2. $p \vee p$ 1, _____
3. p 2, _____

(21) RAA: Second Form:

$(p \rightarrow q) \cdot (p \rightarrow \sim q) = \sim p$
1. $(p \rightarrow q) \cdot (p \rightarrow \sim q) \mid \therefore \sim p$
2. $(\sim p \vee q) \cdot (\sim p \vee \sim q)$ 1, CE
3. $\sim p \vee (q \cdot \sim q)$ 2, DIST
4. $\sim p \vee F$ 3, ExM
5. $\sim p$ 4, TV

(22) COPO: (Contraposition)
[Also called Transposition (TRANS)]

$(p \rightarrow q) = (\sim q \rightarrow \sim p)$
1. $p \rightarrow q \mid \therefore \sim q \rightarrow \sim p$
2. $\sim p \vee q$ 1, _____
3. $q \vee \sim p$ 2, _____
4. $\sim q \rightarrow \sim p$ 3, _____

DN (Double Negation) Applied to Biconditionals:

(23) $p \leftrightarrow q = (\sim p \leftrightarrow \sim q)$
1. $p \leftrightarrow q \mid \therefore \sim p \leftrightarrow \sim q$
2. $(p \rightarrow q) \cdot (q \rightarrow p)$ 1, BE
3. $(\sim q \rightarrow \sim p) \cdot (\sim p \rightarrow \sim q)$ 2, COPO
4. $\sim q \rightarrow \sim p$ 3, BE
5. $\sim p \leftrightarrow \sim q$ 4, COM

(24) $p \leftrightarrow q = \sim(p \leftrightarrow \sim q)$
1. $p \leftrightarrow q \; / \; \therefore \; \sim(p \leftrightarrow \sim q)$
2. $(p \cdot q) \vee (\sim p \cdot \sim q)$ 1, _____
3. $\sim[\sim(p \cdot q) \cdot \sim(\sim p \cdot \sim q)]$ 2, _____
4. $\sim[(\sim p \vee \sim q) \cdot (p \vee q)]$ 3, _____
5. $\sim[(p \to \sim q) \cdot (\sim p \to q)]$ 4, _____
6. $\sim[(p \to \sim q) \cdot (\sim q \to p)]$ 5, _____
7. $\sim(p \leftrightarrow \sim q)$ 6, _____

We now move to six laws of logic which are *tautologous conditionals*, and which, therefore, are *not commutative*. In each of the following six proofs, it will be shown, by a series of step-by-step inferences, that the *conditional considered in its entirety is equivalent to a tautology*. Since each of these six conditionals (SIMP, ADD, MP, MT, DS, and HS) is equivalent to a tautology, the conditional itself is tautological, and thus a law of logic.

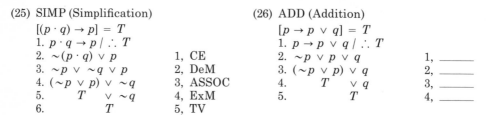

(25) SIMP (Simplification)

$[(p \cdot q) \to p] = T$
1. $p \cdot q \to p \; / \; \therefore \; T$
2. $\sim(p \cdot q) \vee p$ 1, CE
3. $\sim p \vee \sim q \vee p$ 2, DeM
4. $(\sim p \vee p) \vee \sim q$ 3, ASSOC
5. $\quad T \quad \vee \sim q$ 4, ExM
6. $\quad\quad T$ 5, TV

(26) ADD (Addition)

$[p \to p \vee q] = T$
1. $p \to p \vee q \; / \; \therefore \; T$
2. $\sim p \vee p \vee q$ 1, _____
3. $(\sim p \vee p) \vee q$ 2, _____
4. $\quad T \quad \vee q$ 3, _____
5. $\quad\quad T$ 4, _____

CONJ (*Conjunction*). Note the relation of conjunction (CONJ) to SIMP and ASSOC. If the premises of any argument are set up horizontally (rather than vertically), then the premises $p \cdot (q \to s) \cdot r \cdot (r \vee w)$ become by ASSOC: $(p \cdot r) \cdot (q \to s) \cdot (r \vee w)$; and by SIMP: $p \cdot r$, can be derived. However, when premises are arranged vertically, it is customary to call the latter derivation *conjunction*. It is obvious that CONJ is a *rule of procedure*—one which we need not describe here, since it was explained in section 4.1.

(27) MP (Modus Ponens) (Affirming the Antecedent)

$\{[(p \to q) \cdot p] \to q\} = T$
1. $[(p \to q) \cdot p] \to q \; / \; \therefore \; T$
2. $[(\sim p \vee q) \cdot p] \to q$ 1, CE
3. $\sim[(\sim p \vee q) \cdot p] \vee q$ 2, CE
4. $[\sim(\sim p \vee q) \vee \sim p] \vee q$ 3, DeM
5. $[(p \cdot \sim q) \vee \sim p] \vee q$ 4, DeM
6. $[(p \cdot \sim q) \vee (\sim p \vee q)$ 5, ASSOC
7. $(p \cdot \sim q) \vee \sim(p \cdot \sim q)$ 6, DeM
8. $\quad\quad T$ 7, ExM

(28) MT (Modus Tollens) (Denying the Consequent)

$\{[(p \to q) \cdot \sim q] \to \sim p\} = T$
1. $[(p \to q) \cdot \sim q] \to \sim p \; / \; \therefore \; T$
2. $\sim[(p \to q) \cdot \sim q] \vee \sim p$ 1, _____
3. $\sim[(\sim p \vee q) \cdot \sim q] \vee \sim p$ 2, _____
4. $[\sim(\sim p \vee q) \vee q] \vee \sim p$ 3, _____
5. $\sim(\sim p \vee q) \vee (\sim p \vee q)$ 4, _____
6. $\quad\quad T$ 5, _____

Note the economy in steps 4–6 of (28) compared to steps 4–8 of (27). However, both proofs are of equal validity.

Although "$p \lor \sim p$" (ExM) is the most widely used tautology, any other axiom, definition, or law of logic may equally well be replaced by T. Since MP in (27) was shown to be tautological, in step 3 of proof (29): MP $\{[(p \to q) \cdot p] \to q\}$, no less than ExM ($p \lor \sim p$) may be replaced by T, thus completing proof (29).

(29) DS (Disjunctive Syllogism) (Elimination of one Alternant)

$\{[(p \lor q) \cdot \sim p] \to q\} = T$

1. $[(p \lor q) \cdot \sim p] \to q \ / \ \therefore \ T$
2. $[(\sim p \to q) \cdot \sim p] \to q$ 1, CE
3. T 2, MP (as a law of logic).

The usage exemplified by step 2 in proof (29) will not be practiced elsewhere in this book. It is included here simply to illustrate a point.

(30A) HS (Hypothetical Syllogism)

$\{[(p \to q) \cdot (q \to r)] \to (p \to r)\} = T$

1. $(p \to q) \cdot (q \to r) \to (p \to r) \ / \ \therefore \ T$
2. $[(\sim p \lor q) \cdot (\sim q \lor r)] \to (\sim p \lor r)$ 1, _____
3. $\sim[(\sim p \lor q) \cdot (\sim q \lor r)] \lor (\sim p \lor r)$ 2, _____
4. $[\sim(\sim p \lor q) \lor \sim(\sim q \lor r)] \lor (\sim p \lor r)$ 3, _____
5. $[(p \cdot \sim q) \lor (q \cdot \sim r)] \lor (\sim p \lor r)$ 4, _____
6. $[\sim p \lor (p \cdot \sim q)] \lor [r \lor (q \cdot \sim r)]$ 5, _____
7. $[(\sim p \lor p) \cdot (\sim p \lor \sim q)] \lor [(r \lor q) \cdot (r \lor \sim r)]$ 6, _____
8. $[T \cdot (\sim p \lor \sim q)] \lor [(r \lor q) \cdot T]$ 7, _____
9. $(\sim p \lor \sim q) \lor (r \lor q)$ 8, _____
10. $\sim p \lor r \lor (\sim q \lor q)$ 9, _____
11. $\sim p \lor r \lor T$ 10, _____
12. T 11, _____

(30B) HS (Hypothetical Syllogism)

$\{[(p \to q) \cdot (q \to r)] \to (p \to r)\} = T$

1. $[(p \to q) \cdot (q \to r)] \to (p \to r) \ / \ \therefore \ T$
2. $[(p \to q) \cdot (q \to r) \cdot p] \to r$ 1, _____
3. $\{[(p \to q) \cdot p] \cdot (q \to r)\} \to r$ 2, _____
4. $[\quad q \quad \cdot (q \to r)] \to r$ 3, _____
5. $r \quad\quad\quad \to r$ 4, _____
6. $\sim r \quad\quad \lor \quad\quad r$ 5, _____
7. T 6, _____

Observe that, except for proofs (29) and (30B), every step of every proof has been based on a law of logic which is a tautological biconditional; hence all of the above proofs, excepting (29) and (30B), might have been done "backwards" as well as "forwards." For example, the order of steps might have been 5, 4, 3, 2, 1, rather than 1, 2, 3, 4, 5.

Exercise 4.2B. Laws of Logic: Review

Directions: Below, listed in three groups, are abbreviations for the twenty laws (definitions, postulates, rules) of logic studied in exercise 4.2A. This exercise asks you to double-check on your knowledge of these laws. On separate paper, write out the formula (or formulae, since most of these laws have two forms) for each law. Then check your answers either by referring back to exercise 4.2A, or by studying the inside back cover.

(A) *Tautologous Biconditionals,* each having two forms:

(1) COM	(4) ExM	(7) DeM
(2) ASSOC	(5) TAUT	(8) RAA
(3) DIST	(6) ABS	(9) BE

(B) *Other Tautologous Biconditionals:*
    (10) DN   (12) COPO   (14) TV
    (11) CP   (13) CE
(C) *Tautologous Conditionals:*
    (15) SIMP   (17) MP   (19) DS
    (16) ADD   (18) MT   (20) HS
(D) *Rules of Procedure*

Between problems (26) and (27) above, we have already explained why conjunction (CONJ) should be classified as a rule of procedure rather than as a law of logic. It should be realized that our brief informal presentation of "Logic as a Form of Boolean Algebra" has also assumed usages concerning punctuation and the structure of well-formed formulas; rules concerning substitution (replacement); and various other generally accepted usages and procedures.

In section 6.2, three additional rules will be presented, making it possible for the above twenty laws to be applied to subject-predicate (A, E, I, and O-form) statements. A complete listing of all of the laws used in *Logic: Modern and Traditional* may be found on the inside back cover of this book.

Exercise 4.2C.   More Applications of Discursive Reasoning

Directions: Below are eight proofs of the type found in exercises 4.1B and 4.1C. After each step of proof that is not a premise, write in the number(s) and the law of logic justifying that step. In the final steps of each proof you are "on your own."

(1) 1. $(f \cdot \sim a) \to (g \vee \sim f)$
     2. $a \to b$
     3. $\sim b$
     4. $b \vee f \,/ \therefore g$
     5. $\sim a$
     6. f
     7.
     8.
     9.

(2) 1. $h \to \sim k$
     2. $d \vee m$
     3. $m \to k \,/ \therefore \sim h \vee d$
     4. $\sim k \to \sim m$
     5. $h \to \sim m$
     6. $m \vee d$
     7.
     8.
     9.

(3) 1. $z \to (n \to w)$
     2. $w \to y$
     3. $\sim y \,/ \therefore \sim(n \cdot z)$
     4. $\sim w$
     5. $\sim z \vee (n \to w)$
     6. $\sim z \vee (\sim n \vee w)$
     7. $(\sim z \vee \sim n) \vee w$
     8.
     9.
     10.

(4) 1. $(\sim f \vee g) \vee (h \leftrightarrow k)$
     2. $c \vee d \to [(h \vee k) \cdot \sim(h \cdot k)]$
     3. $(g \to f) \cdot (c \vee d) \,/ \therefore f \leftrightarrow g$
     4. $c \vee d$
     5. $(h \vee k) \cdot \sim(h \cdot k)$
     6. $h \leftrightarrow \sim k$
     7. $\sim(h \leftrightarrow k)$
     8. $\sim f \vee g$
     9.
     10.
     11.

(5) 1. $(a \to f) \to (g \vee \sim f)$
     2. $a \to b$
     3. $f \,/ \therefore g \vee k$
     4. $f \vee \sim b$
     5. $\sim b \vee f$
     6. $b \to f$
     7. $a \to f$
     8. $g \vee \sim f$
     9. g
     10. $g \vee k$

(6) 1. $a \to b$
     2. $(a \to f) \to g \cdot b$
     3. $a \cdot b \to f$
     4. $\sim g \,/ \therefore b \cdot$
     5. $\sim g \vee \sim b$
     6. $\sim(g \cdot b)$
     7. $\sim(a \to f)$
     8.
     9.
     10.
     11.

(7)   1. $h \rightarrow k$
    2. $\sim(k \cdot \sim m)$
    3. $(\sim h \leftrightarrow \sim m) \rightarrow f$
    4. $m \rightarrow h$ / $\therefore$ $f \vee \sim g$
    5. $\sim k \vee m$
    6. $k \rightarrow m$
    7. $h \rightarrow m$
    8.
    9.
   10.
   11.

(8)   1. $(w \cdot \sim x) \vee (\sim w \cdot x)$
    2. $y \vee z \rightarrow (x \leftrightarrow w)$
    3. $\sim z$ / $\therefore$ $(\sim y \vee \sim w) \cdot (\sim y \vee x)$
    4. $w \leftrightarrow \sim x$
    5. $\sim x \leftrightarrow w$
    6. $\sim(x \leftrightarrow w)$
    7. $\sim(y \vee z)$
    8.
    9.
   10.
   11.

4.3   CP, RAA, and Proof by Crucial Assignments

CONDITIONAL PROOF (CP).   We now consider a method for handling arguments whose conclusions are conditionals. We begin by proving that:

$$p \rightarrow (q \rightarrow w) = p \cdot q \rightarrow w$$

Here is the proof:

   1. $p \rightarrow (q \rightarrow w)$
   2. $p \rightarrow \sim q \vee w$ 1, CE
   3. $\sim p \vee \sim q \vee w$ 2, CE
   4. $\sim(p \cdot q) \vee w$ 3, ASSOC, DeM
   5. $p \cdot q \rightarrow w$ 4, CE

Since each of the above expressions is equivalent to the others, the first is equivalent to the last, and we have proven that:

$$p \rightarrow (q \rightarrow w) = p \cdot q \rightarrow w$$

The above equivalence is commonly known as the *law of exportation* (EXP); and its application in proof is called conditional proof (abbreviation: CP). The equality sign (=) in the above equation means that

$$[p \rightarrow (q \rightarrow w)] \leftrightarrow [(p \cdot q) \rightarrow w]$$

is a tautologous biconditional. It means, therefore, that the following argument form is valid:

$$p \rightarrow (q \rightarrow w) \ / \ \therefore \ p \cdot q \rightarrow w$$

More important, it means that any argument having the form p / $\therefore$ $q \rightarrow w$ can be restructured to become: $p \cdot q$ / $\therefore$ w.

CP permits us to take the antecedent of the conclusion from the conclusion, and to conjoin it to the other premises.

Suppose for "p" we substitute a series of premises, namely: "$a \cdot b \cdot k \cdot m \cdot p$." Then the law of exportation, which we shall call the method of conditional proof (CP) [which some logicians call the method of *subordinate proof* (SP)] says that:

$$a \cdot b \cdot k \cdot m \cdot p \rightarrow (q \rightarrow w) = a \cdot b \cdot k \cdot m \cdot p \cdot q \rightarrow w$$

The usefulness of this method of proof should be obvious; for, on the one hand, it reduces the conclusion that needs to be proved; and, on the other hand, it provides an added premise to work with.

Here is an example showing the use of CP:

Example A (proof of the hypothetical syllogism as a valid form of argument):

   1. $(q \rightarrow k)$
   2. $(k \rightarrow w)$ / $\therefore$ $q \rightarrow w$

3. q / $\therefore$ w 2, CP
4. k 1, 3, MP
5. w 2, 4, MP

By definition, CP means that the argument's *conclusion* is changed. Hence in line 3 of example A, "2, CP" refers only to the *conclusion* of line 2, namely, to "/ $\therefore$ $q \rightarrow w$."

In the above proof, observe also that premises 1 and 2, followed by "/ $\therefore$ $q \rightarrow w$," are equivalent to premises 1, 2, and 3, followed by "/ $\therefore$ w." The reason should be obvious: the argument forms

$$(q \rightarrow k) \cdot (k \rightarrow w) \mid \therefore q \rightarrow w, \text{ and}$$
$$(q \rightarrow k) \cdot (k \rightarrow w) \cdot q \mid \therefore w \text{ are equivalent.}$$

Hence step 5 completes the proof that the *original* conclusion (/ $\therefore$ $q \rightarrow w$) validly follows from premises 1 and 2.

Here are two other examples showing the correct use of conditional proof.

Example B:

1. $p \rightarrow q$ / $\therefore$ $\sim p \vee (p \cdot q)$
2.   / $\therefore$ $p \rightarrow (p \cdot q)$ 1, CE
3. p / $\therefore$ $p \cdot q$ 2, CP
4. q 1, 3, MP
5. $p \cdot q$ 3, 4, CONJ

Example C applies CP twice:

1. $p \rightarrow (q \rightarrow r)$
2. $q \rightarrow (r \rightarrow w)$ / $\therefore$ $p \rightarrow (q \rightarrow w)$
3. p / $\therefore$ $q \rightarrow w$ 2, CP
4. q / $\therefore$ w 3, CP
5. $q \rightarrow r$ 1, 3, MP
6. $r \rightarrow w$ 2, 4, MP
7. r 4, 5, MP
8. w 6, 7, MP

Exercise 4.3A.   **Using Conditional Proof (CP) to Test the Validity of Arguments**

Directions: On separate paper, write out solutions to each of the following problems. Use conditional proof in at least half of them. You will discover that four of these twelve arguments are invalid.

(1) 1. $a \rightarrow b$
     2. $\sim a \rightarrow c$ / $\therefore$ $\sim b \rightarrow c$

(2) 1. $\sim p \vee r$ / $\therefore$ $p \cdot q \rightarrow r$

(3) 1. $(k \vee p) \rightarrow o$
     2. $\sim m \rightarrow \sim o$ / $\therefore$ $k \rightarrow m$

(4) 1. $s \rightarrow p$
     2. $\sim q \rightarrow \sim m$ / $\therefore$ $s \rightarrow [m \rightarrow (p \cdot q)]$

(5) 1. $o \rightarrow d$
     2. $a \vee (b \cdot o)$ / $\therefore$ $\sim a \rightarrow d$

(6) 1. $\sim(s \rightarrow \sim m) \rightarrow p$
     2. $(\sim p \rightarrow q) \rightarrow q$ / $\therefore$ $s \cdot m \rightarrow q$

7. If the (d)iameter is increased, the (r)adius increases also. If either the (r)adius or the (d)iameter is increased or if the (c)ircumference is larger, then the (a)rea also increases. Therefore, if the (a)rea does not increase, then neither will the (d)iameter.

8. If you have (g)olden hair and (b)lue eyes, then (l)ove is assured. If you have (g)olden hair, you must have (b)lue eyes. Therefore, if you have (g)olden hair, then (l)ove will come your way.

9. If the bank is (l)ocked, but its alarm system is (o)ut of order, then it is in (d)anger

of being robbed. If the bank has no (p)olice protection, it will be (r)obbed. Therefore, if the bank is (l)ocked, then if the alarm system is (o)ut of order and the bank has no (p)olice protection, it will be (r)obbed.

10. If it is true that if (A)llen goes fishing then (B)ill will also go, then it is also true that (C)huck will go fishing too. If (D)ave goes, then (E)ric will not go [fishing]; but if (A)llen goes, (D)ave will go. If (E)ric doesn't go, then (F)red, (G)eorge, and (H)arvey will go. But if the troupe of (F)red, (G)eorge, and (H)arvey all go, then (J)ohn will not go. Therefore, if (J)ohn goes fishing, (C)huck will also go fishing. [*Hint:* Treat $(f \cdot g \cdot h)$ as a unit.]

11. Unless Jim holds on to his (j)ob, he'll either not (b)uy a car or he'll not get (m)arried. Hence, if he gets (m)arried, he'll hold on to his (j)ob.

12. If New Year's resolutions are (r)easonable, and if these resolutions are not (b)roken, then old habits (g)ive way to new habits. Either New Year's resolutions are (r)easonable, or they are (b)roken. Hence, if New Year's resolutions are (b)roken, old habits do not (g)ive way to new habits.

We now introduce a method of proof which will provide a definite proof of invalidity, as well as of validity.

REDUCTIO AD ABSURDUM (RAA). This means, literally, "to reduce to an absurdity"—to show that an assumption cannot be maintained because that assumption entails a self-contradiction. The reductio ad absurdum (RAA) takes two forms:

$$1. \; (\sim p \to p) = p \qquad 2. \; [\sim p \to (q \cdot \sim q)] = p$$

Let us employ rules of inference to prove that these forms are tautologous. (They can also be established as tautologies by truth tables.)

(*RAA*) (First Form)		*RAA* (Second Form)	
1. $\sim p \to p \; / \therefore p$		1. $\sim p \to (q \cdot \sim q) \; / \therefore p$	
2. $p \lor p$	1, CE	2. $p \lor (q \cdot \sim q)$	1, CE
3. p	2, TAUT	3. $p \lor F$	2, ExM
		4. p	3, TV

In ordinary language, the first form means that any proposition which contradicts itself is false, and the second form means that any proposition which entails a self-contradiction is false. The second form may also take the form: $(p \to q) \cdot (p \to \sim q) = \sim p$.

This method of reasoning is very old. Here are two examples of its use by ancient Greek mathematicians. Example A is a theory from Euclid's plane geometry, written about 300 B.C. Example B goes back to Pythagoras, about 500 B.C.

Example A. Theorem: A circle can have at most one center.

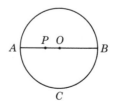

Figure 14

1. Let ABC be a circle with a center O.
2. To prove: there is no other center than O.
3. Suppose, if possible, that the circle has another center P.

4. Draw OP, and let it meet the circle at the points A and B.

5. Since O is a center, $OA = OB$.   5. Radii of a circle are equal.
6. Hence O is the midpoint of AB.   6. Definition of "midpoint."
7. Similarly, P is the midpoint of   7. Reasons (5) and (6).
   AB.
8. But this is impossible unless O 8. By previous theorems, any line
   and P coincide.   can have but one "midpoint."
9. Therefore, a circle has only one
   center.

Example B. In a square, by the Pythagorean theorem, the diagonal a^2 is equal to $b^2 + b^2$, or $a^2 = 2(b^2)$. The early Pythagoreans believed that the ratio a/b could be expressed as a pair of whole numbers, for example, 7/5, 14/9, 71/51. But instead of such a result, one of their members came up with the following proof.

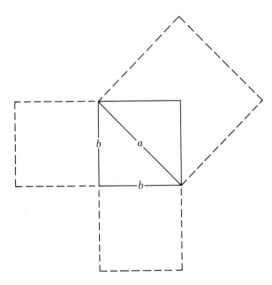

Figure 15

To prove: that it is impossible to find two whole numbers such that the square of one of them is equal to twice the square of the other.

Let $a^2 = 2b^2$, where a and b are whole numbers without any common factor greater than 1.

Part I. If a is *odd*, we have an immediate contradiction, since $2b^2$ is *even*, and we know that the square of an odd number is another odd number.

Part II. If a is *even*, say $2c$, then $4c^2 = 2b^2$, or $2c^2 = b^2$. But this means that b is even, or that a and b have the common factor 2—again a contradiction.

Let us review the argument in Example B. In the equation $a^2 = 2(b^2)$, on the assumption (which the Pythagoreans made) that "a" is a whole number, "a" must be either odd or even. But each of these two alternatives leads to a self-contradiction. Therefore, the assumption that "a" is a whole number (or that the ratio "b/a" is a fraction) is untenable.

THE REDUCTIO AD ABSURDUM (RAA) IN TRUTH-VALUE LOGIC. Briefly, the RAA method of proof rests on the following: Assuming any conditional $p \rightarrow q$ to be tautologous, then the conjunction $p \cdot \sim q$ is self-contradictory. This follows from the fact that, by CE, $(p \rightarrow q) = \sim p \vee q$; and, by DeM, $\sim p \vee q = \sim(p \cdot \sim q)$; hence $(p \rightarrow q) = \sim(p \cdot \sim q)$. Since

$(p \rightarrow q) = \sim(p \cdot \sim q)$, it is obvious that $(p \rightarrow q)$ and $(p \cdot \sim q)$ are self-contradictory, that is, they have complementary sets of truth values.

Letting p signify the antecedent of a conditional, and q the consequent, any conditional statement having the form $p \rightarrow q$ may be changed to an argument having the form p / $\therefore$ q. A *conditional is false* if and only if its antecedent is true and its consequent is false. So, too, an *argument is invalid* if and only if there is one or more assignment of truth values in which the argument's premises are true and the conclusion is false. Accordingly, if we make the tentative assumption that the entire argument is invalid (i.e., that its related conditional would have truth-value F), this tentative assumption can be maintained if and only if we can (on that assumption) find a self-consistent assignment of truth values.

On the other hand, if that assumption cannot be maintained (i.e., if it leads to a self-contradiction), then our tentative assumption that this argument form may be false must be abandoned; and we have established the argument form as valid. Here is an example showing how the method is used, step by step:

Example A:

$p \vee q \rightarrow p$ $\quad\quad\quad F$	Step 1.	Tentatively assume that this conditional is false.
$p \vee q \rightarrow p$ $\quad T \quad\ F\ F$	Step 2.	If we assume that the conditional is false, then its antecedent must be true and its consequent false.
$p \vee q \rightarrow p$ $F\ T \quad\ F\ F$	Step 3.	Transfer the truth value of p—the truth value F which was given to p in step 2.
$p \vee q \rightarrow p$ $F\ T\ T\ F\ F$	Step 4.	Can we assign a truth value to q so that $p \vee q$ will be true? Yes—by making q true. So, we have succeeded in finding a consistent set of truth value assignments, after having assumed that this conditional's antecedent was true and its consequent false. Thus we have shown that the original conditional is not tautologous.
$[p \vee q \ \rightarrow \ p]$ $p \vee q$ / $\therefore p$ $F\ T\ T\ \ F\ \ F$ $3\ 2\ 4\ \ 1\ \ 2$		Putting all this together, we have the form shown on the left. In what follows, however, the first of these four lines will be omitted.

Before proceeding further, review exercises 2.1E, 2.2H, and 2.3B. It will be noted that every problem in these three exercises consisted of a *contingent* statement form like the example shown above. Not a single problem in exercises 2.1E, 2.2H, or 2.3B was a tautologous form. Hence none of them lead to self-contradictions. In contrast, two-thirds of the problems in exercise 4.3B will be tautologous.

Example B:

$p \cdot q$ / $\therefore p \vee q$ $T\ \ T\ \ \ F\ X\ F$ $2\ \ 2\ \ \ 1\ (3)\ 2$	Step 1.	Assume that the entire argument is false.
	Step 2.	Assign truth value F to the consequent, and assign truth value T to *each* premise (for the conjunction of several premises can be true if and only if each separate premise is true).
	Step 3.	Step 3 (in parentheses) would have transferred truth value T from p in the premises to p in the conclusion. But this transfer cannot be made without involving

a self-contradiction namely: it is impossible for the conclusion "$p \lor q$" to be false and at the same time for "p" (in "$p \lor q$") to be true. So, instead of step 3 "T" we mark "X." "X" means "We here run into a self-contradiction."

Examples C and D are the same problem, solved by two different sequences of truth value assignments.

C: $[p \to (q \lor h)] \cdot (h \to w) \cdot \sim w \cdot \sim q \; / \therefore \; \sim p$
 $T\,T \;\; F\,T \;\; T \qquad T\,T\,X \qquad T\,F \qquad T\,F \;\; F \;\; F\,T$
 $4\;2 \;\;\; 6\,5\;\; 7 \qquad 8\;2\;(9) \qquad 2\;3 \qquad 2\;3 \;\;\; 1 \;\; 2\,3$

In C, step 1 assigns truth value F to the total argument form. This can occur only when the antecedent (step 2) is true and the consequent is false. Step 3 transfers the values of $\sim w$ to w, of $\sim q$ to q, and of $\sim p$ to p. Step 4 transfers the value of p. Since the antecedent of the true conditional $p \to (q \lor h)$ has truth value T, either q or h must have truth value T (step 5). But q is already known to have truth value F (step 6); so h must be assigned truth value T (step 7). Step 8 transfers this truth value T of h to the antecedent of $h \to w$. But since $h \to w$ is true, and since its antecedent h is true, its consequent w must also be true (step 9). But this gives contradictory truth values to w. Hence the RAA assumption (step 1) that the total conditional (or argument form) is false cannot be maintained. Thus, indirectly, we have established that this argument is *valid*.

D: $[p \to (q \lor h)] \cdot (h \to w) \cdot \sim w \cdot \sim q \; / \therefore \; \sim p$
 $X\,T \;\; F\,F \;\; F \qquad F\,T \;\; F \qquad F \qquad F \qquad\quad T$
 $(8)\,2 \;\;\; 6\;7\;\; 5 \qquad 4\;2\;\; 3 \qquad 2 \qquad 2 \qquad\quad 2$

In D, steps 2 and 3 (of C) are combined into one step (step 2). This saves time and prevents cluttering. Step 3 transfers the truth value F to w in $h \to w$.

Since a true conditional having a false consequent must have a false antecedent, step 4 now assigns truth value F to h; and step 5 transfers this truth value to the h in $p \to (q \lor h)$; and step 6 transfers the truth value of q to the q in $p \to (q \lor h)$. This means that the alternation $(q \lor h)$ must have truth value F (step 7). Since $q \lor h$ is now a false consequent of a true conditional the antecedent p must be assigned truth value F. But this is inconsistent with the truth value T that p had in step 2. Thus we have again established a self-contradiction, and thereby have proven that the original argument was valid.

Exercise 4.3B should be studied very carefully, because it illustrates a method of proof which, once mastered, may be worked quite easily and quickly. It also illustrates a method of proof which assures us immediately, not only whether an argument is valid, but also whether an argument is invalid.

To use this method of proof, we must *keep the following in mind*: (1) Once any statement p has been established as T or as F, this truth value should be substituted for occurrences of p elsewhere in the formula. (2) The following provide clues to *necessary* inferences, and should be used:

$$(p \cdot q); \quad (p \lor q); \quad (p \to q); \quad (p \cdot q); \quad (p \lor q); \quad (p \to q); \quad (p \to q)$$
$$T \qquad\quad F \qquad\quad F \qquad\quad T\,F \qquad\quad F\,T \qquad\quad T\,T \qquad\quad T\,F$$

(3) The following do *not* provide clues to necessary inferences, and we should delay completing them for as long as possible:

$(p \cdot q);$　　$(p \vee q);$　　$(p \to q);$　　$(p \leftrightarrow q);$　　$(p \leftrightarrow q);$
　　F　　　　　　T　　　　　　T　　　　　　T　　　　　　F

$(p \cdot q);$　　$(p \vee q);$　　$(p \to q);$　　$(p \to q)$
　FF　　　　　T T　　　　　F T　　　　　T T

Exercise 4.3B.　Testing the Validity of Laws of Logic by the Crucial Assignments Method

Remarks: This exercise is designed for two purposes: (A) to review the laws of logic used in this book, and (B) to gain added mastery of the crucial assignments method of proof. You will find that problems 3, 6, 9, 12, 15, 18, 21, 24, 27, and 30 will result in a self-consistent assignment of truth values; hence, they are *not* laws of logic. The other twenty-two problems should result in a self-contradiction, thus showing indirectly that the related conditionals, on which the argument forms are based, are tautological.

Part A.　Directions: In the top answer blank above each even-numbered problem, write the abbreviation for the name of the law of logic proven.

Part B.　Directions: Using the method of crucial assignments, show that the argument is valid or that it is invalid. You will save time if you first study the odd-numbered problems and their solutions; then proceed with the evens.

(1A) ADD
(1B) $a \mid \therefore a \vee b$
　　T　F X F
　　2　1　2

(2A) _____
(2B) $f \cdot g \mid \therefore f$

(3) $w \vee y \mid \therefore w$
　　F T T　F F
　　3 2 4　1 2

(4A) _____
(4B) $\sim(\sim k) \mid \therefore k$

(5A) DN
(5B) $\sim\{\sim[\sim(\sim h)]\} \mid \therefore h$
　　T F T F X　　　F
　　2 3 4 5　　　2

(6) $y \to y \mid \therefore y$

(7A) COM
(7B) $k \vee m \mid \therefore m \vee k$
　　X T F　F F F F
　　2 4　1 3 2 3

(8A) _____
(8B) $a \cdot b \mid \therefore b \cdot a$

(9) $f \vee g \mid \therefore f \cdot g$
　　F T T　F F F T
　　4 2 5　1 3 2 6

(10A) _____
(10B) $a \cdot (b \cdot f) \mid \therefore (a \cdot b) \cdot f$

(11A) ASSOC
(11B) $d \vee (g \vee h) \mid \therefore (d \vee g) \vee h$
　　F T　F X F　F　F F F　F F
　　5 2　6　7　1　4 3 4　2 3

(12)　$\sim d \vee (k \cdot m) \mid \therefore \sim d \cdot (k \cdot m)$

(13A) DeM
(13B) $\sim(f \vee \sim g) \mid \therefore \sim f \cdot g$
　　T FF F T　F FXFT
　　2 4 3 4 5　1 7　2 6

(14A) _____
(14B) $\sim b \vee \sim m \mid \therefore \sim(b \cdot m)$

(15)　$w \cdot (w \vee y) \mid \therefore w \cdot y$
　　T T T T F　F T F F
　　2　6 2 5　1 3 2 4

(16A) _____
(16B) $b \to (f \to g) \mid \therefore b \cdot f \to g$

(17A) EXPORTATION (= CP in reverse)
(17B) $h \cdot k \to m \mid \therefore h \to (k \to m)$
　　TFX T F　F T F　T F F
　　76　2 5　1 3 2　4 3 4

(18)　$a \to \sim a \mid \therefore a$

(19A) RAA
(19B) $\sim a \to a \mid \therefore a$
　　X F T F　F F
　　4 2 3　1 2

(20A) _____
(20B) $b \to (f \cdot \sim f) \mid \therefore \sim b$

(21)　$(w \cdot \sim w) \to z \mid \therefore z$
　　TFFT　T F　F F
　　5 4 7 6　2 3　1 2

(22A) _____
(22B) $f \to g \cdot h \mid \therefore \sim f \vee (g \cdot h)$

(23A) CE
(23B) $\sim a \vee \sim b \mid \therefore a \to \sim b$
　　　 X T T F T F T F F T
　　　 7 2 6 5 1 3 2 3 4

(24)　 $w \to (y \vee z) \mid \therefore \sim w \vee (y \cdot z)$
　　　 T T T T　　 F F T F　　 F F
　　　 4 2 6 5　　 1 3 3 2　　 3 7

In (24) the conclusion is a disjunction, and a disjunction can be false if and only if・
its two disjuncts are false. However, its second disjunct ($y \cdot z$) can be false in three
different ways. So we should select $\sim w$ for our next truth-value assignment. Then,
substituting the truth value of w, we can proceed without difficulty.

Problem (25) is more difficult. Here there are *three* ways in which the premise may
be *true*, and *two* ways in which the conclusion may be *false*. So we set up the problem
twice, and test its conclusion two different ways, thus:

(25A)　BE
(25B–1)　$(f \cdot g) \vee (\sim f \cdot \sim g) \mid \therefore f \leftrightarrow g$
　　　　　 T F F T F T X T F　　 F T F F
　　　　　 4 5 4 2 6 6　　 7 7　　 1 3 2 3

(25B–2)　$(f \cdot g) \vee (\sim f \cdot \sim g) \mid \therefore f \leftrightarrow g$
　　　　　 F F T T T F F X T　　 F F F T
　　　　　 4 5 4 2 7 7 6　　 8　　 1 3 2 3

In (25B–1) and (25B–2) *both* truth-value assignments must result in *inconsistencies*
before (25A) is established as *valid*. On the other hand, as in (27–1) and (27–2), if either
one of the two different truth-value assignments is *consistent*, the argument is shown
to be *invalid*.

(26A)　_____
(26B–1)　$a \leftrightarrow b \mid \therefore (a \to b) \cdot (b \to a)$

(26B–2)　$a \leftrightarrow b \mid \therefore (a \to b) \cdot (b \to a)$

(27–1)　$w \leftrightarrow y \cdot z \mid \therefore (w \leftrightarrow y) \cdot z$
　　　　 T T T T T F T T T F X
　　　　 3 2 4 3 4 1 5 6 5 2

(27–2)　$w \leftrightarrow y \cdot z \mid \therefore (w \leftrightarrow y) \cdot z$
　　　　 F T T F F F F F T F F F
　　　　 3 2 7 3 5 1 4 6 4 2 4

(28A)　_____
(28B–1)　$a \leftrightarrow \sim b \mid \therefore \sim (a \leftrightarrow b)$

(28B–2)　$a \leftrightarrow \sim b \mid \therefore \sim (a \leftrightarrow b)$

(29A)　DN (for $\leftrightarrow$) [Since (29B–1) established validity (29B–2) could have been left
　　　　 undone.]
(29B–1)　$f \leftrightarrow g \mid \therefore \sim f \leftrightarrow \sim g$
　　　　 X T T F T F F F T
　　　　 2 7 1 3 4 2 5 6

(29B–2)　$f \leftrightarrow g \mid \therefore \sim f \leftrightarrow \sim g$
　　　　 X T F F F T F T F
　　　　 2 6 1 3 4 2 3 5

(30–1)　$\sim h \leftrightarrow m \mid \therefore \sim h \leftrightarrow \sim m$

(30–2)　$\sim h \leftrightarrow m \mid \therefore \sim h \leftrightarrow \sim m$

(31A)　Exclusive Disjunction, or Negation of BE
(31B–1)　$(w \vee z) \cdot \sim (w \cdot z) \mid \therefore w \leftrightarrow \sim z$
　　　　　 T　　 T XFT　 F T F F T
　　　　　 2　　 2 6 5　 1 3 2 4 4

(31B–2)　$(w \vee z) \cdot \sim (w \cdot z) \mid \therefore w \leftrightarrow \sim z$
　　　　　 X T F T　　　 F F F T F
　　　　　 6 2 5 2　　　 1 3 2 4 4

(32A)　_____
(32B–1)　$(a \cdot \sim b) \vee (b \cdot \sim a) \mid \therefore a \leftrightarrow \sim b$

(32B–2)　$(a \cdot \sim b) \vee (b \cdot \sim a) \mid \therefore a \leftrightarrow \sim b$

Exercise 4.3C.　Testing Arguments for Validity

Directions: Indicate by V or I whether the following are valid or invalid. It is recommended that you employ two different methods of proof for each problem. Be prepared
to show your work.

_____　1. If grandpa attended the (d)ance, he would not have had his normal amount
　　　　　 of (r)est. And if he went to the (p)arty, he would undoubtedly have (e)aten
　　　　　 too much. But grandpa's health being what it is, either lack of (r)est or
　　　　　 over(e)ating makes him (i)ll. In other words, when grandpa is not (i)ll, we
　　　　　 can be sure that he has had plenty of (r)est and that he has not been

over(e)ating. But look at grandpa now—the day after the party and dance! He's a perfect picture of health. So, we may be pretty sure that he didn't go either to the (d)ance or to the (p)arty.

_____ 2. If Jim studied (p)sychology he would have become (a)ntisocial, and if he had studied (m)ath he would have become (b)ored. If he were either (a)ntisocial or (b)ored, he would not be a (f)raternity officer. Well, he is not a (f)raternity officer. Therefore, he did not study either (p)sychology or (m)ath.

_____ 3. Students are (w)illing to study if and only if their courses are either (h)elpful to them when they seek a job, or are (i)ntrinsically interesting. But these courses are not (i)ntrinsically interesting to students. Therefore, students are not (w)illing to study them.

_____ 4. If Harry loves (B)ess, and if Bess does not love (F)rank, then Harry will be (h)appy. If Bess loves (F)rank, then Frank will not be (r)elieved, and Harry will not be (h)appy. Now we know that Harry is not (h)appy. Therefore, if Harry loves (B)ess, Frank will not be (r)elieved.

_____ 5. If the (s)teel strike is successful, wages will (r)ise. If wages (r)ise, prices of steel will (i)ncrease; and if that happens, the price of automobiles, trucks, tractors, and farm machinery will go (u)p. But this, in turn, will mean an increase in the cost of (f)ood. Therefore, unless there is to be an increase in the cost of (f)ood, the (s)teel strike will not be successful.

_____ 6. The messenger left a telegram for (C)armen, but none for (E)llen, or he left a telegram for (E)llen but none for (R)onald. If the messenger left a telegram for (C)armen, then he (d)elivered it to apartment 6. So, if the messenger did not (d)eliver any telegram to apartment 6, there was no telegram for (R)onald.

_____ 7. If these two men both have (s)teady work, they will both (c)ontribute to the new neighborhood playground. If they both (c)ontribute, then, if their (k)ids will get along, the (m)en will get along too. Hence, since the (k)ids get along but the (m)en don't, at least one of the two men must not have (s)teady employment.

_____ 8. Unless Jim (g)raduates his parents will be (d)isappointed, and unless he gets (m)arried his fiancé will be un(h)appy. So, unless Jim is to have (d)isappointed parents or an un(h)appy fiancé it will be necessary for him both to (g)raduate and to get (m)arried.

_____ 9. If either the (m)other or the (d)aughter paid the auto insurance premium before January 1, then the (p)olicy was in effect and the (c)ost of the collision was covered. If the (c)ost of the collision was covered, they could have taken the (t)rip to Europe. But they weren't able to take the (t)rip. Hence, the (m)other did not pay the auto insurance premium before January 1.

_____ 10. There will be greater (u)nification of knowledge if and only if there is (b)etter communication between the various specialized areas of knowledge. But unless there are (f)ewer symbols used, (b)etter communication will not come about. But (f)ewer symbols will not be used so long as the vast majority of those specializing in one area remain (i)gnorant of the work done by specialists in other areas. Therefore, so long as nearly all specialists remain (i)gnorant of the work done by specialists in other areas, a greater (u)nification of knowledge will not occur.

_____ 11. We ought not to (d)epart from these gracious hosts without giving them our address, unless you don't want them to (v)isit us. But you surely want them to (v)isit us, and, after this long stay, we will have to depart. Therefore, we should give them our address.

_____ 12. Our predicament is this: if we can possibly (m)anage this situation, we must either (p)ay the bill or (r)eturn the groceries. But we cannot (r)eturn the groceries because we ate them, and we cannot (p)ay the bill because we are out of money. What is worse, if we cannot (m)anage this situation, we are both (s)tupid and (i)mprovident. So, the conclusion is obvious: we are (s)tupid and we are (i)mprovident.

_____ 13. If John (r)eceives his A.B. degree this spring, then he will (e)nter law school next fall. If he (r)eceives his A.B. degree this spring and if he (e)nters law school next fall, he must intend to become a (l)awyer. But it is not the case both that he will enter law school this fall and also that he does not intend to become a lawyer. Therefore, John will not receive his A.B. degree this spring.

_____ 14. If Fred caught any (f)ish, they were either (t)rout or (c)atfish. If they were (c)atfish, he would have used (w)orms for bait; and if they were (t)rout, he would have used (m)innows. But Fred told me that he had decided never to fish with (w)orms again, and I know that he didn't catch any (t)rout. That's why I believe that Fred didn't catch any fish.

_____ 15. [Problems 15 and 16 are dilemmas, adapted from Archbishop Whately, *Logic* (London, 1855) 8th ed.] If the blest in heaven have no (d)esires, they will be perfectly (c)ontent. If their desires are (f)ully gratified, they will be perfectly (c)ontent. But the blest in heaven will either have no (d)esires or they will have them (f)ully gratified. Therefore, the blest in heaven will be perfectly (c)ontent.

_____ 16. If this man were (w)ise he would not speak irreverently of the Scripture in (j)est, and if he were (g)ood, he would not do so in (e)arnest. But this man does speak irreverently of the Scripture, either in (j)est or in (e)arnest. Therefore, this man is either not (w)ise or not (g)ood.

_____ 17. All (j)ays are (c)orvidae. All (m)ice are (r)odents. Therefore, if no (m)ice are (j)ays, then no (c)orvidae are (r)odents.

_____ 18. All (f)alcons are (b)irds. No (c)orvidae are (f)alcons. Therefore, if no (a)nnelids are (c)orvidae, then no (a)nnelids are (b)irds.

_____ 19. All (j)ays are (c)orvidae. All (m)ice are (r)odents. Therefore, if no (c)orvidae are (r)odents, then no (m)ice are (j)ays.

_____ 20. All (s)hepherds are (d)ogs; all (d)ogs are (c)anines; all (c)anines are (m)ammals; and all (m)ammals are (v)ertebrates. Therefore, if all (s)hepherds are (m)ammals, all (c)anines are (v)ertebrates.

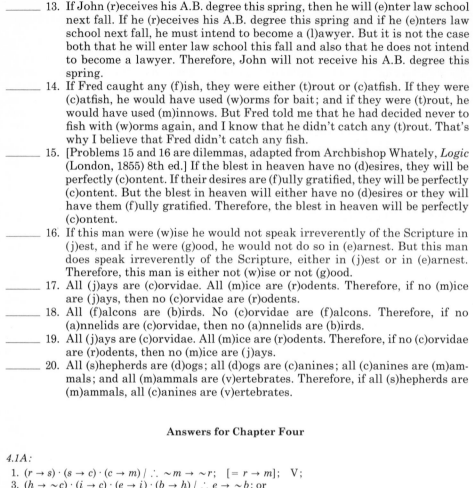

Answers for Chapter Four

4.1A:

1. $(r \to s) \cdot (s \to c) \cdot (c \to m) \mid \therefore \sim m \to \sim r; \quad [= r \to m]; \quad V;$
3. $(h \to \sim c) \cdot (i \to c) \cdot (e \to i) \cdot (b \to h) \mid \therefore e \to \sim b;$ or
$(b \to h) \cdot (h \to \sim c) \cdot (\sim c \to \sim i) \cdot (\sim i \to \sim e) \mid \therefore b \to \sim e; \quad V;$
5. $(w \to t) \cdot (t \to c) \cdot (c \to i) \cdot (i \to \sim s) \mid \therefore w \to \sim s;$ and $(w \to \sim s) \cdot (\sim s \to \sim e) \mid \therefore w \to \sim e; \quad V;$
7. $(b \cdot \sim m \to \sim f) \cdot (\sim f \to \sim p) \cdot (\sim p \to \sim a) \mid \therefore b \cdot \sim m \to \sim a;$
$[= \mid \therefore a \to \sim (b \cdot \sim m) = a \to \sim b \vee m]; \quad V.$

4.1B:

(1) $p, 1, \text{SIMP}; \quad p \vee q, 2, \text{ADD};$
(3) $d, 1, \text{SIMP}; \quad d \vee g, 2, \text{ADD}; \quad f, 1, \text{SIMP}; \quad (d \vee g) \cdot f, 3, 4, \text{CONJ};$
(5) $p, 1, \text{SIMP}; \quad p \vee r, 3, \text{ADD}; \quad x, 2, 4, \text{MP};$
(7) $h, 3, \text{SIMP}; \quad m, 1, 4, \text{MP}; r, 2, 5, \text{DS}; \quad r \vee w, 6, \text{ADD};$
(9) $b, 2, \text{SIMP}; \quad \sim f, 1, 4, \text{MP}; \quad g \cdot (g \to \sim k), 2, \text{SIMP}; \quad \sim k, 6, \text{MP}; \quad \sim f \cdot \sim k, 5, 7, \text{CONJ};$
(11) $h, 2, \text{SIMP}; \quad k \to m, 1, 3, \text{MP}; \quad \sim m, 2, \text{SIMP}; \quad \sim k, 4, 5, \text{MT};$
(13) $\sim a \cdot \sim f, 2, \text{DeM}; \quad \sim a, 3, \text{SIMP}; \quad d \to f, 1, 4, \text{DS}; \quad \sim f, 3, \text{SIMP}; \quad \sim d, 5, 6, \text{MT};$
$\sim d \vee m, 7, \text{ADD};$
(15) $m, 2, \text{SIMP}; \quad w, 2, \text{SIMP}; \quad (y \cdot \sim z) \cdot x, 1, 4, \text{MP};$
$(x \cdot y) \cdot \sim z, 6, \text{ASSOC [concerning ASSOC, review page 20]}; \quad \sim z, 5, \text{SIMP};$
$m \cdot \sim z, 3, 7, \text{CONJ};$
(17) $\sim p, 1, 4, \text{MT}; \quad s, 3, 5, \text{DS}; \quad \sim r \vee \sim s, 2, \text{DeM}; \quad \sim r, 6, 7, \text{DS}; \quad \sim r \vee k, 8, \text{ADD};$
$k \vee \sim r, 9, \text{COM}; \quad \sim k \to \sim r, 10, \text{CE};$
(19) $b \vee b, 2, \text{CE}; \quad b, 4, \text{TAUT}; \quad \sim k \vee \sim k, 1, \text{CE}; \quad \sim k, 6, \text{TAUT}; \quad \sim f, 3, 7, \text{DS}; \quad \sim f \cdot b, 5, 8, \text{CONJ}.$

4.1C:

(1) $2, \text{SIMP}; \quad 1, 3, \text{MT}; \quad f, 2, \text{SIMP}; \quad f \cdot \sim a, 4, 5, \text{CONJ}; \quad (f \cdot \sim a) \vee k, 6, \text{ADD};$

(3) 3, 4, MT; 5, DeM; 6, SIMP; ~f, 2, 7, MT; ~(a ∨ b), 1, 8, MT; ~a · ~b, 9, DeM;
(5) 3, CE; 1, 4, HS; 2, DeM; 6, CE; 5, 7, HS; 8, CE; ~f, 9, TAUT; ~f ∨ k, 10, ADD;
f → k, 11, CE;
(7) 1, DIST; 3, SIMP; 2, SIMP; 4, 5, DS; m, 2, SIMP; k · m, 6, 7, CONJ.

4.1D:
All answers are valid except the following: (2), (8), (12), (14), (15), (16), (18), (21), (22), (25), and (28).

4.1E:

(1) 1. $w → (b → s)$
   2. $w · {\sim}s$ / ∴ ${\sim}b$
   3. w　　　　　　　　　　2, SIMP
   4. $b → s$　　　　　　　　1, 3, MP
   5. ${\sim}s$　　　　　　　　　2, SIMP
   6. ${\sim}b$　　　　　　　　　4, 5, MT

(3) 1. ${\sim}p → a$
   2. $a → {\sim}m$
   3. $m ∨ b$
   4. ${\sim}b$ / ∴ p
   5. m　　　　　　　　　　3, 4, DS
   6. ${\sim}a$　　　　　　　　　2, 5, MT
   7. p [or ${\sim}({\sim}p)$]　　　1, 6, MT

(5) 1. $(g · l) ∨ (w · t)$
   2. ${\sim}g$ / ∴ t
   3. ${\sim}g ∨ {\sim}l$　　　　　　2, ADD
   4. ${\sim}(g · l)$　　　　　　　3, DeM
   5. $w · t$　　　　　　　　　1, 4, DS
   6. t　　　　　　　　　　　5, SIMP

(7) 1. $j ∨ {\sim}b$
   2. $r ∨ {\sim}b → p$
   3. ${\sim}p$ / ∴ j
   4. ${\sim}(r ∨ {\sim}b)$　　　　　2, 3, MT
   5. ${\sim}r · b$　　　　　　　　4, DeM
   6. b　　　　　　　　　　　5, SIMP
   7. j　　　　　　　　　　　1, 6, DS

Problems 9 and 10 of exercise 4.1E are *invalid* arguments. But with our present methods of proof, we can hardly be sure of it; for we may wonder whether we simply failed to think of a good solution. Section 4.3 explains a method of proof whereby we can *know for sure*, not only that an argument is *valid*, but also that an argument is *invalid*.

4.2A:
Answers are given within the exercise itself.

4.2B:
Answers should be written on separate paper and, if possible, without referring to the book.

4.2C:
(1) ~a, 2, 3, MT; f, 3, 4, DS; f · ~a, 5, 6, CONJ; g ∨ ~f, 1, 7, MP; g, 6, 8, DS.
(3) ~w, 2, 3, MT; ~z ∨ (n → w), 1, CE; ~z ∨ (~n ∨ w), 5, CE; (~z ∨ ~n) ∨ w, 6, ASSOC;
~z ∨ ~n, 4, 7, DS; ~n ∨ ~z, 8, COM; ~(n · z), 9, DeM.
(5) f ∨ ~b, 3, ADD; ~b ∨ f, 4, COM; b → f, 5, CE; a → f, 2, 6, HS; g ∨ ~f, 1, 7, MP;
g, 3, 8, DS; g ∨ k, 9, ADD.
(7) ~k ∨ m, 2, DeM; k → m, 5, CE; h → m, 1, 6, HS; h ↔ m, 4, 7, BE; ~h ↔ ~m, 8, DN;
f, 3, 9, MT; f ∨ ~g, 10, ADD.

4.3A:

(1) 1. $a → b$
   2. ${\sim}a → c$ / ∴ ${\sim}b → c$
   3. ${\sim}b$ / ∴ c　　　　　　2, CP
   4. ${\sim}a$　　　　　　　　　1, 3, MT
   5. c　　　　　　　　　　　2, 4, MP

(3) 1. $(k ∨ p) → o$
   2. ${\sim}m → {\sim}o$ / ∴ $k → m$
   3. k / ∴ m　　　　　　　2, CP
   4. $k ∨ p$　　　　　　　　　3, ADD
   5. o　　　　　　　　　　　1, 4, MP
   6. m　　　　　　　　　　　2, 5, MT

(5) 1. $o → d$
   2. $a ∨ (b · o)$ / ∴ ${\sim}a → d$
   3. ${\sim}a$ / ∴ d　　　　　　2, CP
   4. $b · o$　　　　　　　　　2, 3, DS
   5. o　　　　　　　　　　　4, SIMP
   6. d　　　　　　　　　　　1, 5, MP

(7) 1. $d → r$
   2. $[(r ∨ d) ∨ c] → a$ / ∴ ${\sim}a → {\sim}d$
   3. ${\sim}a$ / ∴ ${\sim}d$　　　　　2, CP
   4. ${\sim}[(r ∨ d) ∨ c]$　　　　2, 3, MT
   5. ${\sim}(r ∨ d) · {\sim}c$　　　　4, DeM
   6. ${\sim}(r ∨ d)$　　　　　　　5, SIMP
   7. ${\sim}r · {\sim}d$　　　　　　　6, DeM
   8. ${\sim}d$　　　　　　　　　　7, SIMP

(9) 1. $l · o → d$
   2. ${\sim}p → r$ / ∴ $l → (o · {\sim}p → r)$
   3. l / ∴ $o · {\sim}p → r$　　　2, CP
   4. $o · {\sim}p$ / ∴ r　　　　　3, CP
   5. ${\sim}p$　　　　　　　　　　4, SIMP
   6. r　　　　　　　　　　　2, 5, MP

(11) 1. ${\sim}j → {\sim}b ∨ {\sim}m$ / ∴ $m → j$
   2. m / ∴ j　　　　　　　　1, CP
   3. $m ∨ b$　　　　　　　　　2, ADD
   4. ${\sim}({\sim}m · {\sim}b)$　　　　　3, DeM
   We cannot proceed. The argument is invalid.

The concluding two problems of exercise 4.3A are invalid. The difficulty with saying, "The argument is invalid," is that we may wonder whether there may be some other approach whereby we might have established the arguments as valid. In contrast, the crucial assignments method of proof, which is used in the remainder of section 4.3, makes it immediately evident whether an argument is either valid or invalid.

4.3B:

Answers for odd-numbered problems are given in the text.

Problems 3, 6, 9, 12, 15, 18, 21, 24, 27, and 30 are invalid. All others are valid. Each valid problem is a law of logic. Except for three laws to be explained in chapter 6, these 21 valid problems cover most of the laws used in this text. Try to recognize the laws as you solve the problems. In case you forget, here they are: 1, ADD; 2, SIMP; 4 & 5, DN; 7 & 8, COM; 10 & 11, ASSOC; 13 & 14, DeM; 15, CP [conditional proof—also known as the Law of Exportation (EXP)]; 19 & 20, RAA; 22 & 23, CE (conditional equivalence); 25 & 26, BE (biconditional equivalence); 28 & 29, DN (for ↔); 31 & 32, exclusive disjunction, or the negation of biconditional equivalence.

We leave it to the student to check the validity of TAUT, COPO, DIST, MP, MT, DS, and HS.

The crucial assignments method of proof should also make it very easy to check the validity of the following laws of logic—laws that are *not* used in our text, but which may be found in some other logic books.

(1) Expansion-Contraction: (A) p / ∴ $(p \cdot q) \vee (p \cdot \sim q)$
                            (B) $(p \cdot q) \vee (p \cdot \sim q)$ / ∴ p

(2) Reiteration: p / ∴ $q \to p$
Note: This law could have been used to replace the final three steps of problem (17) of exercise 4.1B.

(3) Laws of Duns Scotus (1265?–1308): $\sim p$ / ∴ $p \to q$
Note: Although Duns Scotus was one of the greatest logicians of all times, he lacked the symbolism to enable him to express this law so concisely. This law would have been usable in the final steps of problem (14) of exercise 4.1B.

(4) The Dam Neck Laws (found in some manuals for computer engineers):
(A) $p \cdot (\sim p \vee q)$ / ∴ $p \cdot q$
(B) $p \vee (\sim p \cdot q)$ / ∴ $p \vee q$

(5) The Distributive Laws applied to the *arrow*. Four forms, two valid and two invalid, are explained in the answers for problems (21A), (22A), (23A), and (24A) of exercise 6.1A.

(6) Absorption: $p \to q$ / ∴ $p \to p \cdot q$
Note: In our system, using the step-by-step method of proof, five steps would be needed to prove $p \to q$ / ∴ $p \to p \cdot q$:

1. $p \to q$	4. $(\sim p \vee p) \cdot (\sim p \vee q)$ (by ExM)
2. $\sim p \vee q$ (by CE)	5. $\sim p \vee (p \cdot q)$ (by DIST)
3. $T \cdot (\sim p \vee q)$ (by TV)	6. $p \to p \cdot q$ (by CE)

Observe that this "law of absorption" is not the same as the laws of absorption used in Boolean algebra, and set forth in problems (8) and (9) of exercise 4.2A.

Since this law is seldom needed, it is not listed among the laws of logic employed in this book (For a summary of these laws, see the inside back cover). But it is definitely a law of logic, and should an instructor so desire, it may be added to the laws available for use.

(7) The Dilemma.
Note: As a rhetorical device, the dilemma was discussed in section 3.5. As a law of logic, it has at least five distinct forms, namely:
(A) Simple constructive: $(p \to q) \cdot (r \to q) \cdot (p \vee r)$ / ∴ q
(B) Complex constructive: $(p \vee q) \cdot (p \to r) \cdot (q \to s)$ / ∴ $r \vee s$
(C) Simple destructive: $(p \to r) \cdot (p \to s) \cdot (\sim r \vee \sim s)$ / ∴ $\sim p$
(D) Complex destructive: $(p \to q) \cdot (r \to s) \cdot (\sim q \vee \sim s)$ / ∴ $\sim p \vee \sim r$
(E) Constructive and Destructive: $(p \to q) \cdot (r \to s) \cdot (p \vee \sim s)$ / ∴ $q \vee \sim r$

4.3C:

(1A) 1. $d \to \sim r$
      2. $p \to e$
      3. $\sim r \vee e \to i$
      4. $\sim i \to r \cdot \sim e$
      5. $\sim i$ / ∴ $\sim (d \vee p)$
      6. $r \cdot \sim e$ 4, 5, MP
      7. r 6, SIMP
      8. $\sim d$ 1, 7, MT

9. ~e   6, SIMP
10. ~p   2, 9, MP
11. ~d · ~p   8, 10, CONJ
12. ~(d ∨ p)   11, DeM
                    Valid

(1B) (d → ~r) · (p → e) · (~r ∨ e → i) · (~i → r · ~e) · ~i | ∴ ~(d ∨ p)
      *F T F T   F T F   F T F F T F   T   T F F F F T X
      10 2 9 9   8 2 7   6 6 5 6 2 4   2   2 2 1 2 11 3

(3A) 1. w ↔ h ∨ i   (3B) (w ↔ h ∨ i) · ~i | ∴ ~w
      2. ~i | ∴ ~w   *T T T T F   T F F F T
      3. (w → h ∨ i) · (h ∨ 'i → w)   3 2 6 4 5   2 2 1 2 2
      We seem to be getting nowhere; so we
      guess that the argument is invalid. But
      to make sure, double check with proof
      (3B).

(5A) This is a polysyllogism, and can probably be seen at a glance to be *valid*. However, it is
      very easy to double check, as is done in (5B).

(5B) (s → r) · (r → i) · (i → u) · (u → f) | ∴ ~f → ~s
      *T T T   T T T   T T T   T T X F T F F F T
      4 2 5   6 2 7   8 2 9   10 2   1 3 3 2 3 3
                        Valid

(7A) 1. s → c
      2. c → (k → m) | ∴ (k · ~m) → ~s
      3. k · ~m | ∴ ~s   CP
      4. c → (~k ∨ m)   2, CE
      5. ~(~k ∨ m)   3, DeM
      6. ~c   4, 5, MT
      7. ~s   1, 6, MT
                    Valid

(7B) (s → c) · [c → (k → m)] | ∴ k · ~m → ~s
      *T T T   T T T T X   F T T T F F F T
      4 2 5   6 2   9 7   1 8 3 8 8 2 3 3

(9A) 1. m ∨ d → p · c
      2. c → t
      3. ~t | ∴ ~m
      4. ~c   2, 3, MT
      5. ~c ∨ ~p   4, ADD
      6. ~(c · p)   5, DeM
      7. ~(m ∨ d)   1, 6, COM, MT
      8. ~m · ~d   7, DeM
      9. ~m   8, SIMP
                    Valid

(9B) (m ∨ d → p · c) · (c → t) · ~t | ∴ ~m
      *T X   T F F   F T F   T F F F T
      7   2 6 5   4 2 3   2 2 1 2 2
                    Valid

(11A) 1. ~(~v) → ~(d · ~g)   (11B) ~(~v) → ~(d · ~g) · v · d | ∴ g
       2. v · d | ∴ g   F T X T F T T T F T T F F
       3. v → ~(d · ~g)   1, DN   7 8   2 6 3 5 4 4 2 2 1 2
       4. v   2, SIMP   Valid
       5. ~(d · ~g)   1, 4, MP
       6. ~d ∨ g   5, DeM
       7. d   2, SIMP
       8. g   6, 7, DS

(13A) 1. r → e   (13B) (r → e) · (r · e → l) · ~(e · ~l) | ∴ ~r
       2. r · e → l   *T T T   T T T T T   T T F F T   F F T
       3. ~(e · ~l) | ∴ ~r   4 2 5   4 7 6 2 8   2 10 3 9 9 1 2 2
       4. ~e ∨ l   3, DeM   Invalid
       5. | ∴ ~r ∨ ~r   3, TAUT
       6. | ∴ r → ~r   5, CE
       7. r | ∴ ~r   6, CP
      Proof (13A) seems to be getting nowhere. We'll check with (13B).

(15A) 1. $\sim d \to c$
     2. $f \to c$
     3. $\sim d \vee f \mid \therefore c$
     4. $\mid \therefore c \vee c$ 3, TAUT
     5. $\mid \therefore \sim c \to c$ 4, CE
     6. $\sim c \mid \therefore c$ 5, CP
     7. d 1, 6, MT
     8. f 3, 7, DS
     9. c 2, 8, MP

(15B) $(\sim d \to c) \cdot (f \to c) \cdot (\sim d \vee f) \mid \therefore c$
      $F\ T\ T\ F$ $F\ T\ F$ $F\ T\ T\ X$ $F\ F$
      $5\ 5\ 2\ 4$ $3\ 2\ 3$ $6\ 6\ 2$ $1\ 2$

(17A) 1. $j \to c$
     2. $m \to r \mid \therefore (m \to \sim j) \to (c \to \sim r)$
     3. $m \to \sim j \mid \therefore c \to \sim r$ 2, CP
     No solution seems possible. Invalid.

(17B) $(j \to c) \cdot (m \to r) \mid \therefore (m \to \sim j) \to (c \to \sim r)$
     $T\ T\ T$ $F\ T\ T$ $F\ \ F\ T\ F\ T\ F$ $T F\ F T$
     $7\ 2\ 6$ $10\ 2\ 5$ $1\ \ 9\ 3\ 8\ 8\ 2$ $4\ 3\ 4\ 4$

In (17B) j might also have truth value F.

(19A) 1. $j \to c$
     2. $m \to r \mid \therefore (c \to \sim r) \to (m \to \sim j)$
     3. $c \to \sim r \mid \therefore m \to \sim j$ 2, CP
     4. $j \to \sim r$ 1, 3, HS
     5. $r \to \sim j$ 4, COPO
     6. $m \to \sim j$ 2, 5, HS
                     Valid

(19B) $(j \to c) \cdot (m \to r) \mid \therefore (c \to \sim r) \to (m \to \sim j)$
     $T\ T\ T$ $X\ T\ F$ $F\ \ T T\ T F\ F$ $T\ F\ F T$
     $5\ 2\ 6$ $2\ 9$ $1\ \ 7 3\ 8 8\ 2$ $4\ 3\ 4\ 4$
                     Valid

chapter 5

INDUCTIVE LOGIC AND SCIENCE

5.1 Scientific Method

The method of science has been succinctly summarized by D. W. Y. Kwok as follows:

> The scientific method operates on four fundamental principles. First, the need for observation, hypothesis, experimentation, and the return to observation: the empirical principle. Second, to achieve exactitude in measurement such a method must employ quantitative means: the quantitative principle. Third, the scientific method deals with causal relations and often uses abstractions to represent them. For this end, it must locate meaningful recurrences of behavior and then formulate general laws or equations which describe and explain such behavior: the mechanical principle of science. Fourth is a general assumption of all scientists which may be called an attitude of mind, a principle inherent in the concept of research: the principle of progress through science . . . [based on what Edgar Zilsel has called] "cooperation for non-personal ends, a cooperation in which all scientists of the past, present, and the future have a part. Today this idea or ideal seems almost self-evident. Yet no Brahmanic, Renaissance humanist, no philosopher or rhetor of classical antiquity ever achieved it. It is a specific characteristic of the scientific spirit and of modern Western civilization."[1]

Section 5.1 will explain in greater detail the meaning of Kwok's "four fundamental principles" of science.

(A) THE EMPIRICAL PRINCIPLE. Empiricism is the belief that knowledge ultimately rests on firsthand, direct, original experience. In the realm of natural science, it means that man's knowledge about a natural phenomenon is attained by attending to, exploring, investigating, and scrutinizing natural phenomena. Any thought or idea is part of the furniture of the mind and is to some extent dependent on human control. But a fact is independent of our control. It is simply there. A fact arises spontaneously out of experience, sometimes quite unexpectedly, and is not arrived at by a chain of reasoning. In contrast to facts, our thoughts result from various processes of sifting, analyzing, and reasoning. Thus facts are immediately and directly given; whereas thoughts and thought processes are indirect: they depend more on the

---

[1] Kwok, D. W. Y., *Scientism in Chinese Thought. 1900–1950* (New Haven: Yale University Press, 1965), pp. 21–22. Reprinted by permission of Yale University Press.

thinker himself. These ideas have been well stated by the famous physiologist, Claude Bernard:

> Experience provides the ultimate test for all scientific beliefs, for a belief cannot rationally be held if it is known to conflict with facts. The sort of experience relevant to science is that of the environment external to the individual observer; it is that of the environment common to all observers, at least potentially. The reason for this concentration on the common, external world is to eliminate the subjective which varies from individual to individual. Thus science becomes impersonal and objective; thereby is the opportunity for cooperative inquiry made possible. "*L'art, c'est* moi; *Le science, c'est* nous." [Art is *me*; science is *we*.][2]

The plight of the person who supposes that truth may be attained merely by a study of *words* may be seen by looking up dictionary definitions of a series of related words. For example:

> *Reason:* normal *mental* powers; a sound *mind.*
> *Mental:* of or for the *mind* or *intellect.*
> *Mind:* the *intellect* in its normal state; *reason.*
> *Intellect:* the ability to *reason*; *mental* ability.
> *Reason:* . . . (Around we go again:)

Dictionaries provide clusters of words and phrases which have somewhat similar meanings. One person may know the meaning of one term ("mind"), a second may know another ("intellect"), a third still another ("reason"), and the dictionary will enable all of them to understand one another. But dictionaries cannot give us "truth," that is, they cannot relate the word being defined to its referent (what the word stands for). Dictionaries can only give meanings—meanings in the sense of "current usage." There is as much *meaning* in "astrology" as in "astronomy," in "alchemy" as in "chemistry." By itself no definition can tell us whether astrology contains as much truth as astronomy; or whether alchemy is as closely in accord with the facts as chemistry is.

Conjoining Reason and Experience. Direct observation of empirical data makes it possible to arrive at a great number of generalizations concerning the world about us; for example, that wood burns; that hens lay eggs; that dogs bark; that carbon and soft iron combine to form steel; that gold has certain characteristic properties; that a gyroscope follows a regular pattern of motion. But what about concepts beyond the pale of ordinary experience—mathematical concepts such as zero, negative numbers, irrational numbers, infinite series; or scientific concepts such as the ego, genes, molecules, atoms, electrons? At first glance, such concepts may seem to consist of "entities" which are as arbitrary as the "tendency" of plants to grow upward, or the "dormitive power" whereby opium puts one to sleep. However, these scientific concepts differ in a most important respect: they lead to predictable results, and these results are empirically observable. For example, Newton reasoned somewhat as follows:

> *If* white light is a mixture of rays differing in refrangibility, and *if* the different colors of the spectrum correspond to these different degrees of refrangibility,
> *then* (1) rays of different colors cannot come to a focus at the same distance from the lens (and this explains the "blurred" images seen through earlier telescopes);

---

[2] Claude Bernard, *An Introduction to the Study of Experimental Medicine* (New York: Dover, 1957), part 1, chap. 2, sec. 4, p. 43. Section 7.1, "Empirical Probability," is also relevant to this discussion of reason and experience.

then (2) for each color there must be a definite and specific amount of refraction (and this amount is measurable in laboratory experiments);

then (3) the permanent colors of natural objects are explained in terms of degrees of refraction;

then (4) mixing in due proportion all the primary colors should produce white light.

Whether a scientist defends the wave theory or the corpuscular theory of light, it should be obvious that neither the waves nor the corpuscles are directly observed. What is observable are the *deductions* which are made on the basis of the theory. Before a scientific hypothesis can be confirmed, predictions must be made from it. These take the form of "if-then" deductions; for example, "If molecules exist, bodies should expand when heated." "If evolution has occurred in the past, then it should occur today also when we study rapidly breeding organisms." Although such deductions may be *valid*, whether or not they are *true* depends, not on formal logic, but on empirical observation. After the deduction tells us what the hypothesis logically implies, the predicted consequences may be subjected to observational or experimental check. If the data turn out as predicted, the hypothesis receives a degree of confirmation—that is, it has been verified; if the data are contrary to what was anticipated on the basis of the hypothesis, the hypothesis is revised or discarded, and a new one invented to replace it.

If we let "h" represent "scientific hypothesis," and let "f" represent "facts which verify that hypothesis," then the "logic of empiricism"—the form of proof employed when facts are used to "prove" a theory—seems to be this: $[(h \rightarrow f) \cdot f] \rightarrow h$. But this is not a tautologous conditional; and hence, it is not a sufficient basis for a rigorous deductive proof. It is for this reason that scientists hold their beliefs tentatively and provisionally as theories or as hypotheses, but not as indisputable truths.[3]

Scientific hypotheses may be viewed as hypothetical constructs—as maps, or models—which the scientist hopes are analogous to the material world. The attitude of the scientific investigator has been aptly described in a well-known passage by Einstein and Infeld:

> In our endeavor to understand reality we are somewhat like a man trying to understand the mechanism of a closed watch. He sees the face and the moving hands, even hears its ticking, but he has no way of opening the case. If he is ingenious he may form some picture of a mechanism which could be responsible for all the things he observes, but he may never be quite sure his picture is the only one which could explain his observations. He will never be able to compare his picture with the real mechanism and he cannot even imagine the possibility or the meaning of such a comparison.[4]

A flat map can never perfectly represent a spherical earth; neither can the simple theories of science perfectly represent all the data of a complex world. Although most of us are inclined to model the world after our inherited conceptual schemes, the scientist is forever seeking to see "through the looking

---

[3] Logically, the indirect proof of science is similar to the circumstantial evidence often used to establish guilt in criminal trials. A classic example of circumstantial evidence is that which led to the conviction of Bruno Hauptmann in the kidnapping of the baby of Charles A. Lindberg. This evidence is described in considerable detail in Philip Wheelwright's *Valid Thinking* (New York: Odyssey, 1962), pp. 269–74. The reasoning of Sherlock Holmes and of other detective stories, both real and imaginary, provides additional examples.

[4] Albert Einstein and Leopold Infeld, *The Evolution of Physics* (New York: Simon and Schuster, 1954), p. 33.

glass" of his inherited preconceptions in order to better understand the world as it really is. Certainly some models (conceptual schemes, maps, theories) fit better than others. However, it is a mistake to suppose that there is only one reasonable or correct model. Minnesota is represented with reasonable accuracy by both the Mercator and the Polar projections. Different maps emphasize different features, but a given set of features may be equally well represented by different maps.

The intelligible structure of nature is not given to man directly or immediately. On this point Galileo was quite clear:

> Nature does not make human brains first and then construct things according to their capacity of understanding, but she first makes things in her own fashion, and then so constructed the human understanding that it, though at the price of great exertion, might ferret out a few of her secrets.[5]

A theoretical scientist formulates various possible structures, whereby from a few assumptions certain conclusions will necessarily follow. The empirical scientist (or the speculative scientist who is also an empirical scientist) then selects that formalized structure which best accounts for the known factual data, and which is most fruitful in providing clues to further investigation. Viewed in a purely formal sense, a scientist's conceptual scheme may be said to prescribe the mathematical or logical conditions to which natural events approximately conform. But this conceptual scheme is a legitimate part of science (and is not mere speculation) only to the extent that natural events do, in fact, occur as the conceptual scheme says they do.

Which of several competing hypotheses is the better one? There is no simple answer to this question, since there are several marks of a good hypothesis. First, a good hypothesis should account for all the known facts. (But facts tend to be ignored when our presuppositions lead us to believe they could not occur.)[6] Second, a good hypothesis should be consistent with other knowledge. (This criterion is difficult to apply, since there have been many revolutionary hypotheses, such as those of Galileo and Darwin, which have caused whole series of revolutions in related areas of knowledge.) Third, a good hypothesis should be simple: it should reduce mental effort; it should bring about intellectual economy. (This criterion is difficult to apply, because what is simple to a Newton or an Einstein may seem unnecessarily complex to John Doe; or what is simple from the viewpoint of physics and astronomy may lead to all kinds of complexities from the viewpoints of theology or metaphysics.) Fourth, a good hypothesis should be fruitful: it should help uncover hitherto unknown truth. (However, some fruitful hypotheses have later been considered quite absurd, even though they undoubtedly inspired the discovery of new truths. For example, the Pythagorean astronomers added much to our knowledge on the hypothesis that the heavenly bodies must number ten.) Finally, a scientific

---

[5] Galileo, *Two Systems*, cited with insightful comments by J. H. Randall, Jr., *The Career of Philosophy* (New York: Columbia University Press, 1962), chap. 13, "Galileo and the Pattern of the New Science."

[6] When the Wright brothers made their historic flight at Kitty Hawk, N.C., on December 17, 1903, no reporter was present, and only one newspaper, the *Norfolk Virginian-Pilot*, gave it more than the briefest mention. Not for five years did New York papers send correspondents to cover their activities. In 1925 Orville Wright said that the failure to credit the accomplishment "was mainly due to the fact that human flight was generally looked upon as an impossibility, and that scarcely anyone believed in it until he actually saw it with his own eyes." This example, and many similar ones, may be found in Harold A. Larrabee, *Reliable Knowledge*, rev. ed. (Boston: Houghton-Mifflin, 1969).

hypothesis—or deductions from that hypothesis—should be verifiable. (Here, again, there is no easy way to determine to what extent "potential energy," "id," "gene," "neutrino," and so forth are verifiable, or to what extent they are employed only in order to make our conceptual schemes more simple, adequate and self-consistent.

By far the most important feature of any hypothesis is the fact that it is held tentatively and provisionally; that it is open to criticism; subject to modification or even to abandonment; and that it is not a rigid dogma or an unalterable prejudice. We shall return to this point when discussing "The Cooperative Principle."

(B) THE QUANTITATIVE PRINCIPLE. If we ask "Why are some areas of knowledge more precise and definite than others?" we soon discover that *measurement* is science's principle means of reducing vagueness in favor of clarity and precision. Historically, the first scientific measurements were of "long–short" *distances* and of "heavy–light" *weights*. Once distance was precisely measured, then the three measurements of length, breadth, and thickness made it possible to also measure *volume*—thus to change the vague polarity of "large—small" into precisely measured amounts.

In short, instead of asking, as Aristotelian logic asked, "What properties?" or "What attributes?" are to be predicated of different classes or kinds of things, Archimedean science asked "To what degree?" and "By what measurable amount?" is one object longer or shorter, heavier or lighter, larger or smaller than some other object, or class of objects, of the same general type. Exercise 5.1A, which builds around one of Archimedes' principles, is designed not to teach natural science, but only to illustrate what is involved when science replaces vague and inexact terms by concepts that are clear and precise, and then, on the basis of such precisely measured terms, is able to make comparisons and relations that would otherwise be impossible.

Exercise 5.1A. Two Types of Knowledge

This exercise deals with one of the oldest laws of physics—Archimedes' principle, which may be stated as follows: *any body immersed in a fluid is buoyed up by a force equal to the weight of the fluid displaced.* A fluid may be a gas such as air, or a liquid such as water. Below are the approximate weights of one cubic foot of several substances:

Solids	pounds per cubic foot	Liquids	pounds per cubic foot	Gases	pounds per cubic foot
Lead	795	Water	62	Air	.0806
Iron	486	Mercury	850	Hydrogen	.0056
Brass	535	Gasoline	49	Helium	.0106
Rubber	67	(These three liquids			
Pine Wood	31	do not mix with each other.)			

Directions: On the basis of the above principle and facts (and ignoring everything else) check each of the following statements as true (T) or false (F).

Example: One cubic foot of brass requires an additional downward force of 315 pounds in order for it to sink in mercury. (This is true (T) since when it sinks it displaces its own weight of 535 pounds, which is 315 pounds less than that of mercury.)

———— 1. Lead will float in mercury.
———— 2. Solid rubber will float in water.
———— 3. Helium will float in hydrogen.
———— 4. A balloon in air filled with a given volume of helium will buoy up only about half as much weight as it would with the same volume of hydrogen.

_____ 5. Pine wood floats lower (i.e., is immersed further) in gasoline than it is
in water.

_____ 6. When a boat is being loaded, the greater the load that is put into that boat,
the deeper the boat will be immersed in the water.

_____ 7. One hundred cubic feet of pine wood will weigh more than five cubic feet
of lead.

_____ 8. When immersed in water, pine wood sinks until about half of its volume
is below the water line.

_____ 9. When weighed in a vacuum, twelve cubic feet of pine wood will weigh
approximately one pound more than when weighed in air.

_____ 10. When weighed in a vacuum, twelve cubic feet of rubber will weigh about
five pounds more than when weighed in air.

The above exercise typified an *exact science* because each of the variables
was measurable in precise numerical amounts. On this account, Archimedes'
principle differs significantly from a vague law such as the law of supply and
demand in economics. The law of supply and demand may be stated thus:
given a *finite supply* of some article of consumption, *the greater the demand,
the higher the price*. But we cannot speak of "demand" in the precise measurable
way that we speak of the weights of lead, iron, water, or air.

In the next exercise, which deals with Ohm's law, problems 1–6 represent a
level of knowledge comparable to that found in the law of supply and demand.
We know in what direction the variation would occur, but we do not know
by what precisely measurable amounts the two (or three) variables are related
to one another. In contrast, problems 7–10 deal with precise amounts, measured
in exact numerical terms by means of ammeters and voltmeters. Problems 7–10
typify the level of precision characteristic of an exact science.

Exercise 5.1B. Concomitant Variations, With and Without Precise Measurement

Remarks: A fundamental law of electrophysics is Ohm's law, which reads:

$$V = IR, \quad \text{or} \quad I = \frac{V}{R}, \quad \text{or} \quad R = \frac{V}{I};$$

where V symbolizes voltage, or "pressure" measured in volts (sometimes symbolized
"E"); where I symbolizes or represents current, measured in amperes; and where R
stands for resistance, measured in Ohms.

From this formula, even without measurements, we can infer many statements such
as 1–6 below.

Directions: (Study the odds, do the evens.) In the answer column on the left, write
D, I, or U to indicate that the blank space in the sentence should contain the word

  D: Decreased,
  I: Increased,
  U: Uncertain (The data is insufficient for an answer in "U").

_____ 1. If the voltage (V) remains constant, and the resistance (R) is increased,
then the current (I) will be _____.

_____ 2. If the voltage (V) remains constant, an increase in the current (I) will
cause the resistance (R) to be _____.

_____ 3. If the voltage (V) is decreased and the resistance (R) is also decreased, the
current (I) will be _____.

_____ 4. If the voltage (V) is increased and the current (I) is increased, the amount
of resistance (R) will be _____.

_____ 5. If the current (I) remains constant while the voltage (V) is increased, the
resistance (R) must be _____.

_____ 6. While the resistance (R) remains constant, an increase in current (I) can
only come about if the voltage (V) is _____.

Remarks: Contrast problems 1–6 with problems 7–10. Note that *precise* answers are possible in problems 7–10 because the variables are not expressed merely in vague terms such as "increased" or "decreased," but are expressed in precise numerical amounts.

_____ 7. Measurement by ammeter shows that a given circuit has a current of 0.01 amperes. Measurement by voltameter shows that the same circuit has a voltage of 0.05 volts. What is the resistance of the circuit?

_____ 8. If the resistance (R) in a circuit is 10 ohms, and if the impressed voltage (V) is 120 volts, how much current (I) (measured in amperes) is flowing through the circuit?

_____ 9. A flashlight bulb has a resistance (R) of 5 ohms, and the battery produces a difference of potential (V) of 1.5 volts. Calculate the current (I) through the bulb.

_____ 10. On a 60-volt line, if the resistance is 1 ohm, how many amperes current will there be?

Measurement. To appreciate the significance of measurement, a brief survey of the history of physics may be of help. Think of kinetics before the time of Galileo and the pendular clock, when the sun dial and the hour glass were the best instruments for measuring time. Once the pendular clock was invented, *motion* (speed, acceleration, "fast–slow") could be precisely understood to mean units of distance (*space*) covered in (divided by) units of duration (*time*). Then, with motion clearly defined, motion (acceleration) multiplied by *mass* (weight) gave a precise meaning to force (*energy*). With its five concepts (space, time, mass, motion, and energy) all precisely defined, kinetics became an exact science.

In contrast to the above five concepts (and the many derivative concepts found in thermal, chemical, electrical, and atomic physics), the following polarities are no more precise than the *yin-yang* of Taoist philosophy:

greater-less (peace of mind)   greater-less (democracy)
greater-less (health)   greater-less (happiness)
greater-less (moral worth)   greater-less (maturity)

The extent to which we are immersed in vague and imprecise terms may better be understood if we choose some terms from law, such as "clear and present danger," "separation of powers," "freedom of speech," "obscenity," or "justice." It is obvious that many of the most important aspects of life do *not* easily lend themselves to precise measurement.

In areas such as law, theology, psychology, sociology, and economics, where precise measurement is lacking, much attention is given to the definition of terms so that all can agree as to their meaning. Here are two examples.

In the *Mishna* there is a section governing the sacrifice of the "red heifer" (see *Numbers* 19:2–9). But how is a "red heifer" to be defined? Five rabbinical schools of thought arose, and as a result a "red heifer" was defined in the following five ways:

1. A heifer is red when every hair on its body is red.
2. A heifer is red when it is almost all red.
3. A heifer is red when the majority of its hairs are red.
4. A heifer is red when a considerable number of its hairs are red.
5. A heifer is red when one hair is red.[7]

Here is an example from modern law (and modern economics):

_____
[7] Herbert J. Searles, *Logic and Scientific Methods*, 2nd ed. (New York: Ronald, 1956), pp. 44–45.

A congressional committee engaged in a study of small business enterprise found it necessary to devise a legal definition of a "small business." Five definitions were proposed: (1) used by the Army, a concern employing 500 persons or less; (2) used by the Navy, a concern employing 100 persons or less; (3) small in comparison with the industry or trade concerned; (4) any company which can prove that it is not a monopoly in its field; and (5) any company which proves that it is not a "dominating unit" in its industry or a subsidiary or affiliate of such a unit.[8]

It should be obvious that words and ideas change as mankind moves from a pastoral, to an agricultural, to an industrial, to a post-industrial civilization; and that the most elusive meanings are those which deal, not with categories or kinds, but with degrees or amounts. When is a man "honest" or "dishonest"? When is a government "democratic" or "totalitarian"? On what basis may we conclude that a person is "altruistic" or "selfish"? At what point does a man become "famous"? "wealthy"? "a security risk"? On what grounds can a family or nation be said to have "a high standard of living"?

In sum, measurement—the quantitative principle—is the criterion which most sharply differentiates the physical sciences from the social and moral sciences. This point should be kept in mind in section 5.2 when we discuss the scope of science.

(C) THE MECHANICAL PRINCIPLE. This represents a perennial issue in philosophy, and lengthy discussions may be found on it in books and articles dealing with "mechanism," "vitalism," "behaviorism," "teleology," "positivism," "determinism," or "freedom." Instead of the usual exposition, we here substitute exercise 5.1C—a series of short quotations.

Exercise 5.1C. The Mechanical Principle

Directions: Study the following quotations. If time permits, study longer references found in the footnote references and in encyclopedia articles. Then be prepared to write a 100 to 400 word explanation of the mechanical principle.

1. *A. R. Hall:*
   The basic axiom of experimental science is that, circumstances being unchanged, a like cause will produce a like result, because the "cause" releases a chain of events following an unchanging pattern. If this is not so, then the experimental method of inquiry is not one that can usefully be applied to the problem.[9]

2. *Henri Poincaré:*
   How was the order of the universe understood by the ancients: for instance, by Pythagoras, Plato or Aristotle? It was either an immutable type fixed once for all, or an ideal to which the world sought to approach. Kepler himself still thought thus when, for instance, he sought whether the distances of the planets from the sun had not some relation to the five regular polyhedrons. This idea contained nothing absurd, but it was sterile, since nature is not so made. Newton has shown us that a law is only a necessary relation between the present state of the world and its immediate subsequent state. All the other laws since discovered are nothing else: they are, in sum, differential equations.[10]

3. *Shirley Jackson Case:*
   The sky hung low in the ancient world. Traffic was heavy on the highway between heaven and earth. Gods and spirits thickly populated the upper air, where they stood in readiness to intervene at any moment in the affairs of mortals. And demonic

---

[8] Harold Larrabee, *Reliable Knowledge*, p. 266.

[9] A. R. Hall, *The Scientific Revolution, 1500–1800*, (London and New York: Longmans, 1954), p. 151.

[10] Henry Poincaré, *The Value of Science* (New York: Science Press, 1907), p. 87.

powers, emerging from the lower world or resident in remote corners of the earth, were a constant menace to human welfare. All nature was alive—alive with supernatural forces.

Supernatural agents were active in every area of man's experience. They guided the sun and the moon and the stars in their course across the heavens. Thunder and lightning were their playthings. By their control of the rain clouds they blest the earth with fruitful showers or deluged it with floods, and parched it with drought. They caused the eruption of angry volcanoes, and they shook the world with violent earthquakes. They let raging storms loose upon land and sea. They gave fertility to the soil, or they withheld its fruits and afflicted its inhabitants with deadly famine.

The common man lived his life under the constant danger of interference by arbitrary supernatural powers. . . .

When Christian missionaries entered the gentile world, preaching the healing power of their risen and heaven-exalted Lord Jesus, they found audiences well prepared to hear their message. . . . Christians were confident that Jesus had been even more effective in his ministrations to the sick than ever could have been the case with any Dionysus or Demeter or Apollo, or Asklepios or Isis or Serapis, or all of them combined. Jesus had excelled all others in restoring health to the sick and had surpassed all rivals in his power to restore the dead to life. Christians had no need for a natural science of medicine because they were confident that supernatural help had been made abundantly available for them through the mediation of their Great Physician.[11]

4. *Edgar Zilsel:*

Experiment requires manual work, and, therefore, in both antiquity and the modern era its use began in handicraft. In antiquity scientific experimentalists were extremely rare. Since rough work was generally done by slaves, contempt of manual labor formed an obstacle that only the boldest of ancient scholars dared to overcome. A similar obstacle, though by scarcity of slaves less unsurmountable, obstructed the rise of experimental science in the modern era.

The educational system under early capitalism took over from the Middle Ages the distinction between liberal and mechanical arts. In the seven liberal arts (grammar, dialectic, rhetoric, arithmetic, geometry, astronomy, and music) thinking and disputing were alone required; on them alone was the education of well-bred men based. All other arts, as requiring manual work, were considered to be more or less plebeian. There are numerous instances to indicate that up to the sixteenth century even the greatest artists of the Renaissance had to fight against social prejudice. And by the same reason the two components of modern scientific method were kept apart: methodical training of intellect was reserved for university scholars and humanistic writers who belonged, or at least addressed themselves, to the upper class; experiment, and to a certain extent observation, was left to lower-class manual workers. Even the great Leonardo [1452–1519], therefore, was not a true scientist. As he had never learned how to inquire systematically, his results form but a collection of isolated, though sometimes splendid, discoveries. In his diaries he several times discusses problems erroneously which he had solved correctly years before. Gradually, however, the technological revolution transformed society and thinking to such a degree that the social barrier between liberal and mechanical arts began to crumble, and the experimental techniques of the craftsmen were admitted to the ranks of the university scholars. Rational training and manual work were united at last: experimental science was born. . . . One of the greatest events in the history of mankind had taken place. . . .

The young experimental science was forced to fight hard battles with prescientific thinking. Primitive man does not distinguish exactly between animate and inanimate objects; he apprehends all natural events as if they were manifestations

---

[11] Shirley Jackson Case, *Origins of Christian Supernaturalism* (Chicago: University of Chicago Press, 1946), pp. 1, 162–63. Reprinted by permission of the publisher.

of striving, loving, and hating beings. This animistic conception of nature is predominant in all civilizations without money economy and dominated medieval thinking too. When a comet appeared in the sky or a monster was born, medieval man questioned rather the meaning, the aim, and the purpose of these events than their causes. The scholars did not think very differently either. Certainly "entelechies" and "substantial forms" of Aristotle and the Scholastics are not primitive ideas; they are complicated and highly rational constructs. Yet their animistic kernel has, as it were, only dried up; something like a soul, striving to reach its aims, still glimmers through the rational hull. The same holds of the "occult qualities" that were liked so well by the Scholastics. These could never be observed but were supposed to adhere to most objects and to produce effects by sympathy and antipathy, as if they were little ghosts. Animistic survivals like these were of no use to modern technology and had to be cleared away. Teleological explanations were gradually replaced by causal ones. Purposes of inanimate things, the meaning of natural events, and soul-like powers of physical objects cannot be ascertained by observation. On the other hand, the regular connection of cause and effect is testable by experience and experiment. Moreover, engineers are able to produce the effects they want if they know the cause. Causal explanation, therefore, became the chief aim of experimental science.

The discarding of teleological explanations may be illustrated by [the suction pump]. . . . The working of suction pumps was explained in the late Middle Ages by the doctrine of *horror vacui*. Water was supposed to rise in pump barrels because nature had an antipathy to empty space. Since the well-diggers of the new era could not calculate from this theory how long they might make their pipes, two pupils of Galileo, Viviani and Torricelli, experimented on pipes filled with mercury and discovered and measured atmospheric pressure.[12]

5. *J. D. Bernal:*

What Harvey established by his close reasoning by experiment had the same revolutionary effect on ancient and Galenic physiology as the discoveries of Galileo and Kepler had on Platonic and Aristotelian astronomy. He showed that the body could be looked at as a hydraulic machine and that the mysterious spirits which were deemed to inhabit it had no place to live in.[13]

6. *Sterling P. Lamprecht:*

The laws of nature are statements of the mechanical phase of nature. They state the uniformities of correlation and sequence which events manifest. The laws of nature are not, however, dictates that compel procedure—they are not statutes or prescriptive enactments. The presence of contingency in nature is not evident at a glance because it is not effectively exploited by inanimate agents. Inanimate agents react to the actual stimulus of the moment; they react, it might be said, to the superficial. Intelligent agents react to more than the actual stimulus; they react to the potentialities of the actual. And these potentialities are always plural. The plural potentialities of nature are the significant basis of human choice. It is insufficient to argue that because things are as they are they will be as they will be. Rather, because things are as they are, an agent who imaginatively foresees the diverse potentialities of things may choose freely within given limits. Freedom is never total—it is not freedom *from* the world. But it is genuine—it is freedom *within* the world. There is at least no supernatural agency introduced into a mechanical nature in order to give man freedom at the expense of nature's laws. Rather there is a natural development in the powers of agents within nature, and with the appearance of the physiologically developed organism of man there emerges the ability to handle materials in the light of alternative possibilities. . . .

---

[12] From an essay by Edgar Zilsel in Georgio de Santillana and Edgar Zilsel, *The Development of Rationalism and Empiricism*, vol. 2, no. 8 of *International Encyclopedia of Unified Science* (Chicago: University of Chicago Press, 1941), excerpts from pp. 52–72. Reprinted by permission of the publisher.

[13] J. D. Bernal, *Science in History*, 3rd. ed. (New York: Hawthorn, 1965), p. 302.

The more we discover of the detail of nature's mechanism the more we are able to predict, guide, control. Through reliance on nature's mechanism we mold nature to our human interests. More than 300 years ago Francis Bacon saw this clearly. Picturing a great center of learning and of scientific research he spoke of the purpose of the institution in these glowing terms, "The end of our foundation is the knowledge of causes, the secret motions of things; and the enlarging of the bounds of human empire, to the effecting of all things possible." These glowing terms are also sober terms. Bacon speaks of the effecting of all things *possible*. He does not let imagination run wild and picture the effecting of all things desired. We control, not through arrogant insistence but through studious observance of nature's ways.[14]

(D) THE COOPERATIVE PRINCIPLE. Kwok's fourth principle of scientific method is "cooperation for nonpersonal ends." In their struggle to overcome prejudice and to gain objectivity, members of the scientific community set forth varied and competing hypotheses—and then await the confirmations or the disconfirmations of these hypotheses by others. A scientist is not a prophet. He does not enunciate a truth from the housetops and expect others to believe him. He reports his assumptions, experimental procedures, and logically derived conclusions as accurately as he can. His colleagues then check these assumptions, and repeat his experiments under various and varied conditions. Only then are his original conclusions accepted, and, in most cases, they are accepted only with further revisions and modifications.

A scientific "publication" is more than a mere statement that "so-and-so" has discovered "such-and-such" facts. Any scientific publication worthy of the name must include a clear and open description of all the relevant details of the methods whereby the data were gathered, or of the thinking and the assumptions on which the deductions were drawn. In this way it is possible for others to *repeat* the observations or the deductions.

The reason for transforming private knowledge into public knowledge is that single individuals are more likely to be mistaken than groups of individuals. Even with the best of intentions, personal prejudices, faulty observations, unconscious assumptions, or unwarranted deductions may need to be verified or corrected by others. In this way science becomes a cooperative endeavor enabling mankind to see "through the looking-glass" and not merely to reflect cultural predispositions, linguistic mind sets, or personal prejudices. The outcome is that knowledge rests, not on tradition or authority, but on a type of proof repeatable and verifiable by others.

Although it is generally true that single individuals are more likely to be mistaken than groups of individuals, sometimes the individual is right and the group is wrong. Many historical cases might be cited, for example, Avogadro, Mendel, or Semmelweiss, but let us consider an imaginary case. Suppose that we live in a society, 99 percent of whose inhabitants are firm believers in spiritualism. Suppose also that spiritualism is a mistaken belief. Now suppose one attends a "seance." Those who believe in spiritualism will see things that are simply not observable to the nonbelievers. Fortified by social custom, it is extremely easy for the 99 percent to see their own prejudices reflected in nature; and it is extremely difficult for the 1 percent to withstand this social pressure.

Now there are relatively few individuals who have the courage and the self-confidence to maintain beliefs contrary to prevailing opinion. Were the personal beliefs of these mavericks restricted to a single community, their

---

[14] Sterling P. Lamprecht, "Man's Place in Nature," in *The American Scholar*, vol. 7 (New York: Scribner's Sons, 1938), pp. 60–77. Reprinted by permission of the publisher. See also S. P. Lamprecht, *Nature and History* (New York: Columbia University Press, 1950), esp. pp. 50–53, and 105–22.

beliefs would very likely die with the believers. But with journals to broadcast such maverick views, "lone thinkers" from various communities may join forces. Not only will they fortify their beliefs psychologically, but through continued communication they will revise and improve their unorthodox views. Thus the off-beat thinking of a small minority may gradually and peacefully modify the viewpoint of the majority, until the intellectual outlook of a culture is greatly changed. This type of change, so characteristic of modern western democracies, has seemed to refute the medieval adage that "the blood of the martyrs is the seed of the church." However, there is abundant sociological data to show that custom, tradition, and social conformity determine most of human behavior—even in the most free and tolerant societies; and there is historical evidence to show that reason alone, when not working in close partnership with observation and experiment, tends merely to rationalize prevailing beliefs. It is only when rationalism and empiricism are combined that men can make real headway against the rigid dogmatisms, narrow legalisms, mechanical rituals, and silly superstitions which impede the full flowering of civilization.

The Self-Corrective Nature of a Mature Mind. Western civilization was born with the discovery among the Greeks that dialectic, as demonstrated in the Socratic dialogues, is a principal method of attaining truth. In any society where overzealous partisans "take the law into their own hands" to compel uniformity of thought, speech, and action—and they are often able to do so because they appeal to pride, group prestige, or to group fear and hysteria— the search for truth is greatly impaired. "The ability to raise searching difficulties on both sides of a subject," wrote Aristotle, "will make us detect more easily the truth and error about the several points that arise." More recently, Judge Learned Hand has written:

> ... wisdom comes as false assurance goes—false assurance, that grows from pride in our powers and ignorance of our ignorance. Beware then of heathen gods; have no confidence in principles that come to us in the trappings of the eternal. Meet them with gentle irony, friendly scepticism and an open soul.[15]

The power of self-correction, the cornerstone of any progressive civilization, is also the most essential feature of science. In the words of Cohen and Nagel:

> Science does not desire to obtain conviction for its propositions in any manner and at *any* price. Propositions must be supported by logically acceptable evidence,

---

[15] Learned Hand, "Democracy: Its Presumptions and Realities," in *Federal Bar Association Journal* 1 (March 1932): 40–45; cited by Irving Dillard, ed., *The Spirit of Liberty: Papers and Addresses of Learned Hand* (New York: Knopf, 1952), p. 101. Consider also the following statement from a eulogy of Judge Learned Hand:
"Judge Hand's belief in reason as a source of law, and his distrust in his own reason's results seem paradoxical at first. Yet they are logically conjoined. He who is least certain is most likely to be receptive to reason. He who is most receptive to reason is least likely to embrace those brethren of certainty—the absolute, the general principle, the formula and the controlling concept. The inquiring mind will continue to inquire." Cited in John J. Cound, "Learned Hand," *Minnesota Law Review*, 44 (1961): 217–21.
For an excellent account of the views of Charles S. Peirce, Josiah Royce, and John Dewey, and their vision of "the great community" as an ideal both of science and of society, read Max H. Fisch, *Classic American Philosophers* (New York: Appleton-Century-Crofts, 1951), "Introduction," pp. 34–39. Such views are by no means confined to American thinkers. In *Science and Human Experience* (London and New York: Macmillan, 1932), p. 14, Sir Herbert Dingle defines science as "the recording, augmentation, and rational criticism of those elements of our experience which are actually or potentially common to all normal people."

which must be weighed carefully and tested by the well-known canons of necessary and probable inference. It follows that the *method* of science is more stable, and more important to men of science, than any particular result achieved by its means.

1. In virtue of its method, the enterprise of science is a self-corrective process. It appeals to no special revelation or authority whose deliverances are indubitable and final. It claims no infallibility, but relies upon the methods of developing and testing hypotheses for assured conclusions. The canons of inquiry are themselves discovered in the process of reflection, and may themselves become modified in the course of study. The method makes possible the noting and correction of errors by continued applications of itself.

2. General propositions can be established only by the method of repeated sampling. Consequently, the propositions which a science puts forward for study are either confirmed in all possible experiments or modified in accordance with the evidence. It is this self-corrective nature of the method which allows us to challenge any proposition, but which also assures us that the theories which science accepts are more probable than any alternative theories. By not claiming more certainty than the evidence warrants, scientific method succeeds in obtaining more logical certainty than any other method yet devised.

3. In the process of gathering and weighing evidence, there is a continuous appeal from facts to theories or principles, and from principles to facts. For there is nothing intrinsically indubitable, there are no absolutely first principles, in the sense of principles which are self-evident or which must be known prior to everything else.

4. The method of science is thus essentially circular. We obtain evidence for principles by appealing to empirical material, to what is alleged to be "fact"; and we select, analyze, and interpret empirical material on the basis of principles. In virtue of such give and take between facts and principles, everything that is dubitable falls under careful scrutiny at one time or another. . . .

5. Scientific method is the only effective way of strengthening the love of truth. It develops the intellectual courage to face difficulties and to overcome illusions that are pleasant temporarily but destructive ultimately. It settles differences without any external force by appealing to our common rational nature. The way of science, even if it is up a steep mountain, is open to all. Hence, while sectarian and partisan faiths are based on personal choice or temperament and divide men, scientific procedure unites men in something nobly devoid of all pettiness. Because it requires detachment and disinterestedness, it is the finest flower and test of a liberal civilization.[16]

Cohen and Nagel's "self-corrective process" of science, like Kwok's "cooperation for nonpersonal ends," suggests that scientific method includes an ethical dimension—one which Jacob Bronowski has described as follows:

The great ethical force of science has proved to be the dissemination of the idea that truth is a thing which will in some way help us all. In this, we don't have to claim that truth is good, or beautiful, or absolute. We simply recognize that men have found that it is easier to run a society made up of independent individuals if they all acknowledge what is true. . . . We have now learned to acknowledge that to be truthful makes it easier for man to be both solitarily creative and socially

[16] From *Logic and Scientific Method* by Morris R. Cohen and Ernest Nagel, copyright, 1934, by Harcourt Brace Jovanovich, Inc., New York; and Routledge & Kegan Paul Ltd., London; renewed, 1962, by Ernest Nagel and Leonora Cohen Rosenfeld. Reprinted by permission of the publishers.

sustained than any alternative behavior. I regard this as a major step that science has made in producing an ethic.[17]

Cooperation and Innovation. The reader may ask, "Have we not overemphasized cooperation to the neglect of innovation?" "Are not historians justified in emphasizing the role of the great creative thinkers—those who challenge prevailing beliefs by proposing new and better theories and hypotheses?"

Certainly creativity—the ability to view an old subject from a new perspective—is indispensable to progress. Indeed, the ability to develop new hypotheses is such a rare ability that even the greatest geniuses manifest that ability in only one or two areas. For the most part, we are social creatures who, in order to exist at all, must accord with the beliefs and assumptions that prevail in our social group. "Common sense" has been well defined as "the inherited assumptions of our ancestors"—false ones as well as true ones—thus partly justifying the view that creative thinkers tend to be lacking in common sense.

However, closer examination of intellectual progress, whether in an individual or in a social group, shows that creative insight is only one of four types of effort required for lasting change. Exercise 5.1D consists of a series of brief statements suggesting that the methodology of science involves not one, but four stages.

Exercise 5.1D.   Creativity and Scientific Discovery: Materials for Study

Directions: Below are several statements having to do with scientific discovery. These and the footnote references may serve as the basis for class discussion on a variety of topics dealing with discovery, creativity and methodology.

1. *Haefele:* Creative thinking usually involves four stages:
   (1) *Preparation:* organization of material; desire to solve.
   (2) *Incubation:* wait after preparation; frustration.
   (3) *Insight:*   birth of clarifying idea; anxiety, followed by thrill of solution, giving rise to the Eureka effect, the "Ah-Ha" experience.
   (4) *Verification:* development and proof; consolidation of new position; study of its implications; elaboration into wider vistas of knowledge.
              The labor of verification brings into light new problems, and the cycle begins again.[18]

2. *Koestler:* Separations and Reintegrations
   There are certain analogies between the characteristic stages in the history of an individual discovery, and the historical development of a branch of science as a whole. Thus a "blocked Matrix" in the individual mind reflects some kind of impasse into which a science has maneuvered itself. The "period of incubation," with its frustrations, tensions, random tries, and false inspirations, corresponds to the critical periods of "fertile anarchy" which recur, from time to time, in the history of every science. These crises have . . . , a destructive and a constructive aspect. In the case of the individual scientist, they involve a temporary retreat to some

---

[17] Jacob Bronowski, *Man and His Future,* ed. Gordon Walstenholme (Boston: Little, Brown, 1963), pp. 370–71. The "inadequacies of our inherited beliefs" discussed in sec. 3.1 and 5.1 imply something that is less inadequate, namely, truth. The search for truth which motivates philosophy and science is based on a confidence in the reality of truth, whether, like Plato, we call this reality the realm of eternal essences, or, like Augustine, the mind of God. In relation to truth, the more we know, the more we know how little we know; for the wider grows man's sphere of knowledge, the greater its contact with the unknown. Hence the spirit of reverence and awe in men like Newton and Einstein.

[18] John Haefele, *Creativity and Innovation* (New York: Reinhold, 1962), pp. 18, 114. Slightly adapted. See also C. S. Whiting, *Creative Thinking* (New York: Reinhold, 1958).

more primitive form of ideation—innocence regained through the sacrifice of hard-won intellectual positions and established beliefs; in the case of a branch of science taken as a whole, the crisis manifests itself in a relaxation of the rigid rules of the game, a thawing of the collective matrix, the breakdown of mental habits and absolute frontiers. . . . The Eureka act proper, the moment of truth experienced by the creative individual, is paralleled on the collective plane by the emergence, out of the scattered fragments, of a new synthesis, brought about by a quick succession of individual discoveries—where, characteristically, the same discovery is often made by several individuals at the same time.

The last stage—verification, elaboration, consolidation—is by far the least spectacular, the most exacting, and occupies the longest periods of time both in the life of the individual and in the historical evolution of science. Copernicus picked up the ancient Pythagorean teaching of the sun as the center of all planetary motions when he was a student in Renaissance Italy (where the idea was much discussed at the time), and spent the rest of his life elaborating it into a system. Darwin hit on the idea of evolution by natural selection at the age of twenty-nine; the remaining forty-four years of his life were devoted to its corroboration and exposition. Pasteur's life reads like a story divided into several chapters. Each chapter represents a period which he devoted to one field of research; at the beginning of each period stands the publication of a short preliminary note which contained the basic discovery in a nutshell; then followed ten or fifteen years of elaboration, consolidation, clarification.

The collective advances of science as a whole, and of each of its specialized branches, show the same alternation between relatively brief eruptions which lead to the conquest of new frontiers, and long periods of consolidation.[19]

3. *Bernard:*

It is an erroneous impression, fostered by sensational popular biography, that scientific discovery is often made by inspiration—a sort of *coup de fondre*—from on high. This is rarely the case. Even Archimedes' sudden inspiration in the bathtub; Newton's experience in the apple orchard; Descartes' geometrical discoveries in his bed; Darwin's flash of lucidity on reading a passage in Malthus; Kekule's vision of the closed carbon ring which came to him on top of a London bus; and Einstein's brilliant solution of the Michelson puzzle in the patent office in Berne, were not messages out of the blue. They were the final co-ordinations, by minds of genius, of innumerable accumulated facts and impressions which lesser men could grasp only in their uncorrelated isolation, but which—by them—were seen in entirety and integrated into general principles.[20]

4. *Oersted:*

In 1822 the Danish physicist, Oersted, at the end of a lecture happened to bring a wire joined at its two extremities to a voltaic cell, to a position above and parallel to a magnetic needle. At first he had purposely held the wire perpendicular to the needle but nothing happened, but when by chance he held the wire horizontally and parallel to the needle he was astonished to see the needle change position. With quick insight he reversed the current and found that then the needle deviated in the opposite direction. Thus by mere chance the relationship between electricity and magnetism was discovered and the path opened for the invention by Faraday of the electric dynamo. It was when telling of this that Pasteur made his famous remark: "In the field of observation chance favours only the prepared mind."

---

[19] Arthur Koestler, *The Act of Creation* (New York: Dell, 1967), pp. 224–25. Reprinted by permission of Macmillan Co., New York, and A. D. Peters & Co., London. See also pp. 121–47, 216–17, 234–35, 674–708.

[20] Hans Zinsser, *As I Remember Him* (Boston: Little, Brown, 1940), pp. 331–32. (A biography of Claude Bernard.) See also Claude Bernard, *An Introduction to Experimental Medicine* (New York: Dover, 1957); Hans Hahn, "The Crisis in Intuition," in *The World of Mathematics* 3, ed. James R. Newman (New York: Simon and Schuster, 1956), pp. 1956–76.

5. *Humphrey:*

A scientific friend of mine ... lay in bed one night trying to piece together certain puzzling results of experiment. Suddenly, like a flash, he had it. The whole thing lay clear before his eyes. He could hardly wait till he got to his laboratory the next morning to try out a test of his insight. Sure enough, the first test was exactly what he had hoped for, and so was the second one. But every experiment he made after that went the opposite way. For months he worked on the problem, and finally disproved his original idea! As he said to me, the only thing that was wrong with that flash of insight was that it wasn't correct.[21]

6. *Pasteur:*

Preconceived ideas are like searchlights which illuminate the path of the experimenter and serve him as a guide to interrogate nature. They become a danger only if he transforms them into fixed ideas. ... Imagination is needed to give wings to thought at the beginning of experimental investigations on any given subject. When, however, the time has come to conclude and to interpret the facts derived from observations, imagination must submit to the factual results of the experiments.[22]

7. *Darwin:*

I have endeavored to keep my mind free so as to give up any hypothesis, however much beloved (and I cannot resist forming one on every subject), as soon as the facts are shown to be opposed to it.

I have also, during many years, followed a golden rule, namely, that whenever a published fact, a new observation or thought came across me, which was opposed to my general results, to make a memorandum of it without fail and at once; for I had found by experience that such facts and thoughts were far more apt to escape from the memory than favorable ones.[23]

8. *P. W. Bridgman:*

The most vital feature of the scientist's procedure has been merely to do his utmost with his mind, *no holds barred*. This means in particular that no special privileges are accorded to authority or to tradition, that personal prejudices and predilections are carefully guarded against, that one makes continued check to assure oneself that one is not making mistakes, and that any line of inquiry will be followed that appears at all promising.[24]

CONCLUSION.　Although we employ logical techniques to solve numerous problems, we "blunder through" many others. Indeed, the phrase "blunder through" emphasizes the fact that our thought processes may be too complex for analysis. This is why W. I. B. Beveridge speaks of the *art* of scientific investigation, and Arthur Koestler compares the abilities of the scientific genius to those of a *sleepwalker*.

Admitting that we know very little for sure about the workings of a creative mind, we offer nevertheless the following tentative generalizations: In its broadest sense, thinking includes all symbolic behavior—all behavior in which symbols are substituted for perceived things, whether in memory and imagination or in rational inquiry. Creative thinking is the production of

---

[21] George Humphrey, *Directed Thinking* (New York: Dodd, Mead, 1948), pp. 134–35. For a clever statement showing the amount of logic involved in so-called "intuition," read by Elizabeth (Colt) Kidd, *Just Like a Woman* (New York: Appleton, 1945), condensed in *Reader's Digest* 58 (May 1951): 143.

[22] Rene J. Dubos, *Louis Pasteur* (Boston: Little, Brown, 1950), pp. 366–67. For a variety of examples illustrating methods of science, read L. W. Beck, *Philosophic Inquiry* (New York: Prentice-Hall, 1952), pp. 109–18; E. A. Burtt, *Right Thinking* (New York: Harper, 1946), chap. 15 and pp. 748–53.

[23] "Darwinisms," cited in Harlow Shapley, Samuel Rapport, and Helen Wright, eds., *A Treasury of Science* (New York: Harper, 1943), pp. 435–36.

[24] P. W. Bridgman, *Reflections of a Physicist* (New York: Philosophical Library, 1950), p. 370. See also W. I. B. Beveridge, *The Art of Scientific Investigation* (New York: Random House, 1955).

new symbols, new mental constructs, new postulational systems, exemplified in such things as maps, classificatory schemes, scientific theories, poems, paintings, and musical compositions. Reason is thinking that is directed toward the solution of a problem. Deductive reasoning deals with inferences and implications—the relations of assumptions to conclusions. Inductive reasoning is a process of evaluation, of critical thinking, whereby certain patterns of deduction are judged as relevant to a particular problem, other patterns judged as irrelevant. These aspects of thinking are inseparable except in theory; and normal thought moves with lightning speed from the creation of postulational schemes, to the derivation of logical inferences from these schemes, or to the testing, transformation, and application of such schemes to the world of experience.

By postulating rational structures, which we call theories or hypotheses, the mind transforms a vast jumble of miscellaneous experiences into a conceptual unity. However, the search for unity amid diversity does not end here. The critical mind is ever eager to test inherited belief against the ever-changing facts and events of the real world. If the hypotheses are validated and confirmed, these hypotheses become theories—the nearest thing to truth that man can possess. But if the hypotheses are shown to be incongruous with factual evidence, then the search begins anew. Thus, striving for unity amid diversity, combining intuitive postulates, rational deduction, and inductive evidence, the mind brings order out of chaos, and gives meaning and significance to what otherwise would remain a medley of varied and disorganized experiences.

5.2   The Scope of Science and Logic

The extension of the ideal of science into economics, politics, ethics, and religion would mean that widespread discussion and deliberation are recognized as the surest and safest way to bring about fair and equitable solutions to disputed issues. This is the principle of "majority rule, minority rights" which, in the words of John H. Hallowell, means:

> It is the *reasoned* judgment of the majority that obligates our compliance with its decisions, not the will of the majority as such. To the extent, therefore, that the rule of the majority becomes more an expression of will and less an expression of reasoned judgment, to that degree it becomes less democratic and more tyrannical.[25]

---

[25] John H. Hallowell, "The Meaning of Majority Rule," *Commonweal* 56 (May 23, 1962): 167–69. See also Henry Steele Commager, ed., *Living Ideas in America* (New York: Harper & Row, 1951), chap. 5, "Democracy: Majority Rule and Minority Rights."

It is very difficult to be reasonable, and especially so in times of rapid change. There is no doubt but that we are living in a period of extremely rapid change in many areas, including changes in basic values. Such changes are more likely to come about in a peaceful manner if there is no rigid orthodoxy, no favored beliefs, no fixed method, no unchanging rules, which might tend to restrict or to prevent the modification of old values to fit new situations. Says Jean François Revel:

> The optimum conditions for the realization of revolution are those in which the forces of change exist in an atmosphere of constitutional benevolence that allows them to make enormous progress without the necessity of provoking an actual civil war. In other words, the more that change is possible through legal means, the better the chance of [peaceful, and therefore, lasting] revolution.

—Jean François Revel, *Without Marx or Jesus* (New York: Doubleday, 1971), p. 185.

In contrasting it with earlier systems of government, Edmund Cahn writes that the American Constitutional system represents a change

	As to Objective	*As to Content*	*As to Sanction*
From:	perpetuity	immutability	appeal to heaven
To:	efficacy	adaptation	appeal to the courts.

—Edmund Cahn, *Confronting Injustice* (Boston: Little, Brown, 1962), p. 68. See also pp. 168–75, 216f.

Unfortunately, many of the basic concepts of economics, politics, morality, philosophy, and religion are vague and ambiguous. None of them are amenable to the precise measurement which characterizes the natural sciences. How, then, can reason operate in such areas?

REASON AND REASONABLENESS.   The quest for truth is greatly impaired when racial and religious prejudice, the struggle for power and prestige, and the compulsion of inherited prejudices all stand as roadblocks to rationality. The great strength of free societies rests in their attempt to keep these roadblocks to a minimum. Alasdair MacIntyre puts the matter thus:

> What then are the true connections between tolerance, rationality, and liberation? The telos of tolerance is not truth, but rationality. Certainly we value rationality because it is by rational methods that we discover truth; but a man may be rational who holds many false beliefs and a man may have true beliefs and yet be irrational. What is crucial is that the former has the possibility of progressing toward truth, while the second not only has no grounds for asserting what he believes, even though it is true, but is continually likely to acquire false beliefs. What is it to be rational? It is a necessary condition of rationality that a man shall formulate his beliefs in such a way as to make clear what evidence would be evidence *against* them, and that he shall lay himself open to criticism and refutation in the light of any possible objection. But to foreclose on tolerance is precisely to cut oneself off from such criticism and refutation. It is to endanger one's own rationality gravely by not admitting one's own fallibility.[26]

In the history of western civilization, after centuries of religious intolerance and persecution, the Age of Reason (1650–1800) emerged as a high-water mark in the attempt to apply reason to the solution of social problems. The Age of Reason was at its zenith when the British and American constitutional systems were initiated. This system rests on the belief that political, economic, and religious revolutions can occur without serious bloodshed; that disputes may be settled by ballots rather than bullets; and that when public opinion is molded by bullets or propaganda rather than free and open discussion, people are more likely to be persuaded by ideas that are false.

SOME DISPUTED ISSUES.   Philosophy begins in wonder and ends in science; science begins in philosophy and ends in technology. The remainder of section 5.2 will move into the area of speculative philosophy as it opens up a few highly controversial issues concerning the scope of science.

Exercise 5.2A.   Measurement and Behaviorism

Directions: Defend or criticize the statement, "Whatever exists does so in some measurable degree"—or the statement's contrapositive, "What cannot be measured does not exist."

Three Viewpoints. To encourage discussion of this problem, we present three opposing viewpoints. Although they may not be needed, specific references are given in the footnotes for each of the three viewpoints.

(1) The behaviorist view, which would restrict psychology and sociology to those aspects of human behavior which are subject to empirical observation and to measurement. This view maintains that "conscious states" or "subjective impressions" can be

---

[26] Alasdair MacIntyre, *Herbert Marcuse: An Exposition and a Polamic* (New York: Viking Press, 1970), concluding pages. See also Albert Guerard, *Bottle in the Sea* (Cambridge, Mass.: Harvard University Press, 1954), chap. 1.

a part of the behavioral sciences only to the extent that such subjective states can be correlated with behavioral acts which may be publicly observed, verified, and measured.[27]

(2) A modified behaviorist view, namely, that many, but not all, facets of human nature may be observed or measured, e.g., E. L. Thorndike's view that the "general goodness" of cities may be measured, though not very accurately.[28]

(3) The view that there are dimensions of man which are beyond the scope of scientific measurement.[29]

In the twentieth century John Dewey (1859–1952) and many others have interpreted a free society to mean one in which reason is free to perform its function of criticizing and analyzing social traditions, and thereby to help bring about a more just and humane civilization. Few Americans would argue against this ideal. However, it should be clearly recognized that social inertia is extremely difficult to combat in areas vitally affecting the economic, political or moral prejudices of any large segment of a society. Even worse, many of the basic terms used in these areas are vague or ambiguous, e.g., "fair wage," "fair trade practices," "monopoly," "minimum living standard" in economics; "clear and present danger," "minority rights," "civil liberties" in politics; "happiness," "well being," "peace of mind," "salvation" in philosophy and religion. Since cooperative thinking is possible only when many people are able to combine their efforts by thinking about the same subject, and since vague and ambiguous terms prevent this from happening, the ability of men to "think together" is far more difficult in social and moral areas than it is in the natural sciences.

Let us summarize. Man's heritage of knowledge—and this includes political, economic, ethical, and religious knowledge no less than science and technology—is always somewhat tentative, and ever subject to reconstruction in the light of new discoveries and of new social situations. The man on the street may say "I think" when he means "I feel," that is, "I am attached to these prejudices." But for a scholar, "I think" is intellectually meaningless unless that thinking has included a fair and impartial study of competing points of view. No pattern of ideas is so sacred that the thinker's mind should be closed to other alternatives. "You are told to prove you are right," said Louis Pasteur, "but I say, try to prove you are *wrong*."

We are all too prone to view science as a *product*, and think of democracy as an *achievement*, forgetting their deeper meanings: science is a *process*, and democracy is a *method* of substituting willing approval for compulsory belief. The advancement of science and democracy signifies the forward march of men and women who are eager for truth and receptive to reason. Anyone receptive to reason is unlikely to embrace those brethren of certainty: the fixed idea, the rigid dogma, the infallible decision, and the unqualified rule. The inquiring mind will continue to inquire; the democratic citizen will continue his struggle for a fuller realization of liberty, equality, and fraternity.

---

[27] This viewpoint is clearly stated in Hans Reichenbach, *Experience and Prediction* (Chicago: University of Chicago Press, 1938), pp. 63–68. *Note:* For each of the three viewpoints we list only one reference. There are many others to be found.

[28] Edward Lee Thorndike, *Man and His Works* (Cambridge, Mass.: Harvard University Press, 1943), chap. 10, "The Welfare of Communities." This chapter is a summary of Thorndike's 1937 book, *Your City*.

[29] A 1971 statement of this view is found in Joseph Uemura, "Measuring Man" reprinted in Henry Ehlers, ed., *Crucial Issues in Education*, 5th ed. (New York: Holt, Rinehart and Winston, 1973), pp. 180–85.

To phrase the matter in religious terms: anyone thoroughly committed to the ideals of science and of democracy will maintain a patient *faith* that reasonable solutions to new and difficult problems are possible; an abiding *hope* that persisting inquiry and open discussion will, sooner or later, resolve these problems; and, however difficult the situation, however heated the controversy, an unfailing attitude of *charity* toward one's fellow humans, particularly toward those whose views seem untenable and repulsive. "The greatest of these is charity" (I *Cor.* 13:13) because, without charity, the future becomes everything, and the present is no longer the focus of life.

On such matters, those who adhere to traditional religious outlooks differ very markedly from positivists, rationalists, and atheists. The selections in exercise 5.2B may help focus attention on a few of the specific areas of agreement and disagreement in such matters.

Exercise 5.2B.   Reason and Religion

Directions: The following statements are intended as springboards for further thought and discussion. Read them carefully. Then give special attention to one or two of them with which you particularly agree or differ. At the instructor's discretion, write a 200- to 500-word editorial essay, or perhaps present a two- to five-minute oral statement, expressing your own point of view.

1. *Blaise Pascal:*

   Man is visibly made to think; this is his whole dignity and his whole merit.

   Reason commands us much more imperiously than a master; for if we disobey the one we are unfortunate, but if we disobey the other we are fools.

   [But] It is the heart which feels God, and not the reason. For that is what faith is, God touching the heart, not the reason.

   There is nothing so conformable to reason as the disavowal of reason in those things which belong to faith. And nothing so contrary to reason as the disavowal of reason in the things that do not belong to faith. There are two excesses equally dangerous: to exclude reason, and to admit reason alone.[30]

2. *H. C. Hockett:*

   Detecting Forgeries: One of the most famous forgeries ever exposed by historical research is that of the "False Credentials." As early as the ninth century, the papal archives contained certain alleged decrees of early popes, as well as a document purporting to be a donation in the fourth century by the Emperor Constantine to Pope Sylvester of the right to govern Italy and the rest of the Roman Empire in the West. Both decretals and donation were accepted as genuine during the Middle Ages, but modern critics have proved their falsity.

   Their form does not correspond to the official form of such documents in the particular papal reigns to which the compiler assigned them. This diplomatics has shown. They use a method of dating which chronology has proved to be unhistorical. Although they supposedly belong to different centuries, their Latin style remains the same, and this the Frankish Latin of the ninth century. Philology has contributed this. It has also been found that their quotations from the scriptures were from the version of Jerome, amended during the time of Charlemagne, and that they contain passages taken bodily from a Frankish council of 829. Finally, they imply the view that the theology of the ninth century was the theology of the second, and that the early bishops of Rome exercised the same wide jurisdiction as the ninth century popes. It is probable that the collection originated in the diocese of Rheims between 847 and 865. Probably the authors believed that by

---

[30] Blaise Pascal (1632–1666), *Thoughts* (reprinted in many editions).

representing the priesthood as an institution going back to the very beginning of the church, they were doing the very best thing they could to make it effective in its holy work.[31]

3. *Albert Schweitzer:*

Christianity has need of thought that it may come to the consciousness of its real self. For centuries it treasured the great commandment of love and mercy as traditional truth without recognizing it as a reason for opposing slavery, witch burning, torture, and all the other ancient and medieval forms of inhumanity. It was only when it experienced the influence of the thinking of the Age of Enlightenment that it was stirred into entering the struggle for humanity. The remembrance of this ought to preserve it forever from assuming an air of superiority in comparison with thought.[32]

4. *Paul Tillich:*

No act of will accepting "right" belief can be properly demanded by any authority. Devotion to truth is supreme; it is devotion to God. There is a sacred element in the integrity that leads to doubt even about God and religion. Indeed, since God is truth, he is the basis and not the object of any question about God. Any loyalty to truth is religious loyalty, even if it leads to a recognition of the lack of truth. Paraphrasing Augustine, the serious doubter may say: "I doubt, therefore I am religious." Even in doubt the divine is present. . . . The only absolutely irreligious attitude, then, is absolute cynicism, absolute lack of earnestness.[33]

5. *Herbert Dingle:*

In science we find ourselves striving more and more to become as literal as possible, until in the most advanced stages of scientific thought we cannot use words at all, but merely *ad hoc* symbols, defined by their relations with other symbols, and when we have to make contact with experience in order to apply our results to everyday life, we make it at the minimum possible number of most unambiguously specifiable points. In religious utterances, on the other hand, we seem not only unable but extremely unwilling to avoid metaphor. "The Light of the World" does not refer to light or to the world; it is more relevant to a single blind man than to the brightest star in the sky. "The Holy Ghost" is not a canonized spectre; a "change of heart" has nothing to do with a surgical operation; "finding Jesus" does not involve excavations in Palestine. Many such phrases, it is true, once had a literal meaning which they have now lost, but we do not try to change them; we seek rather to preserve them. If the scientific part of us were to hear the religious part say, "God's thoughts are not as our thoughts" (Is. 55:6), it would immediately ask, "Then why call them both 'thoughts'?" No one would dream of saying "The lodestone's gravitation is not as the apple's gravitation." The Earth's action on the lodestone we attribute to "magnetism," and its action on the apple we attribute to "gravitation." Again I am not criticizing the language used in

---

[31] This example is adapted from H. C. Hockett, *Critical Method in Historical Research* (New York: Macmillan, 1955), pp. 26–27. Contrast the quest for power, implicit in the last sentence in Hockett, with the quest for truth described on pages 152–54, and implicit in the next two statements by Albert Schweitzer and Paul Tillich.

[32] Albert Schweitzer, *Out of My Life and Thought* (New York: Holt, Rinehart and Winston, 1933), p. 236. Compare with the criticism by W. R. Inge of " . . . the mischievous doctrine that the spiritual eye can only see when the eye of sense is closed."—W. R. Inge, *Christian Mysticism* (London: Methuen, 1899); (New York: Meridian, 1956), p. 299.

[33] Paul Tillich, *The Protestant Era* (Chicago: University of Chicago Press, 1948), pp. 292–93. Contrast this view with the religious pretentions which Dostoyevsky's Grand Inquisitor summed up in his phrase, "miracle, mystery, and authority"; and the orthodox churchman's acquiescence to such authority, which Dietrich Bonhoeffer called "cheap grace."

Concerning "cynicism," read Harry Emerson Fosdick, *A Guide to Understanding the Bible* (New York: Harper & Row, 1938), chap. 2.

either sphere of thought. I am simply pointing out the difference, and suggesting that the involuntary tendency to adopt two contrasted forms of speech may help to convince us of the fundamental nature of the division we have to heal.[34]

6. *Albert Einstein:*

The most beautiful thing we can experience is the mysterious. It is the source of all true art and science. He to whom this emotion is a stranger, who can no longer pause to wonder and stand rapt in awe, is as good as dead; his eyes are closed.

This insight into the mystery of life, coupled though it be with fear, has also given rise to religion. To know that what is impenetrable to us really exists, manifesting itself as the highest wisdom and the most radiant beauty which our dull faculties can comprehend only in their most primitive forms—this knowledge, this feeling, is at the center of true religiousness. In this sense, and in this sense only, I belong in the ranks of devoutly religious men. It is enough for me to contemplate the mystery of conscious life perpetuating itself through all eternity, to reflect upon the marvelous structure of the universe which we can dimly perceive, and to try humbly to comprehend even an infinitesimal part of the intelligence manifested in nature.[35]

7. *George W. Gobel:*

The educated man appreciates both the capabilities and the limitations of the mind in the universal scheme of things. Recognizing his powers, he develops dignity, integrity, and responsibility. Realizing his limitations, he cultivates tolerance, humility and reverence.

The unknowable, the incomprehensible, the insoluble is not merely in the heavens; it is close to us. We experience its effect in our daily lives. Inability to cope with it causes fear, superstition, frustration, suspicion, crime, and war. The education of the future, therefore, must deal with man's attitude toward the unknowable as well as his treatment of the knowable. It must put in finer balance reason and faith.[36]

THE SCOPE OF LOGIC.   In post-Darwinian philosophy much emphasis has been given to what are sometimes called "biological theories of intelligence." In 1877 Charles S. Peirce (1839–1914) argued that Descartes' "universal doubt" is psychologically impossible, since belief, not doubt, is man's basic tendency. Peirce held that the beliefs upon which man guides his actions are more like "bundles of habits" than "intuitive truths." Certainly they are never so "clear and distinct" as to be exempt from criticism and change. Furthermore, man is a social animal to such a degree that the best *test* of truth is the power of thought to get itself accepted in the competition of the market. Here "the market" means "the community of scientific investigators," working, in Kwok's phrase, "for nonpersonal ends."

Two years later (1879), William James insisted that thinking is always purposive: thinking is important because it furthers our aims and interests. This "pragmatic" approach to logic had a long and interesting development,

---

[34] From the book, *The Scientific Adventure*, by Herbert Dingle, pp. 253–54. Copyright © 1952 by Pitman Publishing Corporation. Reprinted by permission of Pitman Publishing Corp. See also William Hordern, *Speaking of God* (New York: Macmillan Co., 1964), p. 7.

[35] Albert Einstein, cited in *Living Philosophers* (New York: Simon & Schuster, 1937), pp. 3–7. For another excellent statement emphasizing the importance of wonder and awe, but written by a man defending a nontheistic viewpoint, read Max Carl Otto, *Science and the Moral Life* (New York: Mentor, 1949), p. 166.

[36] George W. Gobel (then Professor of Law, University of Illinois), cited by William Britton, "Objectives of Higher Education," in *American Association of University Professors Bulletin* 42 (Summer 1956): 256–67.

culminating in John Dewey's 1938 statement, "Nature as it already exists ceases to be something which must be accepted and submitted to, endured or enjoyed, just as it is. It is now something to be modified, to be intentionally controlled."[37]

Dewey (1859–1952) equated logic with scientific method, and considered logic to be a theory of inquiry whose task is to evaluate the various rules and procedures of logic in terms of applicability, simplicity, and utility. Peirce called it "heuristic logic." Others call it the "logic of discovery." The "logic of inquiry" may be considered the theme of chapters 3 and 5 of this book, and we view these two chapters as correlative to, not opposed to, the remaining chapters, which deal almost exclusively with "the logic of argument." Whereas the logic of inquiry is mainly concerned with the dynamics of reasoning, the logic of argument restricts itself to methods of precise statement and of valid proof. Once it is clearly recognized that the postulates or assumptions of any area of knowledge are provisional and tentative, then it is easy to understand why new postulates—new assumptions—provide the dynamism which progress demands, and yet remain in accord with the rules of thinking set forth in formal logic.

NEW ASSUMPTIONS CONCERNING ASSUMPTIONS. The development of non-Euclidean geometries in the nineteenth century has led to radically new assumptions concerning assumptions, i.e., axioms, postulates, definitions, and also concerning the relationship of reason to experience, and of formal logic to empirical science.

For many centuries Euclid's plane geometry was "Exhibit A" for all defenders of rationalism; it was generally agreed that the Euclidean definitions and axioms were self-evident truths. But in the early nineteenth century N. I. Lobachevski and F. Bolyai proposed an alternative geometry; and later in the century G. R. Riemann and F. Klein developed a second non-Euclidean geometry. For the most part, these three geometries all have the same fundamental concepts. However, Euclid and Lobachevski assume that lines may be infinite in length, whereas Riemann does not. In Euclid, one and only one parallel may be drawn; in Lobachevski an infinite number of parallels may be drawn; and in Riemann no parallels are possible. In Euclid, the sum of the angles of a triangle is exactly 180°; in Lobachevski the sum is always less than 180°; in Riemann the sum is always more than 180°.

These rival systems of geometry led to new views concerning deductive systems. Euclid took from ordinary experience "by intuition" such terms as "point," "line," "straight line," "plane," and "congruence"; whereas, about the beginning of the twentieth century, David Hilbert (1862–1942) and other formalists developed systems based entirely on "undefined terms," i.e., terms having no easily recognizable empirical referents. Each of the three above-mentioned systems of geometry is logically coherent; each is a self-consistent geometrical model of what the universe *may* be like. But not one of the three systems was derived inductively from experience. Their origin was primarily rational and logical, not observational or empirical. Formalists insist that laws of logic, such as $\sim(\sim p) = p$, or rules of mathematics, such as $2 + 2 = 4$, are *analytically true*: they are true because an analysis of their basic definitions and postulates makes them logically compelling. This is a radically different

---

[37] For a longer, yet brief, summary of these and similar views, read Max H. Fisch, ed., *Classic American Philosophers* (New York: Appleton-Century-Crofts, 1951), pp. 1–40, "General Introduction."

view from the empiricists' doctrine that "all knowledge originates in experience," e.g., that we believe that $2 + 2 = 4$ simply because we have never experienced an exception to it.

Let us now briefly review the prevailing nineteenth-century empiricist view concerning inductive logic and scientific method. Thomas Henry Huxley (1825–1895) expressed this view when he described "the method of scientific investigation" as follows:

> The method of scientific investigation is nothing but the expression of the necessary mode of working of the human mind. It is simply the mode at which all phenomena are reasoned about, rendered precise and exact. . . .
>
> Suppose you go into a fruiterer's shop, wanting an apple,—you take up one, and, on biting it, you find it is sour; you look at it, and see that it is hard and green. You take up another one, and that, too, is hard, green, and sour. The shopman offers you a third; but, before biting it, you examine it, and find that it is hard and green, and you immediately say that you will not have it, as it must be sour, like those that you have already tried.
>
> Nothing can be more simple than that, you think; but if you will take the trouble to analyze and trace out into its logical elements what has been done by the mind, you will be greatly surprised. In the first place, you have performed the operation of induction. You found that, in two experiences, hardness and greenness in apples went together with sourness. It was so in the first case, and it was confirmed by the second. True, it is a very small basis, but still it is enough to make an induction from; you generalize the facts, and you expect to find sourness in apples where you get hardness and greenness. You found upon that a general law, that all hard and green apples are sour; and that, so far as it goes, is a perfect induction. Well, having got your natural law in this way, when you are offered another apple which you find is hard and green, you say, "All hard and green apples are sour; this apple is hard and green, therefore this apple is sour." That train of reasoning is what logicians call a syllogism, and has all its various parts and terms—its major premise, its minor premise, and its conclusion. And, by the help of further reasoning, which, if drawn out, would have to be exhibited in two or three other syllogisms, you arrive at your final determination, "I will not have that apple." So that, you see, you have, in the first place, established a law by induction, and upon that you have founded a deduction, and reasoned out the special conclusion of the particular case. [38]

MILL'S METHODS.   Mill's methods of induction (John Stuart Mill, 1806–1873) may be viewed as a refinement of the preceding statement. Mill called

---

[38] Excerpt from T. H. Huxley, *Darwiniana* (London, 1863). For an excellent evaluation of Mill's methods, read *John Stuart Mill's Philosophy of Scientific Method*, edited with an introduction by Ernest Nagel (New York: Hafner, 1950), pp. xv–xlviii. For recent restatements of Mill's methods, accompanied by criticisms of them, read I. M. Copi, *Introduction to Logic*, 4th ed. (New York: Macmillan, 1972), chap. 12; J. D. Carney and R. K. Scheer, *Fundamentals of Logic* (New York: Macmillan, 1964), part 3; N. Rescher, *Introduction to Logic* (New York: St. Martin's, 1964), part 4; Herbert L. Searles, *Logic and Scientific Methods* (New York: Ronald, 1948, 1956), pp. 201–332.

It should be noted that Huxley's example of scientific reasoning is an example of analogical reasoning: Because apples A, B, and C have properties G (green), H (hard) and S (sour), therefore apple D, which has properties G and H, will also have property S. But this is not an adequate explanation of scientific method. For in science the fruitfulness of analogies depends on whether consequences can be deduced from them which can be observed and tested, and this in turn depends on whether the resemblance selected is analogous in a fundamental way. Although analogies are extremely helpful in providing clues and insights, analogies are often misleading, since things can be analogous in a superficial way. On this point recall the analogical reasoning of the pigeon in section 3.1, namely: because Alice and serpents both ate eggs and both had long necks, therefore Alice must be some kind of a serpent. The aim of scientific investigation is to distinguish (a) those resemblances between sets of phenomena which are accidental, from (b) those based on some law or principle common to both sets of phenomena. The history of any branch of science the method illustrated, in the previous example by Huxley, the *Method of Agreement*: when two phenomena are observed constantly to occur together, we have a clue that they may be causally related. But Mill moved on from here to his *Method of Difference*: when the *absence* of a given phenomenon in an antecedent is invariably followed by the absence of that same phenomenon in its consequent, we have proof of the absence of causal relationship.[39] Mill put these two methods together in his famous "Method of Agreement and Difference": "If events having property a are invariably followed by events having property b, and if the absence of a is invariably accompanied by the absence of b, then a may be said to be the cause of b."

Let us use logical symbols to summarize these three methods:

> Method of Agreement: If a, then b: $a \to b$
> Method of Difference: If $\sim a$, then $\sim b$: $\sim a \to \sim b$
> Method of Agreement and Difference: $(a \to b) \cdot (\sim a \to \sim b)$

Applying COPO and BE, $(a \to b) \cdot (\sim a \to \sim b) = (a \to b) \cdot (b \to a) = (a \leftrightarrow b)$. In words: if and only if a, then and only then b.

Here is an illustration of the use of Mill's Method of Agreement and Difference:

To test the effects of vitamin A on health, a scientist performed the following experiments: (1) he observed that rats fed on a normal diet containing vitamin A were healthy. (2) But when members of this group of rats were given a diet deficient in vitamin A, they became sick. Then, to insure a fair sample, he reversed the diets of the sick and healthy rats, and (3) he found that those who had been sick but who were not fed a normal diet regained their health; (4) whereas the healthy ones, after being placed on a diet deficient in vitamin A, became sick.

Let us employ the symbolism of truth-value logic to summarize this experiment.

> Let a = The rats ate food containing vitamin A;
> Let $\sim a$ = The rats ate food not containing vitamin A;
> Let h = The rats were (or became) healthy;
> Let $\sim h$ = The rats were (or became) nonhealthy, i.e., sick.

Now the four steps in this scientist's experiments may be symbolized thus:

> (1) $a \to h$;   (2) $\sim a \to \sim h$;   (3) $a \to h$; and (4) $\sim a \to \sim h$.

Conjoining these four statements, and applying COPO to (2) and (4) yields:

$$(a \to h) \cdot (h \to a) \cdot (a \to h) \cdot (h \to a); \text{ or, by TAUT and BE:}$$
$$a \leftrightarrow h$$

This suggests that Mill's Method of Agreement and Difference for discovering cause and effect relations between events in the world of space-time-matter may also be expressed in terms of the biconditional of truth-value logic.

Exercise 5.2C.   Symbolizing "Mill's Method of Agreement and Difference"

Directions: Following the preceding example, i.e., the experiment with vitamin A, express each of the following in symbolic form.

---

represents a movement from (a) to (b), and such a movement involves much more than analogical thinking.

[39] Mill's Method of Concomitant Variations may be considered as an extension of his Method of Agreement, and Mill's Method of Residues may be viewed as an extension of his Method of Difference.

1. Goldscheider had his arm suspended in a special frame and moved about by an assistant. His muscles, therefore, had no share in these movements. Yet he could distinguish as small an angle of movement of this arm as when his own muscles moved and supported it. He concluded that muscular (s)ensations play no important role in our (c)onsciousness of the movements of our limbs.

2. The presence of (a)ir is somehow causally related to the transmission of (s)ound because, when an electric bell is placed so that air may be added or removed at will, we can hear (s)ounds when (a)ir is present, but cannot hear (s)ounds when there is no (a)ir.

3. [Sachs found that] when (l)ight is excluded from a plant, then, although all other conditions remained the same, no (s)tarch was formed; but when the plant was exposed to light again, then there was a renewed formation of starch. Similarly, when certain portions of the leaves of an illuminated plant were covered with black paper, then no starch was formed in those portions. Sachs concluded that starch is formed in plants by the decomposition of carbon-dioxide gas in chlorophyll under the influence of light.

4. Two monkeys were made drunk, one with raw spirits (whiskey), the other with matured spirits. The first became angry; it spat and swore. The second was merely foolish and amiable in its intoxication. A week later the doses were reversed, and once more the monkey which had the (r)aw whiskey became (q)uarrelsome, while the monkey which had the matured [= nonraw] whiskey was genial and good-humored [= nonquarrelsome]. This seemed to prove that, at least for monkeys, the effects resulting from the drinking of raw spirits are far worse than those which result from drinking matured spirits.

Answers for Chapter Five

5.1A:
1. T;   3. F;   5. T;   7. F;   9. T.

5.1B:
1. D;   3. U;   5. I;   7. 5 ohms (Solution: $R = V/I = 0.05/0.01 = 5$ ohms);
9. 0.3 amperes (Solution: $I = V/R = 1.5/5 = 0.3$ amperes).

5.1C and 5.1D
   No answers are given for these exercises.
   As a summary of section 5.1, the following take-home assignment is suggested:
   Write a 300- to 500-word essay on "Inductive Logic and Science." In this essay, give particular emphasis to "the empirical principle" and show how this principle is implemented and perfected by means of (a) the quantative, (b) the mechanical, and (c) the cooperative principles.

5.2A:
No answers are given for this exercise.

5.2B:
No answers are given for this exercise.

5.2C:
   1. Let m signify "muscular movement occurred," let $m \cdot s$ signify "muscular movement initiated by the self occurred," and let $m \cdot \sim s$ signify "muscular movement initiated by someone other than the self occurred." Let c signify "the subject was conscious of the movement." Then,

$$[(m \cdot s) \to c] \cdot [(m \cdot \sim s) \to c]$$

(To see why the first two lines are equivalent, study (21A) under 6.1 on page 209.)

$$= [(m \cdot s) \vee (m \cdot \sim s)] \to c$$
$$= [m \cdot (s \vee \sim s)] \to c \quad \text{(by DIST)}$$
$$= m \to c \quad \text{(by ExM, TV)}$$

Another conclusion: s and $\sim s$ are irrelevant. They are unrelated to c.

   3. Let "l" signify the presence of light; "$\sim l$" the absence of light. Let "s" signify "Starch was formed"; and let "$\sim s$" signify "Starch was not formed." Then, $(l \to s) \cdot (\sim l \to \sim s) \mid \therefore (l \leftrightarrow s)$.

chapter 6

SUBJECT-PREDICATE LOGIC

6.1 Symbolizing the A-, E-, I-, and O- Forms of Traditional Logic

REVIEW AND OVERVIEW.   In chapters 2 and 4, where the entire emphasis was on the *truth values* of statements, lower-case letters were used to symbolize many different types of sentences. Thus the single letter s could have been used, in different contexts, to symbolize the universal "All tenors are (s)ingers," the existential "Some pianists are (s)ingers," the singular "John is a (s)inger," or the indefinite "Birds are (s)ingers." But now we require a different symbolism, one which clearly represents the subject and predicate of every statement, and one which clearly differentiates universals, existentials, and singulars. The following seven examples may serve as an overview of several symbolisms, including the new symbolism we will use here.

Statement	Truth Value	Boolean	Set Theory	New
1. All (d)ogs are (m)ammals.	m	$D \cdot \sim M = \emptyset$	$D \subset M$	$d \to m$
2. No (w)itches are (f)airies.	$\sim f$	$W \cdot F = \emptyset$	$W \subset \sim F$	$w \to \sim f$
3. Tom is a (b)oy.	b	$\{t\} \cdot \sim B = \emptyset$	$t \in B$, or $\{t\} \subset B$	Bt
4. Tom and Dick are (b)oys.	b	$\{t \cdot d\} \cdot \sim B = \emptyset$	$\{t \cdot d\} \subset B$	$Bt \cdot Bd$
5. Some (s)wans are (p)ets.	p	$S \cdot P \neq \emptyset$		$Sx \cdot Px$
6. Some (s)wans are not (p)ets.	$\sim p$	$S \cdot \sim P \neq \emptyset$		$Sy \cdot \sim Py$
7. Dogs are (p)ets.	p	(Statement 7 would need to be reworded, so it could be clearly known to be either $d \to p$ or $Dx \cdot Px$.)		

Students should realize that there are several different symbolisms used in twentieth-century logic, and that the one used in this chapter is simpler than the ones which are more generally used. However, although the different symbolisms may *seem* to be quite different, the underlying reasoning behind them is very similar. Hence any student who understands the symbolism used here should be able in an evening's time to adapt what he knows to the Polish notation, or to any one of the several Anglo-American symbolisms to be found in other logic books.[1]

---

[1] For a brief explanation of various symbols representing the same essential ideas, read Samuel D. Guttenplan and Martin Tamny, *Logic: A Comprehensive Introduction* (New York: Basic Books, 1971), pp. 367–70; Gerald J. Massey, *Understanding Symbolic Logic* (New York: Harper and Row, 1970), pp. 118–22, "Alternative Notations."

What distinguishes chapter 6 from earlier chapters in this book is the use of *singular* and *existential* statements—categorical assertions about nonempty sets. Thus, "Px" means "There exists at least one P," or "The set P has one or more members." "$Px \cdot Qx$" means "There are one or more P's that are also Q's." As subscripts for existentials we shall employ the three lower-case letters "x," "y," and "z." For example, "Some (d)ogs are (w)hite" ($Dx \cdot Wx$); "Some (d)ogs are (b)lack" ($Dy \cdot By$); "Some (d)ogs are neither (w)hite nor (b)lack" $\{(Dz \cdot \sim Wz \cdot \sim Bz)$ or $[Dz \cdot \sim (Wz \vee Bz)]\}$. The fact that we use three different subscripts (x, y, and z) makes it clear that we are referring to three different subsets within the larger set "Dogs."[2]

Without these *subscripts* the conjunction of $d \cdot w$ ("Some dogs are white") and $d \cdot b$ ("Some dogs are black") would yield $(d \cdot w) \cdot (d \cdot b)$; which, by DIST, yields $d \cdot (w \cdot b)$, or "Some dogs are both white and black." But with distinct symbols for $Dx \cdot Wx$, and for $Dy \cdot By$, such confusions may be avoided. The new symbolism is especially helpful for dealing with singular propositions.

SINGULARS.   In set theory, "Tom is a boy" would be symbolized "$t \in B$" or "$\{t\} \subset B$." But we shall now symbolize it "Bt." Here the lower-case letter "t" represents the statement's subject "Tom," and the capital letter "B" represents the statement's predicate, "is a member of the set 'Boys,'" or "has the attribute 'Boyness.'"

Suppose we learn more about Tom, namely, "Tom is a (b)oy, Tom is a (s)inger, and Tom is a (f)ootball player." This represents the conjunction of these three statements and would be symbolized $Bt \cdot St \cdot Ft$. Suppose we were to speak about three different boys, as in "Tom is a (p)ianist, Dick is a (b)ugler, but Harry is not a (m)usician." We symbolize this "$Pt \cdot Bd \cdot \sim Mh$."

In traditional logic, singulars were treated as if they were universals. Consider what is probably the most famous syllogism of medieval logic:

All men are mortal; Socrates is a man; Therefore, Socrates is mortal.

In this syllogism, "Socrates is a man" and "Socrates is a mortal" were classified as universals. The reasoning of medieval logicians is not difficult to understand. First, since the one-membered set "Socrates" referred to the entire membership of the subject class, "Socrates is a man" was considered to be of the same type as "All Swedes are men" or "All dogs are mammals." Second, since *every* statement was taken to mean a categorical statement about nonempty sets, universals as well as singulars and existentials were interpreted to be categorical affirmations about existential reality. We shall return to this point in sections 6.2 and 6.3. Before proceeding, it will be well to study quite carefully the manner in which universals, singulars, and existentials are to be symbolized.

Exercise 6.1A.   Symbolizing Statements

Directions: Before each problem, circle A, B, or C to indicate which of the three symbolisms is correct. At least one of the three symbolisms for each problem will be correct. You are to consider an equivalent symbolism as a correct one, e.g., "$\sim p \vee q$" for "$p \rightarrow q$." If in doubt, complete all odd-numbered problems before doing the evens.

A   B   C   1. John is not a (p)lumber.   A. $\sim Pj$ B. $\sim (Pj)$ C. $P \sim j$

---

[2] For the rare existential having a name beginning with the letter "x," "y," or "z," we *stipulate* some other letter as a subscript. Thus "Xerxes was a king" could be symbolized "Ka"; "Yucatan is a peninsula" by "Pb"; and "Zeno is a stoic" by "Sc." These are rare cases, and will not occur at all in this book.

A B C   2. Tom and Dick are (t)all.   A. $Tt \cdot Td$ B. $(t \cdot d) \to t$
C. $\sim(\sim Tt \vee \sim Td)$

A B C   3. Each (i)ndividual is (s)ubstantial.   A. $Ix \cdot Sx$ B. $i \to s$
C. $\sim s \to \sim i$

A B C   4. No (s)ubstance is an (a)ttribute.   A. $s \to \sim a$ B. $\sim s \to a$
C. $\sim s \vee \sim a$

A B C   5. Dave and Frank are not both (m)arried.   A. $\sim(Md \cdot Mf)$
B. $\sim Md \vee \sim Mf$ C. $\sim Md \to \sim Mf$

A B C   6. Tom, Dick, and Harry are not all (b)aritones.   A. $Tx \cdot Dx \cdot Hx \to Bx$
B. $\sim Bt \vee \sim Bd \vee \sim Bh$ C. $\sim(Bt \cdot Bd \cdot Bh)$

A B C   7. Some (b)oys are not (t)all, and some (g)irls are (t)all.   A. $\sim Tb \cdot Tb$
B. $(Bx \cdot \sim Tx) \cdot (Gy \cdot Ty)$ C. $(Bx \cdot \sim Tx) \vee (Gx \cdot Tx)$

A B C   8. Some (p)oliticians are (h)onest; others are dishonest.
A. $(Px \cdot Hx) \cdot (Py \cdot \sim Hy)$ B. $Px \cdot Hx \to Py \cdot \sim Hy$
C. $(p \cdot h) \cdot \sim(h \cdot p)$

A B C   9. Many (d)reamers are im(p)ractical, but no (d)reamers are (b)oring.
A. $Dx \cdot \sim Px \cdot (d \to \sim b)$ B. $(d \to \sim p) \cdot (d \to \sim b)$
C. $(Dx \cdot \sim Px) \cdot (Dy \cdot \sim By)$

A B C   10. If all (s)eniors (g)raduated, some of them carried (o)verloads.
A. $(s \to g) \to Sx \cdot Ox$ B. $(Sx \cdot Gx) \cdot (Sy \cdot Oy)$
C. $\sim(Sx \cdot Ox) \to \sim(s \to g)$

A B C   11. Many (a)thletes are (h)onor students, and Bill is one of them.
A. $Ax \cdot Hx \cdot Ba \cdot Bh$ B. $Ax \cdot Hx \cdot Ab \cdot Hb$ C. $(a \to h) \cdot Ax \cdot Hb$

A B C   12. "Tom is a (d)ancer" implies "At least one (d)ancer exists."
A. $Td \to Xd$ B. $Dt \to Dx$ C. $\sim Dx \to \sim Dt$

A B C   13. Unless there is a typographical (e)rror, every (p)roblem in this exercise has at least one (c)orrect answer.   A. $\sim e \to (p \to c)$
B. $\sim e \cdot p \to c$ C. $e \vee p \to c$

A B C   14. If "No (b)oys are (g)irls" is true, then "If Tom is a (b)oy then Tom is not a (g)irl" is also true.   A. $\sim b \cdot g \to Tb \cdot T \sim g$
B. $(b \to \sim g) \to (Bt \to \sim Gt)$ C. $(g \to \sim b) \to (Gt \to \sim Bt)$

A B C   15. Since Einstein was a (g)enius, and since he lived in the (t)wentieth century, there must be at least one (t)wentieth century (g)enius.
A. $Te \cdot Ge \to Tx \cdot Gx$ B. $Eg \cdot Et \mid \therefore Xt \cdot Xe$ C. $Ge \cdot Te \to Tx \cdot Gx$

A B C   16. Every (p)arable is (m)eaningful if you (s)tudy it.   A. $s \to (p \to m)$
B. $p \to (s \to m)$ C. $Sp \leftrightarrow Mp$

A B C   17. The parable of the Prodigal Son is (m)eaningful, if you (s)tudy it.
A. $s \to (p \to m)$ B. $Sp \to Mp$ C. $\sim Mp \to \sim Sp$

A B C   18. If Washington was a (g)eneral, then some (p)residents were (g)enerals.
A. $(w \to g) \to (Px \cdot Gx)$ B. $Gw \to (Px \cdot Gx)$ C. $\sim Gw \vee (Px \cdot Gx)$

A B C   19. If all (g)enerals were (t)all men, then Napoleon was a (t)all man.
A. $(g \to t) \to Tn$ B. $\sim Tn \leftrightarrow \sim(g \to t)$ C. $Tn \vee \sim(g \to t)$

A B C   20. Some (s)nakes are (p)ets and some (s)nakes are not (p)ets.
A. $(s \cdot p) \cdot (s \cdot \sim p)$ B. $(Sx \cdot Px) \cdot (Sy \cdot \sim Py)$
C. $(Px \cdot Sx) \cdot (\sim Py \cdot Sy)$

A B C   21. All (s)quirrels and (b)eavers are (r)odents.   A. $s \vee b \to r$
B. $(s \to r) \cdot (b \to r)$ C. $s \cdot b \to r$

A B C   22. If this animal is an (e)lephant, then it is a (m)ammal and it is (h)erbivorous.   A. $(e \to m) \cdot (e \to h)$ B. $e \to m \cdot h$ C. $e \to m \vee h$

A B C   23. If this is a (b)ig mammal and if it is (h)erbivorous, then it is probably an (e)lephant.   A. $b \cdot h \to e$ B. $(b \to e) \vee (h \to e)$ C. $b \vee h \to e$

A B C   24. If any job (p)ays well, then it either requires exceptional (s)kill or it demands many hours of (w)ork.   A. $p \to s \vee w$
B. $(p \to s) \vee (p \to w)$ C. $(p \to s) \cdot (p \to w)$

A major purpose of *Logic: Modern and Traditional* is to show that the traditional Aristotelian-scholastic logic is only one step removed from modern logic, and that the two logics can be united into a single system. In order to combine traditional and modern logic into one system, it is first necessary to understand the logical structures underlying the subject-predicate grammar used in Indo-European languages.

THE A-, E-, I-, AND O- FORMS OF TRADITIONAL LOGIC.   In traditional logic, simple statement forms were analyzed into their component elements as follows:

Subject and Predicate. Each simple statement has a subject (*S*) and a predicate (*P*) called *terms*. This is true of all Indo-European languages.

Quantifiers. The subject term is preceded by one of three quantifiers: "All," "No," or "Some."

Copula. The verbs "is," "are," "is not," and "are not" indicate either (a) that *S* is included in *P*, or (b) that *S* is excluded from *P*.

These quantifiers and copulas make it possible to discover meanings and relationships between subjects and predicates that might not otherwise be evident. Thus the sentence "Students exercise too little" would be changed to the statement "Some students are persons who exercise too little." This sentence can now be seen to have the same meaning as "Some persons who exercise too little are students," or as "Some persons who exercise too little are not non-students," or as "Some students are not persons who do not exercise too little."

UNIVERSALS.   The two forms "All *S* is *P*" and "No *S* is *P*" are called *universals* because they refer to each and every member of the subject set. We here treat universals as conditionals, so that "All (d)ogs are (m)ammals" is understood to mean "If any animal is a (d)og, it is a (m)ammal" ($d \rightarrow m$), and "No (h)orses are (t)igers" is taken to be equivalent to "If any animal is a (h)orse, it is not a (t)iger" ($h \rightarrow \sim t$). To interpret universals as conditionals is to recognize that universals often speak in an abstract or hypothetical manner, so that universals do not necessarily imply that members of the subject set actually exist. For example, "All mermaids are aquatic creatures"; "If anyone could show us how to square the circle, he would be a phenomenal genius"; "All chiligons are hundred-sided polygons."

EXISTENTIALS.   Propositions of the form "Some *S* is *P*" or "Some *S* is not *P*" are called *existential* because they assert that we are speaking about one or more actually existing members. Thus, "Some grass is brown" affirms that, in the world of existing realities, the conjunction of grasses with brown objects is not an empty set. "Some creatures in fairy-tale books are dwarfs" asserts the existence of one or more dwarfs, at least in the sense that they exist in fairy-tale books. Observe that the quantifier "some" is very indefinite, and includes such varied meanings as "a few," "about half," "nearly all," "1 percent," "50 percent," "99 percent," and "perhaps 100 percent." In traditional logic all such shades of meaning are reduced to the single quantifier "some." We define "Some *S* is *P*" to mean "At least one *S* is a *P*" or "One or more *S*'s are *P*'s."

The combination of universals ("All *S* . . . ") ("No *S* . . . "), and existentials ("Some *S*"), with affirmatives ("is," "are"), and negatives ("is not," "No *S* are _____"), produces exactly four types of simple propositions. Following medieval logicians, we symbolize these four types by the letters "A," "E," "I," and "O." *A* and *I*—the first two vowels of the Latin word *affirmo* ("I affirm")—signify affirmative propositions. E and O—the two vowels of the Latin word *nego* ("I deny")—signify negative propositions. Let the subject and predicate terms be represented by "*S*" and "*P*" respectively. This produces the following four types of categorical statements:

A: *Universal Affirmative* (total inclusion):   All *S* is *P*
    If *x* is an *S*, then *x* is a *P*. $(s \rightarrow p)$
E: *Universal Negative* (total exclusion):   No *S* is *P*
    If *x* is an *S*, then *x* is not a *P*. $(s \rightarrow \sim p)$
    or If *x* is an *S*, then *x* is a $\sim P$. $(s \rightarrow \sim p)$
I: *Existential Affirmative* (partial inclusion):   Some *S* is *P*
    There exists at least one element (represented by the subscript *x*) that is in both *S* and *P*. $(Sx \cdot Px)$
O: *Existential Negative* (partial exclusion):   Some *S* is not *P*.
    There exist one or more *S*'s that are not *P*'s. $(Sx \cdot \sim Px)$
    or There exists at least one *S* that is not a *P*. $(Sx \cdot \sim Px)$

Keep clearly in mind the distinction between the A, E, I, and O *statement forms*, and the two *terms* (*S* and *P*) within any statement. For example, each of the following are E-form *statements*, but none of the four have the same subject and predicate *terms*: "No *S* is *P*," "No $\sim S$ is *P*," "No *S* is $\sim P$," and "No $\sim S$ is $\sim P$."

Exercise 6.1B.   Structure of A-, E-, I-, and O- Propositions

Part I.   Directions: On the left side of the number in the answer column, write A, E, I, or O to show the structure or form of the proposition. On the right side of the number in the answer column, write S, P, C, or Q to indicate whether the underscored word or phrase is the subject term (S), the predicate term (P), the copula (C), or the quantifier (Q).

1. Some sentences *are not* propositions.   _____ 1. _____
2. Some subject terms *are* singular terms.   _____ 2. _____
3. *Some* sentences are expressions of ideas whose meaning becomes clearly intelligible only when restated in one of the A-, E-, I-, or O- forms.   _____ 3. _____
4. No universal proposition is *one beginning with the quantifier* "*some.*"   _____ 4. _____
5. All *singular propositions* are sentences without quantifiers.   _____ 5. _____
6. Some sentences having different forms are *sentences having equivalent meanings.*   _____ 6. _____
7. *Some* so-called "singular" propositions are sentences whose subject contains more than a single name or idea.   _____ 7. _____
8. *No* A- or E-form propositions are existential propositions.   _____ 8. _____
9. No *universal propositions* are I- or O-form propositions.   _____ 9. _____
10. No I- or O-form statement *is* a universal proposition.   _____ 10. _____

Part II: Now reverse the procedure: underscore the word or words asked for.

11. No sentence beginning with the quantifier "No" is an affirmative proposition.   11. Subject
12. Some verbs are words whose brevity may contribute to ambiguity.   12. Predicate
13. Some logical propositions are rather stilted forms of expression because of the stipulation that they must make explicit the quantifier, the copula, and the subject and predicate sets.   13. Copula
14. Some statements in normal English are sentences whose meanings are ambiguous precisely because the statements do not make clear the quantifier, the copula, the subject set, and/or the predicate set.   14. Quantifier
15. All attributes in traditional logic are sets of objects which have similar properties.   15. Predicate

16. Some students are misinformed persons who suppose that the
values of logical precision and linguistic clarity negate the values
of poetic symbolism and ritualistic expression.   16. Predicate

Each sentence in exercise 6.1B was clearly expressed as an A-, E-, I-, or O-
form. In ordinary language, on the other hand, brevity often takes precedence
over clarity, and the copula or quantifier may be omitted. This means that the
structure of sentences in ordinary language is often vague and indefinite.
Before such indefinite sentences may be used in logical arguments, they must
be restructured into an A-, E-, I-, or O- form. Exercise 6.1C asks the reader to
do this.

Exercise 6.1C.   Transforming Vague Statements Into A-, E-, I-, and O- Forms

Remarks: In everyday speech and writing, the quantifiers "All," "No," and "Some"
are frequently omitted. This usually occurs for the sake of brevity, but it also occurs
when there is a desire to substitute half truths and clichés for precise statements. The
A-, E-, I-, and O- forms of traditional logic help to eliminate this type of ambiguity.

Directions: First work the odd numbered problems and compare your solutions with
the answers provided. Next do the evens. Use separate paper, and make sure that
each A-, E-, I-, or O- form has a clearly defined subject term, predicate term, copula, and
quantifier.

1. Every man dies.
2. Without exception, children love to play.
3. Any man can do that.
4. Whales are mammals.
5. Gentlemen prefer blondes.
6. Freshmen are insufficiently prepared.
7. Indians are not sociable.
8. Americans are law breakers.
9. People don't think logically.
10. We Americans are a God-fearing people.
11. Swedes are blondes.
12. There are college seniors who have never learned to read carefully.
13. At least one student in this class is an honor student.
14. About half of all college graduates are not equal in ability to the top ten percent
of high school seniors.
15. An occasional malcontent becomes a revolutionary.
16. Law floats in morality but sinks in hypocritical piety.
17. There are some freshmen who are not unprepared.
18. There are a number of habits that will ruin a person's character.
19. No one walks who can afford a car.
20. None are free who do not govern themselves.

Exercise 6.1D.   Writing Equivalent A-, E-, I-, and O- Forms

Remarks: In exercise 2.2G, emphasis was placed on the equivalence of $p \rightarrow q$,
$\sim q \rightarrow \sim p$, $q \vee \sim p$, $\sim p \vee q$, $\sim (p \cdot \sim q)$, and $\sim (\sim q \cdot p)$. Exercise 6.1D has a similar
purpose, except that we now deal with the A-, E-, I-, and O- forms of traditional subject-
predicate logic. This exercise should help the student to understand how, using two
A-forms and two E-forms, any universal may be expressed in four equivalent ways;
or how, using two I-forms and two O-forms, any existential may be expressed in four
equivalent ways.

Directions: Carefully study the *Answers* for problems 15, 17, and 19 of exercise 6.1C.
Observe that each group of four equivalent statements contains two affirmatives and
two negatives. Observe also that the subject terms are alike in each of two pairs of
any four equivalent statements.

Now, on separate paper, copy the following eight sentences, and express each of them in four equivalent ways. In each case you should end up either with two A-form and two E-form statements, all universals; or with two I-form and two O-form statements, all existentials.

1. All horses are mammals.
2. No dogs are fish.
3. No baby less than a year old is a fast runner.
4. All persons who win honors are hard workers.
5. Some floors are not dirty.
6. Some geese are pets.
7. Some people who work hard are unsuccessful.
8. Some students who are on probation are not unintelligent people.

Exercise 6.1E should be quite easy, for it merely requires that A- and E- forms (universals) of traditional logic be interpreted as conditionals, and it then applies to these conditionals the rules of the hypothetical syllogism studied in section 2.5. Thus, problem 2 of exercise 6.1E should be restated to read:

If anyone is not (w)ell adjusted, he is a (m)isfit.   1. $\sim w \rightarrow m$
If anyone is (w)ell adjusted, he is not a juvenile
  (d)elinquent.   2. $w \rightarrow \sim d \, (= d \rightarrow \sim w)$
Therefore, if anyone is a juvenile (d)elinquent,
  he is a (m)isfit. $/ \therefore d \rightarrow m$

Exercise 6.1E.   Arguments Employing Only Universals

Directions: Symbolize the following ten arguments as conditionals. Then, in the answer blanks, write V or I to indicate whether the argument is valid or invalid.

_____ 1. No (g)entlemen are (r)ude, because all (b)arbarians are rude, and no barbarian is a gentleman.

_____ 2. All juvenile (d)elinquents are (m)isfits, because no person who is (w)ell adjusted is a juvenile (d)elinquent, and anyone who is not (w)ell adjusted is a (m)isfit.

_____ 3. All (sp)onges are (s)ensitive, and no (b)otannical species is (s)ensitive. Hence, no (sp)onge is a (b)otannical species.

_____ 4. All (sp)onges are (s)ensitive, hence all sponges are (z)oological species, for all zoological species are sensitive.

_____ 5. Every law (b)reaker is a (r)ascal; hence, every (t)hief is a law breaker, because every thief is a rascal.

_____ 6. All (m)ums are (p)lants. No mums are (e)xtinct species. So no extinct species are plants.

_____ 7. All (c)etaceans are (m)ammals. No cetaceans are (u)ngulates. Therefore, no ungulates are mammals.

_____ 8. No (w)alruses are (u)ngulates. We know, therefore, that no (w)alruses are (c)etaceans, because no ungulates are (c)etaceans.

_____ 9. All (u)ngulates are creatures having (h)oofs. No hoofed creatures have (f)ins. Therefore, no ungulates have fins.

_____ 10. No (k)angaroos are non-(m)arsupials. No (m)arsupials are non-(b)lixes. Therefore, all kangaroos are blixes.

SOME ALTERNATIVE WAYS OF EXPRESSING UNIVERSALS.

There are many and varied ways in which the A- and E- forms of traditional logic are expressed in ordinary language. These forms are neither ambiguous, nor vague, nor subtle; they are simply different ways of expressing the same ideas. Here are four groups of such forms of expression. All of them are widely used in English.

Only if S, then P; Only S is P; None but S is P; None except S is P; S alone is P.

These sentences all mean "No non-*S* is *P*," or "No *P* is non-*S*" or "All *P* is *S*." In brief, "Only *S* is *P*" becomes "All *P* is *S*." For example, "None except birds are robins" becomes "All robins are birds"; "Only the strong survive" becomes "If you survive, then you are strong."

The only S is P. Sentences beginning with "The only" are quite different. The article "the" changes the meaning completely. For example, "The only Evergreens in our city park are Spruce" means "All (the) Evergreens in our city park are Spruce"; whereas "Only nondeciduous trees are evergreens" means "All evergreens are nondeciduous." The article "the" is usually used when referring to classes having a rather restricted membership, as in "The only sophomores in this room are physics majors" which means "All (the) sophomores in this room are physics majors."

All but S is P (or *all except S is P*). Statements of this type are to be interpreted to mean "All non-*S* is *P*" or "All ~ *S* is *P*." They should not be confused with sentences of the type "None but *S* are *P*" or "None except *S* are *P*." Thus "All but (c)hildren must (p)ay full fare" means "All non-children must pay full fare" ($\sim c \rightarrow p$); or, by COPO, "All who are not required to (p)ay full fare are (c)hildren ($\sim p \rightarrow c$). Again, "All except the (a)ged or the (d)isabled must (b)ear arms" means "All persons who are not either (a)ged or (d)isabled are persons required to (b)ear arms" [$\sim(a \vee d) \rightarrow b$; or $\sim b \rightarrow (a \vee d)$].

An S is a P means "All *S* is *P*," and is probably a contraction of the form "[If anything is] an *S* [it] is a *P*." Thus "A dog has a tail" means "If any creature is a dog, it has a tail," or "All dogs have tails" ($d \rightarrow t$).

Exercise 6.1F. Transforming Statements From Ordinary Language Into A- and E- Forms

Directions: Without seriously altering the meaning, rewrite the following, expressing each sentence as an A-form or an E-form proposition.

1. Only babies cry.
2. Only women bear children.
3. Only freshmen are excluded.
4. Only the ignorant pretend to despise knowledge.
5. None think the great unhappy but the great. (= None but the great think the great unhappy).
6. All except cripples must work.
7. None but children are admitted free.
8. Heaven favors only kindly desires.
9. Except ye repent, ye cannot be saved.
10. None except men play varsity football.
11. No one was admitted without a passport.
12. No cross, no crown.
13. Only water is a truly refreshing drink.
14. The only world champions are young men.
15. The only people out of work are the uneducated or the sick.
16. The only student who really fails is the one who doesn't try.
17. Only tragedy can result if you try to make an engineer out of a moron.
18. All but women and children wore uniforms.
19. Any man who was not disabled or who was not a pacifist carried arms.
20. A whale is a cetacean.
21. No dogs, except those on leashes, are permitted in this park.
22. No student fears an exam except one who is unprepared.

23. Among mammals, only cetaceans live in water.
24. The only persons who made the honor roll are seniors.

Exercise 6.1G. Testing Arguments for Validity

Directions: On separate paper, reformulate each of the following problems. Then, using any method of proof you prefer, decide whether the argument is valid or invalid, and write V or I in the answer blank.

_____ 1. All non-(m)arsupials are nonbandicoots. Hence, no (b)andicoots are non-opposums; for all (o)pposums are marsupials.

_____ 2. All (l)iberals are unorthodox. Only (o)rthodox people support established (t)raditions. So, no liberals support established traditions.

_____ 3. Only persons who (s)ave string are (m)iserly. Only (p)oor people save string. Hence, none but the poor are miserly.

_____ 4. A (f)lickertail is not a (c)orvidae. Only creatures that live in the Dakota (p)rairies are (f)lickertails. Therefore, no (c)orvidae are (f)lickertails.

_____ 5. All members of our (f)aculty are (c)ertified teachers; because, only (g)raduates are on our faculty, and only nongraduates are uncertified.

_____ 6. Only un(i)ntelligent creatures are in(v)ertebrates. None except (v)ertebrates possess any marked (a)bility to communicate. Therefore, any animal possessing any marked ability to communicate is a vertebrate.

_____ 7. A (w)hale is a (c)etacean, and only (h)ighly intelligent creatures are (c)etaceans. None except creatures with (b)rains are (h)ighly intelligent. A (b)rainy creature is one (p)ossessing a vertebrate cranium that is responsible for the interpretation of sensory impulses, the coordination and control of bodily activities, and the exercise of emotion and thought. None except creatures (p)ossessing such a vertebrate cranium are (s)eals. Therefore, only (c)etaceans are (s)eals.

_____ 8. None except those who failed to (g)raduate are required to (r)epeat this course. All who graduated are now (m)arried. So, none except nonmarried persons are required to repeat this course.

_____ 9. No animals except (m)ammals are covered with (h)air. None but hair-covered animals have two successive sets of (t)eeth. It follows that all animals that do not have two successive sets of teeth are nonmammals.

_____ 10. All except those who are (s)ick have to (w)ork; and all who work are to be given three (m)eals each day. Therefore, only persons who are not given three meals each day are sick.

Exercise 6.1H. Eight Lewis Carroll Polysyllogisms³

Directions:
(A) Restate and interpret each statement in the following arguments as an A-form, an E-form, or as a conditional.
(B) Symbolize each statement, using the suggested symbols.
(C) Write down the valid conclusion which follows from each set of premises. (*Note:* In problems 1 and 2 the valid conclusions are given.)

(1) 1. Anyone who breaks his promises is un(d)ependable.
    2. Every (w)ine-drinker is very (c)ommunicative.
    3. Any man who keeps his (p)romises is (h)onest.
    4. No teetotalers are pawn(b)rokers.
    5. One can always (d)epend on a very communicative person.
    Therefore, no pawnbrokers are dishonest.

---

³ The polysyllogisms of exercise 6.1H—all valid—are slightly adapted from the mathematical recreations of Lewis Carroll (author of *Alice in Wonderland* and *Through the Looking Glass*) in his book, *Symbolic Logic*, republished by Dover Publications, Inc., New York, 1955. Ten Lewis Carroll polysyllogisms, similar to these, may be found in R. T. Purtill, *Logic for Philosophers* (New York: Harper & Row, 1971), pp. 182–85.

(2) Universe of discourse: Animals.
   1. Animals that do not (k)ick are un(e)xcitable.
   2. (D)onkeys have no (h)orns.
   3. A (b)uffalo can always (t)oss one over a gate.
   4. No animals that kick are (s)afe for children.
   5. No hornless animal can toss one over a gate.
   6. All animals are excitable, except buffaloes.
      Therefore, no donkeys are safe for children.
(3) 1. No Gentiles (o)bject to pork.
   2. No one who (a)dmires pigsties ever (s)tudies Lewis Carroll's *Symbolic Logic.*
   3. No (M)andarin is able to (r)ead Hebrew.
   4. Unless objecting to pork, everyone admires pigsties.
   5. No (J)ew is unable to read Hebrew.
      Therefore, _____
(4) Universe of discourse: Plum pudding.
   1. A plum pudding that is not really (s)olid is mere (p)orridge.
   2. Every plum pudding served at my (t)able has been (b)oiled in cloth.
   3. Any plum pudding that is mere (p)orridge is in(d)istinguishable from soup.
   4. No plum puddings are really solid, except those that are served at my table.
      Therefore, _____
(5) 1. The only kinds of food that my (d)octor allows me to eat are those that are not very (r)ich.
   2. Nothing that (a)grees with me is un(s)uitable for supper.
   3. Wedding (c)akes are always very (r)ich.
   4. My (d)octor allows me to eat all foods that are (s)uitable for supper.
      Therefore, _____
(6) 1. No kitten that (l)oves fish is (u)nteachable.
   2. No kitten without a (t)ail will (p)lay with a gorilla.
   3. Kittens with (w)hiskers always love fish.
   4. No teachable kitten has (g)reen eyes.
   5. No kittens have tails unless they have whiskers.
      Therefore, _____
(7) Universe of discourse: Logic exercises.
   1. When I work a logic exercise without (g)rumbling, you may be sure it is one that I can (u)nderstand.
   2. These (p)olysyllogisms are not (a)rranged in regular order like the arguments I am used to.
   3. No (e)asy problems give me a (h)eadache.
   4. I cannot understand arguments not arranged in regular order like the ones I am used to.
   5. I never grumble at a problem unless it gives me a headache.
      Therefore, _____
(8) Universe of discourse: Fish.
   1. No (s)hark ever (d)oubts that it is well fitted-out.
   2. A fish that cannot dance a (m)inuet is (c)ontemptible.
   3. No fish is quite certain that it is well fitted-out, unless it has (t)hree rows of teeth.
   4. All fishes, except (s)harks, are (k)ind to children.
   5. No (h)eavy fish can dance a minuet.
   6. A fish with three rows of teeth is not to be despised.
      Therefore, _____

CONCLUDING COMMENT. Teachers or students who are familiar with traditional logic will note that section 6.1 has not employed some of the terms found in most traditional logic textbooks, notably: *obversion, conversion,* and *immediate inference.* If we symbolize various equivalent A, E, I, and O statement forms, we see that *obversions* are instances of *double negation,* thus:

In (All S is P) = (No S is non-P), $(s \to p) = [s \to \sim(\sim p)]$ by DN;
In (Some S is P) = (Some S is not non-P), $Sx \cdot Px = Sx \cdot \sim(\sim Px)$ by DN.
In (Some S is not P) = (Some S is non-P), $(Sx \cdot \sim Px = Sx \cdot \sim Px)$. Here it makes no difference whether the negation of P is expressed by "non" or by "not."

Conversions of E-forms are instances of *Contraposition.*
Thus, in (No S is P) = (No P is S), $(s \to \sim p) = (p \to \sim s)$ by COPO.

Conversions of I-forms are instances of *Commutation.*
Thus, in (Some S is P) = (Some P is S), $(Sx \cdot Px) = (Px \cdot Sx)$ by COM.

Contrapositives of A-forms are simply symbolized as *contrapositives.*
Thus, in (All S is P) = (All non-P is non-S), $(s \to p) = (\sim p \to \sim s)$ by COPO.

Contrapositives of O-forms are equivalent by *Commutation* and *Double Negation.*
Thus, in (Some S is not P) = (Some $\sim P$ is not $\sim S$), $(Sx \cdot \sim Px) = [\sim Px \cdot \sim(\sim Sx)]$ by COM and by DN.

Immediate Inference will be discussed in sections 6.2, 6.3, and 6.4.

6.2   Three New Laws of Logic: PART, QE, and SING-EX

CONJOINING UNIVERSALS WITH SINGULARS AND EXISTENTIALS. In the memories of every normal adult are stored countless items of information, such as "Dogs have tails," "Tadpoles turn into frogs," "Paris is in France," "My hair needs cutting," "My office is on Main Street," "There is skin on my finger," and "Hot things burn." When we face concrete situations, we draw on this huge store of information and use whatever portions of it that seem relevant to our immediate concerns. Thus if I know, as stored information, that "If I touch a hot object, it will burn me," and conjoin it with the categorical statement "This red stove burner is hot," the stored information is changed to "If I touch this red stove burner, it will burn me"—and the inference proceeds. This section will explain the logical principles by which such inferences are made.

Particularization (PART) is the basic rule which makes it possible to apply to specific events the more general truths contained in conditionals. Application of PART to singulars is shown in these examples: If "All (d)ogs are (m)ammals" $(d \to m)$ is true, then by PART "If Fido is a (d)og, Fido is a (m)ammal" $(Df \to Mf)$ is also true. Similarly, by PART, "If Rover is a (d)og, then Rover is a (m)ammal" $(Dr \to Mr)$ will also be true.

Here is a valid argument, showing the use of PART:

In Symbols:

Minor Premise: Jumbo is an (e)lephant.	1. Ej
Major Premise: All (e)lephants are (h)erbivorous.	2. $e \to h \mid \therefore Hj$
Revised Major Premise (by PART):	3. $Ej \to Hj$ 2, PART
If Jumbo is an (e)lephant, then Jumbo	4. Hj 1, 3, MP
is (h)erbivorous.	
Conclusion: Hence, Jumbo is (h)erbivorous.	

*Crucial Assignments
Method of Proof:*

Original Symbolism: $(Ej) \cdot (e \to h) \mid \therefore Hj$
Revised symbolism, after PART is applied: $Ej \cdot (Ej \to Hj) \mid \therefore Hj$
$\quad\quad\quad\quad\quad\quad\quad\quad\quad\quad$ T $\quad$ X T F $\quad$ F F

The revised symbolism makes it clear that the two premises and the conclusion all refer to the same thing (namely, Jumbo); so the argument has unity, and can be tested for validity. Each problem in exercise 6.2A requires application of the law of particularization (PART) to the major premise. In this way, the major premise, the minor premise, and the conclusion all have the same subscript, and the argument can be judged to be either valid or invalid.

Exercise 6.2A.   Arguments Applying PART to Singulars

Directions: Symbolize each of the following arguments, and indicate whether it is valid or invalid.

1. All (l)iberals (s)upport education. Senator (B)rown is not a (l)iberal. So, he does not (s)upport education.
2. Every (s)urgeon must also be a (p)hysician who knows something about general medicine. But Karl is a (s)urgeon. So, Karl is also a (p)hysician who knows something about general medicine.
3. Any applicant (a)dmitted to medical school must have had (g)ood grades. So, (P)aul must not have had (g)ood grades, for he was not (a)dmitted.
4. If Reverend Church were a man of (i)ntegrity, he would (p)ractice what he preaches. But he doesn't do this. So, he lacks (i)ntegrity.
5. Anyone who has (r)eplaced a dictatorship with a democratic regime has made (s)weeping changes in his government. (F)idel Castro has made (s)weeping changes in his government. Therefore, Fidel Castro has (r)eplaced a dictatorship with a democratic regime.
6. Anyone who is a (c)oward, does not deserve military (h)onors. But (G)unshot is not a (c)oward. So he deserves military (h)onors.
7. Either an argument employs the principle of (t)ransitivity or it is not a (s)yllogism. But the (a)rgument you are reading does not employ the principle of (t)ransitivity. Therefore, this argument is a (s)yllogism.
8. All (p)orpoises are (m)ammals. So, if (t)his Disneyland "fish" is not a (p)orpoise, it must not be a (m)ammal.
9. Unless a man has (c)ourage, he will not (s)peak out on behalf of unpopular causes. But (J)ones certainly has not (s)poken out on behalf of a number of causes that were extremely unpopular. So, (J)ones must not be a man of (c)ourage.
10. [Adapted from David Hume (1711–1776)]: If any idea is un(r)elated to human experience, it is without (m)eaning to man. But (t)his theologian's ideas of divine attributes are un(r)elated to human experience. Therefore, (t)his theologian's ideas are without (m)eaning to man.
11. If any creature is a (w)inged horse, it can (f)ly. Hence, since Pegasus was a (w)inged horse, Pegasus could (f)ly.
12. If any creature is a (w)inged horse, it can (f)ly. Therefore, Pegasus could (f)ly, for Pegasus was a (w)inged horse.
13. All of the (e)lves [in *The Sleeping Beauty*] were (a)cquainted with the Sleeping Beauty. Therefore, if Grumpy was one of the (e)lves, Grumpy was (a)cquainted with the Sleeping Beauty.
14. All of the (e)lves were (a)cquainted with the Sleeping Beauty. Therefore, if Mickey Mouse was not (a)cquainted with the Sleeping Beauty, Mickey Mouse was not one of the (e)lves.
15. St. Augustine did not (b)elieve that a serpent spoke to Eve, because St. Augustine did not interpret every statement in the Bible (l)iterally, and anyone who interprets every statement in the Bible (l)iterally (b)elieves that a serpent spoke to Eve.
16. Bertrand Russell did not interpret the Bible (l)iterally, because anyone who interprets the Bible (l)iterally (b)elieves that a serpent spoke to Eve, and Bertrand Russell certainly did not believe that such a conversation took place.

Particularization (PART) is a restatement of Aristotle's *dictum de omni et nullo*: Whatever is affirmed (as in an A-form) or affirmed *not* to be so (as in an

E-form) of *all* members of a subject set must also be affirmed of any particular member, or of any group of members, within that set. However, modern logic attaches an important *proviso* to Aristotle's *dictum de omni et nullo*: some other premise must assure us that the universal (or the conditional) refers to a nonempty set. Let us see why this proviso is necessary.

Even as ancient and medieval arithmetic dealt exclusively with positive whole numbers, so traditional logic was built around categorical statements, with hypothetical or conditional statement forms largely ignored. Accordingly, medieval logicians would have reasoned thus: "If 'All *S* is *P*' is true, then the related I-form 'Some *S* is *P*' is also true." Similarly, "If 'No *S* is *P*' is true, then 'Some *S* is not *P*' is also true."

Modern logic does *not* admit such inferences. The reason modern logicians do *not* attribute existence to conditionals, or to A- or E-form statements, may be seen in the following inferences:

1. No (p)hysicist is an (i)nventor of a perpetual motion machine. ($p \rightarrow \sim i$)
2. No (i)nventor of a perpetual motion machine is a (p)hysicist. ($i \rightarrow \sim p$)
3. All (i)nventors of perpetual motion machines are non-(p)hysicists. ($i \rightarrow \sim p$)
4. Some (i)nventors of perpetual motion machines are non-(p)hysicists.

$$(Ix \cdot \sim Px)$$

Modern logic assumes that universals, such as 1, 2, and 3 above, may refer to the empty set, but that statement 4 is a categorical statement about empirically observable events in the existential world. By definition, the existential $Ix \cdot \sim Px$ means "There *exists* at least one person who is both an inventor of perpetual motion machines and a nonphysicist." In contrast, "$i \rightarrow p$" means merely that *if* any such inventor exists (whether in actuality or as a pure possibility) then such an inventor *would be* (not *is*) a nonphysicist. Hence, modern logic recognizes statements 1, 2, and 3 as equivalent; but will not allow statement 4 to be derived from them.

Unlike traditional logic, modern logic does not assume that all statements are existential: it is simply not the case that all A and E propositions are categorical statements about the real world. In modern logic, the contrast between "All" and "Some" signifies a contrast between the *hypothetical* (conditional, conjectural, ideational, definitional—found in the A- and E- forms) and the *existential* (read, actual, empirical, verifiable—expressed in the I- and O- forms). Hence, from an *A-form*, e.g., "All Chiligons are Polygons," the *related I-form*, e.g., "Some Chiligons are Polygons" (which means "There *exists* at least one 100-sided Polygon") *may be derived only if some other premise in the argument explicitly states that the A-form refers to a nonempty set.*

We now formally state the rule of PART (Particularization) in its two forms: First, as we have already noted, as it applies to singulars; and second, as we are about to see, as it applies to existentials:

PART (*Particularization*):

(a) applied to singulars: $(s \rightarrow p) \cdot Sa \rightarrow (Sa \rightarrow Pa)$
$(s \rightarrow p) \cdot Sb \rightarrow (Sb \rightarrow Pb)$

(b) applied to existentials: $(s \rightarrow p) \cdot Sx \rightarrow (Sx \rightarrow Px)$
$(s \rightarrow p) \cdot Sy \rightarrow (Sy \rightarrow Py)$

Two Restrictions: (1) PART may be applied to universals of an argument only if some other premise is an existential or a singular; (2) PART may *not* be applied to the *conclusion* of any argument.

ARGUMENTS CONTAINING EXISTENTIALS.   In exercise 6.2A we studied
arguments of the type "All (d)ogs are (m)ammals. Fido is a (d)og. So, Fido is a
(m)ammal." Exercise 6.2B deals with problems very much like this, except that
existentials replace singulars. Let us suppose that we know that "All (s)nakes
are (c)rawling creatures," ($s \to c$) but we cannot name any individual snake
or snakes. However, we do know "Some (d)esert creatures are (s)nakes"
($Dx \cdot Sx$). The following proofs show how, from these two premises, the conclusion "Some (d)esert creatures are (c)rawling creatures" ($Dx \cdot Cx$) may be
derived.

(A–1) 1. $s \to c$
     2. $Dx \cdot Sx$ / $\therefore Dx \cdot Cx$
     3. $Sx \to Cx$ 1, PART
     4. Sx 2, SIMP
     5. Cx 3, 4, MP
     6. Dx 2, SIMP
     7. $Dx \cdot Cx$ 5, 6, CONJ

Once the thinking involved in Proof
(A–1) is thoroughly understood, the
proof may be abbreviated by writing
down two steps at a time, as in (A–2):

(A–2) 1. $s \to c$
     2. $Dx \cdot Sx$ / $\therefore Dx \cdot Cx$
     3. $Sx \to Cx$ 1, PART
     4. Cx 2, SIMP; 3, MP
     5. $Dx \cdot Cx$ 2, SIMP; 4, CONJ

(B–1) Proof by Crucial Assignments:
Original: $(s \to c) \cdot (Dx \cdot Sx)$ / $\therefore Dx \cdot Cx$
Revision: $(Sx \to Cx) \cdot Dx \cdot Sx$ / $\therefore Dx \cdot Cx$
       T T T T T F X FT
       3 2 4 2 2 1 $2\ 5$

The amount of paperwork for the proof by
crucial assignments may be somewhat reduced by listing the existentials only once,
thus:

(B–2) Proof by Crucial Assignments
(shortened):
     Top line: $(s \to c)$
Second line: $(Sx \to Cx) \cdot Dx \cdot Sx$ / $\therefore Dx \cdot Cx$
         T T T T T F T FX

But this shortened version should not let us
forget that PART may be applied to universals
only if there are other premises which are
categorical (i.e., singulars or existentials).
Only thus can we be sure that the argument
deals with nonempty sets.

Exercise 6.2B.   Arguments Containing Existentials

Directions:

(A) Symbolize each of the following arguments.
(B) Using any method or methods you wish, determine each argument's validity. Be
prepared to show your proofs.
(C) In the answer blank before each problem, write V or I (valid or invalid).

_____ 1. Some (b)irds have (n)ails. All (b)irds are (f)eathered. Therefore, some
(f)eathered creatures have (n)ails.

_____ 2. All (f)ighters are (p)ugnacious, and some (f)ighters are (l)osers. Consequently, some (p)ugnacious persons are (l)osers.

_____ 3. All Nobel prize (w)inners are men of (g)enius. Hence, some (F)ascists were
(g)eniuses, because several (F)ascists were Nobel prize (w)inners.

_____ 4. Some (s)aints are (p)roud, because some (M)oguls are (s)aints, and all
(M)oguls are (p)roud.

_____ 5. There are (f)ootball fans who are not (o)pera fans. All (o)pera fans are
(l)overs of music. So, there are (f)ootball fans who are not (l)overs of music.

_____ 6. All (m)istakes are (f)orgivable, and many (m)istakes are not (s)inful. Therefore, there are (s)ins which are not unforgivable.

_____ 7. Anyone who loves (d)emocracy (h)ates dictatorship. But there are members
of this (p)arty who do not love (d)emocracy. Hence, there are members of
this (p)arty who do not (h)ate dictatorship.

_____ 8. All (c)riminals are (d)angerous. Some un(i)ntelligent men are (c)riminals.
So, some (d)angerous persons are not (i)ntelligent.

_____ 9. All (m)ermaids live in (w)ater. Any creature that lives in (w)ater can (s)wim.
Therefore, there are (m)ermaids that can (s)wim.

_____ 10. All (g)ods are (d)ivine. Every (d)ivine being is deserving of (w)orship. Therefore, there are (g)ods that are deserving of (w)orship.
_____ 11. Some (c)orundums are (s)apphires. All (s)apphires are (v)aluable. Therefore,
all (c)orundums are (v)aluable.
_____ 12. No (w)ild creatures make good (p)ets. There are some (k)ittens that are
(w)ild. Therefore, no (k)ittens make good (p)ets.

CONTRADICTION, QUANTIFICATION EQUIVALENCE (QE).   Two statements are contradictory if and only if the truth of one guarantees the falsity
of the other (and if and only if the falsity of one guarantees the truth of the
other). Below are examples of I-form and E-form statements which have the
same subject and predicate terms and are contradictory. Study carefully these
two statements, their accompanying Venn diagrams, Boolean equations, and
modern symbolisms.

In all of these symbolisms, "x" signifies the *existence* of one or more substantial individuals—individuals verifiable in the world of empirical reality.

I: Some Swans are Pets
$(Sx \cdot Px)$
$= \sim(\sim Sx \lor \sim Px)$
$= \sim(Sx \to \sim Px)$

E: No Swans are Pets
$(s \to \sim p)$
$= (\sim s \lor \sim p)$
$= \sim(s \cdot p)$

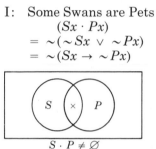

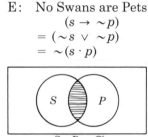

Figure 16 $S \cdot P \neq \emptyset$ $S \cdot P = \emptyset$ **Figure 17**

Observe that the three symbolisms for the I-form "Some Swans are Pets"
$[(Sx \cdot Px) = \sim(\sim Sx \lor \sim Px) = \sim(Sx \to \sim Px)]$ are all categorical statements—
statements having existential or empirical referents. Similarly the three
symbolisms for the contradictory E-form "No Swans are Pets" $[(s \to \sim p) =
(\sim s \lor \sim p) = \sim(s \cdot p)]$ all represent truth-value statements—statements
having an ideological, hypothetical, or conditional plane of existence.

Now study the following pair of O-form and A-form statements, and they
will also be seen to be contradictory:

O: Some Swans are not Pets
$(Sx \cdot \sim Px)$
$= \sim(\sim Sx \lor Px)$
$= \sim(Sx \to Px)$

A: All Swans are Pets
$(s \to p)$
$= (\sim s \lor p)$
$= \sim(s \cdot \sim p)$

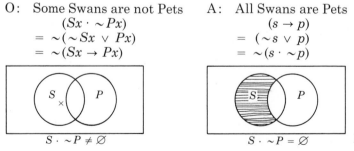

Figure 18 $S \cdot \sim P \neq \emptyset$ $S \cdot \sim P = \emptyset$ **Figure 19**

Again, observe that in the O-form statements, $Sx \cdot \sim Px$, $\sim(\sim Sx \lor Px)$
and $\sim(Sx \to Px)$ refer to existential or categorical statements about reality;
whereas in the A-form statements, $s \to p$, $\sim s \lor p$, and $\sim(s \cdot \sim p)$ refer only to
the truth values of statements—statements considered purely on an ideo-
logical or hypothetical plane.

Let us call two statements "related" if and only if they have the same subject and predicate terms. Then the following two rules summarize the *laws of quantification equivalence* (QE):

An A-form ($s \rightarrow p$) is true if and only if its related O-form ($Sx \cdot \sim Px$) is false.

An E-form ($s \rightarrow \sim p$) is true if and only if its related I-form ($Sx \cdot Px$) is false.

Observe that related A- and E- forms may both be false; hence the falsity of a universal (e.g., "No Swans are Pets") does not guarantee the truth of its related universal (e.g., "No Swans are Pets"). Hence A- and E- forms are not contradictories. (In traditional logic they were called "Contraries.") Similarly, related I- and O- forms may both be true (e.g., "Some Swans are Pets" and "Some Swans are not Pets"), and are not contradictories. More will be said on this topic before studying exercise 6.4B.

Exercise 6.2C. Equivalent, Contradictory, and Independent Statements

Definitions: Two statements are *equivalent* if and only if they have the same sets of truth values, and *contradictory* if and only if they have complementary sets of truth values. A-, E-, I-, and O-form statements can be equivalent or contradictory only if they have the same subject terms and the same predicate terms. Statements which are neither equivalent nor contradictory are *independent* of one another, and the truth or falsity of either of two independent statements leaves us *doubtful* concerning the truth or falsity of the other. In other words, given that statement *A* is true, and that statement *A* is the only premise on which our reasoning is based, then statement *B* will be either (1) equivalent, hence *true*; (2) contradictory, hence *false*; or (3) neither (1) nor (2), hence (3) *doubtful*.

Directions: Below are 32 pairs of statements. First symbolize each statement. Then, assuming that the first statement is *true*, circle T, F, or D to indicate whether the paired statement is True, False, or Doubtful. Read "$\sim S$" as "non-*S*," and read "$\sim P$" as "non-*P*."

1A. An *S* is a *P*.	T F D	1B. None but $\sim S$ are $\sim P$.	
2A. All *S* is *P*.	T F D	2B. All $\sim P$ is $\sim S$.	
3A. "No *S* is *P*" is false.	T F D	3B. Some *P* is not *S*.	
4A. No $\sim S$ is $\sim P$.	T F D	4B. Any $\sim S$ is a *P*.	
5A. Some *S* is not *P*.	T F D	5B. Some $\sim P$ is not $\sim S$.	
6A. There are *S*'s that are *P*'s.	T F D	6B. Only if P, then $\sim S$.	
7A. Some $\sim P$ is not $\sim S$.	T F D	7B. There are *P*'s that are not *S*'s.	
8A. Some *S* is not *P*.	T F D	8B. Some non-*S* is not *P*.	
9A. It is false that all crows are black.	T F D	9B. Some crows are not black.	
10A. Some swans are white.	T F D	10B. Some swans are not non-white.	
11A. Some birds are not singers.	T F D	11B. It is not true that all birds are singers.	
12A. All pigs are porkers.	T F D	12B. All nonporkers are nonpigs.	
13A. All metals are conductors.	T F D	13B. Some metals are nonconductors.	
14A. Some plastics are not non-conductors.	T F D	14B. Some conductors are not plastics.	
15A. All unreal things are ideal.	T F D	15B. No unreal things are ideal.	
16A. Some MD's are not surgeons.	T F D	16B. No nonsurgeons are MD's.	
17A. Some nonmetals are non-salts.	T F D	17B. Some salts are metals.	
18A. All unfortunate events are undesirable.	T F D	18B. All desirable events are unfortunate.	
19A. All moral acts are free.	T F D	19B. All free acts are moral.	
20A. All criminal acts are reprehensible.	T F D	20B. No criminal acts are acts that are not reprehensible.	

21A. All edible plums are ripe.	T F D	21B. No unripe plums are edible.
22A. All dogs are canines.	T F D	22B. "All canines are dogs" is false.
23A. "No gases are heavy" is false.	T F D	23B. Some heavy things are not gases.
24A. All Swedes are blondes.	T F D	24B. Some blondes are non-Swedes.
25A. Some pilots are heroes.	T F D	25B. Some unheroic people are pilots.
26A. Some Finns are poetic.	T F D	26B. It is false that no poetic people are Finns.
27A. All persons you know are persons you cannot hate.	T F D	27B. No persons you can hate are persons you know.
28A. All times when X is Y are times when P is Q.	T F D	28B. No times when P is not Q are times when X is not Y.
29A. Some persons who read are persons who do not study.	T F D	29B. Some persons who do not study are not persons who do not read.
30A. Some illiterate people are not unintelligent.	T F D	30B. Some intelligent people are illiterate.
31A. No existential is a universal.	T F D	31B. To believe that some universals are not existentials is to be mistaken.
32A. Some persons who work hard are not very successful.	T F D	32B. Some persons who are very successful are persons who do not work hard.

Before proceeding, two important points should be noted. First, keep in mind that every valid argument is based on the assumption that if all of its premises are *true* then its conclusion must also be *true*. Given a premise that is stated to be false, for example, "It is false that all dogs are pets" [$\sim(d \rightarrow p)$], it should immediately be changed to a true premise, namely, "Some dogs are not pets ($Dx \cdot \sim Px$). This application of quantification equivalence (QE) can occur in exactly four ways:

1. Symbolize "It is false that no (w)omen are (s)tudents" as well as "Some (w)omen are (s)tudents," by ($Wx \cdot Sx$) rather than by $\sim(w \rightarrow \sim s)$.
2. Symbolize "It is false that all (m)en are (t)all" as well as "Some men are not tall," by ($Mx \cdot \sim Tx$) rather than by $\sim(m \rightarrow t)$.
3. Symbolize "It is false that some (b)oys are (m)ature" as well as "No boys are mature," by ($b \rightarrow \sim m$) rather than by $\sim(Bx \cdot Mx)$.
4. Symbolize "It is false that some (g)irls are not (p)retty," as well as "All (g)irls are pretty," by ($g \rightarrow p$) rather than by $\sim(Gx \cdot \sim Px)$.

All S is not P. A second difficulty related to QE arises from an ambiguous usage found in the English form "All S is not P." In such forms, although the "not" precedes the predicate term, it should be thought of as preceding the entire statement. With this slight change, "All Swans are *not* Pets" would be recognized to have the same meaning as "*Not* (All Swans are Pets)" [$\sim(s \rightarrow p)$, or $Sx \cdot \sim Px$].

It should be realized that this form, in various contexts, has different meanings. Thus, "Not all dogs are pets" would usually be interpreted to mean *two* things: (a) "Some dogs are not pets," but also (b) "Some dogs are pets."

Now consider the following example. Suppose you were attending a professional basketball game and say (perhaps to yourself) "Some members of this team are not whites" ... "Most members of this team are not whites" ... "All members of this team are not whites." In this context, the concluding statement would mean "All members of this team are nonwhites" or "No members of this team are whites." This E-form "No members of this team are whites" contradicts the I-form "Some members of this team are whites." Since, under some circumstances, the E-form seems to be a reasonable interpretation of the form "All S is not P", whereas under other circumstances the contradictory I-form "Some S is P" seems to be implicit in the statement, it is possible for these two interpretations to nullify one another. Note, however, that "Some S is not P" is implicit in either interpretation. Thus we are left with "Some S is not P" as the minimal, necessary meaning contained in statements having the form "All S is not P."

To avoid endless ambiguity, logic books *stipulate* that the form "All S is not P" shall be given exactly one meaning—its minimal meaning contained in the O-form "Some S is not P." However, because of its ambiguity, the sentence "All S is not P" cannot be said to be strictly equivalent to the statement "Some S is not P." Only its *stipulated* meaning is strictly equivalent.

Exercise 6.2D. Testing Validity of Arguments

Directions: First do the odd-numbered problems, and check your solutions against those shown in the *Answers.* Then do the evens. Use any method of proof you prefer, and be prepared to show your proof. Then write V or I to indicate whether the argument is valid or invalid.

_____ 1. It is simply not the case that there are American (b)ankers who do not support (c)apitalism. But it is equally false to say that all (j)ournalists support (c)apitalism. Therefore, there are no (j)ournalists who are (b)ankers.

_____ 2. It is false that no (c)riminals are (i)ntelligent. It is also false that some (m)orons are intelligent. So, we know positively that some criminals are not morons.

_____ 3. There is not a modern (b)iologist who has not (r)ead Darwin. Moreover, some readers of Darwin are (a)theistic in their religious outlook. Therefore, not every modern biologist is nonatheistic in his religious outlook.

_____ 4. There are (g)eniuses who are (p)sychotic; and it is false that no Australian (a)borigines are geniuses. Hence, there are Australian (a)borigines who are psychotic.

_____ 5. No one who (p)aid his dues is un(e)mployed; so, all of our (g)raduates are (e)mployed, since not one of them failed to pay his dues.

_____ 6. There are (s)portsmen who are not (a)thletes; because every (a)thlete is a person with (p)hysical skill, and not every (s)portsman has (p)hysical skill.

_____ 7. The only (h)onor students in his school are (s)eniors. Now it is not the case that there are (s)eniors who are also (f)reshmen. Hence, the only students in his school who were not (h)onor students are (f)reshmen.

_____ 8. There are no (u)pright animals that are also (q)uadrupeds; and there are no (h)orses that are not (q)uadrupeds. Hence, all (h)orses are (u)pright animals.

_____ 9. All our (g)raduates are (a)ble and (c)ompetent; but not every graduate is a (s)cholar. Therefore, not all persons who are able and competent are scholars.

_____ 10. All (p)ets are (t)ame but every (d)og is not a pet. Therefore, not every (t)ame creature is a (p)et.

We come now to the third new rule for subject-predicate logic:

SING-EX: *Singulars are existentials.*[4]

Thus, "Abe is a sailor" implies "At least one sailor exists" ($Sa \rightarrow Sx$); and

---

[4] For an elaboration of the view that singular terms need *not* be existential, read Karel Lambert and Bas C. vam Fraassen, *Derivation and Counterexample: An Introduction to Philosophical Logic* (Belmont, Cal.: Dickinson, 1972), chaps. 6 and 7, "The Logic of Singular Terms," pp. 127–62, 216–22 (Bibliography). See also pp. 193–95 in section 6.3 of this text.

"Bill is a tall man" implies "Some men are tall" ($Mb \cdot Tb \to Mx \cdot Tx$). By COPO, $Sa \to Sx$ yields $\sim Sx \to \sim Sa$, and $Tb \cdot Mb \to Mx \cdot Tx$ yields $\sim(Mx \cdot Tx) \to \sim(Mb \cdot Tb)$.

Since $\sim(Sx \cdot \sim Px) \to \sim(Sa \cdot \sim Pa)$, and since, by QE, $(s \to p) = \sim(Sx \cdot \sim Px)$, it follows, by HS, that $(s \to p) \to \sim(Sa \cdot \sim Pa)$. On the other hand, although by QE $\sim(s \to p) = Sx \cdot \sim Px$, since *SING-EX is not commutative*, we cannot derive a singular from the negation of a universal.

This point is so important that it may be well to review QE: $Sx \cdot Px = \sim(s \to \sim p); (s \to \sim p) = \sim(Sx \cdot Px); Sx \cdot \sim Px = \sim(s \to p); (s \to p) = \sim(Sx \cdot \sim Px)$. In all these forms of QE, the range of referents for "x" in $Sx \cdot Px$ or in $Sx \cdot \sim Px$ is exactly the same as it is for the universals $s \to \sim p$ or $s \to p$.

In contrast, note how narrow and restricted is the range of "x" when any existential is derived from a singular. Thus, from the true singular "Carl (G)ustaf is a (t)wentieth-century (k)ing" ($Tg \cdot Kg$), we may validly derive the true singular "At least one (t)wentieth-century (k)ing exists" or "Some (t)wentieth-century men are (k)ings" ($Tx \cdot Kx$). Here $Tx \cdot Kx$ would be true even if the only referent for "x" in "$Tx \cdot Kx$" happened to be King Carl Gustaf of Sweden.

On the other hand, the *negation* of the singular "It is false that John (D)oe is a (t)wentieth-century (k)ing" [$\sim(Td \cdot Kd)$] will *not* yield the broad and unrestricted existential [$\sim(Tx \cdot Kx)$], since, by QE, this would mean "It is false that there are *any* (t)wentieth-century (k)ings" ($t \to \sim k$).

The above examples suggest that SING-EX is a rule of logic which must be qualified. Here is the rule and the qualifications:

SING-EX: *Singulars are existentials.*
In symbols: $Sa \to Sx; Sa \cdot Pa \to Sx \cdot Px$
Hence, by COPO: $\sim Sx \to \sim Sa; \sim(Sx \cdot Px) \to \sim(Sa \cdot Pa)$

Note the use of different subscripts (a topic to be considered again in section 6.4): $Sa \to Px, Sb \to Py; (Sa \cdot Pa) \cdot (Sb \cdot Qb) \to (Sx \cdot Px) \cdot (Sy \cdot Qy)$.
   Two Restrictions for SING-EX: (1) QE does not apply to singulars. (2) QE may not be applied to negations of existentials derived from singulars.

To reemphasize the need for these two restrictions, study the "proof" shown to the right. In this so-called proof, "$\sim Wa$" signifies "Abe is not a (w)oman" and "Ka" signifies "Abe is a king." The argument's conclusion is invalid because step 5 violates our second restriction.

1.	$\sim Wa \mid \therefore w \to k$	
2.	$\sim Wa \vee Ka$	1, ADD
3.	$\sim Wx \vee Kx$	2, SING-EX
4.	$\sim(Wx \cdot \sim Kx)$	3, DeM
5.	$w \to k$	4, QE

Here is an argument illustrating the proper use of SING-EX:

(T)om and (B)ill are (W)elshmen. (T)om is a (s)culptor. All (s)culptors are (a)rtists. So, some (a)rtists are (W)elshmen.

1.	$Wt \cdot Wb$		
2.	St		
3.	$s \to a \mid \therefore Wx \cdot Ax$		
4.	Sx	2, SING-EX	
5.	$Sx \to Ax$	3, PART	
6.	Ax	4, 5, MP	
7.	Wx	1, SIMP; SING-EX	
8.	$Ax \cdot Wx$	6, 7, CONJ	

The adaptation shown below embodies some of the same reasoning contained in the above 8-step proof.

Original: $(Wt \cdot Wb) \cdot St \cdot (s \to a) \mid \therefore Wx \cdot Ax$
Adaptation: Wx $\cdot Sx \cdot (Sx \to Ax) \mid \therefore Wx \cdot Ax$
             T T $T \, T$ $F \, T \, FX$
             2 2 $3 \ 2 \ 4$ $1 \ 5 \ 2$

Exercise 6.2E will require application of these principles.

Exercise 6.2E.   Arguments Containing Singulars

Directions: First solve the odd-numbered problems, and compare your solutions with the answers given. Then solve the even-numbered problems. Use any method of proof you desire to prove the argument valid or invalid. Be prepared to show your proofs.

1. Either Tom or Bill will (w)in. Anyone is (l)ucky who (w)ins. Therefore, either Tom or Bill will be (l)ucky.
2. No (S)wedes are persons whose language is not (I)ndo-European. Therefore, if Awana is one who speaks a (M)uskhogean dialect, and if no (M)uskhogean dialects are (I)ndo-European, then Awana is not a (S)wede.
3. Many (b)eautiful (w)omen marry for (m)oney. But surely Jane would not be called (b)eautiful. So, Jane must not have married for (m)oney.
4. All (g)eniuses are (e)xceptional persons. Steinmetz was a (g)enius who was (p)hysically handicapped. Therefore, some (p)hysically handicapped persons are (e)xceptional persons.
5. No (s)urgeons or (d)octors are (i)diots. But if anyone cannot (p)ass this simple exam, he is surely an (i)diot, and Joe (R)attlebrain certainly cannot (p)ass it. Therefore, Joe (R)attlebrain is neither a (s)urgeon nor a (d)octor.
6. No (h)ermit is (s)ociable. Anthony is an (a)scetic (h)ermit. Therefore, it is false that all (a)scetics are (s)ociable.
7. Someone at the (h)otel (s)tole an expensive fur coat. Anyone who (s)tole such a coat would have left the (h)otel lest he be caught with the coat. Also, the person who (s)tole the coat spent the (e)vening with Smith. Jones left the hotel, and Jones spent the evening with Smith. Therefore, Jones (s)tole the coat.
8. All (c)ompetent (g)overnors are (s)table. Therefore, since Governor Bob is an (a)lcoholic, and since no (a)lcoholics are (s)table, Bob is not a (c)ompetent (g)overnor, and not all governors are competent.

FROM ARISTOTLE TO QUINE.

FROM ARISTOTLE TO QUINE.   Aristotelian logic began with substantial and concrete objects; and Aristotle's subject-predicate logic involved the predication of certain attributes to these objects. Thus "John is tall" would have been interpreted to mean "The quality 'tallness' is predicated of John." "My house is red" would be interpreted to mean "The property 'redness' is attributed to my house." Sometimes attributes were attached to other attributes, as in "All red things are colored (things)"; which would become "All objects which have the attribute of being red also have the property of being colored."

Beginning with the A-, E-, I-, and O- forms of medieval logic, modern thought has gradually moved away from this subject-attributed approach to logic to an approach which W. V. Quine has described as follows:

> Numerals name numbers. The symbol "12" names 12. . . . What is 12? It is how many Apostles there were, how many months in a year, how many eggs in a carton. But 12 is not merely a property of a dozen eggs, months, and Apostles, it is the property common to the class of a dozen eggs, the class of a dozen months, and the class of a dozen Apostles.
>
> One of the sources of clarity in mathematics is the tendency to talk of classes rather than properties. Whatever is accomplished by referring to a property can generally be accomplished at least as well by referring to the class of all things that have that property. Clarity is gained because for classes we have a clear idea of sameness and difference; it is a question simply of their having or not having the same members.
>
> In particular, then, we do best to explain 12 not as the property of being a dozen but as the class of all dozens, the class of all 12-member classes.[5]

---

[5] W. V. Quine, "The Foundations of Mathematics," in *Scientific American* 211 (September 1964): 112–27.

Aristotle distinguished universals from particulars (what traditional logic called "particulars" we call "existentials"); but it was a distinction of *quantity*, not of *quality*. For Aristotle believed that universals as well as existentials were categorical statements about existential reality. Aristotle believed that universals were derived from existentials in a manner somewhat as follows: we observe that "Fido barks," that "Rover barks," that "King barks," and that "Lassie barks." Then, after a reasonable number of such observations, we make an "inductive leap" to the universal "All dogs bark" ($d \rightarrow b$). Modern logic is in general accord with Aristotle except on one point: the universal "All dogs bark" is not another categorical statement; rather, it is a hypothesis, and it should be formulated as a conditional. To reemphasize the reason for this, consider these empirically observable generalizations: "No canines lay eggs," "No felines lay eggs," "No rodents lay eggs," "No ruminants lay eggs"; and the inductive leap to "No mammals lay eggs." (See problem 10 of exercise 2.5A.)

This brings us to a basic weakness in traditional logic, and to what is perhaps the most fundamental difference between traditional and modern logic. In traditional logic, assuming "All winged horses can fly" ($w \cdot h \rightarrow f$) is *true*, then by "immediate inference" the related I-form "Some winged horses can fly" ($Wx \cdot Hx \cdot Fx$) would also be true. In modern logic, this inference is valid only if we are sure that "winged horses" does not refer to the empty set.

Thus, if we assume (or *assert*) as an additional premise that "Dogs exist," (Dx), then from the A- form "All dogs are (m)ammals" ($d \rightarrow x$) we may employ PART, MP, and CONJ to derive the conclusion "Some (d)ogs are (m)ammals." Similarly, if one premise of an argument affirms that horses exist (Hx), then given another premise in the E-form, "No (h)orses are (t)igers," ($h \rightarrow \sim t$), we may validly derive the related O-form "Some (h)orses are not (t)igers" ($Hx \cdot \sim Tx$). Surely there is nothing unreasonable about making such assumptions. But also, there is surely nothing unreasonable about insisting that such assumptions be *stated*. It is only on this final point that modern logic differs from traditional logic. Exercise 6.2F is designed to show that this point is not altogether academic.

Exercise 6.2F. "Immediate Inference" in Modern Logic

Directions: In this exercise each group of problems is headed by two italicized statements, each correctly symbolized, and each assumed to be true. The remaining statements in each group are to be understood as conclusions, which may be either true, false, or doubtful. If the statement necessarily follows from the two italicized statements, circle *T* for true. If the statement contradicts either of the italicized statements, circle *F* for false. If, on the basis of the two italicized premises, the statement cannot be shown to be either true or false, circle *D* for doubtful. Be prepared to show your proofs.

Group I. (A) *All (m)ermaids live in (w)ater.*   ($m \rightarrow w$)
         (B) *There exist many (c)reatures that live in (w)ater.*   ($Cx \cdot Wx$) | $\therefore$

1. There are no mermaids that do not live in water.   1. *T   F   D*
2. There are mermaids that do not live in water.   2. *T   F   D*
3. Either there are creatures that live in water or there are no mermaids.   3. *T   F   D*
4. If there are mermaids then there are creatures that live in water.   4. *T   F   D*
5. All creatures that do not live in water are nonmermaids.   5. *T   F   D*

Group II. (A) *If Daisy (g)oes to the prom with Daffy, I'll (e)at my hat.* ($Gd \rightarrow Ei$)
         (B) *I'll not (e)at my hat.*   ($\sim Ei$) | $\therefore$

6. All times when Daisy goes to the prom with Daffy are times when I'll eat my hat.   6. *T   F   D*
7. No times when I do not eat my hat are times when Daisy goes to the prom with Daffy.   7. *T   F   D*
8. Either I'll not eat my hat, or Daisy goes to the prom with Daffy.   8. *T   F   D*
9. It will never happen both that I'll eat my hat and that Daisy will go to the prom with Daffy.   9. *T̊   F   D*
10. There are times when I eat my hat, and these occur when Daisy goes to the prom with Daffy.   10. *T   F   D*

Group III.   (A) *No person (p)roclaiming scientific truth on the basis of private conversa-*
            tions with the angel Gabriel is a (s)cientist. $(p \rightarrow \sim s)$
          (B) *Both scientists and nonscientists exist.* $(Sx \cdot \sim Sy) \mid \therefore$

11. If anyone proclaims scientific truth on the basis of private conversations with the angel Gabriel, he is not a scientist.   11. *T   F   D*
12. All persons proclaiming scientific truth on the basis of private conversations with the angel Gabriel are scientists.   12. *T   F   D*
13. Some persons proclaiming scientific truth on the basis of private conversations with the angel Gabriel are nonscientists.   13. *T   F   D*
14. It is false that there ever existed a scientist who proclaimed scientific truth on the basis of private conversations with the angel Gabriel.   14. *T   F   D*
15. Any person proclaiming scientific truth on the basis of private conversations with the angel Gabriel is a nonscientist.   15. *T   F   D*

Group IV.   (A) *All (m)ath majors who have I.Q. (s)cores under 50 are to be (e)xcused*
            from taking the calculus exam. $(m \cdot s \rightarrow e)$ or $[(m \rightarrow e) \vee (s \rightarrow e)]$
          (B) *There are many (m)ath majors; and there are also many people with*
            I.Q. scores under 50. $(Mx \cdot Sy) \mid \therefore$

16. Any person not to be excused from taking the calculus exam is either not a math major or he does not have an I.Q. score under 50.   16. *T   F   D*
17. Some math majors who have I.Q. scores under 50 are to be excused from taking the calculus exam.   17. *T   F   D*
18. It is false that there are math majors with I.Q. scores under 50 who are not to be excused from taking the calculus exam.   18. *T   F   D*
19. No math majors who have I.Q. scores under 50 are to be excused from taking the calculus exam.   19. *T   F   D*

Group V.   (A) *All (p)rofessors who (t)each logic classes while dead-drunk are to (r)eceive*
            salary increments. $(p \cdot t \rightarrow r)$
          (B) *There are professors who are not to receive salary increments.*
            $(Px \cdot \sim Rx) \mid \therefore$

20. Some professors who teach logic classes while dead-drunk will not receive salary increments.   20. *T   F   D*
21. Some professors who do not receive a salary increment are professors who teach logic classes while dead-drunk.   21. *T   F   D*
22. No professor who does not teach logic classes while dead-drunk will receive a salary increment.   22. *T   F   D*
23. Some professors who teach logic classes while dead-drunk are to receive salary increments.   23. *T   F   D*
24. Some professors who teach logic classes while dead-drunk are not to receive salary increments.   24. *T   F   D*

SOME COMMENTS ON SYMBOLISM.   In the development of logic, there have been many ways in which the same essential ideas have been symbolized. These different symbolisms tend to change the manner in which sentences are formulated. For example, medieval logicians restructured statements into the A-, E-, I-, and O- forms; most modern logicians tend to emphasize conditionals;

computer engineers eliminate conditionals in favor of conjunctions and disjunctions so as to better use the wedge, the dot, and the tilde.

In this text, exactly the same symbols are used for *universals* as were used in truth-value logic (see chapters 2 and 4). The more crucial differences occur with respect to symbolizing singulars and existentials, and in relating them to universals. The following short argument will serve to illustrate major differences:

Example: All (m)iners are (p)eople. Miners exist. Therefore, people exist.

Prevailing Contemporary Symbolism:		*Symbolism Used in This Text:*	
1. $(x) Mx \rightarrow Px$ [or $(x) Mx \supset Px$]		1. $m \rightarrow p$	
2. $(\exists x) Mx \mid \therefore Px$		2. $Mx \mid \therefore Px$	
3. Ma	2, EI	3. $Mx \rightarrow Px$	1, PART
4. $Ma \rightarrow Pa$ [or $Ma \supset Pa$]	1, UI	4. Px	2, 3, MP
5. Pa	3, 4, MP		
6. Px	5, EG		

$$\text{or } (m \rightarrow p) \dots$$
$$(Mx \rightarrow Px) \cdot Mx \mid \therefore Px$$
$$X \quad T \quad F \quad T \qquad F$$

In the "prevailing symbolism," the same subscript "x" is used for the universal (premise 1) and for the existential (premise 2). In order to find a common meeting ground for these two premises, two rules are needed: EI (*Existential Instantiation*, used in step 3) and UI (*Universal Instantiation*, used in step 4). With this common subscript "a," premises 3 and 4 may be conjoined, and the law of *Modus Ponens* applied to them, yielding Pa in premise 5. Then, using a third rule, EG (*Existential Generalization*), Px is derived from Pa (step 6).

In the symbolism used in this text, exactly the same symbols are used for *universals* as were used in truth-value logic. This usage is also employed by other logicians when they deal with truth-value logic. Therefore, the most significant difference in the two symbolisms is the use of PART in place of EI, UI, and EG.

Observe that the symbolism used in this text makes it possible to apply the method of crucial assignments to arguments containing I- and O- forms—something which cannot be done when the prevailing symbolism is employed.

However, what is of genuine importance is not the symbolism used, but the basic concepts of logic studied. These concepts are common to the several logics, however different their symbolisms. Any student who understands the basic concepts should have little or no difficulty adapting what he knows to the "Polish notation" or to other widely used symbolisms in logic.

Before proceeding to exercise 6.2G, carefully review the laws of logic (i.e., the forms of argument) emphasized in this book. These are listed on the inside back cover. Give special attention to the final group, "Three Added Rules for Subject-Predicate Logic." These are the rules studied in section 6.2, and applied in exercise 6.2G.

Exercise 6.2G.   Recognizing Laws of Logic

Directions: In the answer blanks, fill in (a) the number or numbers of previous steps in the proof that are being used, and (b) the law that is applied to this step or to these steps. This exercise is similar to the exercises studied in section 4.1, except that it requires the use of PART, QE, and SING-EX as well as the laws of truth-value logic that were used in chapter 4.

(1) 1. $Ha \cdot Ma$
  2. $(Kb \cdot Wb) \vee (Kb \cdot Rb)$
  3. $\sim f \rightarrow \sim m \mid \therefore Ha \cdot Fx \cdot Ky$
  4. $Hx \cdot Mx$ _____

(2) 1. $Va \mid \therefore \sim v \rightarrow w$
  2. $Va \vee Wa$ _____
  3. $\sim(\sim Va \cdot \sim Wa)$ _____
  4. $\sim(\sim Vx \cdot \sim Wx)$ _____

5. Mx _____
6. $\sim Fx \rightarrow \sim Mx$ _____
7. Fx _____
8. Ha _____
9. $Kb \cdot (Wb \vee Rb)$ _____
10. Kb _____
11. Ky _____
12. $Ha \cdot Fx \cdot Ky$ _____

(3)   1. $\sim Ha \cdot Ma$
     2. $\sim g \vee \sim m$
     3. $\sim(g \rightarrow h)$ / $\therefore$ $\sim Mx \cdot \sim Gy$
     4. $Gx \cdot \sim Hx$ _____
     5. $\sim Gx \vee \sim Mx$ _____
     6. Gx _____
     7. $\sim Mx$ _____
     8. $\sim Hy \cdot My$ _____
     9. $\sim Gy \vee \sim My$ _____
     10. My _____
     11. $\sim Gy$ _____
     12. $\sim Mx \cdot \sim Gy$ _____

5. $\sim v \rightarrow \sim(\sim w)$ _____
6. $\sim v \rightarrow w$ _____

Remarks. In problem (2), step 5 violates one of the restrictions to the use of SING-EX: "QE may not be applied to negations of existentials derived from singulars," explained above on page 185. Hence this "proof" is invalid, and steps 5 and 6 should not be filled in. We leave it to the reader to decide whether or not these restrictions are ignored in problems (3) and (4).

(4)   1. $\sim Fb \rightarrow \sim Gb$ / $\therefore$ $g \rightarrow f$
     2. $Fb \vee \sim Gb$ _____
     3. $Fx \vee \sim Gx$ _____
     4. $\sim(\sim Fx \cdot Gx)$ _____
     5. $\sim f \rightarrow \sim g$ _____
     6. $g \rightarrow f$ _____

6.3   Some Paradoxes of Modern Logic

PARADOXES RESULTING FROM AMBIGUITY. In ordinary English usage, "paradox" is sometimes understood to mean any seemingly absurd or self-contradictory statement which nevertheless expresses a truth. Following this definition, a paradox is often revealed to be nothing more than a concealed ambiguity, or a sudden and dramatic shift in the meaning of a word or phrase which compels the hearer to think, that is, to harmonize the seeming self-contradiction. Socrates employed this rhetorical device when he declared that he was the wisest man in Athens because he knew that he knew nothing. Communication fails unless his hearers realized that Socrates was not contradicting himself, but only giving a graphic statement of the truth that all human knowledge is as naught as compared with the vast realm of mystery and indefiniteness which remains beyond our present knowledge. Likewise, "For whosoever will save his life shall lose it" (Mark 8:35) implies no logical contradiction, since the saving and losing have to do with different levels of being. Paradoxes of this type are useful as long as we look for the truth, not in them, but in a new rational synthesis behind them.

Here are eight examples of "paradoxes" built around ambiguities. The italicized words should help you locate the word whose meaning is ambiguous:

1. "Many that are *first* shall be last; and the last shall be first" (Matt., 19:30).
2. If *you* have a fight with *your* conscience, and lose—*you* win.
3. The *shortest* way there is the *longest* way around.
4. The *rest* of your *days* depend on the *rest* of your nights.
5. Proper diet adds years to your *life* and *life* to your years.
6. "There is only one thing worse than *being talked about*, and that is—not *being talked about*" (Oscar Wilde).
7. "An arrow in flight is in the same *space* during every instant of its flight; therefore, it is at rest during the entire flight" (Zeno).
8. A leader is best when people hardly know that he *exists* (Lao Tzu).

PARADOXES RESULTING FROM UNSTATED OR CONTRADICTORY ASSUMPTIONS. More generally, paradoxes occur because of unstated, yet contradictory, assumptions behind a process of reasoning. As an example of this type, consider the following proof that $2 = 1$:

1. Let $a = b = 1$.	1. We begin with these assumptions.
2. Then $a^2 = ab$.	2. Multiply equals by equals. Multiply a and b by a.
3. Then $a^2 - b^2 = ab - b^2$.	3. Subtract equals from equals.
4. Then $(a + b)(a - b) = b(a - b)$.	4. Factor, using distributive law.
5. Then $(a + b) = b$.	5. Divide equals by equals.
6. Therefore, $2 = 1$.	6. Substituting equals for equals, where $a = b = 1$.

Does this really "prove" that $2 = 1$? Of course not. What it proves is that the method of proof employed is fallacious. Analysis of step 5 will show that [since $a = b = 1$, by assumption] $a - b = 1 - 1 = 0$. But another rule of arithmetic tells us that we cannot divide by zero. Hence, this so-called proof is invalid, for it violates a fundamental rule of arithmetic.

Just as violation of a basic rule of arithmetic led to the "proof" that $2 = 1$, so violation of an equally basic rule of logic—that PART may not be applied to the *conclusion* of an argument—might lead to a specious "proof" such as the following:

Premise: Some (d)ogs are (p)ets. $Dx \cdot Px \mid \therefore d \rightarrow p$

Conclusion: Hence, all (d)ogs are (p)ets. $Dx \cdot Px \mid \therefore Dx \rightarrow Px$

                                           $T \quad T \quad F\,T \quad F\,X$

Obviously, this does not prove that "All dogs are pets" may logically be derived from "Some dogs are pets." It merely shows that a basic restriction concerning the use of the rule of particularization (PART) has been ignored.

In the history of every branch of science there are times when new ideas are partly accepted while old ideas—often contradictory ones—are retained. The ancient proof that the diagonal of a square can be neither an even nor an odd number (section 4.3) seemed utterly paradoxical as long as the earlier belief that the entire domain of arithmetic is confined to positive whole numbers was retained.

In the fifth century B.C. Zeno of Elea set forth many paradoxes. One of them dealt with the relation of part to whole. It is assumed as axiomatic that any collection of parts, taken separately, should be equal to the same collection, taken as a whole. But drop a grain of millet seed and it makes no noise; then drop a bag of millet seed and a sound is heard. Weigh a grain of millet seed and the scale remains unchanged; yet weigh a bag of millet seed and a definite weight is registered. Until better scales were developed, and until psychologists learned more about minimal threshholds of perception, there were no satisfactory resolutions of this paradox.

Again, during the sixteenth and seventeenth centuries, for those who assumed that the earth was the only center of the universe, Jupiter's moons seemed strange and paradoxical. On the other hand, until the concept of impetus or inertia was clarified, the Copernican hypothesis that "the earth moves" left unexplained some readily observable facts, e.g., that a body thrown straight up into the air returns to the exact place where it was thrown.

Similarly, in eighteenth-century chemistry, before oxygen was discovered and the nature of combustion was understood, the best chemists of the day found it necessary to assign "negative weight" to certain substances—a puzzling paradox.

In the social sciences, such contradictions seldom manifest themselves so clearly. Nevertheless, Rudyard Kipling stated a basic truth when he wrote:

> It is not learning, grace or gear
>   Nor easy meat and drink,
> But bitter pinch of pain and fear
>   That makes creation think.[6]

In any area of knowledge, scientific or nonscientific, whenever new discoveries challenge traditional beliefs, compelling the most basic assumptions of a field of knowledge to be reexamined, we may say of the thinker what the British psychoanalyst R. D. Laing says of his patient:

> There must be something the matter with him
>   because he would not be acting as he does
>   unless there was
>   therefore he is acting as he is
>   because there is something the matter with him
>
> He does not think there is anything the matter
>   with him because
>   one of the things that is
>   the matter with him
>   is that he does not think that there is anything
>   the matter with him
>
> Therefore
>   we have to help him realize that,
>   the fact that he does not think there is anything
>   the matter with him
>   is one of the things that is
>   the matter with him[7]

SELF-REFERENTIAL PARADOXES.   Consider the following example:

> Once a crocodile stole a baby from a mother who was washing her clothes along the banks of the Ganges. In response to the mother's plea, the crocodile promised to restore the baby provided the mother would give the right answer to this question, "Is the crocodile going to restore the baby?"
> The mother answered "No," and continued: "If *No* is the *wrong* answer, this means that you were intending to restore the baby to me when you asked the question. But if *No* is the *right* answer, then you must restore the baby in order to keep the promise you just made. So, in either case, you must restore my baby."
> To which the crocodile replied, "If *No* is the *right* answer, this makes it a simple fact that I am not going to give back the baby. And if *No* is the *wrong* answer, then my promise does not hold. So, I am not going to restore your baby."[8]

The student will see the similarity of this mother-crocodile dialogue to the Protagoras-Euathlus dilemma (problem 16, exercise 3.4A). In both cases, the argument itself is such an integral part of its own "proof" that reasoning cannot proceed in a rational manner until the problem has been reformulated.
Consider a paradox cited in *Timothy* 1:12: Epimenides, the Cretan, declared "All Cretans are liars." To make this statement self-consistent, we must assume either that Epimenides was an *ex*-Cretan, or that he was using the

---

[6] Rudyard Kipling, "The Benefactors," stanza 5, in Bartlett's *Familiar Quotations*.

[7] From *Knots*, by R. D. Laing. Copyright ©️ 1970 by the R. D. Laing Trust. Reprinted by permission of Pantheon Books, a Division of Random House, Inc., New York, and Tavistock Publications Ltd., London. Cited by James S. Gordon, "Who is Mad? Who is Sane?" *Atlantic* 227 (January 1, 1971): 50–61.

[8] Slightly adapted from J. G. Brennan, *Handbook of Logic* (New York: Harper and Row, 1961), p. 93. See also Robert L. Martin, ed., *The Paradox of the Liar* (New Haven, Conn.: Yale University Press, 1970).

quantifier "All" to mean "Nearly all." Otherwise his statement involved a self-contradiction, and may have been intended as a joke.

When Aristotle declared "All generalizations are false—including this one" he was probably trying to dramatize the fact that, in an extremely complex and changing world, it is practically impossible to find a generalization which does not admit of some exceptions. For, if we attempt to interpret Aristotle's statement literally, we run into a self-contradiction.

Let us see why. Let g symbolize the generalization "All (g)eneralizations are false." Assuming g to be true, we immediately derive another statement which we will symbolize by the letter t: "The generalization 'All generalizations are false' is (t)rue." But if t is a true proposition, it necessarily implies $\sim g$. Thus we have two implications: (1) $g \rightarrow t$, and (2) $t \rightarrow \sim g$. But, by COPO, (2) becomes (3): (3) $g \rightarrow \sim t$. Combining (1) and (3) gives the following RAA: $[(g \rightarrow t) \cdot (g \rightarrow \sim t)] \leftrightarrow \sim g$.

Thus, when we conjoin the A-form "All generalizations are false," to the existential and logically derivative, yet incompatible, proposition, "The statement 'All generalizations are false' is true," we arrive at a self-contradiction. These two statements can be simultaneously "true" only with respect to the empty set.

To resolve paradoxes of this sort, Russell and Whitehead proposed a "theory of types" which operates somewhat as follows: for the statement form "All generalizations are false" substitute the equivalent statement form "If x is a generalization, then x is false." Obviously, in this new form the variable "x" may be replaced by many substitutional instances. For example, let x signify "All logicians are rational." Then, by substitution, we would have "If 'All logicians are rational' is a generalization, then 'All logicians are rational' is false." Thousands of other such substitutions could be made. But we can never substitute for x the proposition itself, namely, "If x is a generalization, then x is false." In brief, no function of the form $f(x) = k$ may take the form $f(f) = k$; for when we do this we are confusing the form f with the content x which fills that form. Constants and variables must be kept clear and distinct. Using the terminology of set theory: sets should never be confused with members of sets; and this confusion may easily occur if the universal set U is not clearly defined. Indeed it was his use of the ambiguous "set of all sets" which led to "Russell's paradox."[9]

THE PARADOX OF MATERIAL IMPLICATION.   The late George Conger, for many years professor and head of the Department of Philosophy at the University of Minnesota, once told of an incident which occurred in the 1930s when Bertrand Russell (1872–1970) was there as a guest speaker. Anticipating that the audience would be small and rather selective, the lecture was scheduled in a room which seated approximately two hundred students. When Russell had finished his lecture, he asked for questions from the audience. After some hesitation, a student stood up and asked, "Mr. Russell, what do you think about things in general?" Without a second's hesitation, Russell answered, "In general, I don't think about things in general."

[9] For a brief explanation of the ambiguity which led to "Russell's paradox," (and thus showing that this paradox does not undercut the foundations of set theory) read A. H. Lightstone, *The Axiomatic Method: An Introduction to Mathematical Logic* (Englewood Cliffs, N. J.: Prentice-Hall, 1964), p. 44. For summary statements concerning paradoxes, read W. V. Quine, "Paradox," in *Scientific American* 206 (April 1962): 84–96; J. D. Carney and R. K. Scheer, *Fundamentals of Logic* (New York: Macmillan, 1964), chap. 6. See also "Logical Paradoxes" in Paul Edwards, ed., *The Encyclopedia of Philosophy* (New York: Macmillan, 1967), vol. 5, pp. 45–51; Morris Kline, *Mathematics in Western Culture* (New York: Oxford, 1964), chap. 25, "The Paradoxes of the Infinite."

At Minnesota, Russell spoke the language of common sense, and he was correct. Earlier in his career, however, when criticizing Gottlob Frege (1848–1925), Russell postulated "the set of all sets" (which is the most universal of all possible universal sets), and then he also postulated an element outside that set. Since "define" means "to place within limits," and since "the set of all sets" cannot thus be defined, Russell's paradox arose from his failure to stipulate the universe of discourse in which his thinking was occurring. The law of excluded middle means that every set has a complimentary set—*within some universal set*. Since the complement of a universal set is the null set, we may not even *assume* that the null set contains an element.

Committed to a philosophy of realism, Russell gave considerable attention to statements such as the following: "All twentieth-century French (k)ings are (b)ald," i.e., "If anyone is a twentieth-century French (k)ing, he is (b)ald" $(k \rightarrow b)$. From this statement we can, by quantification equivalence (QE), derive the verifiable statement "It is false that there exists any twentieth-century French (k)ing who *is not* (b)ald." $[\sim(Kx \cdot \sim Bx)]$. Equally verifiable, however, is the statement "It is false that there exists any twentieth-century (k)ing who *is* (b)ald" $[\sim(Kx \cdot Bx)]$; which by QE means "No twentieth-century French (k)ings are (b)ald" $(k \rightarrow \sim b)$.

Thus we have established that two related A- and E-forms $(k \rightarrow b)$ and $(k \rightarrow \sim b)$ are both true. However, as the following Venn diagrams clearly show, their "truth" concerns the empty set:

$\sim(Kx \cdot \sim Bx)$
$k \rightarrow b$

All K are B:
$K \cdot \sim B = \varnothing$

$\sim(Ky \cdot By)$
$k \rightarrow \sim b$

No K are B:
$K \cdot B = \varnothing$

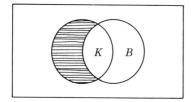

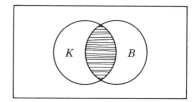

Figure 20

Figure 21

$\sim(Kx \cdot \sim Bx) \cdot \sim(Ky \cdot By)$
$(k \rightarrow b) \quad \cdot \quad (k \rightarrow \sim b)$

All K are B *and* No K are B:
$K = \varnothing$

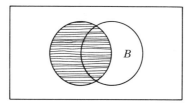

Figure 22

Employing CE, DIST, ExM, and TV, the conjunction $(k \rightarrow b) \cdot (k \rightarrow \sim b)$ yields $\sim k$:

$$(k \rightarrow b) \cdot (k \rightarrow \sim b) = (\sim k \vee b) \cdot (\sim k \vee \sim b)$$
$$= \sim k \vee (b \cdot \sim b) = \sim k \vee F = \sim k$$

Thus we have established that the two related A- and E- forms $(k \to b)$ and $(k \to \sim b)$ are both true, if and only if "k" is false, i.e., if and only if it is false that there are any twentieth-century French kings.

However, since the symbol "$\sim k$" is completely lacking in context, it is therefore ambiguous, and thus gives rise to further puzzling ambiguities. If we were to employ the symbolism explained in section 6.2, it would be obvious at once that the conjunction of $(k \to b)$ with $(k \to \sim b)$ cannot occur on the existential plane. For, by PART, $k \to b$ would yield $Kx \to Bx$, whereas $k \to \sim b$ would yield $Ky \to \sim By$. Since they have different subscripts, the conjunction of $Kx \to Bx$ with $Ky \to \sim By$ is obviously impossible.

What does the fact that we can talk as easily and as glibly about twentieth-century French kings as we do about seventeenth-century French kings prove to us? It proves that we can speak easily and glibly about the empty set.

Even though both of the preceding statements about twentieth-century French kings are *true* in the sense that no referents can be found to prove them to be *false*, they are *not true* in the sense that empirical observation can be used to *verify* them.

The paradox of material implication results mainly from the fact that everyday language employs "If . . . then" not only to represent clearly defined sets of *truth values*, but also to signify *causal relations*. Unless we clearly differentiate the truth values of statements from their *meanings*, we may quite easily and unintentionally shuttle back and forth between two entirely different usages of "If . . . then." Certainly the following three statement forms

$$p \cdot \sim p \to q \cdot \sim q; \qquad p \cdot \sim p \to q; \qquad p \cdot \sim p \to q \vee \sim q$$

all have truth value T. But this defined meaning of the arrow does *not* mean that a self-contradiction $(p \cdot \sim p)$ is a *cause* of an event. In truth-value logic, when the *antecedent* of any conditional is *false*, then that *conditional considered as a whole* necessarily has truth value T. But when we employ "If . . . then" to refer to *causal relations in the world of physical reality*, we cannot interpret a self-contradictory state of affairs to be a cause.

It would seem that the Hegelian-Marxian dialectic shuttles back and forth between these two usages of "If . . . then." The "truth" of this dialectic, or rather, its "grain of truth," consists in the rule of logic that from self-contradictory premises *any conclusion whatsoever logically follows*. If, like Marx, we define "society" as a group of people living in peace and harmony; and if the presence of large numbers of alienated citizens leads to social chaos, disharmony, and "self-contradiction," then, out of such self-contradiction *something* in the way of change is likely to occur. However, as John H. Randall, Jr., has shown, it is only *hindsight*, not foresight, that can tell us *what actually does ensue.*[10] The following tongue-in-check exercise is intended to emphasize this basic truth contained in the Hegelian-Marxist dialectic.

---

[10] John H. Randall, Jr., *The Career of Modern Philosophy* (New York: Columbia University Press, 1966), vol. 2. On p. 311 Randall writes:

You cannot possibly *predict* anything by [Hegelian] dialectic—Hegel never attempts any prediction of the future. Dialectic, in fact, is not a method to be employed for the discovery of any new fact or existence or idea, but rather a method of criticizing the ideas you already have. It is a method, that is, not of scientific inquiry and prediction, but of clarification and understanding.

A somewhat similar, and considerably less lucid, defense of the Marxian dialectic by Friedrich Engels may be found in Irving M. Copi and James A. Gould, eds., *Readings in Logic* (New York: Macmillan, 1964), pp. 155–62.

Exercise 6.3A.   Deriving Conclusions From Self-Contradictory Premises

Directions: The following "multiple-choice exam" is designed to emphasize a fundamental principle of truth-value logic: from self-contradictory premises, *anything*—any conclusion whatsoever—"follows." Answers are not given, since each inference is *valid*, but none is necessarily *true.*

1. In modern algebra, the empty set (for example, the set "All Dogs that are also non-Dogs") is a subset of
   (A) the set of "All Dogs that are non-Dogs" (the empty set).
   (B) the set "All creatures that are either Dogs or non-Dogs" (the universal set).
   (C) each and every other set (for example, the sets "Chairs," "Stars," "Lions").
2. In truth-value logic, given self-contradictory statements as premises (e.g., "X is a dog" *and* "X is not a dog"), we may validly derive from this:
   (A) any other self-contradictory statement (e.g., "X is a cat *and* X is not a cat").
       $[(d \cdot \sim d) \rightarrow (c \cdot \sim c)]$
   (B) any tautologous statement (e.g., "X is a cat *or* X is not a cat").
       $[(d \cdot \sim d) \rightarrow (c \vee \sim c)]$
   (C) any statement whatsoever (e.g., "Fido is a dog."). $[(d \cdot \sim d) \rightarrow Df]$
3. In Fichte's romantic philosophy, the Ego (Thesis) posits its own self-contradiction the non-Ego (Anti-Thesis); and this logically leads to:
   (A) the Superego $[(t \cdot \sim t) \rightarrow s]$
   (B) Nirvana $[(t \cdot \sim t) \rightarrow n]$
   (C) anything whatsoever
4. In Hegelian dialectic a contradiction is assumed when Being (Thesis) is conjoined with non-Being (Antithesis). This contradiction leads logically to:
   (A) the Creation of the World
   (B) the Annihilation of the World
   (C) something or other, which Hegel called the "Synthesis."
5. In Marxian dialectic, when Thesis (i.e., a society based on a set of norms, such as those of fourteenth-century Austria, or of nineteenth-century Russia) is followed by Antithesis [internal difficulties and maladjustments because of changed economic conditions]; it is assumed that such internal "contradictions" necessarily result in a new Synthesis (a different type of social order), which might well be:
   (A) the Holy Roman Empire   (D) Communism
   (B) Nationalism   (E) Totalitarianism
   (C) Capitalism   (F) Anarchism

PARADOXES RESULTING FROM AMBIGUOUS CONTEXT. The first rule of thinking is a very simple one: "*Stick to the point.*" This means "Specify the *context.*" "Define the universal set." "Make clear the universe of discourse within which your statements are to be understood." Any thinking which lacks a specified domain of discourse is headed for ambiguity and paradox, even when it rigorously adheres to other rules of logic.

For example, let *s, m, p, d,* and *g* represent the following five propositions:

> John is a (s)tudent.
> John is a (m)usic major.
> John is a (p)hilosophy major.
> Columbus (d)iscovered America.
> Grass is (g)reen.

Now assume that *s, m,* and *p* are within the domain of discourse, but that *d* and *g* are not. Then, in the series of inferences below, steps 2, 3, 4, 5, and 6 are legitimate inferences; but steps 7, 8, 9, and 10 bring in propositions outside the domain of discourse and are therefore fallacious.

Premise: 1. s
Valid Inferences: 2. $s \lor \sim m$ 1, ADD
                   3. $\sim m \lor s$ 2, COM
                   4. $m \to s$ 3, CE
                   5. $\sim p \lor s$ 1, ADD, COM
                   6. $p \to s$ 5, CE
Invalid Inferences: 7. $\sim d \lor s$ 1, ADD, COM
                   8. $d \to s$ 7, CE
                   9. $\sim g \lor s$ 1, ADD, COM
                   10. $g \to s$ 9, CE

Context helps us understand why, even though the two statements are logically equivalent, English usage recommends one statement form in preference to another. For example, by the law of commutation (COM) $g \lor \sim b = \sim b \lor g$. Yet "Either Al is in Germany or Al is not in Berlin" is preferable to "Either Al is not in Berlin or Al is in Germany." Why? Because "Germany" provides the general context of this statement, and good usage demands that this context come in the first rather than the last clause of the statement. Similar reasons explain why we would condemn "Either Fido is not a (d)og or Fido is a (m)ammal," but would approve "Either Fido is a (m)ammal or Fido is not a (d)og," even though, by COM, $\sim d \lor m = m \lor d$. On the other hand, the two contrapositives "If Fido is a dog, then Fido is a mammal" ($d \to m$) and "If Fido is not a mammal, then Fido is not a dog" ($\sim m \to \sim d$) are both correct; as are "If Al is in Berlin, then Al is in Germany" ($b \to g$) and "If Al is not in Germany, then Al is not in Berlin" ($\sim g \to \sim b$). In English usage, for purposes of context, "either . . . or" statements require that we move from the general to the specific; whereas, "if . . . then" statements may move in either direction.

As our next example of paradoxes arising from ambiguous context, consider the so-called "Raven Paradox." By COPO, "All Ravens are Black" has the same truth values as its contrapositive "All non-Black things are non-Ravens." But do these two statements have the same *meanings*? Do they have the same *referents*? If it is not immediately evident that they do not, consider the following analogous example. Suppose our context (our universal set) is "Living persons," and suppose that this universal set has 4 billion members. Within this universal set, consider the following two subsets: (1) "persons now in this (b)uilding" and (2) "members of my (f)amily." Let us suppose that there are now exactly 100 persons in this building, and that my family consists of exactly 4 members. Then, to *verify* the statement "All members of my (f)amily are in this (b)uilding" ($f \to b$), not more than 100 persons would need to be found. But to verify the contrapositive "All persons not in this building are persons not in my family" ($\sim b \to \sim f$) we might need to search until we had located as many as 3,999,999,900 persons.[11]

The Raven Paradox reminds us, once more, that *the meanings of statements are not to be identified with their truth values.* Thus the two statements "My dog is an animal" and "My dog is a female collie that is closely related to the Lassie of the movies" may both have truth value *T*; but the more *specific* statement, the one whose context is narrower, is the *more meaningful.*

Similarly, the statement "All non-Black things are non-Ravens" becomes increasingly meaningful if we reduce "non-black *things*" to "*birds* that are not black," i.e., if we limit our discussion to ornothology. It would be more

---

[11] For a detailed analysis of the Raven Paradox from the standpoint of statistical analysis, read Satoni Watanabe, *Knowing and Guessing* (New York: Wiley, 1969), p. 184 f.

meaningful still if we narrowed the context to the relatively small family of birds, *corvidae*. Since only Ravens, Jays, Magpies, and Crows are *corvidae*, the statement "All non-Black *corvidae* are non-Ravens" would be more meaningful, and incomparably more amenable to verification, than "All non-black *things* are non-ravens."

Let us return to the paradox of material implication, this time analyzing it from the viewpoint of context. In *Symbolic Logic*, Lewis and Langford cite this example:

> If p implies q, then it is not the case that p is true and q is false. $\{(p \rightarrow q)$
> $[= (\sim p \vee q)] = \sim (p \cdot \sim q)\}$. The converse cannot be proved by our postulates . . .
> Let p = "Roses are red" and q = "Sugar is sweet." It is here not the case that p
> is true and q is false—since q is true . . . But p does not imply q: "Sugar is sweet"
> cannot be inferred from "Roses are red."[12]

Let us see what happens when the sentences "Roses are red" and "Sugar is sweet" are replaced by statements and *symbols which make clear subject-predicate relationships*. Let us replace "Roses are (r)ed" ("r") by "Some (r)oses are (m)aroon" ($Rx \cdot Mx$), and replace "Sugar is (s)weet" ("s") by "All (s)ugar is (p)alatable" ($s \rightarrow p$). With such subject-predicate statement forms, there would be no possibility of getting entangled in paradoxes of the type described by Lewis and Langford.

The importance of context is implicit in the scholastic thesis, "Logical truth is found imperfect and incomplete in simple apprehension, perfect and complete in the judgment." This thesis says, in effect, that until statements have a subject and a predicate, they are not clear. Thus, the ejaculation "pain" or "painful" is less clear and meaningful than "For all x, x is painful" $[(x) (Px)]$ or than "For some x, x is painful" $[(\exists x) (Px)]$; but these forms are still lacking in precise context, hence they are less clear and meaningful than the subject-predicate statements "Some (b)ruises are (p)ainful" ($Bx \cdot Px$), "All (w)ounds are (p)ainful" ($w \rightarrow p$), or "This toothache is (p)ainful" (Pt).

It may be logically correct to say "Everything is real" and to symbolize it $(x) (Rx)$, but logical symbolism would be closer to the usage of ordinary thought and language if the statement were revised to become an A-form "All (t)hings are (r)eal"; which could be then symbolized $t \rightarrow r$ [or $(x) (Tx \supset Rx)$]. With this formulation, we could then proceed to ask "Is there some *(t)hing* that is not (r)eal?" And our restatement of the problem would tend to make us ask: Do "things" include "ideas" or "possibles"? By expressing the judgment as a subject-predicate judgment, we could move ahead with our inquiry—and not be caught up in paradox because of a faulty symbolism.

In short, from the standpoint of meaning and clarity, we should recognize the advantages of the traditional A-, E-, I-, and O-form statements over the modern atomic type. As N. L. Wilson once wrote " . . . the sentence 'No individuals exist' . . . does not describe a possible state of affairs, nor does the sentence 'There are individuals' record a fact."[13]

---

[12] C. I. Lewis and C. H. Langford, *Symbolic Logic*, 2nd ed. (Goucester, Mass.: Peter Smith, 1959), p. 122.

[13] N. L. Wilson, *The Concept of Language* (Toronto: University of Toronto Press, 1959), p. 104. We agree with Kant, that existence is not an attribute; and with Aristotle, that anything which exists must fall within some category, within some domain of discourse. Accordingly, for an assertion such as "Pegasus exists" to be sufficiently meaningful as a part of logic, it should be reformulated into another statement, e.g., "Pegasus is a winged horse" ($Wp \cdot Hp$), or "Pegasus is a mythological character" (Mp), or "Pegasus is a zoological creature" (Zp).

Properties, if they exist at all, exist only as a result of attaching names to, or designating, distinctive types of experience. If there were no red *things*, we would not know about the property "red." This last sentence needs qualification. Perhaps we could postulate "red" as the color which best complements yellow; or as a range of colors somewhere between infra-red and indigo. But were we to say "Everything is red" we would not be communicating anything intelligible, for the "red" would have no property which makes it distinctive or recognizable. Our ordinary perceptions consist mainly of the fitting of sense experiences into general categories, and it is important that logical symbolism be so constituted as to incorporate this basic psychological fact. Hence rather than employ a phraseology (and a related symbolism) such as "Everything is red" or "For all x, x is red" [(x) Rx], we will do better to express this idea thus: "All (r)ed things are (c)olored objects" ($r \rightarrow c$) or "Every (r)ed color [is a color which] falls (b)etween infra-red and indigo" ($r \rightarrow b$). We should also take note of the fact that "Everything is red" admits of no contradiction: for if we once admit that everything is red, we should not even attempt to look for something that is not red. On the other hand, "Some red objects are heavy," "No red things are white," and so on, can be verified as true or false statements, thus meriting a place among those concepts and symbolisms which deserve a place in our scientific heritage.

Exercise 6.3B.   Context, Paradox, and the Limitations of Reason

Directions: Defend or criticize the following statements.[14]

A. [Dewey wrote:] " . . . the significant business of philosophy is the disclosure of the context of beliefs."
[Dewey] considers both temporal and spatial aspects of background and comes to the conclusion that the whole contextual background can never come into question at once, with the corollary that something is always being taken for granted or is "understood." What he calls "selective interest" has been known by the more common philosophical term, "subjective," which, he says, is equivalent to individuality or uniqueness. He sees individuality as a "mode of selection which determines subject-matter." . . . [For Dewey:] All thinking must take place in a context, and thinking about thought without reference to context, as Dewey puts it, "is in the end but a beating of wings in the void."

B. [Camus wrote:] "In psychology as in logic, there are truths but no truth. . . . I realize that if through science I can seize phenomena and enumerate them, I cannot, for all that, apprehend the world."
The terrible paradox that Camus perceives is that man has lucidity *and* seemingly definite walls around him. We are lucid enough to perceive the walls but we are unable to see a way out or even guess why the walls are there.

---

[14] Statements A and B are reprinted from *Tough and Tender Learning* by David Nyberg by permission of Mayfield Publishing Company, formerly National Press Books, 1971, pp. 55–60. The John Dewey quotations are from *Experience, Nature and Freedom* (New York: Bobbs-Merrill, 1960). The Albert Camus quotations are from *The Myth of Sisyphus* (New York: Knopf, 1955). The two definitions in C are from Spinoza's *Ethics*.

For a statement emphasizing the importance of context in structuring educational curricula, read John Walton, "A Confusion of Contexts: The Interdisciplinary Study of Education," in *Educational Theory* 24 (Summer 1974): 219–46. Mature students wishing to study context from the most comprehensive and philosophical point of view should read John H. Randall, Jr., *Hellenistic Ways of Deliverance and the Making of the Christian Synthesis* (New York: Columbia University Press, 1970), chap. 7: "The Intelligible Universe of Plotinus."

For Camus, the sole significant datum is the absurd, but it is not the world itself which constitutes the absurd. The absurd depends as much upon man as upon the world. To understand the world one must apprehend all of its events in all of their relations. This is impossible for, as Dewey suggests, the limits of man's knowledge due to the effects of context are finite, though indefinite. Nonetheless, as Camus vividly illustrates, there is in man a nostalgia, a wild longing for clarity, a need for familiarity, an appetite for certainty. "The absurd is essentially a divorce [between the man considering the world and the world considered]. It lies in neither of the elements compared; it is born of their confrontation. The absurd is lucid reason noting its limits."

C. Wonder is the thought of anything which brings the mind to a standstill—because the concept in question has no connection with other concepts.—*Spinoza*

Humility is pain arising from a man's contemplation of his own weakness of body and mind.—*Spinoza*

CONCLUDING COMMENTS.   Modern logic runs into paradoxes when (a) it deals with statements which turn out to be self-contradictory and which have no referents; and (b) when it operates within a context (within a universal set) that is not clearly defined. We can illustrate (a) with a single example:

> These concluding comments are written for all and only those readers for whom no concluding comments are ever written.

We can illustrate (b) by two statements:

1. Everything (p)ossible is a kind of (b)eing, and anything that has (b)eing is possible. $(p \to b) \cdot (b \to p)$, or $(p \leftrightarrow b)$
2. Everything that is (s)ubstantial (existential, actual, within the realm of space-time-matter) is also (p)ossible (ideational, conceivable); but not everything (p)ossible is also (s)ubstantial. $[\sim(p \to s)$ or $(Px \cdot \sim Sx)]$.

Here the expression $Px \cdot \sim Sx$ places the subscript "x" under "P" ("possible") whereas, by definition, "x" is properly used only with things that are (s)ubstantial. Stated otherwise, the rules of quantification equivalence (QE) do not seem to apply to concepts which represent the *entire* range of (b)eing.

Thus, the empty set (including self-contradictory statement forms) at the one extreme, and "the set of all sets" (any statements that are so abstract and general that they are not amenable to definition, i.e., they cannot be "placed within limits") on the other, are easy-to-form combinations of words or symbols. But they are extremely difficult to deal with. Perhaps we move a tiny step forward when we recognize the necessity of keeping thought within a definite context.

Exercise 6.3C.   Deciphering the Meanings of Ordinary Language Statements

Comments: This exercise is a review of ideas previously covered in exercises 6.1F, 6.1G, 6.1H, 6.2C, and 6.2D. It is designed to emphasize the fact that, for most students, interpreting the precise meanings contained in sentences is the most difficult feature of logic. Stated otherwise, once the meaning of statements has been clearly expressed so as to be readily understood, it is relatively easy to judge whether *arguments* based on such statements are valid or invalid. The ambiguities in this exercise are far less subtle, difficult, and puzzling than those which give rise to paradoxes.

Directions: Following the directions for exercise 6.2F, circle T, F, or D after each problem. This will indicate whether, on the basis of the italicized sentence heading each group, that statement may be inferred to be true (T) or false (F), or whether its truth or falsity remains doubtful (D).

Group A. *Some dogs are not pets.*

1. Not all dogs are pets.	1. T F D
2. Only if *x* is a dog is *x* a pet.	2. T F D
3. All except dogs are nonpets.	3. T F D
4. There are pets that are not dogs.	4. T F D
5. No dogs are nonpets.	5. T F D

Group B. *A whale is a cetacean.*

6. Every whale is a cetacean.	6. T F D
7. Everything other than cetaceans are nonwhales.	7. T F D
8. All nonwhales are noncetaceans.	8. T F D
9. All creatures are nonwhales except cetaceans.	9. T F D.
10. "Some whales are not cetaceans" is false.	10. T F D

Group C. *Only A-students are honor students.*

11. All A-students are honor students.	11. T F D
12. Some A-students are honor students.	12. T F D
13. No honor students are persons who are not A-students.	13. T F D
14. There are honor students who are not A-students.	14. T F D
15. The only A-students are honor students.	15. T F D

Group D. *All is not gold that glitters.*

16. Some gold does not glitter.	16. T F D
17. Some gold glitters.	17. T F D
18. Some things that glitter are not gold.	18. T F D
19. All nongold glitters.	19. T F D
20. Some things that are not gold are not things that do not glitter.	20. T F D

6.4 Review and More Difficult Problems

We begin this final section of chapter 6 with an exercise reviewing the varied types of proof studied earlier in the book. Problems 1 and 2 of exercise 6.4A are similar to those studied in section 2.5. Problems 3–7 are similar to those studied in chapter 4. Problems 8–20 are of the type studied in section 6.1.

Exercise 6.4A. Testing for Validity: Review

Directions: In this exercise, you are not only to indicate whether the argument is valid or invalid, but are also to show your proofs. Write them on separate paper.

1. If the consequent of any conditional is a (t)autology, then it cannot be (f)alse. But unless the consequent of a conditional is (f)alse, that conditional considered as a (w)hole is necessarily true. Therefore, whenever the consequent of any conditional is a (t)autology, that conditional considered as a (w)hole is necessarily true.

2. If the antecedent of a conditional is (a)bsurd, it must also be (f)alse. But if the antecedent of a conditional is (f)alse, then that conditional considered as a whole must have (t)ruth value *T*. Hence, if any conditional considered as a whole does not have (t)ruth value *T*, that conditional's antecedent cannot be (a)bsurd.

3. If and only if an argument form [for example, $p \cdot q \mathbin{/} \therefore \sim(\sim p)$] is (v)alid, then and only then is its related conditional [for example, $p \cdot q \to p$] or biconditional [for example, $\sim(\sim p) \leftrightarrow p$] (t)autologous. If and only if the conditional or biconditional is (t)autologous, then and only then does the crucial assignments method result in an (i)nconsistency. Therefore, if and only if the crucial assignments method does not result in an (i)nconsistency is the original argument form in(v)alid.

4. Given our present (e)conomic system, if any group of people doing essentially the same kind of work is well (o)rganized, that group can somehow manage either to secure (l)egislation which gives special benefits to their group, or they can devise quasi-monopolistic (t)rade agreements to keep their prices high, or, in the case of labor, they can (s)trike and get their special demands by paralyzing the entire

economy. Now it doesn't much matter whether these things happen because of (l)egislation favorable to one special group or because of quasi-monopolistic (t)rade agreements between large companies, or because of (s)trikes by powerful unions—any one, two, or three of them gives special (a)dvantages to one segment of society as against other segments. Therefore, if we don't want such special (a)dvantages to occur, we must either find ways to make it more difficult for special interest groups to become so well (o)rganized, or we will have to give up our present (e)conomic system.

5. If grammar is to become an authentic (s)cientific discipline, it will have to be organized and structured on some clear (l)ogical basis. But such a (l)ogical organization is not likely to come about unless grammarians study (m)odern developments in mathematical logic. There is another condition without which such a (l)ogical organization of grammar will not come about, namely, the condition that (m)odern developments in mathematical logic and (a)pplications to the field of grammar and semantics should be joined. Therefore, unless grammarians study (m)odern mathematical logic, and unless ways can be found to (a)pply this logic to grammar and semantics, grammar will remain an area of study that cannot truly be called (s)cientific.

6. All (j)ays are (c)orvidae. All (m)ice are (r)odents. Therefore, if no (m)ice are (c)orvidae, then no (j)ays are (r)odents.

7. All (t)igers are (f)elines. All (m)ammals are (v)ertebrates. Therefore, if all (t)igers are (v)ertebrates, then all (f)elines are (m)ammals.

8. There have certainly been many (m)artyrs in the history of mankind. Now, every (m)artyr is a person who places his ideals (a)bove life itself. But anyone who places any ideal (a)bove life itself is following an ideal that cannot properly be considered (n)atural. Hence, if any ideal that cannot properly be considered (n)atural is defined as a (s)upernatural ideal, then there are many (m)artyrs who have followed (s)upernatural ideals.

9. All (c)ollies are (d)ogs, and all (d)ogs are (v)ertebrates. Therefore, since Fido is not a (c)ollie, Fido is not a (v)ertebrate.

10. All (s)hepherds are (d)ogs and no (d)ogs are (c)orvidae. Therefore, since Rover is a (s)hepherd, Rover is not a (c)orvidae.

11. All (c)ollies are (d)ogs. All (d)ogs are (m)ammals, and all (m)ammals are (v)ertebrates. Therefore, since King is a (c)ollie, some (v)ertebrates are (d)ogs.

12. There are some teachers who are not (s)ociable even though they are (p)olite. Anyone who is (p)olite is (w)ell bred. And anyone who is un(k)ind is not (w)ell bred. Therefore, there are some (k)ind people who are not (s)ociable. [*Note:* In this argument the context, or the universe of discourse, is "teachers." Hence "(t)each-ers" need not be symbolized—although symbolizing it would do no harm other than to require extra steps in the proof.]

13. There are men who are both im(p)olite and un(g)entlemanly. It is not the case that there is anyone who is (r)efined who is not also (p)olite. If a man is dis(h)onest then he is not a (g)entleman. Furthermore, if a man is truly (w)ell bred, then he is either (r)efined or he is a (g)entleman. Therefore, there are men who are not truly (w)ell bred.

14. No (s)tudents are (i)lliterate. Alex is a (m)oron. Therefore, if every (m)oron is (i)lliterate, Alex is not a (s)tudent.

15. Any activity that is (s)timulating is (b)eneficial to one's mental health. Some activities, although (s)timulating, are (h)azardous. Therefore, some (b)eneficial things are (h)azardous.

16. The (f)allacy of false conversion [of an A-form proposition] is something every student of (t)raditional logic should understand. (H)elen understands the (f)allacy of false conversion. So, (H)elen must have studied (t)raditional logic.

17. All (s)cholars are (r)ational. Hence, if there exist (M)artians who are (b)arbaric, and if no (b)arbaric (M)artians are (r)ational, then there are (b)arbaric (M)artians who are not (s)cholars.

18. Every member of our (t)eam is a (g)ood student. If a (g)ood student cannot (s)tudy, he (c)omplains. There are members of our (t)eam who cannot (s)tudy. Therefore, there are members of our (t)eam who are (g)ood students and who (c)omplain.

19. If (M)arx was a (l)iberal, then every (u)topian is a (l)iberal. If all (u)topians are (l)iberals, then Viscomte de (B)oland must have been a (l)iberal. But obviously he was not. Therefore, it is false that all (u)topians are (l)iberals, and it is also false that (M)arx was a (l)iberal.

20. Bill and Don are both (g)ood students and both are members of our (t)eam. Any (g)ood student who cannot (s)tudy will (c)omplain. Therefore, there are members of our (t)eam who will (c)omplain.

The next exercise is a review and a continuation of exercise 6.2C. It deals with what traditional logic calls "immediate inference." In part I, QE, DN, COM, and COPO should help us to decide whether a statement is equivalent to, contradictory to, or independent of the model. But in part II an added existential premise makes it possible, in some cases, to also relate universals to existentials by means of PART, SIMP, MP, MT, and CONJ.

Exercise 6.4B.   Review of Particularization (PART) and Quantification Equivalence (QE)

Part I.   Directions: This exercise contains four groups of statements, each group headed by a *model* which you are to assume to be *true*. Then, in the answer blanks, write T, F, or D where

> T signifies "This statement is *equivalent* to the model, hence *true.*"
> F signifies "This statement *contradicts* the model, hence is *false.*"
> D signifies "This statement is neither equivalent to nor contradictory to the model; hence the truth-value of the model (our only premise) leaves us *doubtful* concerning the truth value of this statement."

In Part I, the one premise given in the *model* is the *only* premise on which the inferences are to be based.

Model A: No S is P $(s \rightarrow \sim p)$

_____ 1. All S is P.
_____ 2. All S is $\sim P$.
_____ 3. All P is not $\sim S$.
_____ 4. It is false that some S is not P.
_____ 5. It is false that all S is $\sim P$.
_____ 6. No S is non-P.
_____ 7. Some P is S.
_____ 8. Some $\sim S$ is P.

_____ 9. All S is not $\sim P$.
_____ 10. No P is S.
_____ 11. Some $\sim P$ is not S.
_____ 12. It is false that all P is non-S.
_____ 13. All P is $\sim S$.
_____ 14. Some P is not non-S.
_____ 15. Some P is not S.
_____ 16. It is false that some non-S is not non-P.

Model B: *It is false that some persons who do not (t)ry are (g)eniuses.*

_____ 17. All geniuses are persons who try.
_____ 18. No geniuses are persons who do not try.
_____ 19. No persons who do not try are geniuses.
_____ 20. Some persons who do not try are geniuses.
_____ 21. "No persons who do not try are geniuses" is false.
_____ 22. It is simply not the case that there are genuine geniuses who are also persons who really do not try.
_____ 23. Some persons who try are geniuses.
_____ 24. Some geniuses are persons who try.

Model C: *It is false that there are (u)nicorns that do not have goats' (h)eads.*
[$\sim(Ux \cdot \sim Hx)$;   or $u \rightarrow h$]

_____ 25. Any creature that does not have a goat's head is a unicorn.
_____ 26. Some unicorns are creatures with the heads of goats.
_____ 27. No creatures that do not have goats' heads are unicorns.
_____ 28. Some creatures that have goats' heads are unicorns.
_____ 29. Some creatures that are not unicorns are creatures that do not have goats' heads.
_____ 30. It is false that no unicorns have goats' heads.
_____ 31. It is false that there are creatures that have goats' heads that are not unicorns.
_____ 32. It is untrue that there are creatures with goats' heads that are unicorns.

Model D: *All (d)ogs are (m)ammals.*

_____ 33. Some dogs are mammals.
_____ 34. Some dogs are not nonmammals.
_____ 35. Some mammals are dogs.
_____ 36. Some mammals are not creatures other than dogs.
_____ 37. No dogs are mammals.
_____ 38. All dogs are nonmammals.
_____ 39. No mammals are dogs.
_____ 40. All mammals are nondogs.

Part II.   Directions: In this part revise each of the above four models, so that each of them consists of two statements, or two premises. On the basis of these *two* statements you are now to derive inferences (T, F, or D) for the same 32 problems.

Model A: 1. No S is P.
            2. At least one S exists.
Model B: 1. It is false that some persons who do not (t)ry are (g)eniuses.
            2. There are many (s)tudents (perhaps because of boredom or fatigue) who do not (t)ry.
Model C: 1. All (u)nicorns have goats' (h)eads.
            2. Some of the creatures (m)entioned in ancient and medieval literature are (u)nicorns.
Model D: 1. All (d)ogs are (m)ammals.
            2. Some (d)ogs are (p)ets.

Ordinary language expresses ideas in many different ways, only a few of which are clear. In applying formal logic to everyday language, the greatest difficulty is to decide precisely what statements mean. Once this decision has been reached, it is a relatively simple matter to symbolize the statement. We believe, however, that there is no better way to learn to read the English language with care and understanding than to do the type of problems illustrated in exercise 6.4C.

Exercise 6.4C.   Symbolizing Statements

Directions: Each problem in this exercise is followed by three symbolizations, at least one of which is correct. In the *Answers* column, circle A, B, or C to indicate the proper answers.

Answers

1. Unless it contains a (t)ypographical error, every (p)roblem in this exercise has at least one (c)orrect answer: A, B, or C.
   (A) $\sim t \cdot p \leftrightarrow Ca \lor Cb \lor Cc$
   (B) $\sim t \to (p \to Ca \lor Cb \lor Cc)$
   (C) $\sim t \cdot p \cdot c \to a \lor b \lor c$ A   B   C
2. If no girls are beautiful, then some men are disillusioned.
   (A) $\sim Bg \to Dm$
   (B) $(g \to \sim b) \to (Mx \cdot Dx)$
   (C) $\sim (Gx \cdot Bx) \to (m \to \sim d)$ A   B   C

3. Only persons (t)alented as children become (g)eniuses as adults.
   (A) $g \rightarrow t$
   (B) $t \rightarrow g$
   (C) $\sim(Gx \cdot \sim Tx)$ A B C
4. Only if a president makes (h)istorically significant decisions is that president (o)utstanding.
   (A) $o \rightarrow h$
   (B) $h \rightarrow o$
   (C) $\sim(Ox \cdot \sim Hx)$ A B C
5. The only (o)utstanding presidents were men who made (s)ignificant decisions.
   (A) $o \rightarrow s$
   (B) $\sim(Ox \cdot \sim Sx)$
   (C) $o \vee \sim s$ A B C
6. Some days are rainy, other days are sunny, but all days pass away.
   (A) $Rd \cdot Sd \cdot (d \rightarrow p)$
   (B) $(Dx \cdot Rx) \cdot (Dy \cdot Sy) \cdot (d \rightarrow p)$
   (C) $(r \vee s) \cdot p$ A B C
7. All men are earthbound except astronauts.
   (A) $m \cdot \sim a \rightarrow e$
   (B) $\sim e \rightarrow a \vee \sim m$
   (C) $(m \rightarrow e) \cdot (a \rightarrow \sim e)$ A B C
8. If Bob is both dumb and lazy then he is neither smart nor industrious.
   (A) $Db \cdot Lb \rightarrow \sim Sb \vee \sim Lb$
   (B) $Db \cdot Lb \rightarrow \sim(Sb \vee Ib)$
   (C) $Sb \vee Ib \rightarrow \sim Db \vee \sim Lb$ A B C
9. If anyone is (s)mart, then only if he is (a)mbitious will he be (i)ndustrious.
   (A) $s \rightarrow (a \rightarrow i)$
   (B) $Sa \cdot Aa \rightarrow Ia$
   (C) $s \rightarrow (i \rightarrow a)$ A B C
10. Whether (b)lack or (w)hite, if any man is (s)tarving or if he is completely (a)lienated from society, he will (r)ob.
    (A) $(b \vee w) \cdot (s \vee a) \rightarrow r$
    (B) $(Bx \vee Wx) \cdot [(Sx \vee Ax) \rightarrow Rx]$
    (C) $(b \cdot s) \vee (w \cdot s) \vee (b \cdot a) \vee (w \cdot a) \rightarrow r$ A B C
11. If (w)olves, (d)ogs, and (f)oxes are (c)anines, and if (s)quirrels, (b)eavers, and (m)uskrats are (r)odents, then there are lots of (c)anines and (r)odents.
    (A) $[(w \vee d \vee f \rightarrow c) \cdot (s \vee b \vee m \rightarrow r)] \rightarrow Cx \cdot Rx$
    (B) $[(w \cdot d \cdot f \rightarrow c) \cdot (s \cdot b \cdot m \rightarrow r)] \rightarrow Cx \cdot Bx$
    (C) $\sim(Cx \cdot Rx) \rightarrow (w \cdot d \cdot f \rightarrow \sim c) \cdot (s \cdot b \cdot m \rightarrow \sim r)$ A B C
12. Among (w)ell-known (b)irds, only (o)striches and (e)mus and (d)omestic fowl do not (f)ly.
    (A) $w \cdot b \rightarrow (o \cdot e \cdot d \rightarrow \sim f)$
    (B) $w \cdot b \rightarrow (\sim f \rightarrow o \vee e \vee d)$
    (C) $\sim f \cdot w \cdot b \rightarrow o \cdot e \cdot d$ A B C
13. If there is plenty of (f)ood, then, even if industrial production is not (h)igh, most (A)mericans will (e)njoy a high standard of living.
    (A) $f \cdot \sim h \rightarrow Ax \cdot Ex$
    (B) $f \vee \sim h \rightarrow Ax \cdot Ex$
    (C) $f \rightarrow (\sim h \rightarrow Ax \cdot Ex)$ A B C
14. Unless there are (s)aints who are (p)erfect, no (m)en are (p)erfect, and your beloved Kate is im(p)erfect too.
    (A) $\sim(Sx \cdot Px) \rightarrow [(\sim m \rightarrow p) \cdot \sim Pk]$
    (B) $\sim(Sx \cdot Px) \rightarrow [(m \rightarrow \sim p) \cdot \sim Pk]$
    (C) $(s \rightarrow \sim p) \rightarrow [m \rightarrow \sim p] \cdot \sim Pk$ A B C

15. Either Bob is smart but not industrious, or he is industrious but not smart.
    (A) $i \leftrightarrow \sim s$
    (B) $Ib \leftrightarrow \sim Sb$
    (C) $(Ib \cdot \sim Sb) \vee (Sb \cdot \sim Ib)$ A B C
16. If all (t)hings are (r)eal, then it is false that Bill's (h)allucination is un(r)eal.
    (A) $(t \rightarrow r) \rightarrow \sim(Hb \cdot \sim Rb)$
    (B) $(t \rightarrow r) \rightarrow \sim(\sim Rb \cdot \sim Hb)$
    (C) $(t \rightarrow r) \rightarrow (Hb \rightarrow Rb)$ A B C
17. Admitting that "all (m)en are (r)ational" means merely that "all (m)en behave rationally approximately (o)ne percent of the time," then "all (m)en are (r)ational" means that "all (m)en, viewed in terms of their highest (p)otentialities, are (r)ational."
    (A) $[(m \rightarrow r) \leftrightarrow (m \rightarrow o)] \rightarrow [(m \rightarrow r) \leftrightarrow (m \cdot p \rightarrow r)]$
    (B) $[(m \rightarrow r) \leftrightarrow (m \rightarrow o)] \rightarrow [(m \rightarrow r) \leftrightarrow (\sim m \vee \sim p \vee r)]$
    (C) $[(m \rightarrow r) \leftrightarrow (m \rightarrow o)] \rightarrow [(m \rightarrow r) \leftrightarrow \sim(Mx \cdot Px \cdot \sim Rx)]$ A B C
18. All men are (r)ational, except those who are (d)ominated by irrational or subrational impulses.
    (A) $\sim d \rightarrow (m \rightarrow r)$
    (B) $\sim d \cdot m \rightarrow r$
    (C) $m \rightarrow r \cdot \sim d$ A B C
19. Granted that every (m)an has innumerable (p)otentialities, there are (t)imes in life when men are children of (l)ight, but there are also (o)ccasions in life when these same men are children of (d)arkness.
    (A) $(m \rightarrow p) \rightarrow (Tx \cdot Lx) \cdot (Ox \cdot Dx)$
    (B) $(m \rightarrow p) \rightarrow (Tx \cdot Lx) \cdot (Oy \cdot Dy)$
    (C) $[(m \rightarrow p) \rightarrow (Tx \cdot Lx)] \cdot [(m \rightarrow p) \rightarrow (Ox \cdot Dx)]$ A B C
20. If every (p)ossibility is also a (r)eality, then all (t)hings are (r)eal, even if some (p)ossibilities never (h)appen as events in time.
    (A) $[(p \rightarrow r) \cdot (Px \cdot \sim Hx)] \rightarrow (t \rightarrow r)$
    (B) $(p \rightarrow r) \rightarrow (t \rightarrow r) \cdot (Px \cdot \sim Hx)$
    (C) $\sim(p \rightarrow h) \cdot (p \rightarrow r) \rightarrow (t \rightarrow r)$ A B C

ARGUMENTS CONTAINING MORE THAN ONE EXISTENTIAL.   In most arguments not more than one or two singulars or existentials occur. The reason for this is fairly obvious. The very nature of any argument is to apply general knowledge (expressed as universals or conditionals) to particular situations (i.e., to singulars or particulars), and we cannot focus these generalizations in very many different directions at the same time. Nevertheless, there are arguments which contain more than one existential, and sometimes more than one singular. When they do, different subscripts must be used, as in "John is tall" (Tj); "Harry is not tall" ($\sim Th$); "Some boys are not tall, but some girls are tall" ($Bx \cdot \sim Tx) \cdot (Gy \cdot Ty)$. Since different subscripts may not be combined into a single statement, no confusion is possible with this symbolism. Of course, if we were to say "These men are lazy" ($Mx \cdot Lx$), and then say "These *same* men are bureaucrats," we would use the same subscripts for both existentials.

Problem 1 of exercise 6.4D illustrates what was said in the above paragraph; since problem 1 really consists of *two arguments*, both of which employ the universal $(d \rightarrow m) \cdot (b \rightarrow m)$ [or $(d \vee b \rightarrow m)$] as a common premise.

In setting up an argument having more than one existential, we should indicate that the conclusion is valid if either one or the other of the two existentials may be established, thus:

Example A: All (r)ubies are (p)recious stones. Some (c)orundums are not (r)ubies. Some (c)orundums are (r)ubies. Therefore, some (p)recious stones are (c)orundums.

1. $r \rightarrow p$
2. $Cx \cdot \sim Rx$
3. $Cy \cdot Ry$ / $\therefore (Px \cdot Cx) \vee (Py \cdot Cy)$
4. Cy 3, SIMP
5. Ry 3, SIMP
6. $Ry \rightarrow Py$ 1, PART
7. Py 5, 6, MP
8. $Py \cdot Cy$ 4, 8, CONJ
9. $(Px \cdot Cx) \vee (Py \cdot Cy)$ 8, ADD, COM
                 Valid

To employ the crucial assignments method, every premise and conclusion must have the same subscript; so this problem must be set up in two ways:

Part I. $(r \rightarrow p) \cdot Cx \cdot \sim Rx$ / $\therefore Px \cdot Cx$
        $(Rx \rightarrow Px) \cdot Cx \cdot \sim Rx$ / $\therefore Px \cdot Cx$
         F T F   T   T F   F F FT
         6 2 5   2   2 2   1 4 23
                Invalid

Part II. $(r \rightarrow p) \ldots$
        $(Ry \rightarrow Py) \cdot Cy \cdot Ry$ / $\therefore Py \cdot Cy$
        T T X   T   T   F F FT
               Valid

Part II of the crucial assignments method establishes $Py \cdot Cy$ as valid; hence, by ADD, $(Py \cdot Cy) \vee (Px \cdot Cx)$ is also valid.

Before beginning the final exercise, let us recall a few basic principles involved when arguments contain existentials as well as universals. With respect to particularization (PART): PART may be applied to a universal premise only if some other premise indicates that this universal is related to a nonempty set. Following is an example, with three solutions:

Example B: All (s)oldiers are (m)en. Bob is a (t)all (s)oldier. Therefore, Bob is a (t)all (m)an.

(B–1)   1. $s \rightarrow m$
        2. $Tb \cdot Sb$ / $\therefore Tb \cdot Mb$
        3. $Sb \rightarrow Mb$ 1, PART
        4. Tb 2, SIMP
        5. Mb 3, 4, MP
        6. $Tb \cdot Mb$ 4, 5, CONJ

(B–2) $(s \rightarrow m) \cdot (Tb \cdot Sb)$ / $\therefore Tb \cdot Mb$
        $(Sb \rightarrow Mb) \cdot Tb \cdot Sb$ / $\therefore Tb \cdot Mb$
        T T T   T   T   F T FX
        3 2 4   2   2   1 5 2

(B–3) $(Sb \rightarrow Mb) \cdot Tb \cdot Sb$ / $\therefore Tb \cdot Mb$
        X T F   T   T   F T FF
        2 5   2   2   1 3 24

In solutions (B–2) and (B–3) observe that the crucial assignments method is usable only after (using PART) each and every statement has the same subscript. Note also that different orders of steps are followed in proofs (B–2) and (B–3).

It should be obvious that PART may *not* be employed when all premises are universal. Also, PART may not be applied to a conclusion, because doing so would change that conclusion's meaning. Thus, in example C there is no way in which we can derive an existential conclusion from two universal premises.

Example C: All (m)ermaids are (a)quatic creatures. Any creature either resides in (w)ater or it is not (a)quatic. So, some (m)ermaids reside in (w)ater.

(C–1)   1. $m \rightarrow a$
      2. $(w \vee \sim a) \: / \: \therefore \: Mx \cdot Wx$
      3. $a \rightarrow w$ 2, COM, CE
      4. $m \rightarrow w$ 1, 3, HS

(C–2) $(m \rightarrow a) \cdot (w \vee \sim a) \: / \: \therefore \: Mx \cdot Wx$
Since we cannot proceed with a proof, the argument is invalid.

In applying SING-EX, no less than in applying PART, great care must be exercised, lest we *assume* more than is warranted. For example, if we know that "Mary is a (h)istory student, and Kate is studying (p)hysics" ($Hm \cdot Pk$), we must interpret them as two separate existentials ($Hx \cdot Py$), even though it *could* be that both Mary and Kate were studying both history and physics.

Exercise 6.4D.   More Difficult Problems

Directions: Symbolize each of the following arguments, and test for validity.

1. All (d)ogs and (b)eavers are (m)ammals. Some (p)ets are (m)ammals. Some (p)ets are not (m)ammals. Hence, some (p)ets are not (d)ogs.

2. All (m)ice are (s)mall. Some (r)odents are not (s)mall. Some (r)odents are (s)mall. So, some (m)ice are not (r)odents.

3. Among (b)usinessmen, a person is (s)uccessful if and only if he (m)akes money. Many (b)usinessmen possess (p)roperty. Many (s)uccessful men (m)ake money. Therefore, there are (b)usinessmen who (m)ake money.

4. Some (I)rishmen are (a)ggressive and others are not. Now it is well known that there are no (a)ggressive persons who are not (b)ullies. Furthermore, the notion that there are some (b)ullies who need not be regarded with (s)uspicion is simply untenable. Hence, there are (I)rishmen who need not be regarded with (s)uspicion.

5. All (h)onor students are either (b)rilliant or (d)iligent. No (b)rilliant student is (d)iligent. Paul is an (h)onor student and Paul is (d)iligent. Therefore, some (h)onor students are not (b)rilliant.

6. There are (t)eachers who are (e)xperienced but who are (i)ncompetent. No incompetent person (d)eserves tenure. All (u)niversity professors (d)eserve tenure. There are persons who (d)eserve tenure who are not (u)niversity professors. Therefore, not all persons who (d)eserve tenure are (e)xperienced.

7. To be (a)dmitted into this course, a student must either be enrolled as a (g)raduate, or he must be an (u)pperclassman whose grades are (e)xceptional. John is an (u)pperclassman whose grades are (e)xceptional. Therefore, at least one (u)pperclassman will be (a)dmitted into this course.

8. There is nothing made of (g)old that is not (e)xpensive. No dental (f)illings are made of (d)iamonds. All (d)iamonds are (e)xpensive. Not all dental (f)illings are (e)xpensive. Therefore, there are in(e)xpensive things that are not made from either (g)old or (d)iamonds.

9. If public (e)xposure of this scandal means that an (i)nvestigation will be launched, and if repression of the story (i.e., if there is no public exposure) means that (c)orruption will continue as before, then one of these two outcomes will occur: either public exposure accompanied by a decrease in corruption, or else repression of the story accompanied by continued corruption. But a public (i)nvestigation is not going to be launched. Therefore, corruption will continue as before.

10. There are philosophers who are not mathematicians. But there are no mathematicians who are ignorant of logic. Therefore, some of those who are ignorant of logic are philosophers.

11. Bob was the (b)atter and Sam was the (s)econd baseman. If Bob (h)it a grounder toward second base, then either Sam (f)ielded the ball or there was an (e)rror. But Sam did not (f)ield the ball. Therefore, either Bob did not (h)it a grounder toward second base or there was an (e)rror.

12. At a certain college, all students receive a (s)atisfactory grade if and only if they pass the (f)inal exam. There are a number of students at that college who are (a)bsent much of the time, and Betty is one of them. Therefore, if we can be sure that there is not a single student at the college who, although frequently (a)bsent,

did not, on that account, receive an un(s)atisfactory grade, then, if Betty passed her (f)inal exams, Betty must have received (s)atisfactory grades.

13. If anyone (p)honed for repair service, then (I)ke would have (w)orked tonight. Anyone who (w)orks tonight will (s)leep late tomorrow. Now, we know that (G)eraldine (p)honed for repair service. So, someone will (w)ork tonight and (s)leep late tomorrow.

14. Only (j)uniors and (s)eniors are (e)ligible for this course. There are some (p)oor students who are not (e)ligible for this course. Ted is one of them and Ted is a (j)unior. Therefore, only (s)eniors are (e)ligible for this class.

15. If all (p)ills are (d)irty, then all (s)lovenly (a)pothecaries are (b)lameworthy. If there are any (p)ills which are (d)irty, then all (p)ills are (d)irty and (r)isky. All vitamin (t)ablets are (p)ills. Only the (s)lovenly are (c)areless. Therefore, if any (a)pothecary is (c)areless, then, if some vitamin (t)ablets are (d)irty, then he is (b)lameworthy.

16. All persons attending the carnival were either (g)rownups or (c)hildren accompanied by their parents. All of the (g)rownups who stayed past (m)idnight (e)njoyed themselves. But some of those attending the carnival who stayed past (m)idnight did not (e)njoy themselves, and Buster was one of them. Therefore, anyone who did not (e)njoy himself either left the carnival before (m)idnight, or he was not a (g)rownup. Furthermore, if Buster did not (e)njoy himself, he was not a (g)rownup.

Answers for Chapter Six

6.1A:

1. A, B (*Note:* the tilde before the parenthesis in B negates everything within that parenthesis $[\sim(Pj)]$; but this is not different than the negation of P by itself ($\sim Pj$);
3. B, C;   5. A, B;   7. B;   9. A;   11. B;   13. A, B;   15. A, C;   17. B, C;
19. A, C;   21. A, B;   23. A, B.

A study of the following four proofs will show why, in problems 21, 22, 23, and 24, answers A and B are equivalent in meaning. Observe also that, although the arrow is distributive over the dot and over the wedge, neither the dot nor the wedge are distributive over the arrow.

(21A) 1. $(s \rightarrow r) \cdot (b \rightarrow r)$
     2. $(\sim s \vee r) \cdot (\sim b \vee r)$ 1, CE
     3. $(\sim s \cdot \sim b) \vee r$ 2, DIST
     4. $\sim(s \vee b) \vee r$ 3, DeM
     5. $(s \vee b) \rightarrow r$ 4, CE

(22A) 1. $e \rightarrow m \cdot h$
     2. $\sim e \vee (m \cdot h)$ 1, _____
     3. $(\sim e \vee m) \cdot (\sim e \vee h)$ 2, _____
     4. $(e \rightarrow m) \cdot (e \rightarrow h)$ 3, _____

(23A) 1. $b \cdot h \rightarrow e$
     2. $\sim(b \cdot h) \vee e$ 1, CE
     3. $(\sim b \vee \sim h) \vee e$ 2, DeM
     4. $\sim b \vee \sim h \vee e \vee e$ 3, TAUT
     5. $(\sim b \vee e) \vee (\sim h \vee e)$ 4, ASSOC
     6. $(b \rightarrow e) \vee (h \rightarrow e)$ 5, CE

(24A) 1. $(p \rightarrow s) \vee (p \rightarrow w)$
     2. $(\sim p \vee s) \vee (\sim p \vee w)$ 1, _____
     3. $(\sim p \vee \sim p) \vee (s \vee w)$ 2, _____
     4. $\sim p \vee (s \vee w)$ 3, _____
     5. $p \rightarrow s \vee w$ 4, _____

6.1B:

1. 0, C;   3. I, Q;   5. A, S;   7. I, Q;   9. E, S;
11. Sentence beginning with the quantifier "No";   13. are;
15. Sets of objects which have similar properties.

6.1C:

1. All men are creatures that die; or, All men are persons who die ($m \rightarrow d$).
3. All men are persons who can do that ($m \rightarrow d$).
5. Some gentlemen are persons who prefer blondes ($Gx \cdot Px$). *Note:* There may be differences of interpretation of the meanings embodied in several of these sentences, for they are unclear in their present form. However, if your answer to problem 5 was "All gentlemen are persons who prefer blondes," how would you explain the preference of some gentlemen for brunettes? Problems 5–11 are all of the same type, and illustrate the substitution of cliché thinking for accurate statements.
13. Some students in this class are honor students ($Sx \cdot Hx$). Problems 13–16 change what are surely more precise expressions of "quantity" to the catchall "Some" of traditional logic.

However, as the answers to problems 15 and 17 will show, once the quantifier "Some" is used, along with a copula and along with clearly defined subject and predicate terms, other equivalent I- and O-form statements can readily be constructed. Observe also that the vague "Some *S* is *P*" forms of problems 12–16 are less ambiguous than the indefinite forms in problems 5–11. Modern probability theory, briefly explained in chapter 7, may be viewed as an attempt to make more precise the "quantity" of the quantifier "Some."

For each of the next three problems, we provide four different answers, all equivalent to one another, and all correct:

15. Let *M* signify "persons who were (m)alcontents"; let $\sim M$ signify "persons who were not (m)alcontents"; let *R* signify "persons who became revolutionaries" and let $\sim R$ signify "persons who did not (b)ecome revolutionaries." Then, using two I-forms and two O-forms, problem 15 can be expressed in four equivalent ways:

Some *M* are *B* $(Mx \cdot Bx)$;   Some *M* are not $\sim B$ $[Mx \cdot \sim (\sim Bx)]$;
Some *B* are *M* $(Bx \cdot Mx)$;   Some *B* are not $\sim M$ $[Bx \cdot \sim (\sim Mx)]$.

17. Let *F* signify "(f)reshmen; let $\sim F$ signify "persons other than (f)reshmen"; let *P* signify "persons who are (p)repared"; and let $\sim P$ signify "persons who are not (p)repared." Then, the four equivalent forms—two I's and two O's—are:

Some *F* are not $\sim P$ $[Fx \cdot \sim (\sim Px)]$;   Some *F* are *P* $(Fx \cdot Px)$;
Some *P* are *F* $(Px \cdot Fx)$;   and Some *P* are not $\sim F$ $[Px \cdot \sim (\sim Fx)]$.

19. The four equivalent universals will consist of two A-forms and two E-forms, namely:

No persons who can (a)fford a car are persons who (w)alk. $(a \to \sim w)$.
All persons who can (a)fford a car are persons who do not (w)alk. $(a \to \sim w)$;
All persons who (w)alk are persons who cannot (a)fford a car. $(w \to \sim a)$; and
No persons who (w)alk are persons who can (a)fford a car. $(w \to \sim c)$.

6.1D:

1. All horses are mammals $(h \to m)$; No horses are nonmammals $[h \to \sim (\sim m)]$; No nonmammals are horses $(\sim m \to \sim h)$; All nonmammals are nonhorses $(\sim m \to \sim h)$.

3. Let *B* = baby less than a year old, and let *F* = fast runner. Then the four equivalent forms are: No *B* are *F* $(b \to \sim f)$; No *F* are *B* $(f \to \sim b)$; All *F* are $\sim B$ $(f \to \sim b)$; and All *B* are $\sim F$ $(b \to \sim f)$. [Let $\sim B$ = "people who are not fast runners."]

5. Some floors *are not* dirty surfaces $(Fx \cdot \sim Dx)$; Some floors *are* surfaces that are not dirty $(Fx \cdot \sim Dx)$; Some surfaces that are not dirty *are* floors $(\sim Dx \cdot Fx)$; Some surfaces that are not dirty *are not* surfaces that are not floors $[\sim Dx \cdot \sim (\sim Fx)]$.

7. Let *W* = people who work hard; let *S* = successful people. Then the four equivalent forms are Some *W* are $\sim S$ $(Wx \cdot \sim Sx)$; Some $\sim S$ are *W* $(\sim Wx \cdot Sx)$; Some $\sim S$ are not $\sim W$ $[\sim Sx \cdot \sim (\sim Wx)]$; Some *W* are not *S* $(Wx \cdot \sim Sx)$. [Let $\sim S$ = "unsuccessful," and let $\sim W$ = "persons who do not work hard."]

   Note: To a modern logic student, accustomed to DN, COM, and COPO, exercise 6.1D may seem somewhat pedantic. But in traditional logic, which employed no such laws and which confined itself entirely to verbal statements, the four equivalent A- and E-forms, and the four equivalent I- and O-forms, were extremely important.

6.1E:

Note: If there is any question concerning validity, review the three rules for the hypothetical syllogism (HS) in section 2.5.

1. $(b \to r) \cdot (b \to \sim g) \mathbin{/} \therefore g \to \sim r \; [/ \therefore r \to \sim g]$;   Invalid;
3. $(sp \to s) \cdot (b \to \sim s) \mathbin{/} \therefore (sp \to \sim b) = (sp \to s) \cdot (s \to \sim b) \mathbin{/} \therefore (sp \to \sim b)$;   Valid;
5. $(b \to r) \cdot (t \to r) \mathbin{/} \therefore (t \to b)$;   Invalid;
7. $(c \to m) \cdot (c \to \sim u) \mathbin{/} \therefore (u \to \sim m) \; [/ \therefore m \to \sim u]$;   Invalid;
9. $(u \to h) \cdot (h \to \sim f) \mathbin{/} \therefore (u \to \sim f)$;   Valid.

6.1F:

Note: The answers for exercise 6.1F include a symbolization of each statement. Note that A- and E-forms are symbolized in exactly the same way that their related conditionals were symbolized in chapter 2. This practice will be maintained throughout.

1. All persons who (c)ry are (b)abies. $(c \to b)$
3. All persons (e)xcluded are (f)reshmen. $(e \to f)$
5. All persons who (t)hink the great unhappy are (g)reat persons. $(t \to g)$
7. All persons admitted (f)ree are (c)hildren. $(f \to c)$
9. All persons who do not (r)epent are persons who cannot be (s)aved. $(\sim r \to \sim s)$ or $(s \to r)$
11. All persons without (p)assports were persons not (a)dmitted; or No persons who were (a)dmitted were persons without (p)assports. $(\sim p \to \sim a)$ or $(a \to p)$

13. All truly (r)efreshing drinks are (w)ater; or, If a drink is truly refreshing, it is water. $(r \rightarrow w)$
15. All persons out of (w)ork are persons who are either un(e)ducated or (s)ick. $(\sim w \rightarrow \sim e \lor s)$
17. All times when you try [or, If you try] to (m)ake an engineer out of a moron, (t)ragedy is the result. $(m \rightarrow t)$
19. All men who were not (d)isabled or who were not (p)acifists were persons who bore (a)rms. $(\sim d \lor \sim p \rightarrow a)$
21. No (d)ogs that are not on (l)eashes are (p)ermitted in the park. $(d \cdot \sim l \rightarrow \sim p)$ or All (d)ogs that are (p)ermitted in the park are dogs on (l)eashes. $[d \rightarrow (p \rightarrow l)]$
23. All (m)ammals that live in (w)ater are (c)etaceans. $(m \cdot w \rightarrow c)$

6.1G:

(1A) 1. $\sim m \rightarrow \sim b$
　　 2. $o \rightarrow m$ / $\therefore$ $b \rightarrow \sim(\sim o)$
　　 3. $b \rightarrow m$ 　　　　　　 1, COPO
　　 Since $b \rightarrow \sim(\sim o) = b \rightarrow o$, the argument has exactly 3 terms. But the middle term is on the right side of the arrow in both premises.

(1B) $(\sim m \rightarrow \sim b) \cdot (o \rightarrow m)$ / $\therefore$ $b \rightarrow \sim(\sim o)$
　　 $F\ T\ \ T\ F\ T\ \ \ \ F\ T\ T\ \ \ \ F\ T\ F\ F\ F\ T$
　　 $7\ 7\ \ 2\ 6\ 6\ \ \ \ 5\ 2\ 8\ \ \ \ 1\ 3\ 2\ 3\ \ 4\ 5$
　　　　　　　　 Invalid

(3A) 1. $m \rightarrow s$
　　 2. $s \rightarrow p$ / $\therefore$ $m \rightarrow p$
　　 3. $m \rightarrow p$ 　　　　　　 1, 2, HS
　　　　　　 Valid

(3B) $(m \rightarrow s) \cdot (s \rightarrow p)$ / $\therefore$ $m \rightarrow p$
　　 $X\ T\ F\ \ \ \ F\ T\ F\ \ \ \ \ \ T\ F\ F$
　　 $2\ 6\ \ \ \ \ 5\ 2\ 4\ \ \ \ \ 1\ 3\ 2\ 3$

(5A) 1. $f \rightarrow g$
　　 2. $\sim c \rightarrow \sim g$ / $\therefore$ $f \rightarrow c$
　　 3. $g \rightarrow c$ 　　　　　　 2, COPO
　　 4. $f \rightarrow c$ 　　　　　　 1, 3, HS
　　　　　　 Valid

(5B) $(f \rightarrow g) \cdot (\sim c \rightarrow \sim g)$ / $\therefore$ $f \rightarrow c$
　　 $T\ T\ T\ \ \ \ F\ X\ T\ F\ T\ \ \ F\ T\ F\ F$
　　 $4\ 2\ 5\ \ \ \ 8\ \ \ 2\ 7\ 6\ \ \ 1\ 3\ 2\ 3$

(7A) We leave a step-by-step proof to any student who may prefer that method of proof.

(7B) $(w \rightarrow c) \cdot (c \rightarrow h) \cdot (h \rightarrow b) \cdot (b \rightarrow p) \cdot (s \rightarrow p)$ / $\therefore$ $s \rightarrow c$
　　 $F\ T\ F\ \ \ F\ T\ T\ \ \ T\ T\ T\ \ \ T\ T\ T\ \ \ T\ T\ T\ \ \ F\ T\ F\ F$
　　 $6\ 2\ 5\ \ 10\ 2\ 9\ \ \ 8\ 2\ 8\ \ \ 7\ 2\ 7\ \ \ 3\ 2\ 4\ \ \ 1\ 3\ 2\ 3$
　　　　　　　　 Invalid

(9A) 1. $h \rightarrow m$
　　 2. $t \rightarrow h$ / $\therefore$ $\sim t \rightarrow \sim m$
　　 3. $\sim m \rightarrow \sim h$ 　　　　 1, COPO
　　 4. $\sim h \rightarrow \sim t$ 　　　　 2, COPO
　　　　　　 Invalid

(9B) $(h \rightarrow m) \cdot (t \rightarrow h)$ / $\therefore$ $\sim t \rightarrow \sim m$
　　 $T\ T\ T\ \ \ \ F\ T\ \ \ \ \ \ F\ TF\ F\ F\ T$
　　 $F\ 2\ 4\ \ \ \ 5\ 2\ \ \ \ \ \ 1\ 33\ 2\ 33$
　　 6
　　 As Step 6, "h" could be assigned either truth-value T or truth-value F.
　　　　　　 Invalid.

6.1H:

1. $(\sim p \rightarrow \sim d) \cdot (w \rightarrow c) \cdot (p \rightarrow h) \cdot (\sim w \rightarrow \sim b) \cdot (c \rightarrow d)$ / $\therefore$ $b \rightarrow \sim(\sim h)$
　 $= (b \rightarrow w) \cdot (w \rightarrow c) \cdot (c \rightarrow d) \cdot (d \rightarrow p) \cdot (p \rightarrow h)$ / $\therefore$ $b \rightarrow h$ [or, $b \rightarrow \sim(\sim h)$]
3. $(\sim j \rightarrow \sim o) \cdot (a \rightarrow \sim s) \cdot (m \rightarrow \sim r) \cdot (\sim o \rightarrow a) \cdot (j \rightarrow r)$
　 $= (m \rightarrow \sim r) \cdot (\sim r \rightarrow \sim j) \cdot (\sim j \rightarrow \sim o) \cdot (\sim o \rightarrow a) \cdot (a \rightarrow \sim s)$ / $\therefore$ $(m \rightarrow \sim s)$
　 Conclusion:　No Mandarin studies Lewis Carroll's *Symbolic Logic.*
5. $(d \rightarrow \sim r) \cdot [a \rightarrow \sim(\sim s)] \cdot (c \rightarrow r) \cdot (s \rightarrow d)$
　 $= (a \rightarrow s) \cdot (s \rightarrow d) \cdot (d \rightarrow \sim r) \cdot (\sim r \rightarrow \sim c)$ / $\therefore$ $a \rightarrow \sim c$, or $c \rightarrow \sim a$,
　 Hence, wedding cakes always disagree with me; or No wedding cakes agree with me.
7. $(\sim g \rightarrow u) \cdot (p \rightarrow \sim a) \cdot (e \rightarrow \sim h) \cdot (\sim a \rightarrow \sim u) \cdot (\sim h \rightarrow \sim g)$
　 $= (e \rightarrow \sim h) \cdot (\sim h \rightarrow \sim g) \cdot (\sim g \rightarrow u) \cdot (u \rightarrow a) \cdot (a \rightarrow \sim p)$ / $\therefore$ $e \rightarrow \sim p$,
　 or, $p \rightarrow \sim e$, or, These polysyllogisms are not easy; or, If these are Lewis Carroll's polysyllogisms, they are not easy.

6.2A:

(A)　Using Step-by-Step Method:
(1A) 1. $l \rightarrow s$
　　 2. $\sim Lb$ / $\therefore$ $\sim Sb$
　　 3. $Lb \rightarrow Sb$ 　　　　　　 1, PART
　　　　　　 Invalid

(B)　Using the Crucial Assignments Method:
(1B) $(l \rightarrow s) \cdot \sim Lb$ / $\therefore$ Sb
　　 $(Lb \rightarrow Sb) \cdot \sim Lb$ / $\therefore$ Sb
　　 $F\ \ T\ F\ \ \ \ T\ F\ \ \ \ F\ \ F$
　　 $3\ \ 2\ 4\ \ \ \ \ 2\ \ \ \ \ 1\ \ 2$
　　　　　　 Invalid

(3A)
1. $a \rightarrow g$
2. $\sim Ap$ / $\therefore \sim Gp$
3. $Ap \rightarrow Gp$ 1, PART
     Invalid

(3B) $(a \rightarrow g) \cdot \sim Ap$ / $\therefore \sim Gp$
$(Ap \rightarrow Gp) \cdot \sim Ap$ / $\therefore \sim Gp$
$\quad F \quad T \ T \quad\quad T \ F \quad\quad F \ F \ T$
$\quad 4 \quad 2 \ 3 \quad\quad 2 \ 2 \quad\quad 1 \ 2 \ 2$

(5A)
1. $r \rightarrow s$
2. Sf / $\therefore Rf$
3. $Rf \rightarrow Sf$ 1, PART
     Invalid

(5B) $(r \rightarrow s) \cdot Sf$ / $\therefore Rf$
$(Rf \rightarrow Sf) \cdot Sf$ / $\therefore Rf$
$\quad F \ T \ T \quad\quad T \quad\quad F \ F$
$\quad 3 \ 2 \ 4 \quad\quad 2 \quad\quad 1 \ 2$

(7A)
1. $t \lor \sim s$
2. $\sim Ta$ / $\therefore Sa$
3. $Ta \lor \sim Sa$ 1, PART
4. $\sim Sa$ 2, 3, DS
     Invalid

(7B) $(t \lor \sim s) \cdot \sim Ta$ / $\therefore Sa$
$(Ta \lor \sim Sa) \cdot \sim Ta$ / $\therefore Sa$
$\quad F \quad T \ T \ F \quad\quad T \ F \quad\quad F \ F$
$\quad 4 \quad 2 \ 3 \ 3 \quad\quad 2 \ 2 \quad\quad 1 \ 2$

(9A)
1. $\sim c \rightarrow \sim s$
2. $\sim Sj$ / $\therefore \sim Cj$
3. $\sim Cj \rightarrow \sim Sj$ 1, PART
4. $Sj \rightarrow Cj$ 3, COPO
5. $\sim Sj \lor Cj$ 4, CE
     Invalid

(9B) $(\sim c \rightarrow \sim s) \cdot \sim Sj$ / $\therefore \sim Cj$
$(\sim Cj \rightarrow \sim Sj) \cdot \sim Sj$ / $\therefore \sim Cj$
$\quad F \ T \quad T \ T \ F \quad\quad T \ F \quad\quad F \ F \ T$
$\quad 4 \ 4 \quad 2 \ 3 \ 3 \quad\quad 2 \ 2 \quad\quad 1 \ 2 \ 2$

(11A)
1. $w \rightarrow f$
2. Wp / $\therefore Fp$
3. $Wp \rightarrow Fp$ 1, PART
4. Fp 2, 3, MP
     Valid

(11B) $(w \rightarrow f) \cdot Wp$ / $\therefore Fp$
$(Wp \rightarrow Fp) \cdot Wp$ / $\therefore Fp$
$\quad T \quad T \ X \quad\quad T \quad\quad F \ F$
$\quad 3 \quad 2 \quad\quad\quad 2 \quad\quad 1 \ 2$

(13A)
1. $e \rightarrow a$ / $\therefore Eg \rightarrow Ag$
2. Eg / $\therefore Ag$ 1, CP
3. $Eg \rightarrow Ag$ 1, PART
4. Ag 2, 3, MP
     Valid

(13B) $e \rightarrow a$ / $\therefore Eg \rightarrow Ag$
$(e \rightarrow a) \cdot Eg$ / $\therefore Ag$
$(Eg \rightarrow Ag) \cdot Eg$ / $\therefore Ag$
$\quad X \ T \ T \quad\quad T \quad\quad F \ F$

In (13A) remember that CP is a method of *indirect proof*; so we have *not* established Ag as a *conclusion*. Rather, having established Ag by using CP, we have established the *original* conclusion: $Eg \rightarrow Ag$.

The top lines of page 180 explain why CP must be applied in the second line of answer (13B).

(15A)
1. $\sim La$
2. $l \rightarrow b$ / $\therefore \sim Ba$
3. $La \rightarrow Ba$ 2, PART
     Invalid

(15B) $\sim La \cdot (l \rightarrow b)$ / $\therefore \sim Ba$
$\sim La \cdot (La \rightarrow Ba)$ / $\therefore \sim Ba$
$\quad T \ F \quad F \ T \ T \quad\quad F \ F \ T$
$\quad 2 \ 2 \quad 3 \ 2 \ 4 \quad\quad 1 \ 2 \ 2$

6.2B:

(A) Step-by-Step Method:

(1A)
1. $Bx \cdot Nx$
2. $b \rightarrow f$ / $\therefore Fx \cdot Nx$
3. Nx 1, SIMP
4. $Bx \rightarrow Fx$ 2, PART
5. Bx 1, SIMP
6. Fx 4, 5, MP
7. $Fx \cdot Nx$ 3, 6, CONJ
     Valid

(B) Crucial Assignments Method:

(1B) $(Bx \cdot Nx) \cdot (b \rightarrow f)$ / $\therefore Fx \cdot Nx$
$(Bx \cdot Nx) \cdot (Bx \rightarrow Fx)$ / $\therefore Fx \cdot Nx$
$\quad T \quad T \quad\quad T \ T \ T \quad\quad F \ T \ F X$
$\quad 2 \quad 2 \quad\quad 3 \ 2 \ 4 \quad\quad 1 \ 5 \ 2$

(3A)
1. $w \rightarrow g$
2. $Fx \cdot Wx$ / $\therefore Fx \cdot Gx$
3. $Wx \rightarrow Gx$ 1, PART
4. Gx 2, SIMP; 3, MP
5. $Fx \cdot Gx$ 2, SIMP; 4, CONJ
     Valid

(3B) $(w \rightarrow g) \cdot (Fx \cdot Wx)$ / $\therefore Fx \cdot Gx$
$(Wx \rightarrow Gx) \cdot Fx \cdot Wx$ / $\therefore Fx \cdot Gx$
$\quad T \quad T \ T \quad\quad T \quad T \quad\quad F \ X \ F \ T$
$\quad 3 \quad 2 \ 4 \quad\quad 2 \quad 2 \quad\quad 1 \quad 2 \ 5$

(5A)
1. $Fx \cdot \sim Ox$
2. $o \rightarrow l$ / $\therefore Fx \cdot \sim Lx$
3. $Ox \rightarrow Lx$ 2, PART
Neither MP nor MT is possible.
     Invalid

(5B) $(Fx \cdot \sim Ox) \cdot (o \rightarrow l)$ / $\therefore Fx \cdot \sim Lx$
$(Fx \cdot \sim Ox) \cdot (Ox \rightarrow Lx)$ / $\therefore Fx \cdot \sim Lx$
$\quad T \quad T \ F \quad\quad F \ T \ T \quad\quad F \ T \ F F T$
$\quad 2 \quad 2 \ 2 \quad\quad 3 \ 2 \ 6 \quad\quad 1 \ 4 \ 2 5 5$

(7A) 1. $d \rightarrow h$
    2. $Px \cdot \sim Dx$ / $\therefore Px \cdot \sim Hx$
    3. $Dx \rightarrow Hx$ 1, SIMP
                             Invalid

(7B) $(d \rightarrow h) \cdot (Px \cdot \sim Dx)$ / $\therefore Px \cdot \sim Hx$
      $(Dx \rightarrow Hx) \cdot Px \cdot \sim Dx$ / $\therefore Px \cdot \sim Hx$
        F T T T T F F T $F F T$
        3   2 6   2   2 2   1 4 2 5 5

(9A) 1. $m \rightarrow w$
    2. $w \rightarrow s$ / $\therefore Mx \cdot Sx$

(9B) $(m \rightarrow w) \cdot (w \rightarrow s)$ / $\therefore Mx \cdot Sx$

In both (9A) and (9B) there is no existential premise. Hence PART cannot be applied to either premise, and it is impossible to derive any existential conclusion. Invalid. Later, we shall say more about inferences of this type.

(11A) 1. $Cx \cdot Sx$
     2. $s \rightarrow v$ / $\therefore c \rightarrow v$
     3. Sx 1, SIMP
     4. $Sx \rightarrow Vx$ 2, PART
     5. Vx 3, 4, MP
     6. Cx 1, SIMP
     7. $Cx \cdot Vx$ 5, 6, CONJ
                        Invalid

(11B) $(Cx \cdot Sx) \cdot (s \rightarrow v)$ / $\therefore c \rightarrow v$
    In (11B) we cannot apply PART to the *conclusion*; so the proof cannot proceed. Invalid.
    Problem 11 illustrates a rule of traditional logic: "If either premise of a syllogism is an existential, the conclusion must also be existential."

6.2C:

(1A) $s \rightarrow p$; (1B) $\sim p \rightarrow \sim s$; T;   (3A) $\sim (s \rightarrow \sim p) = Sx \cdot Px$; (3B) $Py \cdot \sim Sy$; D;
(5A) $Sx \cdot \sim Px$; (5B) $\sim Px \cdot \sim (\sim Sx)$; T;   (7A) $\sim Px \cdot \sim (\sim Sx)$; (7B) $Py \cdot \sim Sy$; D;
(9A) $\sim (c \rightarrow b) = Cx \cdot \sim Bx$; (9B) $Cx \cdot \sim Bx$; T;
(11A) $Bx \cdot \sim Sx$; (11B) $\sim (b \rightarrow s) = Bx \cdot \sim Sx$; T;   (13A) $m \rightarrow c$; (13B) $Mx \cdot \sim Cx$; F;
(15A) $(u \rightarrow i)$; (15B) $(u \rightarrow \sim i)$; D;   (17A) $\sim Mx \cdot \sim Sx$; (17B) $Sy \cdot My$; D;
(19A) $m \rightarrow f$; (19B) $f \rightarrow m$; D;   (21A) $e \rightarrow r$; (21B) $\sim r \rightarrow \sim e$; T;
(23A) $\sim (g \rightarrow \sim h) = Gx \cdot Hx$; (23B) $Hy \cdot \sim Gy$; D;   (25A) $Px \cdot Hx$; (25B) $\sim Hy \cdot Py$; D;
(27A) $k \rightarrow \sim h$; (27B) $h \rightarrow \sim k$; T;   (29A) $Rx \cdot \sim Sx$; (29B) $\sim Sx \cdot \sim (\sim Rx)$; T;
(31A) $e \rightarrow \sim u$; (31B) $\sim (Ux \cdot \sim Ex) = u \rightarrow e$; D.

Note: In the answers for problems 3, 7, 17, 23, and 25, the two different subscripts are meant to indicate that the two existentials may refer to different individuals. More will be said on this point in section 6.4.

Remember that the A-form "All dogs are pets" ($d \rightarrow p$) and its related E-form "No dogs are pets" ($d \rightarrow \sim p$) may both be *false*; hence they are not contradictories. In problem 18, since $d \rightarrow f$ and $d \rightarrow \sim f$ are not contradictory, the correct answer is D. More will be said on this point in section 6.3.

6.2D:

(1A) 1. $b \rightarrow c$
    2. $Jx \cdot \sim Cx$ / $\therefore j \rightarrow \sim b$
    3. $Bx \rightarrow Cx$ 1, PART
    4. $\sim Bx$ 2, SIMP; 3, MP
    5. $Jx \cdot \sim Cx$

For most logic teachers (but not for most contemporary logic students) problem 1 recalls one of the eight rules of the syllogism in traditional logic: if either premise of a syllogism is an existential, the conclusion must be an existential.

A more definite proof of this argument's invalidity is shown in Proof (1B).

(1B) $(b \rightarrow c) \cdot Jx \cdot \sim Cx$ / $\therefore j \rightarrow \sim b$
    $(Bx \rightarrow Cx) \cdot Jx \cdot \sim Cx$ / $\therefore$ We *cannot* apply PART to the conclusion.

(3A) 1. $b \rightarrow r$
    2. $Rx \cdot Ax$ / $\therefore Bx \cdot Ax$
    3. $Bx \rightarrow Rx$ 1, PART
    We cannot derive Bx
                    Invalid

(3B) $(b \rightarrow r) \cdot (Rx \cdot Ax)$ / $\therefore Bx \cdot Ax$
    $(Bx \rightarrow Rx) \cdot Rx \cdot Ax$ / $\therefore Bx \cdot Ax$
    F T T T T F F $F T$
    5   2 6   2   2   1 4 2 3

(5A) 1. $p \rightarrow e$
    2. $g \rightarrow p$ / $\therefore g \rightarrow e$
    3. $g \rightarrow e$ 1, 2, HS
                    Valid

(5B) $(p \rightarrow e) \cdot (g \rightarrow p)$ / $\therefore g \rightarrow e$
    F T F X T F F $T F F$
    5 2 4   2 6   1 3 2 3

(7A) 1. $h \rightarrow s$
    2. $s \rightarrow \sim f$ / $\therefore \sim h \rightarrow f$
    3. / $\therefore \sim f \rightarrow h$ 3, COPO
    We have succeeded in giving the syllogism exactly three terms; but the arrow points the wrong way!

(7B) $(h \rightarrow s) \cdot (s \rightarrow \sim f)$ / $\therefore \sim h \rightarrow f$
    F T F $F T$ T F $T F F F$
    T F
    5 2 6   6 2 4 4   1 3 3 2 3
                    Invalid

(9A)
1. $g \to a \cdot c$
2. $Gx \cdot \sim Sx \mid \therefore Ax \cdot Cx \cdot \sim Sx$
3. Gx 2, SIMP
4. $Gx \to Ax \cdot Cx$ 1, PART
5. $Ax \cdot Cx$ 3, 4, MP
6. $\sim Sx$ 2, SIMP
7. $Ax \cdot Cx \cdot \sim Sx$ 5, 6, CONJ

(9B) $g \to a \cdot c$

$(Gx \to Ax \cdot Cx) \cdot Gx \cdot \sim Sx \mid \therefore (Ax \cdot Cx) \cdot \sim Sx$
$\quad T \;\; TT \;\; TT \quad\quad T \quad TF \quad F\;T\;TT\;\;FXF$
$\quad 3 \;\; 2\;4\;\; 44 \quad\quad 2 \quad 2\;2 \quad 1\;\;5\;\;55\;\;2\;\;6$
                            Valid

6.2E:

(1)
1. $Wt \lor Wb$
2. $w \to l \mid \therefore Lt \lor Lb$
3. $\mid \therefore \sim Lt \to Lb$ 2, CE
4. $\sim Lt \mid \therefore Lb$ 3, CP
5. $Wt \to Lt$ 2, PART
6. $\sim Wt$ 4, 5, MT
7. Wb 1, 6, DS
8. $Wb \to Lb$ 2, PART
9. Lb 7, 8, MP
                      Valid

When an argument contains more than one singular or more than one existential, great care must be exercised in using the crucial assignments method, and the step-by-step method of proof will generally be easier to handle.

(3)
1. $Bx \cdot Wx \cdot Mx$
2. $\sim Bj \mid \therefore \sim Mj$
3. $\sim By$ 2, SING-EX

In step 3, we cannot be sure that "Jane" is included among the women mentioned in premise 1; hence in step 3, we must give a different subscript ("y" rather than "x"). But this will not help us conjoin the premises, so the argument is invalid.

(5A)
1. $s \lor d \to \sim i$
2. $\sim p \to i$
3. $\sim Pr \mid \therefore \sim (Sr \lor Dr)$
4. $\sim Pr \to Ir$ 2, PART
5. Ir 3, 4, MP
6. $Sr \lor Dr \to \sim Ir$ 1, PART
7. $\sim (Sr \lor Dr)$ 5, 6, MT
                      Valid

(5B)
1. $(s \lor d \to \sim i) \cdot (\sim p \to i) \cdot \sim Pr \mid \therefore \sim (Sr \lor Dr)$
2. $(Sr \lor Dr \to \sim Ir) \cdot (\sim Pr \to Ir) \cdot \sim Pr \mid \therefore \sim (Sr \lor Dr)$
$\quad X \quad\quad T\;F\;T \quad\quad TF\;\;TT \quad\;\; TF \quad F\;F \quad\quad T$
$\quad\quad\quad\quad 2\;6\;6 \quad\quad 4\;4\;\;2\;5 \quad\quad 2\;2 \quad 1\;2 \quad\quad 3$

(7A)
1. $Hx \cdot Sx$
2. $s \to \sim h$
3. $s \to e$ (or, $Sx \cdot Ex$)
4. $\sim Hj \cdot Ej \mid \therefore Sj$
5. $Sj \to \sim Hj$
6. $Sj \to Ej$
(If premise 3 means $Sx \cdot Ex$, Ex would not necessarily be the same person as Ej.)

(7B) $(s \to \sim h) \cdot (s \to e)$

$(Sj \to \sim Hj) \cdot (Sj \to Ej) \cdot \sim Hj \cdot Ej \mid \therefore Sj$
$\;\; F \quad T\;T\;F \quad\quad F\;\;T\;\;T \quad TF \quad\;T \quad\quad F$
                     Invalid

Invalid; for we can neither affirm the antecedent nor deny the consequent. Observe that premise 1 was not usable in the proof.

Problem 7 might serve as a springboard for a discussion of "circumstantial evidence."

6.2F:

1. T; $m \to w$;
3. T; Premise B is symbolized $Cx \cdot Wx$. By ADD, this yields $(Cx \cdot Wx) \lor (c \to \sim m)$;
5. T; $\sim w \to \sim m$, or $m \to w$;   7. D; $e \to \sim g$, or $g \to \sim e$;   9. D; $\sim (Ex \cdot Gx)$, or $(e \to \sim g)$;
11. T; $(p \to \sim s)$;   13. D; $(Px \cdot \sim Sx)$;   15. T; $(p \to \sim s)$;   17. D; $(Mz \cdot Sz \cdot Ez)$;
19. D; $(m \cdot s \to \sim e)$;   21. D; $(Py \cdot \sim Sy \cdot Ty)$; we could validly derive $\sim (Px \cdot Tx)$;
23. D; we cannot derive $Px \cdot Tx \cdot Rx$.

6.2G:

1. 1, SING-EX; 4, SIMP; 3, PART; 5, 6, MT; 1, SIMP; 2, DIST; 9, SIMP; 10, SING-EX; 8, 7, 11, CONJ.
3. 3, QE; 2, PART; 4, SIMP; 5, 6, DS; 1, SING-EX; 2, PART; 8, SIMP; 9, 10, DS; 7, 11, CONJ.

6.3A:

No answers are given, since each inference is *valid* (but none is necessarily *true*).

6.3B:

No answers are given for this exercise since it consists of subjective questions.

6.3C:

[*Group* A: $Dx \cdot \sim Px$];   1. $\sim(d \to p) = Dx \cdot \sim Px; T$;   3. $\sim d \to \sim p; D$;   5. $d \to \sim(\sim p); F$;
[*Group* B: $w \to c$];   7. $\sim c \to \sim w; T$;   9. $\sim c \to \sim w; T$;
[*Group* C: $h \to a$];   11. $a \to h; D$;   13. $h \to \sim(\sim a); T$;   15. $a \to h; D$;
[*Group* D: $\sim(gl \to go) = Glx \cdot \sim Gox$];   17. $Gox \cdot Glx; D$;   19. $\sim go \to gl; D$.

6.4A:

(1) $(t \to \sim f) \cdot (\sim f \to w) \ / \therefore t \to w$ Using HS, problem (1) could easily be solved
$\quad X\,T\;F\;T \quad F\,T\;T\;F \quad F\;T\,F\;F$ Valid   by the step-by-step method.
$\quad\; 2\;6\;6 \quad\;\; 5\,5\;2\;4 \quad\;\; 3\;2\;3$

(3A) 1. $v \to t$
     2. $t \to i \ / \therefore \sim i \to \sim v$
     3. $v \to i$ 1, 2, HS (twice)
     4. $\sim i \to \sim v$ 3, COPO (twice)

(3B) $(v \leftrightarrow t) \cdot (t \leftrightarrow i) \ / \therefore (\sim i \leftrightarrow \sim v)$
$\quad T\,T\;T \quad T\,T\;X \quad F \;\; T\,F\,F\;F\,T$
$\quad 4\;2\;5 \quad\;\; 6\;2 \quad\quad 1 \;\; 3\,3\;2\;3\;3$
$\qquad\qquad\qquad\qquad$ Valid

Reminder: The crucial assignments method of proof works least well where there is more than one possible assignment, e.g.:

$$p \to q; \quad p \vee q; \quad p \cdot q; \quad p \leftrightarrow q; \quad \text{or } p \leftrightarrow q$$
$$\quad T \qquad\quad T \qquad\quad F \qquad\quad T \qquad\qquad F$$

The crucial assignments method works best (and you should choose your order of steps accordingly), when there is only one possible assignment of truth values, e.g.:

$$p \to q; \quad p \vee q; \quad p \cdot q; \quad p; \quad \sim q.$$
$$\quad F \qquad\quad F \qquad\quad T \qquad T \qquad F$$

(5) $(s \to l) \cdot (\sim m \to \sim l) \cdot [l \to (m \cdot a)] \ / \therefore [(\sim m \cdot \sim a) \to \sim s]$
$\quad X\,T\;F \qquad\quad T \qquad\quad F\,T\;F\,F\,F \quad F \quad\; T\,F\,T\,T\,F\;F\;F\,T$
$\quad\; 2\;9 \qquad\qquad\; 2 \qquad\quad\;\; 8\;2\;\;6\,7\,5 \quad\;\; 1 \quad\; 4\;4\,3\,4\,4\;\,2\;3\,3$
$\qquad\qquad\qquad\qquad\qquad$ Valid

(7) $(t \to f) \cdot (m \to v) \ / \therefore (t \to v) \to (f \to m)$
$\quad F\;T\;T \quad\; F\;T\;F \quad\; F\,F\,T\,F\,F\,F\,T\,F\,F$
$\quad 10\;2\;6 \quad\; 5\;\,2\;7 \quad\; 1\;9\,3\,8\;2\,4\;3\;4$
$\qquad\qquad\qquad$ Invalid

(9A) 1. $c \to d$
     2. $d \to v$
     3. $\sim Cf \ / \therefore \sim Vf$
$\qquad\qquad\qquad\qquad\qquad\qquad$ Invalid

(9B) $(c \to d) \cdot (d \to v) \cdot \sim Cf \ / \therefore \sim Vf$
$\quad (Cf \to Df) \cdot (Df \to Vf) \cdot \sim Cf \ / \therefore \sim Vf$
$\quad\; F\;\;T\;F \quad\;\; F\;\;T\;T \quad\;\; T\,F \quad\; F\,F\,T$
$\quad\; 4\;\;\;2\;5 \quad\;\; 6\;\;\;2\;3 \quad\;\; 2\;2 \quad\; 1\;2\;2$
$\qquad\qquad\qquad\quad$ Invalid

(11A) 1. $c \to d$
      2. $d \to m$
      3. $m \to v$
      4. $Ck \ / \therefore Vx \cdot Dx$
      5. Cx 4, SING-EX

      6. $Cx \to Dx$ 2, PART
      7. Dx 5, 6, MP
      8. $d \to v$ 2, 3, HS
      9. $Dx \to Vx$ 8, PART
    10. Vx 7, 9, MP
    11. $Vx \cdot Dx$ 7, 10, CONJ
$\qquad\qquad\qquad\qquad\qquad\qquad\qquad$ Valid

The crucial assignments method of proof for (11) may be set up two ways:

$\qquad\quad (c \to d) \cdot (d \to m) \cdot (m \to v) \cdot Ck \ / \therefore Vx \cdot Dx$
(11B–1) $(Ck \to Dk) \cdot (Dk \to Mk) \cdot (Mk \to Vk) \cdot Ck \ / \therefore Vk \cdot Dk \ (/ \therefore Vx \cdot Dx)$; or
(11B–2) $(Cx \to Dx) \cdot (Dx \to Mx) \cdot (Mx \to Vx) \cdot Cx \ / \therefore Vx \cdot Dx$
$\qquad\qquad\;\; T\;\;T\;T \quad\;\; T\;\;T\;T \quad\;\; T\;\;T\;T \quad\; T \quad F\,T\;F\,X$
$\qquad\qquad\;\; 3\;\;\;2\;4 \quad\;\; 5\;\;\;2\;6 \quad\;\; 7\;\;\;2\;8 \quad\; 2 \quad\; 1\;9\;2$
$\qquad\qquad\qquad\qquad\qquad$ Valid

(13A)   1. $\sim Px \cdot \sim Gx$
        2. $r \to p$
        3. $\sim h \to \sim g$
        4. $w \to (r \vee g) \ / \therefore \sim Wx$
        5. $Rx \to Px$ 2, PART
        6. $\sim Px$ 1, SIMP
        7. $\sim Rx$ 5, 6, MT
        8. $\sim Gx$ 1, SIMP
        9. $\sim Rx \cdot \sim Gx$ 7, 8, CONJ
      10. $\sim(Rx \vee Gx)$ 9, DeM

11. $Wx \rightarrow (Rx \vee Gx)$ 4, PART
12. $\sim Wx$ 10, 11, MP
                    Valid

$$(r \rightarrow p) \cdot (\sim h \rightarrow \sim g) \cdot (w \rightarrow r \vee g)$$

(13B) $\sim Px \cdot \sim Gx \cdot (Rx \rightarrow Px) \cdot (\sim Hx \rightarrow \sim Gx) \cdot [Wx \rightarrow Rx \vee Gx] \mid \therefore \sim Wx$
         $T\,F$ $T\,F$ F $T\,F$ T X $T\,F$ $F\,F$ $F\,F\,T$
         $2\;2$ $2\;2$ 4 $2\;3$ 2 $2\;5$ $7\;6$ $1\;2\;2$

(15A) 1. $s \rightarrow b$ (15B) $(s \rightarrow b) \cdot Sx \cdot Hx \mid \therefore Bx \cdot Hx$
       2. $Sx \cdot Hx \mid \therefore Bx \cdot Hx$ $(Sx \rightarrow Bx) \cdot Sx \cdot Hx \mid \therefore Bx \cdot Hx$
       3. Sx 2, SIMP X $T\,F$ T T $F\,F\,F\,T$
       4. $Sx \rightarrow Bx$ 1, PART $2\;5$ 2 2 $1\;4\;2\;3$
       5. Bx 3, 4, MP   Valid
       6. $Bx \cdot Hx$ 2, SIMP; 5, CONJ

(17A) 1. $s \rightarrow r \mid \therefore [(Mx \cdot Bx) \cdot (b \cdot m \rightarrow \sim r)] \rightarrow Bx \cdot Mx \cdot \sim Sx$
       2. $(Bx \cdot Mx) \cdot (b \cdot m \rightarrow \sim r) \mid \therefore Bx \cdot Mx \cdot \sim Sx$ 1, COM, CP
       3. $(Bx \cdot Mx) \cdot (Bx \cdot Mx \rightarrow \sim Rx)$ 2, PART
       4. $\sim Rx$ 3, MP
       5. $Sx \rightarrow Rx$ 1, PART
       6. $\sim Sx$ 4, 5, MT
       7. $Bx \cdot Mx$ 3, SIMP
       8. $Bx \cdot Mx \cdot \sim Sx$ 6, 7, CONJ

(17B) To apply the crucial assignments method of proof, and also to adhere to the rule that PART
       may be applied to premises only if some other premise affirms existence, it would be necessary
       to first apply CP to the argument. If this is done, it should be remembered (as was true also
       in 17A) that this proof would establish only the original *conditional* conclusion. Referring
       to the first three lines of (17A) we set it up thus:

$$(Sx \rightarrow Rx) \cdot Mx \cdot Bx \cdot (Bx \cdot Mx \rightarrow \sim Rx) \mid \therefore (Bx \cdot Mx) \cdot \sim Sx$$
            $F\;\;T\,F$ T T T T $T\,T\,F$ $F\;\;T\,T\;\;F\,X\,F$
            $6\;\;2\;5$ 2 2 3 3 $2\;4\;4$ $1\;\;7\;8\,7\;\;2\;\;9$

(19) *Remarks:* Although chemists are able to symbolize *elements*, chemists often find it helpful
     to deal with *combinations of elements*, e.g., the ammonium ion ($NH_4 +$), the sulphate group
     (SO_4), the methyl group (CH_3), or the benzine ring (the phenyl group: C_6H_5). Similarly,
     logicians sometimes find it helpful to treat a complex statement as a single unit. This is
     done with "$u \rightarrow l$" in the following proofs for problem (19).

(19A) 1. $Lm \rightarrow (u \rightarrow l)$ 5. $\sim Lm$ 3, 4, MT
       2. $(u \rightarrow l) \rightarrow Lb$ 6. $\sim (u \rightarrow l)$ 2, 3, MT
       3. $\sim Lb \mid \therefore (Ux \cdot \sim Lx) \cdot \sim Lm$ 7. $Ux \cdot \sim Lx$ 6, QE
       4. $Lm \rightarrow Lb$ 1, 2, HS   8. $(Ux \cdot \sim Lx) \cdot Im$ 5, 7, CONJ

(19B) $[Lm \rightarrow (u \rightarrow l)] \cdot [(u \rightarrow l) \rightarrow Lb] \cdot \sim Lb \mid \therefore \sim (u \rightarrow l) \cdot \sim Lm$
        $F\;\;T\;\;\;F$ $F\;\;\;\;T\,F$ $T\,F$ $T\,F$ F $F\,X\,F$
        $6\;\;2\;\;\;5$ $F\;\;\;\;4$ $2\;3$ $2\;2$ $1\;8$ $7\;\;2\;\;9$

[*Note:* Although Proof (19B) "works", we recommend the step-by-step method of proof in
arguments where a variety of subscripts occur; because, when using the crucial assignments
method of proof in such cases, one may easily violate some of the restrictions set forth in section 6.2.]

6.4B:

Part I. Note: In this exercise you may save time by first writing eight equivalent forms of each
model. Thus, *model A* would yield: No S is P ($s \rightarrow \sim p$); All S is $\sim P$ ($s \rightarrow \sim p$); All P is $\sim S$ ($p \rightarrow \sim s$);
No P is S ($p \rightarrow \sim s$); It is false that some S is P [$\sim (Sx \cdot Px)$]; It is false that some P is S [$\sim (Px \cdot Sx)$];
It is false that some P is not $\sim S$ {$\sim [Px \cdot \sim (\sim Sx)]$}; It is false that some S is not $\sim P$
{$\sim [Sx \cdot \sim (\sim Px)]$}.

Model A: 1. D;   3. F [*Note:* For "All S is not P" read the paragraphs immediately preceding
exercise 6.2D];   5. F;   7. F;   9. F;   11. D;   13. T;   15. D;
Model B: 17. T;   19. T;   21. F;   23. D;
Model C: 25. D;   27. T;   29. D;   31. D;
Model D: 33. D;   35. D;   37. D;   39. D.

Part II.
Model A: 1. F;   3. F;   5. F;   7. F;   9. F;   11. D;   13. T;   15. D;
Model B: 17. T;   19. T;   21. F;   23. D;
Model C: 25. D;   27. T;   29. D;   31. D;
Model D: 33. T;   35. T;   37. F;   39. F.

6.4C:

(1) B;   (3) A, C;   (5) A, B;   (7) A, B;   (9) C;   (11) A;   (13) A, C;   (15) B, C;
(17) A, B, C;
(19) B. Problem (19) illustrates the fact that the same subject, *in different contexts*, may manifest contradictory properties. Hence we employ one subscript for one context $(Tx \cdot Lx)$, but use a different subscript for a different context $(Oy \cdot Dy)$.

6.4D:

(1A)

1. $(d \rightarrow m) \cdot (b \rightarrow m)$
2. $Px \cdot Mx$
3. $Py \cdot \sim My \mathbin{/} \therefore (Px \cdot \sim Dx) \vee (Py \cdot \sim Dy)$
4. $Dy \rightarrow My$ 1, SIMP, PART
5. $\sim My$ 3, SIMP
6. $\sim Dy$ 4, 5, MP
7. Py 3, SIMP
8. $Py \cdot \sim Dy$ 7, 6, CONJ
9. $(Px \cdot \sim Dx) \vee (Py \cdot \sim Dy)$ 8, ADD, COM
      Valid

(1B) Proof by Crucial Assignments Method:

Part A: $[(Dx \vee Bx) \rightarrow Mx] \cdot Px \cdot Mx \mathbin{/} \therefore Px \cdot \sim Dx$
          T   T   T T   T   T   F T FFT

Part A admits of a consistent assignment of truth values, hence its conclusion is not valid.

Part B: $[(Dy \vee By) \rightarrow My] \cdot Py \cdot \sim My \mathbin{/} \therefore Py \cdot \sim Dy$
          F   F   T F   T   T F   F X FT F

Part B results in an inconsistent assignment of truth values, so its conclusion is valid. (Hence, by ADD, $(Px \cdot \sim Dx) \vee (Py \cdot \sim Dy)$ is also valid.

(3A)

1. $b \rightarrow (s \leftrightarrow m)$
2. $Bx \cdot Px$
3. $Sy \cdot My \mathbin{/} \therefore (Bx \cdot Mx) \vee (By \cdot My)$
4. Bx 3, SIMP
5. $Bx \rightarrow (Sx \rightarrow Mx)$ 1, PART
6. $Sx \leftrightarrow Mx$ 4, 5, MP
    We seem to be getting nowhere.

(3B–1) $Bx \rightarrow (Sx \leftrightarrow Mx) \cdot Bx \cdot Px \mathbin{/} \therefore Bx \cdot Mx$
      T   T F   T F   T   T   F T FF
      6   2   8   7 5   2   2   1 3 24
          Invalid

(3B–2) $By \rightarrow (Sy \leftrightarrow My) \cdot Sy \cdot My \mathbin{/} \therefore By \cdot My$
      F   T   T   T T   T   T   F F FT
      5   2   7   8 6   2   2   1 4 23
          Invalid

(5A)

1. $h \rightarrow b \vee d$
2. $b \rightarrow \sim d$
3. $Hp \cdot Dp \mathbin{/} \therefore Hx \cdot \sim Bx$
4. Dp 3, SIMP
5. $Bp \rightarrow \sim Dp$ 2, PART
6. $\sim Bp$ 4, 5, MT
7. $Hp \cdot \sim Bp$ 3, SIMP; 6, CONJ
8. $Hx \cdot \sim Bx$ 7, SING-EX

(5B) $(h \rightarrow b \vee d) \cdot (b \rightarrow \sim d) \cdot Hp \cdot Dp \mathbin{/} \therefore Hx \cdot \sim Bx$
Knowing that $Hp \cdot Dp \rightarrow Hx \cdot Dx$, we change this to:
$(Hx \rightarrow Bx \vee Dx) \cdot (Bx \rightarrow \sim Dx) \cdot Hx \cdot Dx \mathbin{/} \therefore Hx \cdot \sim Bx$
      T   F   T F   T   T   T   F T FX   F
      2   5   2 4   4   2   2   1 3 2   6
          Valid

(7A)

1. $a \rightarrow g \vee (u \cdot e)$
2. $Uj \cdot Ej \mathbin{/} \therefore Ux \cdot Ax$
      Invalid

(7B) $[a \rightarrow g \vee (u \cdot e)] \cdot Uj \cdot Ej \mathbin{/} \therefore Ux \cdot Ax$
                   $\ldots Ux \cdot Ex \ldots$
$[Ax \rightarrow Gx \vee (Ux \cdot Ex)] \cdot Ux \cdot Ex \mathbin{/} \therefore Ux \cdot Ax$
   F   T   T T TT   T   T   FT FF
   5   2   8 6 76   2   2   1 3 24

(9A)

1. $(e \rightarrow i) \cdot (\sim e \rightarrow c) \rightarrow (e \cdot \sim c) \vee (\sim e \cdot c)$
2. $\sim i \mathbin{/} \therefore c$
Since SIMP cannot be applied to premise 1, there seems to be no way to establish this conclusion. Invalid.

(9B) $[(e \rightarrow i) \cdot (\sim e \rightarrow c) \rightarrow (e \cdot \sim c) \vee (\sim e \cdot c)] \cdot \sim i \mathbin{/} \therefore c$
  T F FF T FF F   T   FFT F   F   TFFF   TF   F F
  5 7 69 5 58 2   1   44 2 2   4   44 3 2   11   1 1
          Invalid

Observe the complex thinking involved in step 4. This choise of truth values for e and $\sim e$ insures that the consequent of the lengthy first premise will have truth-value F, and thus makes it more likely that a self-contradiction will show up later. However, a choice of truth-value T for e would also have resulted in a self-consistent assignment of truth values.

(11A) 1. $h \to f \vee e$
      2. $\sim\!f$ / ∴ $\sim\!h \vee e$
      3. $\sim\!h \vee f \vee e$ 1, CE
      4. $(\sim\!h \vee e) \vee f$ 3, ASSOC
      5. $\sim\!h \vee e$ 2, 4, DS
           Valid

In Problem (11) observe that "Bob" and "the batter" are terms which may be substituted for one another; and the same is true of "Sam" and "the second baseman." Hence, we can ignore this substitution, and symbolize the argument in the simplest possible way, as is done here.

(11B) $(h \to f \vee e) \cdot \sim\!f$ / ∴ $\sim\!h \vee e$
      $X\,T\,FF\,F\quad TF\quad F\,FT\,F\,F$

(13) *Note:* In the first premise of problem (13) "anyone" means "at least one person"; whereas in the second premise "anyone" means "everyone."

      1. $Px \to Wi$
      2. $w \to s$
      3. Pg / ∴ $(Wx \cdot Sx) \vee (Wy \cdot Sy)$
      4. Px 3, SING-EX
      5. Wi 1, 4, MP
      6. Wy 5, SING-EX
      7. $Wy \to Sy$ 2, PART
      8. Sy 6, 7, MP
      9. $Wy \cdot Sy$ 6, 8, CONJ
    10. $(Wx \cdot Sx) \vee (Wy \cdot Sy)$ 9, ADD

In proof (13), step 6, observe that SING-EX yields Wy, and not Wx. It may not be until after steps 6, 7, 8, and 9 have been completed that it is realized just how the conclusion of this argument should be set up.

Because such problems occur in applying SING-EX to proofs containing more than one existential, the step-by-step method of proof is safer in such cases than the method of crucial assignments.

(15)   1. $(p \to d) \to [(s \cdot a) \to b]$
      2. $(Px \cdot Dx) \to [p \to (d \cdot r)]$
      3. $t \to p$
      4. $c \to s$ / ∴ $(Ay \cdot Cy) \to [(Tx \cdot Dx) \to By]$
      5. $Ay \cdot Cy$ / ∴ $Tx \cdot Dx \to By$ CP
      6. $Tx \cdot Dx$ / ∴ By CP
      7. $Tx \to Px$ 3, PART
      8. Px 6, SIMP; 7, MP
      9. Dx 6, SIMP
    10. $Px \cdot Dx$ 8, 9, CONJ
    11. $p \to (d \cdot r)$ 2, 10, MP
    12. $\sim\!p \vee (d \cdot r)$ 11, CE
    13. $(\sim\!p \vee d) \cdot (\sim\!p \vee r)$ 12, DIST
    14. $p \to d$ 13, SIMP, CE
    15. $(s \cdot a) \to b$ 1, 14, MP
    16. $(Sy \cdot Ay) \to By$ 15, PART
    17. $Cy \to Sy$ 4, PART
    18. Sy 5, SIMP; 17, MP
    19. Ay 5, SIMP
    20. $Sy \cdot Ay$ 18, 19, CONJ
    21. By 16, 20, MP*

* Using a different notation, a solution to a problem very similar to problem 15 may be found in Irving M. Copi, *Symbolic Logic*, 3rd ed. (New York: Macmillan, 1967), pp. 119–20.

chapter 7

PROBABILITY

7.1 Empirical Probability

INTRODUCTION. Our discussion of probability will be quite elementary. It omits any discussion of permutations and combinations, since these would require knowledge of Pascal's triangle and the binomial theorem. It says nothing about the theory of limits, for this theory involves infinite series of events, and requires a knowledge of calculus. And it says nothing about statistics or about frequency distribution.

The study of probability may be viewed as an attempt to give the vague quantifier, "some," more precise meaning, and thus to transform vague guess-work into reasonable predictions. Consider the following syllogism: "If any Chinese-speaking people voted here, they are American citizens, but *some* Chinese-speaking people did vote here. Therefore, some Chinese-speaking people are American citizens." This argument is both valid and sound. But it does not tell us in any way whether the number of Chinese-speaking people who voted here was 10; 100; 1000; 10,000; 100,000; or 1,000,000. A study of probability should help us to be more precise.

PROBABILITY, SCIENCE, AND PREDICTION. Like science, probability accepts the fact that human knowledge is limited, hence that estimates of probability made under one set of circumstances need not apply somewhere else. For example, in tossing a fair coin, the probability of heads is the same as the probability of tails, which could mean that in *a long series of tosses we will turn up approximately as many heads as tails*. But suppose the coin were tossed on the moon, or on some other satellite where the pull of gravity is many times less than it is on the earth. Or suppose the coins tossed were four or five times thicker than the coins now used. Under such circumstances, we might discover that approximately one coin in twenty-five lands on its edge; and we would then estimate future results as follows:

$p(E)$ (probability that coins land on Edge):   1/25
$p(H)$ (probability of Heads):   12/25
$p(T)$ (probability of Tails):   12/25

This example illustrates a feature that probability has in common with inductive knowledge: induction is the use of knowledge to gain more knowledge. What we can learn on any one occasion is always limited by what we already know, but there is a continuity in the development of knowledge, and we may hopefully work toward greater degrees of accuracy in forecasting. Just as the tools man makes are limited by the tools he has on hand to make them with, so man's knowledge of future events is limited by the inadequacies of his present knowledge.

Probability helps us to make predictions that are usable in numerous ordinary life situations. For example, what is the probability that an August day spent at Yellowstone Park will be a rainy day? What is the probability that a child vaccinated with antipolio shots will nevertheless have polio during the ensuing year? What would be a fair rate for an insurance company to charge for insurance against an automobile accident during the coming year? If a groceryman, who orders twenty-five boxes of cereal each week, runs out of this cereal on the average of once every three weeks, how many boxes should he order to run out not more than about once in ten weeks? What is the probability that a lethal ray (or "what percentage of lethal rays") will penetrate a lead wall one inch thick? These questions need more precise statement. But they indicate the type of questions with which probability theory deals. They are such practical questions, that any theory which provides even imperfect answers to them is of tremendous value.

EMPIRICAL PROBABILITY.   Future events are seldom precisely the same as past events, but they are sufficiently alike to enable reasonable men to learn to apply to the future what they have learned from the past. The application of past experience to future conduct is a type of thinking which shapes most of our lives. Probability is merely a precise, mathematical approach to "learning from experience."

In a complex world of changing and varied events, it is far easier to prove an existential proposition than to prove a universal law. For example, it is easier to prove "There exists at least one mammal (my dog!) which does not lay eggs" than to prove "No mammals lay eggs." Probability theory begins with concrete events, or with clusters of such events. In contrast to traditional deductive logic, it does not begin with properties or attributes assumed to be essential to all members of a class. It begins with specific, observable events of a certain type; and it assesses whether or not these observed events may reasonably be assumed to be "fair samples" of larger clusters of events. On the assumption that they are, the theory of probability enables us to predict with what likelihood future events of the same type will occur. Consider the following simple example of empirical probability.

Using seeds taken from a variety of different ears of his seed corn, a farmer tested a sample of 30 grains, with results as follows (where *G* signifies "Germinated," and *N* signifies "Not Germinated"):

GGGGGGGGGGNGGGGNGNGNGGGGGGGNGGGGN

On the basis of this sample, he estimated that about 24 out of every 30 (or 4 out of every 5) grains of seed corn from this crop would germinate.

Obviously a larger number of seeds, tested with varying degrees of moisture, temperature, and other variables, would have produced a more reliable sample. Even at best, however, the sample is merely an "estimate." Although it is neat and precise to *say* "About 80 out of 100 seeds should germinate," the meaning of the statement would be more accurately expressed as "Probably somewhere between 70 percent and 90 percent of the seeds will germinate."

From Euclid to Newton, the mathematical approach to the physical sciences was a priori and deductive. After careful reflection on the knowledge available, certain broad principles or generalizations—sometimes called "self-evident principles"—were affirmed as axioms, and from these many theorems were deduced. In section 4.2 we applied this method to formal deductive logic. However, this a priori deductive approach has not worked well in the social sciences, or in other areas where there are so many variables or unknowns that it is impossible to judge any single element or elements as dominant.

Consider the following problem. Jones, age 50, wants to pay an insurance company an annual premium so that, either when Jones reaches age 70, or when Jones dies (if he dies before reaching age 70), Jones' wife or children shall receive $10,000. What annual premium should the insurance company ask of Jones?

To answer this question the company might consult Jones' doctors; search out Jones' medical records or the medical histories of both sides of Jones' family; study the hazards of the occupation he is in; and so forth. But since it is axiomatic that no one can judge when a *particular* individual is going to die, this approach would be ineffectual.[1]

Instead, the insurance company could approach the problem by dealing with random events as follows. It could study the death records of 10,000 men who had reached age 50, and find out how many of these 10,000 men died before reaching age 70. Suppose the company finds that 5,801 of the 10,000 men studied died before reaching age 70. Then the company could conclude that the *probability* of Jones dying before the age of 70 was 5,801/10,000, or 0.58. With this information, a fair premium could be established. The key to this approach is that the company *first appeals to experience*, and only on the basis of experience does it set up any estimate concerning probabilities.

If we define "rationality" as any deliberate effort to learn from past experience, probability is extremely rational. However, the word "experience" cannot then be belittled as "sense experience"—something to be sharply contrasted with "reason." For some of the early writers on probability, the traditional doctrine of matter and form had come to mean that the created world of material objects and events was patterned after ideal forms in the mind of God, and that human reason represented man's ability, as a child of God, to abstract these eternal forms from his sense perceptions of concrete objects. Thus man's sense organs were thought to experience the quantitative and material aspects of objects and events, while man's reason was believed to understand the eternal properties and universal attributes, on the basis of which material objects were assumed to have been patterned.

Probability is a method of reasoning whereby, on the basis of past events of a certain type, the mind extrapolates, or guesses about, future events which are, hopefully, of a somewhat similar type. Probability is closely allied to empirical science inasmuch as its conclusions are never fixed and unalterable, but are ever subject to revision in the light of future experience. Like scientific measurements, probability samples represent successive degrees of approximation to an ideal figure.

The "ideal figure" is more easily studied in theory than in practice, or in situations, such as tossing coins or dice, where the number of possibilities may be precisely defined. In probability theory "precisely defined" means much more than a definition in terms of attributes or properties. It means *measurable* degrees of likelihood. For example, suppose you are to take a plane trip from New York to Paris. There are only two possible outcomes: either you'll arrive safely, or you won't. But this does not mean that the probability of arriving

---

[1] Morris Kline discussed probability under the chapter heading "The Mathematical Theory of Ignorance: The Statistical Approach to the Study of Man." See Morris Kline, *Mathematics in Western Culture* (New York: Oxford University Press, 1964), p. 340 f.

safely is only 1/2 because the one outcome (arriving safely) is far more probable than the other outcome (not arriving safely). Thus any meaningful explanation of probability necessarily involves an understanding of quantity, or measure.

THE NUMBER OF ELEMENTS IN A SET (THE CARDINALITY OF FINITE SETS). In order to answer the questions "How much?" or "How many?" we will now consider sets (and we restrict our discussion to finite sets) with respect to the number of elements in a set, or in a pair of sets. Consider the following two sets: the set of vowels in the English language, and the set of the Great Lakes. We list the elements of these two sets: {a, e, i, o, u} and {Lake Erie, Lake Huron, Lake Michigan, Lake Ontario, Lake Superior}. Although these two sets are not equal, they do possess the common property of having the same number of elements. We could count the number of elements in each set and then observe that each set has exactly five elements; and we could then place the five elements of the two sets in a one-to-one correspondence, thus:

> Set of the Great Lakes: G = {Erie, Huron, Michigan, Ontario, Superior}
> Set of English vowels: V = {a,   e,   i,   o,   u}

If we wish to describe "quantity" in terms of "quality," we may say that the above two sets possess the quality (or property, or attribute) of having the same cardinality. This means that, with respect to the *number* of elements in each set, the two sets are the same.

Not all sets can be put into a one-to-one correspondence. For example, the set {a, e, i, o, u} cannot be put into a one-to-one correspondence with the set {1, 2, 3}. In fact, two finite sets can be put into a one-to-one correspondence if, and only if, they have exactly the same number of elements.

In order to proceed, we now introduce a useful and standard notation: for any finite set A, we let $n(A)$ be the notation for the number of elements of A. For example, if A = {a, b, c}, then $n(A)$ = 3. Clearly, $n(\varnothing)$ = 0.

Exercise 7.1A.   The Number of Elements in a Set

Part A.   Below is a Venn Diagram showing all of the elements in three sets A, B, and G. In this diagram U = {a, b, g, r, o, x, y, z}, A = {a, x}, B = {b, o, y}, and G = {g, r, a, y}.

Directions: Study the diagram; then complete the following:

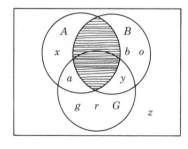

Figure 23

(1) $n(U)$ =	(5) $n(\sim A \lor \sim G)$ =	(9) $n(A \lor B \lor G)$ =
(2) $n(A)$ =	(6) $n(G \lor B)$ =	(10) $n(\sim A \lor B \lor G)$ =
(3) $n(A \cdot B)$ =	(7) $n(\sim G \lor B)$ =	(11) $n(A \lor \sim B \lor G)$ =
(4) $n(A \cdot G)$ =	(8) $n(G \cdot \sim B)$ =	(12) $n(\sim A \cdot B \cdot G)$ =

Although our treatment of probability will be as nonmathematical as possible, the student should note the following equations, and observe how they are exemplified in the diagram for exercise 7.1A.

1. $n(A) + n(\sim A) = n(U)$
2. $n(A \vee B) = n(A) + n(\sim A \cdot B)$
3. $n(B) = n(A \cdot B) + n(\sim A \cdot B)$ [Compare $q = (p \cdot q) \vee (\sim p \cdot q)$]
3X. $n(\sim A \cdot B) = n(B) - n(A \cdot B)$

Substituting 3X in 2 gives:

4. $n(A \vee B) = n(A) + n(B) - n(A \cdot B)$

This is a mathematical way of saying that when we add up the elements in the set $A \vee B$ we must not count the conjunction $A \cdot B$ twice.

Here is the formula for three sets, which you can easily check against the above diagram:

$$n(A \vee B \vee G)$$
$$= n(A) + n(B) + n(G) - n(A \cdot B) - n(A \cdot G) - n(B \cdot G) + n(A \cdot B \cdot G)$$

Exercise 7.1B.

Part A. In a certain freshman class of 700 students, 200 students take mathematics and 350 students take history. If 50 students take both mathematics and history, determine (1) how many students are taking history or not taking mathematics, (2) how many students are taking history and not taking mathematics, (3) how many students are taking neither mathematics nor history, and (4) how many students who are not taking history are also not taking mathematics. To solve these four problems, it may be helpful to use the following diagram:

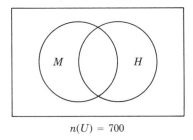

$n(U) = 700$ **Figure 24**

Part B. If, in addition to the information given in exercise 7.1B, it is known that 75 freshmen take physics and that all of these physics students take mathematics, but only 15 take history, then (1) determine how many students are taking mathematics, but not physics or history; (2) determine how many students are taking mathematics and history but not physics. Observe that the diagram for part A must be changed considerably before it can be used for part B.

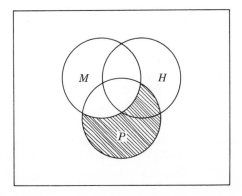

Figure 25

Exercise 7.1C.

A small coeducational college enrolled exactly 100 girls. A survey revealed the following information: 74 of the girls dated Freshmen $[n(F) = 74]$; 70 dated Sophomores $[n(S) = 70]$; 53 dated Juniors $[n(J) = 53]$; 56 dated Freshmen and Sophomores $[n(F \cdot S) = 56]$; 44 dated Sophomores and Juniors; 42 dated Freshmen and Juniors; 38 dated Freshmen, Sophomores, and Juniors. How many of these 100 girls did not date either Freshmen, Sophomores, or Juniors? $[n(\sim F \cdot \sim S \cdot \sim J) = ?]$

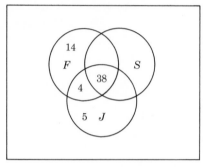

$$n(U) = 100$$ **Figure 26**

Hint: To arrive at the answer to this problem, you must follow the following order:

1. $n(F \cdot S \cdot J) = 38$ 5. $n(F \cdot \sim S \cdot \sim J) =$
2. $n(F \cdot S \cdot \sim J) =$ 6. $n(\sim F \cdot S \cdot \sim J) =$
3. $n(F \cdot \sim S \cdot J) =$ 7. $n(\sim F \cdot \sim S \cdot J) =$
4. $n(\sim F \cdot S \cdot J) =$ 8. $n(\sim F \cdot \sim S \cdot \sim J) =$ [the answer]

Before proceeding, we interpose an exercise which (for those who understand the make-up of a deck of cards) should serve as a helpful review of conjunction, alternation, and complementation—three operations which are as basic to probability as they are to set theory or to logic.

Exercise 7.1D.   Combinations of Sets and Subsets
in a Deck of Playing Cards

For the few readers who do not understand cards, we list the following classes and subclasses in a normal deck of 52 playing cards. Assume that "Ace is low," that is, classify the ace with the numbered cards, and do not include the ace among the face cards.

		B		*R*
	S	*C*	*H*	*D*
F	*K*	*K*	*K*	*K*
	Q	*Q*	*Q*	*Q*
	J	*J*	*J*	*J*
N	10	10	10	10
	9	9	9	9
	(8, 7, 6, 5, 4, 3)			
	2	2	2	2
	1	1	1	1

Symbols: *R*—red cards (26); *B*—black cards (26); *F*—face cards (12); *N*—numbered cards (40); *S*—spades (13); *H*—hearts (13); *D*—diamonds (13); *C*—clubs (13); *K*—kings (4); *Q*—queens (4); *J*—jacks (4).

Directions: Indicate the number of cards in each of the following sets:

_____ 1. $K \cdot Q$
_____ 2. $K \vee Q$
_____ 3. $K \cdot N$
_____ 4. $N \cdot B$
_____ 5. $(R \cdot B) \vee (R \cdot N)$
_____ 6. $(R \cdot K) \vee (B \cdot Q)$
_____ 7. $(R \cdot N) \vee (B \cdot N)$
_____ 8. $N \vee (R \cdot B)$
_____ 9. $(R \vee B)$
_____ 10. $(R \vee D) \vee (K \cdot Q \cdot J)$
_____ 11. $(R \vee Q) \cdot (R \cdot Q)$
_____ 12. $(N \cdot R) \vee (N \cdot B)$

_____ 13. $(R \cdot F) \vee (B \cdot F)$
_____ 14. $(N \vee R) \vee (N \vee B)$
_____ 15. $(K \cdot N) \vee (Q \cdot N)$
_____ 16. $(F \cdot Q) \vee (F \cdot K)$
_____ 17. $(C \cdot D) \vee (H \cdot S)$
_____ 18. $(S \vee H) \vee (D \vee C)$
_____ 19. $(F \vee N) \cdot C$
_____ 20. $B \vee K \vee J$
_____ 21. $(F \cdot Q) \vee (B \cdot Q)$
_____ 22. $\sim R$
_____ 23. $\sim (R \vee K)$
_____ 24. $\sim [(R \cdot K) \vee (B \cdot Q)]$

FROM NUMBERS TO PROBABILITIES.   Suppose we draw a card from a shuffled deck of 52 ordinary playing cards. What is the probability of selecting an ace? We shall assume that we have a fair deck; that is, each of the 52 cards is equally as likely to appear as any other card. Then since the card which is drawn could be any one out of the 52 cards in the deck, and since four of these cards are aces, our intuition tells us that the probability of drawing an ace is 4/52 or 1/13. Similarly, the probability of drawing a spade is 13/52 or 1/4, and the probability of drawing the ace of spades is 1/52.

If we let U denote the set of 52 playing cards, A denote the subset of 4 aces, and S denote the subset of 13 spades, then $n(U) = 52$, $n(A) = 4$, $n(S) = 13$. Finally, if we let $p(A)$ denote the probability of obtaining an element of the set A (an ace), $p(S)$ denote the probability of obtaining an element of the set S (a spade), and let $p(A \cdot S)$ denote the probability of obtaining an element of the set $A \cdot S$ (a card which is both an ace and a spade), then we can write:

$$p(A) = \frac{n(A)}{n(U)}, \qquad p(S) = \frac{n(S)}{n(U)}, \qquad \text{and } p(A \cdot S) = \frac{n(A \cdot S)}{n(U)}$$

Clearly $p(\emptyset) = 0$, and $p(U) = 1$, and for any proper subset of A of U, $p(A)$ is a number between 0 and 1. Hence, the probability of any event ranges between 0 and 1: 0 probability means the event cannot happen; a probability of 1 means that the event necessarily happens. A probability of 0.3 means that there are 3 chances in 10 that the event will happen. A probability of 0.9 means that there are 9 chances in 10 that the event will happen; or 1 chance in 10 that the event will not happen.

With these facts in mind, let us now restate the problem of exercise 7.1C. Instead of there being exactly 100 girls in this college, let there be 1,000 girls, 1,100 girls, or any number of girls. Then instead of stipulating that 74 (out of 100) girls dated Freshmen, say instead that 74 percent of the girls dated Freshmen. Similarly, say that 70 percent dated Sophomores; 53 percent dated Juniors; and so on.

Let us formulate this idea in a more general manner: consider a universe containing an arbitrary number of elements, say "a." Then, $n(U) = a$. If 74 percent of the girls dated Freshmen, then $0.74\ n(U) = 0.74a$. The probability that a girl dated a freshman is still covered by our basic formula:

$$p(F) = \frac{n(F)}{n(U)} = \frac{0.74a}{a} = 0.74$$

Thus the probability of an event can be thought of as a percentage because, in the fraction that gives the probability, "the number of elements, $a, \ldots$" will always cancel.

For simplicity, the number of elements in the universe can be supposed to be just 1: $n(U) = 1$. On this supposition, probabilities of events correspond to percentages of cases (or times) in which the events occur. $p(F) = 0.74$ can be read "74 percent of all the girls dated F"; or as "The probability that any girl, chosen at random, dated F is 0.74."

Exercise 7.1E.

Part A. If the probability that a student takes art is 0.30, that he takes biology is 0.46, and that he takes both art and biology is 0.20, find the probability that a student will take: (1) either art or biology; (2) art but not biology; (3) biology but not art; (4) neither art nor biology.

Fill in the percentages in the diagram:

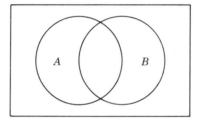

Figure 27

Part B. To continue the same problem, add the following assumptions: the probability that a student takes music is 0.25; that he takes both music and biology is 0.12; that he takes both music and art is 0.0 (that is, that no student is permitted to take both music and art). Find the probability that a student will take: (5) either music or biology; (6) either art or music; (7) either art, music, or biology; (8) neither art, nor music, nor biology; (9) neither art nor music; (10) neither biology nor music.

Fill in the above data in the diagram:

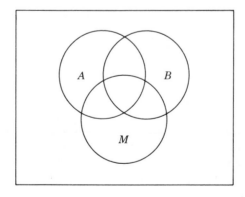

Figure 28

Before proceeding to a more detailed analysis of the specifics of probability, let us note a few common misunderstandings. The first thing to remember is that induction and probability cannot be justified in the same way that deductive inferences are justified. There are no truth tables, no tautologies, no self-contradictory statement forms. There is no attempt in probability or statistics to explain *specific* events in terms of *specific* causes; for the entire "logic" is built around large groups or collections of events. Whatever understanding we have of specific events comes about only from our understanding of large groups of events, of which a specific event may be a member.

To illustrate this point, suppose you are a bridge player, and suppose you have wanted all your life to be dealt a "perfect" hand, say, a hand of 13 spades. The probability of being dealt *that* hand is about one in 1,000,000,000,000. However, the probability of getting *any* other previously specified hand, say, a hand containing four 2s, four 3s, four 4s, and a 5 of clubs would also be about one in 1,000,000,000,000. In short, a noteworthy hand—one to which we give particular *note*—is no less probable, and no more probable, than any other hand in the total array of about 1,000,000,000,000 possible hands. For people trained in probability, such "noteworthy" events are judged to be "extremely improbable" rather than "miraculous" events.

Another point to keep in mind is that probabilities may be compared, even when each is very small. Let us suppose that the probability of the average American driver in any given year becoming involved in a fatal accident is one in 8,000; whereas the probability for a reckless driver is one in 2,000. Suppose a reckless driver then says, "I have been a reckless driver and I'm still around; but Jones, who was a very cautious driver, was just killed in an automobile accident." This man fails to note that the probability that he will have a fatal accident is only one in 2,000—compared to Jones' one in 8,000. In brief, the probability that either man will be involved in a fatal accident is so slight that comparisons between two *individual* cases is meaningless.

We complete these introductory remarks with one more example. Suppose a coin is dropped 10 times, showing heads 6 times, and tails 4 times. Now suppose the coin is dropped 100 times, and shows heads 54 times and tails 46 times. Finally, suppose the coin is dropped 1,000 times, and shows heads 520 times and tails 480 times. Note that the percentage of heads moves from 0.6 to 0.54 to 0.52—closer and closer to the ideal or a priori figure of 0.50. But note also that on the tenth toss the coin is only one off; on the one-hundredth toss it is four off; and on the 1,000th toss it is twenty off the "norm." If a coin were tossed 100,000 times—and this experiment has been conducted many times—the total of heads showing would be extremely close to 50 percent. Even so, each toss is an "Independent Event," wholly unrelated to previous events.

The "gambler's fallacy" is to assume that, because a coin shows heads five or six times in a row, the next toss *must* be tails. The fallacy consists of confusing statistical knowledge (i.e., knowledge about percentages and averages applied to *large groups of events*, or to large collections of data) with causal knowledge (knowledge of cause-effect relations) pertaining to *specific events*. This truth is contained in the saying, "The dice have no memories."

In sum, "the law of averages" (e.g., that heads will "in the long run" show 50 percent of the time) is a "law," not in the a priori sense that it is defined to be true, or in the sense that it is a tautologous statement form. Rather, it is a "law" in the sense that it is a truth based on experience: its truth depends on the observation of many, many specific events. For this reason, probability is properly classified under induction and experimental science. Nevertheless, as we shall now discuss, such inductive thinking is not as far removed from deductive, a priori, thinking as is sometimes supposed.

7.2 Independent, Complementary, Mutually Exclusive, and Alternative Events

INDEPENDENT EVENTS. We begin with a few key definitions and theorems.

Definition: Two events are *mutually exclusive* if both of them cannot occur in a single trial. Thus in a draw from a deck of playing cards, the two events of obtaining a spade and a heart are mutually exclusive; whereas the two events of obtaining a spade and an ace are not mutually exclusive.

Definition: Two events are *independent* if the probability of the occurrence of one is not influenced by the occurrence of the other. Otherwise these events are *dependent*. Thus if every time a card is drawn from a 52-card deck, that card is replaced, then each successive draw is an independent event. But if the cards are not replaced, the second draw depends on the result of the first draw, and the two events are dependent. Thus there is a probability of 1/13 that the first card drawn from a 52-card deck will be an ace. If this ace is not put back into the deck (not replaced), then the probability of getting another ace on the second draw will be 3/51, or 1/17. Thus the second draw is dependent on, or conditioned by, the first draw.

Conjunction of independent events. If two events are independent, then the probability that *both* events will occur is equal to the product of the occurrence of each separate event. Letting A and B signify two independent events:

$$p(A \cdot B) = p(A) \times p(B)$$

Here is a more general theorem concerning the conjunction of independent events.

Theorem: If $A, B, \ldots, N$ are independent events, then
$$p(A \cdot B \ldots N) = p(A) \times p(B) \ldots \times p(N).$$

For example, in three successive tosses of a die, the probability of three 2s is $1/6 \times 1/6 \times 1/6$, or 1/216. Again, in three successive tosses of a coin, the probability of three heads is $1/2 \times 1/2 \times 1/2 = 1/8$.

To see the practical meaning of these formulae, consider the eight possible outcomes of *one throw of three coins* (a penny, a nickle, and a dime). Such a throw gives the set $U = \{(h, h, h), (h, h, t), (h, t, h), (h, t, t), (t, h, h), (t, h, t), (t, t, h), (t, t, t)\}$. Now instead of one throw of three coins, consider the possible outcomes of *three consecutive throws of one coin*. It should be obvious that there will be the same eight possible outcomes; because, even as the penny, nickle, and dime fell independently of one another, so each of the three successive throws of any one coin fall independently of one another. In short, the probability of getting three heads is 1/8.

If events are independent of one another, the probability of many separate events all happening is the product of their separate probabilities. This principle has been verified empirically by thousands of tosses of coins and of dice. But the theorem is so basic to probability theory that it should be viewed as a fundamental postulate, which is asserted (assumed) but not proved on the basis of other principles more basic. Let us now study some examples of the application of this theorem.

Example A. A restaurant menu lists 2 soups, 3 beverages, 4 meats, 5 vegetables, and 6 desserts. How many possible combinations of 1 soup, 1 beverage, 1 meat, 1 vegetable, and 1 dessert does this menu provide? *Answer:* $2 \times 3 \times 4 \times 5 \times 6 = 720$.

In how many ways could a man order a meal consisting of 1 soup, 1 beverage, and 1 dessert? *Answer:* $2 \times 3 \times 6 = 36$ different ways.

If we assume that each choice is equally probable (an unlikely assumption!) what is the probability that a customer would order a particular soup (for example, pea soup), a particular beverage (for example, tea) *and* a particular dessert (for example, apple pie)? *Answer:* $1/2 \times 1/3 \times 1/6 = 1/36$, or one chance in 36. Stated otherwise, the odds would be 35 to 1 that he would *not* order all three.

Example B. A student takes a multiple-choice exam in which, for each question, there are 3 wrong answers and 1 right answer. Assuming that the student answers entirely by chance, what is the probability that he will: (1) answer the first three questions right? (*answer:* $1/4 \times 1/4 \times 1/4 = 1/64$); (2) answer the first three questions wrong? (*answer:* $3/4 \times 3/4 \times 3/4 = 27/64$); (3) answer the first two questions right, and the third question wrong? (*answer:* $1/4 \times 1/4 \times 3/4 = 3/64$); (4) answer exactly two of the first three questions wrong? (*answer*—observe that we now have three *alternatives*, namely $\{(R, W, W), (W, R, W), (W, W, R)\}$:

$$p(R, W, W) = 1/4 \times 3/4 \times 3/4 = 9/64$$
$$p(W, R, W) = 3/4 \times 1/4 \times 3/4 = 9/64$$
$$p(W, W, R) = 3/4 \times 3/4 \times 1/4 = 9/64$$

Hence, $p\{(R, W, W), (W, R, W), (W, W, R)\} = 9/64 + 9/64 + 9/64 = 27/64$.

Example C. Suppose that a man wishes to go from town A through town F to town I; and suppose there are four roads (B, C, D, and E) between A and F; and two roads (G and H) between F and I. In how many ways could the man go from A to I by way of F? *Answer:* There are four different roads he could take from A to F. For *each* of these roads taken (from A to F) he could take two other roads (G and H) from F to I. Hence, the total number of possible routes would be $4 \times 2 = 8$.

Now suppose he wishes to continue from I to M, and that there are exactly three roads (J, K, and L) between I and M. In how many different ways could he go from A, by way of F and I, to M? *Answer:* For *each* of the eight possible routes from A via F to I, he can now choose three new roads from I to M; so the total number of possible routes from A to M via F and I is $8 \times 3 = 24$. Or, putting the entire problem into a single formula, $4 \times 2 \times 3 = 24$.

Exercise 7.2A.

Directions: Assume a multiple-choice exam, each question of which contains three answers, two of which are wrong, one right. Assume that a student answers this test entirely by chance, that is, that he is as likely to choose one answer as another. Now compute the probability that this student will answer:

1. any given question right.   1. _____
2. any given question wrong.   2. _____
3. the first two questions wrong.   3. _____
4. the first two questions right.   4. _____
5. the first three questions right.   5. _____
6. the first four questions wrong.   6. _____
7. the first right and the second wrong.   7. _____
8. the first two right and the third wrong.   8. _____
9. the first right, the second wrong, and the third right.   9. _____
10. the first wrong, the next two right.   10. _____

COMPLEMENTARY EVENTS. The use of complementary events was implicit in exercise 7.2A. For if the probability of getting a right answer was $1/3$, then the probability of getting a wrong answer was $1 - 1/3 = 2/3$. Again, if a coin is tossed three times, the probability of getting three successive heads is $1/2 \times 1/2 \times 1/2 = 1/8$; and the probability of *not* getting three heads is $1 - 1/8$, or $7/8$.

Odds. The above problems are sometimes phrased as follows: in a toss of three coins, what are the *odds* for getting at least one tail? Since the probability of getting at least one tail is 7/8, and the probability of *not* getting at least one tail is 1/8, the odds are 7/8 to 1/8, or 7 to 1 in favor of getting at least one tail.

MUTUALLY EXCLUSIVE EVENTS.   Two events A and B are mutually exclusive if and only if they cannot occur together. This means: $A \cdot B = \emptyset$, or $\sim(A \cdot B) = U$. For two mutually exclusive events, A and B, the formula is this:

$$p[(A \vee B) \cdot \sim(A \cdot B)] = p[(A \vee B) \cdot \sim(\emptyset)] = p(A \vee B) = p(A) + p(B)$$

When dealing with mutually exclusive events, these formulas may be extended as follows:

$$p(A \vee B \vee C \vee \cdots \vee N) = p(A) + p(B) + p(C) + \cdots + p(N)$$

Exercise 7.2B.

From a pile of 26 letters of the alphabet, a letter is chosen at random. What is the probability that the letter selected will be:

(1) a vowel, where "vowel" is stipulated to mean $\{a, e, i, o, u\}$.
(2) a consonant.
(3) a vowel between the letters j and n (in alphabetical order).
(4) any consonant that precedes the letter e (in alphabetical order).
(5) a vowel or a consonant.
(6) any vowel that precedes the letter k.

Exercise 7.2C.

A single die is cast and a single coin is thrown. Study the table below, noting the twelve equally likely outcomes in the universal set U.

$(h, 1)$	$(t, 1)$
$(h, 2)$	$(t, 2)$
$(h, 3)$	$(t, 3)$
$(h, 4)$	$(t, 4)$
$(h, 5)$	$(t, 5)$
$(h, 6)$	$(t, 6)$

Now determine the following probabilities:

(1) a six and a head   (2) a six or a head
(3) an even number   (4) an even number and a tail
(5) an even number or a tail   (6) an even or odd number and a tail
(7) a number less than two and a tail (8) a number not less than two and a tail

Exercise 7.2D.

Below are four premises of an argument, with the probability that each premise is true indicated by an equation. Estimate the probability that the conclusion is true.

p(The wise man is a temperate man) $= 9/10$
p(The temperate man is constant) $= 9/10$
p(The constant man is imperturbable) $= 8/9$
p(The imperturbable man is without sorrow) $= 8/9$
Therefore,
    p(The wise man is without sorrow) $=$

Exercise 7.2E.

A set of pool balls (15 balls, numbered 1 through 15) is placed in an urn. If one ball is drawn out, what is the probability that it is:

(1) an 8 or a 9
(2) an even number
(3) a number less than 5
(4) a number divisible by 4

(5) a number divisible by 5 or 6
(6) a number divisible by 6, 7, or 8
(7) a 16
(8) a two-digit number

Consider the possibilities of throwing a pair of dice—one red, the other green. The following array shows the complete set of possibilities.

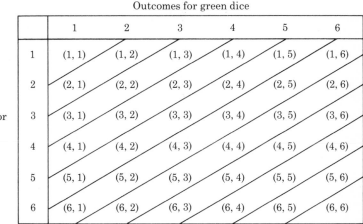

Figure 29

We will suppose that the 36 outcomes of the universal set U are equilikely.

If we want to determine the probability of obtaining a seven with a single toss of two dice, we let A be that subset of U consisting of all outcomes which give a total of seven on the two dice. Examining our table, we see that $A = \{(1, 6), (2, 5), (3, 4), (4, 3), (5, 2), (6, 1)\}$. Thus the desired probability is given by $p(A) = n(A)/n(U) = 6/36 = 1/6$. What is the probability that the numbers on the two dice will total 12? The chart shows exactly one such possibility, namely (6, 6). Within the set U of 36 possible outcomes, let T (for "Twelve") represent the subset $\{(6, 6)\}$. Then: $p(T) = n(T)/n(U) = 1/36$.

Similarly, within U, if we let E (for "Eleven") signify the subset which consists of these two possible outcomes, then $E = \{(5, 6), (6, 5)\}$, and $p(E) = n(E)/n(U) = 2/36 = 1/18$. Continuing this line of analysis leads to the following totals and their probabilities:

Totals: 2   3   4   5   6   7   8   9   10   11   12
Probabilities: 1/36 2/36 3/36 4/36 5/36 6/36 5/36 4/36 3/36 2/36 1/36

Before going further, let us note a relationship between propositional logic, set theory, and simple probability. Let q and r be propositions having associated sets Q and R, respectively. If $p(Q)$ and $p(R)$ denote, respectively, the probability that propositions q and r are *true*, then:

$p(Q \lor R)$ is the probability that the proposition $q \lor r$ is true;
$p(Q \cdot R)$ is the probability that the proposition $q \cdot r$ is true;
$p(\sim Q)$ is the probability that the proposition $\sim q$ is true; and so on.

Remember that every proposition is either true or false; there is no middle ground. If we say "The *probability* of the statement 'This coin will show heads' is 0.5" we are *not* saying "The *statement* is 0.5 true!"

ALTERNATIVE EVENTS.   Suppose we ask, "What is the probability that the numbers on the two dice will total either (e)leven *or* (t)welve"? Since $p(E \cdot T) = 0$, this question would be expressed in mathematical language as follows:

$$p(E \lor T) = p(E) + p(T) = n(E)/n(\text{U}) + n(T)/n(\text{U}) = 2/36 + 1/36$$
$$= 3/36 = 1/12$$

"What is the probability that the numbers on the two dice will total either 12 or a number greater than 11?" Obviously, we are repeating ourselves, and asking for $p(T \lor T)$. Since $T \lor T = T$, the answer is $p(T) = 1/36$. But suppose the question is this: "What is the probability that the numbers on the two dice will total either twelve or a number greater than ten?" Note that "a number greater than ten" includes the possibility of either an eleven or a twelve. Using symbols, "twelve or a number greater than ten" = $T \lor (E \lor T) = [(E \lor (T \lor T)] = E \lor T$. And, as we have seen, $p(E \lor T) = p(E) + p(T) = 2/36 + 1/36 = 3/36 = 1/12$.

We may solve this problem by using a formula introduced earlier:

$$n(A \lor B) = n(A) + n(B) - n(A \cdot B)^2$$

For A, substitute the set T (the outcome "twelve"); for B substitute $E \lor T$ (the two possible outcomes "eleven or twelve"). Then this formula could be applied thus:

$$n[T \lor (E \lor T)] = n(T) + n(E \lor T) - n[T \cdot (E \lor T)] = n(T) + n(E \lor T)$$
$$- n(T) = n(E \lor T) = n(E) + n(T) = 2 + 1 = 3$$

Since the probability always equals $n(F)/n(\text{U})$, the answer is 3/36, or 1/12.

Consider another example: In the single toss of a pair of dice (a red die and a green die), what is the probability that either the number turned up on the red die is less than 3 or that the number turned up on the green die is greater than 4? To solve this problem, we let A be that subset of U for which the number turned up on the red die is less than 3, and let B be that subset of U for which the number turned up on the green die is greater than 4. By examining our table, we see that $A = \{(1, 1), (1, 2), (1, 3), (1, 4), (1, 5), (1, 6), (2, 1), (2, 2), (2, 3), (2, 4), (2, 5), (2, 6)\}$ and $B = \{(1, 5), (2, 5), (3, 5), (4, 5), (5, 5), (6, 5), (1, 6),$

---

[2] $n(A \lor B) = n(A) + n(B) - n(A \lor B)$ is the basic formula, not only for alternative events, but also for mutually exclusive events which were discussed earlier. For, if events A and B are mutually exclusive, then $A \cdot B = 0$. So the formula

$n(A \lor B) = n(A) + n(B) - n(A \cdot B)$ becomes $n(A \lor B) = n(A) + n(B) - 0$; and
$p(A \lor B) = p(A) + p(B) - p(A \cdot B)$ becomes $p(A \lor B) = p(A) + p(B) - 0$;
        or simply $p(A \lor B) = p(A) + p(B)$

The above formulas and their numerical applications call attention to a basic difference between logic and mathematics: nearly every branch of mathematics deals with quantity and with numerical measurement; whereas not only traditional logic, but most areas of modern logic, deal only with classes or sets of objects. The great strength of mathematics lies in the fact that quantitative measurement is a tremendous aid, not only to scientific precision, but also to precise definition. Because the study of probability requires the repeated use of numerical calculations, probability is usually classified as a branch of mathematics. But it relates to logic in so many ways that no introduction to modern logic would be complete if it did not provide some basic understanding of probability.

(2, 6), (3, 6), (4, 6), (5, 6), (6, 6)}. In this case, $n(A) = 12$, $n(B) = 12$, $n(A \cdot B) = n\{(1, 5), (1, 6), (2, 5), (2, 6)\} = 4$. Thus $p(A \lor B) = p(A) + p(B) - p(A \cdot B) = n(A)/n(U) + n(B)/n(U) - n(A \cdot B)/n(U) = 12/36 + 12/36 - 4/36 = 20/36 = 5/9$.

Sometimes probabilities are related in such a way that we can compute one from others. Suppose the probability that horse A will win the first race is 1/3; the probability that A will win the first race and B will win the second is 1/12; and the probability that at least one of the two horses will win their respective races is 1/2. What is the probability that B will win the second race?

First, let us express the above data in symbols: $p(A) = 1/3$; $p(A \cdot B) = 1/12$; $p(A \lor B) = 1/2$. To find $p(B)$, use the formula $p(A \lor B) = p(A) + p(B) - p(A \cdot B)$. This formula becomes $p(B) = p(A \lor B) + p(A \cdot B) - p(A) = 1/2 + 1/12 - 1/3 = 6/12 + 1/12 - 4/12 = 3/12 = 1/4$.

The probability that B will win the second race is 1/4.

Exercise 7.2F.

Given a throw of two dice, what is the probability that the sum of the two upturned dice will be:

(1) 6	(2) 5
(3) 6 or 5	(4) 6 or 5 or 2
(5) an even number	(6) an odd number
(7) a number greater than 8	(8) a number less than 8
(9) any number except 7	(10) any number except 11 or 12
(11) one	(12) a number greater than 1

Exercise 7.2G.

A pair of dice are tossed twice. Restudy the chart and find the following probabilities:

1. two consecutive "sevens."
2. two consecutive "elevens."
3. a "seven" followed by an "eleven."
4. a "seven" and an "eleven."
5. at least one "seven."
6. at least one "eleven."
7. exactly one "seven."
8. exactly one "eleven."

Exercise 7.2H.

Assume a multiple-choice exam, in which each question contains three answers: two which are wrong, one right. Assume that a student answers this test entirely by chance, that is, that he is as likely to choose one answer as another. Now compute the probability that this student will answer:

1. exactly one of the first three right. 1. _____
2. exactly two of the first three wrong. 2. _____
3. one, but not both, of the first two right. 3. _____
4. one, but not both, of the first two wrong. 4. _____
5. at least one of the first two wrong. 5. _____
6. one or more of the first two right. 6. _____
7. at least two of the first three right. 7. _____
8. at least two of the first three wrong. 8. _____
9. not more than one of the first three wrong. 9. _____
10. not more than one of the first three right. 10. _____
11. exactly two of the first four right, exactly two wrong. 11. _____
12. exactly one of the first four right, exactly three wrong. 12. _____

7.3   Dependent Events and Conditional Probability

INDEPENDENT EVENTS.   We have seen that the probability of drawing an ace in a single draw from an ordinary deck of shuffled playing cards is $4/52 = 1/13$. Thus the probability of drawing two aces in two successive drawings of a single card, replacing the first card and shuffling the deck before drawing the second card, is given by the product $(1/13) \times (1/13) = 1/169$. If this second card is also replaced and the deck again shuffled before drawing a third card, then the probability of drawing three aces is given by the product $(1/13) \times (1/13) \times (1/13) = 1/2197$. Note that since the drawn card was replaced each drawing was independent of the previous drawing.

DEPENDENT EVENTS.   Even though the drawn cards are not replaced, we are still able to compute probabilities. In the previous example, if the first card is not replaced, then the outcome of the first drawing does have an effect on the probability of obtaining an ace on the second drawing. For if the first card drawn is an ace, then we are left with a deck of 51 cards containing only three aces, and the probability of drawing an ace from this deck is $3/51 = 1/17$. Similarly, the probability of drawing three aces in three successive drawings, without replacement, is given by the product $(4/52) \times (3/51) \times (2/50) = (1/13) \times (1/17) \times (1/25) = 1/5525$.

Suppose we draw two cards, without replacement, and wish to compute the probability that the first card is not an ace but that the second card is an ace. Since the probability that the first card is an ace has been computed to be $1/13$, the probability that it is not an ace is $1 - 1/13 = 12/13$. Moreover, if the first card were not an ace, then we have seen that the probability of the second card being an ace is $4/51$. Thus the desired probability is given by the product $(12/13) \times (4/51) = 16/221$. The probability that the first card is an ace $(4/52)$ and that the second card is not an ace $(48/51)$ is easily seen to be the same as the probability just computed $(16/221)$. Thus if we wanted to determine the probability of obtaining one and only one ace in two successive drawings without replacement, we observe that this may occur in two different independent ways: a non-ace on the first draw and an ace on the second, or an ace on the first draw and a non-ace on the second. Since these two pairs of events are mutually exclusive, the desired probability is given by the sum $(16/221) + (16/221) = 32/221$. Observe that this problem combines independent events (the first drawings), dependent events (the second drawings), and alternative events (the combinations of the two pairs of drawings).

CONDITIONAL PROBABILITY.   Now consider the following problem: in a toss of a Red die and a Green die (R and G), what is the probability that the Red die turns up a "1"? The answer is $1/6$. Now let us rephrase the question: what is the probability that the Red die turns up a "1," given that the total of $R + G$ is less than 4? Given this condition "that the total is less than 4," our problem is no longer concerned with 36 possible outcomes, but only with the subset $\{(1, 2), (1, 1), (2, 1)\}$. In two of the three elements of this set, $R = 1$. Hence, given the condition that "$R + G$ is less than 4," the answer to our problem is $2/3$.

We now state a formal *definition of conditional probability*: Let A and B be subsets of a universal set U, such that $p(A) \neq 0$. The conditional probability of B, given A, is denoted by $p(B/A)$, and is defined by the equation:

$$p(B/A) = \frac{p(A \cdot B)}{p(A)}$$

In words: "The conditional probability of B, given A, is the ratio of the probability of *both A and B* to the probability of *A* alone.

Let us apply this formula to the above example concerning the red and green dice.

$$p(B/A) = \frac{p(A \cdot B)}{p(A)} = \frac{p[\{(1, 2), (1, 1), (2, 1)\} \cdot \{(1, 2), (1, 1)\}]}{p\{(1, 2), (1, 1), (2, 1)\}}$$
$$= \frac{p\{(1, 2), (1, 1)\}}{p\{(1, 2), (1, 1), (2, 1)\}} = \frac{2}{3}$$

Consider the following problem. An urn contains 60 red balls, 25 white balls, and 15 green balls. Since the probability of drawing a red ball in one random selection from the urn is 60/100, or 3/5, the probability of drawing a red ball in each of two successive drawings, where the first ball is replaced before the second ball is drawn, is given by the product 3/5 × 3/5, or 9/25. Similarly, the probability of drawing three red balls in three successive drawings, replacing each ball before the next drawing, is given by the product 3/5 × 3/5 × 3/5, or 27/125.

Suppose now that we draw two balls, replacing the first before drawing the second. What is the probability that both balls will be of the same color? This probability will be the sum of the probabilities of the independent occurrences of two red, two white, or two green balls. The probability of two red balls has been computed to be 9/25. Similarly, the probability of two white balls is (1/4) (1/4) = 1/16, and the probability of two green balls is (3/20) (3/20) = 9/400. Thus the probability that both balls are of the same color is given by the sum (9/25) + (1/16) + (9/400) = (144/400) + (25/400) + (9/400) = 178/400 = 89/200.

To determine the probability that the two balls will be of a different color, we could take the sum of the probabilities of the separate independent events (first ball white and second ball green, first ball green and second ball red, and so forth). However, it is much easier to compute this probability by observing that the occurrence of two balls of the same color and the occurrence of two balls of a different color are complementary events, and thus the sum of their separate probabilities is one. Thus the probability of obtaining two balls of a different color is given by 1 − (89/200) = 111/200.

Now let us turn from independent events to dependent events. Suppose two balls are drawn in succession, the first one not being replaced before drawing the second. What is the probability that both are red? If A and B denote the occurrences of a red ball on the first and second drawings, respectively, then we want to determine $p(A \cdot B)$. By our formula, it is sufficient to compute $p(A)$ and $p(B/A)$, and then take their product. Both of these latter probabilities are easily computed as follows: $p(A)$ = 60/100 = 3/5, $p(B/A)$ = 59/99 (since if A occurred, then we have only 99 balls left of which 59 are red.) Hence the required probability $p(A \cdot B)$ = $p(A)$ × $p(B/A)$ = (60/100) × (59/99) = (3/5) × (59/99) = 59/165.

Exercise 7.3A.

A card is drawn at random from an ordinary deck of shuffled playing cards. Find the following probabilities:

1. the card is a spade given that the card is red
2. the card is a spade given that the card is black
3. the card is a seven of spades given that the card is black

4. the card is a seven given that the card is a spade
5. the card is a seven of spades given that it is a spade
6. the card is a seven of spades given that the card is a 2, 3, 4, 5, 6, 7, 8, 9, or 10

Exercise 7.3B.

In a single toss of a pair of dice (one die red and the other die green), find the following probabilities:

1. a total of ten
2. a total of ten given that the red die is a six
3. a total of ten given that the top numbers on the two dice are the same
4. a total of ten given that the red die is a two
5. a total of ten given that the top number on the red die differs from the top number on the green die
6. a total of ten given that the previous three throws also totaled ten

Exercise 7.3C.

Remarks: Below are the sixteen combinations of truth values previously listed in exercise 2.3G:

A. *TTTT*	E. *FTTT*	I. *FTTF*	M. *FTFF*
B. *TTTF*	F. *TTFF*	J. *FTFT*	N. *FFTF*
C. *TTFT*	G. *TFTF*	K. *FFTT*	O. *FFFT*
D. *TFTT*	H. *TFFT*	L. *TFFF*	P. *FFFF*

Part A.   Review of section 7.2.

Directions: Assume that each of the above sixteen truth values is equally probable. Then, choosing at random any one of the sixteen options, what is the probability that:

1. the statement is tautologous?
2. the statement is self-contradictory?
3. the statement is contingent?
4. exactly two of its four truth values is T?
5. exactly one of its four truth values is T?
6. the statement has truth value T at least twice?
7. the statement is false more often than it is true?
8. the statement has truth value T exactly three times?

Part B.   Conditional Probability.

9. Given that the statement has exactly two truth values T, what is the probability that it can be expressed by a single letter without using a tilde?
10. On the same conditions as problem 9, what is the probability that the statement could be expressed by a single letter either with or without a tilde?
11. Given that the statement is a biconditional or an exclusive disjunction, what is the probability that its first truth value will be F?
12. Given that the statement is a simple conjunction, what is the probability that its first truth value will be T?
13. Given that a statement has exactly one truth value, T, what is the probability that its truth value will be $FFTF$?
14. Given that a statement is contingent, what is the probability that the statement will be true exactly as often as it is false?
15. Given that a statement is not contingent, what is the probability that it will be true exactly as often as it is false?
16. Given that a statement is false more often than it is true, what is the probability that its first truth value will be T?

Exercise 7.3D.

A, B, C, and *D* in order throw a die exactly one time each. The first one to throw a "7" wins. What is the probability that:

1. none will win?
2. *A* will win?
3. *B* will win?
4. *C* will win?
5. *D* will win?

Exercise 7.3E.

From a piggy bank containing 1 quarter, 2 dimes, 3 nickles, and 4 pennies, two coins are shaken out. What is the probability that their total value will be exactly:

(1)   2¢   (6) 16¢
(2)   6¢   (7) 20¢
(3) 10¢   (8) 26¢
(4) 11¢   (9) 30¢
(5) 15¢   (10) 35¢

Exercise 7.3F.

For a certain baseball player it is estimated that over a season he gets a hit 30 percent of his times at bat, gets on base 35 percent of his times at bat, and scores 10 percent of his times at bat. If this player is at bat four times during a game, find the following probabilities:

1. that he obtains four hits ("goes four for four")
2. that he obtains at least one hit
3. that he scores no runs
4. that he scores at least one run
5. that he goes hitless (compare problem 2 above)
6. that he obtains at least one hit in three successive games
7. that he obtains at least one hit for 56 consecutive games

Note: Change problem 7 so the batting average is 0.325 because Joe DiMaggio, whose lifetime batting average was 0.325, holds the major league batting record for hitting safely in 56 consecutive games. Then look at the *answer* for problem 7. Do not do all the complex calculation that the problem would require.

Exercise 7.3G.

A and *B* are two newspaper reporters. *A*'s reports are factually correct 3 times out of 4; *B*'s reports are factually correct 2 times out of 3. Assuming their reports on the same incident are made independently, yet are the same, what is the probability that their reports:

1. are both right?
2. are both wrong?

Answers for Chapter Seven

7.1A:
 (1) 8;   (3) 0;   (5) 7;   (7) 5;   (9) 7;   (11) 6.

7.1B:
Part A: (1) 550;   (3) 200.
Part B: (1) 90.

7.1C: (Answers for odd-numbered problems also shown in the diagram:)

(1) $n(F \cdot S \cdot J) = 38$;   (3) $n(F \cdot \sim S \cdot J) = 4$;   (5) $n(F \cdot \sim S \cdot \sim J) = 14$;
(7) $n(\sim F \cdot \sim S \cdot J) = 5$.

7.1D:

(1) 0;   (3) 0;   (5) 20;   (7) 40;   (9) 52;   (11) 2;   (13) 12;   (15) 0;   (17) 0;
(19) 13;   (21) 4;   (23) 24.

7.1E:

Part A:

(1) 56 percent. Using the diagram for problems 1 to 4 below, first fill in areas $A \cdot B$; $A \cdot \sim B$; and $B \cdot \sim A$; then add the three figures. Using the formula, $p(A \vee B) = p(A) + p(B) - p(A \cdot B) = 0.30 + 0.46 - 0.20 = 0.56$.

(3) 26 percent. Using the diagram, $B \cdot \sim A = p(B) - p(B \cdot A) = 0.46 - 0.20 = 0.26$.

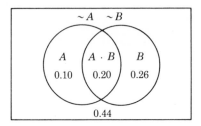

Figure 30

Part B:

(5) 59 percent. Using the diagram for problems 5 to 10 below, $p(M \vee B) =$ the sum of all the areas contained in either M or B, not counting any areas twice. Using the formula, $p(M \vee B) = p(M) + p(B) - p(M \cdot B) = 0.25 + 0.46 - 0.12 = 0.59$.

(7) $p(A \vee M \vee B) = p(A) + p(M) + p(B) - p(A \cdot M) - p(A \cdot B) - p(M \cdot B) + p(A \cdot M \cdot B) = 0.30 + 0.25 + 0.46 - 0 - 0.20 - 0.12 + 0 = 0.69$.

(9) $p[\sim(A \vee M)] = 1.00 - p(A \vee M) = 1 - [p(A) + p(M) - p(A \cdot M)] = 0.45$.

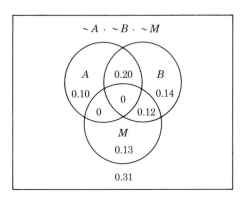

Figure 31

7.2A:

(1) 1/3;   (3) $[2/3 \times 2/3] = 4/9$;   (5) $[1/3 \times 1/3 \times 1/3 =] 1/27$;   (7) $[1/3 \times 2/3 =] 2/9$;
(9) $[1/3 \times 2/3 \times 1/3 =] 2/27$.

7.2B:

(1) 5/26;   (3) 0;   (5) 1.

7.2C:

(1) 1/12;   (3) 1/2;   (5) 3/4;   (7) 1/12.

7.2D:

(9/10) (9/10) (8/9) (8/9) = 64/100.

7.2E:

(1) 2/15;   (3) 4/15;   (5) 5/15, or 1/3;   (7) 0.

7.2F:

(1) 5/36;   (3) 5/36 + 4/36 = 9/36 = 1/4;   (5) 1/2;   (7) 5/18;   (9) 5/6;   (11) 0.

7.2G:

(1) $1/6 \times 1/6 = 1/36$;   (3) $1/6 \times 1/18 = 1/108$;

(5) First Solution: $(1/6 \times 5/6) + (5/6 \times 1/6) + (1/6 \times 1/6) = 11/36$;
    Second Solution: $1/6 + 1/6 - (1/6 \times 1/6) = 11/36$;

(7) $(1/6 \times 5/6) + (5/6 \times 1/6) = 10/36 = 5/18$.

7.2H:

(1) Add up the three answers for $[(R, W, W) \vee (W, R, W) \vee (W, W, R)]$ or (more briefly) triple the probability of (R, W, W), giving $3[1/3 \cdot 2/3 \cdot 2/3] = 4/9$;

(3) $[1/3 \cdot 2/3] + [2/3 \cdot 1/3] = 4/9$;

(5) The answer is the same as $1 - $ "the first two are right," or $1 - 1/9$, or 8/9;

(7) $(1/3 \times 1/3 \times 1/3) + (2/3 \times 1/3 \times 1/3) + (1/3 \times 2/3 \times 1/3) + (1/3 \times 1/3 \times 2/3) = 1/27 + 2/27 + 2/27 + 2/27 = 7/27$;

(9) 7/27 (Note that problems 7 and 9 are the same);

(11) Let R and W signify "right" and "wrong." Then there are six possible combinations of two right and two wrong: $(R, R, W, W), (R, W, R, W), (R, W, W, R), (W, R, R, W), (W, R, W, R), (W, W, R, R)$; or $6 (1/3 \times 1/3 \times 2/3 \times 2/3)$; or $6 (4/81)$; or 24/81; or 8/27.

7.3A:

(1) 0;   (3) 1/26;   (5) 1/13.

7.3B:

(1) 1/12;   (3) 1/6;   (5) 1/15.

7.3C:

Part A:

(1) 1/16;   (3) 14/16, or 7/8;   (5) 4/16, or 1/4;   (7) 5/16.

Part B:

(9) 2/6, or 1/3 (Here U = Cases F, G, H, I, J, K);   (11) 1/2, (U = Cases H and I);

(13) 1/4;   (15) 0.

7.3D:

(1) $(5/6)^4 = 625/1296$;   (3) $5/6 \cdot 1/6 = 5/36$;   (5) $1/6 \cdot 5/6 \cdot 5/6 \cdot 5/6 = 125/1296$

7.3E:

(1) $(4/10 \times 3/9) = 12/90 = 2/15$;   (3) $(3/10 \times 2/9) = 6/90 = 1/15$;

(5) $(2/10 \times 3/9) + (3/10 \times 2/9) = 2/15$;   (7) $(2/10 \times 1/9) = 2/90 = 1/45$;

(9) $(1/10 \times 3/9) + (3/10 \times 1/9) = 6/90 = 1/15$.

7.3F:

(1) $(3/10)^4 = 81/10,000 = 0.0081$

(3) $(9/10)^4 = 6561/10,000 = 0.6561$

(5) $(1 - 0.3)^4 = (0.7)^4 = 0.2401$

(7) $[(1 - (0.675)^4]^{56} = 0.000002193$

7.3G:

(1) $p(A \cdot B)$ given that $(A \cdot B) \vee (\sim A \cdot \sim B)$; or $(6/12)/(7/12) = 6/7$.

Note: Of the four possibilities $[(R, R), (R, W), (W, R), (W, W)]$, this problem restricts itself to (R, R) and (W, W).

Index

RULES AND DEFINITIONS OF LOGIC: A SUMMARY

Observe that each law in Group A and Group B yields *two* valid argument forms. For example, since the statement form $p = \sim(\sim p)$ is tautologous, *two* argument forms $[p \mathbin{/} \therefore \sim(\sim p); \text{ and } \sim(\sim p) \mathbin{/} \therefore p]$ are valid. The economy resulting from a liberal use of tautologous biconditionals should be obvious. Further economy results from the fact that nearly all of the laws in Group A are widely used in mathematics, and that most of them have dual forms.

Numbers in braces indicate sections in this book where the law is explained, for example, DN [1.3; 2.2].

A. Tautologous Biconditionals Common to Set Theory and to Logic.

COM (Commutation): $p \cdot q = q \cdot p; p \vee q = q \vee p$ [1.3; 2.2]
  COM applied to Biconditionals: $p \leftrightarrow q = q \leftrightarrow p$ [2.3]
ASSOC (Association): $p \cdot (q \cdot r) = (p \cdot q) \cdot r; p \vee (q \vee r) = (p \vee q) \vee r$ [1.3]
DIST (Distribution): $p \cdot (q \vee r) = (p \cdot q) \vee (p \cdot r);$
$\qquad\qquad\qquad\quad p \vee (q \cdot r) = (p \vee q) \cdot (p \vee r)$ [1.3]
DN (Double Negation): $\sim(\sim p) = p$ [1.3; 2.2]
  Applied to Biconditionals and to Exclusive Alternations: [2.3]
$\quad (p \leftrightarrow q) = (\sim p \leftrightarrow \sim q) = \sim(p \leftrightarrow \sim q) = \sim(\sim p \leftrightarrow q)$
$\quad \sim(p \leftrightarrow q) = \sim(\sim p \leftrightarrow \sim q) = (p \leftrightarrow \sim q) = (\sim p \leftrightarrow q)$
TAUT (Tautology): $p \cdot p = p; p \vee p = p$ [1.3]
ExM (Excluded Middle):
  (1) Set Theory formulation: $P \cdot \sim P = \varnothing; P \vee \sim P = U$ [1.3]
  (2) Truth Value formulation: $p \cdot \sim p = F; p \vee \sim p = T$ [4.2]
DeM (DeMorgan): $\sim(p \cdot q) = \sim p \vee \sim q; \sim(p \vee q) = \sim p \cdot \sim q$ [1.3; 2.2]
COPO (Contraposition; Transposition): $p \rightarrow q = \sim q \rightarrow \sim p$ [2.2]
CP (Law of Exportation—used mostly in Conditional Proof):
  $p \rightarrow (q \rightarrow r) = p \cdot q \rightarrow r$ [4.3]
RAA (Reductio ad Absurdum): $(\sim p \rightarrow p) = p; \sim p \rightarrow (q \cdot \sim q) = p$ [4.3]
TV (Rules for sets of Truth Values where T and F replace U and $\varnothing$, and where
  p and q replace A and B):
  $F \cdot T = F; \quad p \cdot F = F; \quad p \cdot T = p; \quad \sim T = F$
  $F \vee T = T; \quad p \vee T = T; \quad p \vee F = p; \quad \sim F = T;$ [2.1; 4.2]

B. Laws and Definitions Used Only in Logic
(Tautologous Biconditionals).

CE (Conditional Equivalence): $p \rightarrow q = \sim p \vee q$ [2.2]

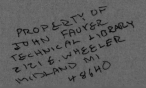